Leadership and Uncertainty Management in Politics:
Leaders, Followers and Constraints in Western
Democracies

Palgrave Studies in Political Leadership seeks to gather some of the best work
on political leadership broadly defined, stretching from classic areas such as
executive, legislative and party leadership to understudied manifestations
of political leadership beyond the state. Edited by an international board of
distinguished leadership scholars from the United States, Europe and Asia, the
series publishes cutting-edge research that reaches out to a global readership.

Leadership and Uncertainty Management in Politics

Leaders, Followers and Constraints in Western Democracies

Edited by

Agnès Alexandre-Collier
Professor of British Studies at the University of Burgundy, Dijon, France

and

François Vergniolle de Chantal
Professor of American Politics at Paris Diderot University, France

First published 2015 by
PALGRAVE MACMILLAN

Palgrave Macmillan in the UK is an imprint of Macmillan Publishers
Limited, registered in England, company number 785998, of Houndsmills,
Basingstoke, Hampshire RG21 6XS.

Palgrave Macmillan in the US is a division of St Martin's Press LLC,
175 Fifth Avenue, New York, NY 10010.

Palgrave Macmillan is a global academic imprint of the above companies
and has companies and representatives throughout the world.

Palgrave® and Macmillan® are registered trademarks in the United States,
the United Kingdom, Europe and other countries.

ISBN 978–1–137–43923–9 hardback

This book is printed on paper suitable for recycling and made from fully
managed and sustained forest sources. Logging, pulping and manufacturing
processes are expected to conform to the environmental regulations of the
country of origin.

A catalogue record for this book is available from the British Library.

A catalog record for this book is available from the Library of Congress.

Typeset by MPS Limited, Chennai, India.

Contents

Tables, Figures and Boxes

Tables

Figures

Box

Acknowledgements

This book was inspired by an International Conference held at the University of Burgundy on 9–10 November 2012 under the auspices of the Centre Interlangues, Texte, Image, Langage (EA 4182). In addition, we would like to thank the Regional Council of Burgundy (Conseil Régional de Bourgogne) and the University of Paris-Diderot, which partly financed the project.

The purpose of this conference was to bring together some specialists of key Western democracies to address the various facets of political leadership from a multidisciplinary perspective. The common thread of all chapters is more particularly the notion of uncertainty management. Anxiety/Uncertainty Management (AUM) theory was introduced by Dr William B. Gudykunst to define how human communication based on the balance of anxiety and uncertainty in social situations works. Gudkykunst believed that this was a key for successful intercultural communication. Even though this theory is not the main object of the book, we are grateful to the scholars who shaped and developed the concept which, it seemed to us, could fit usefully into the wider frame of political leadership.

We have been extremely fortunate to have as contributors a varied and dynamic team of scholars who agreed to address political leadership from this perspective.

We are also particularly grateful to our British and American colleagues who provided excellent translations of some texts: David Karol, Mark Niemeyer and Margaret Tomarchio. In addition, we would like to thank Kenin Nonin and Julie Murrell for their work on the manuscript. We are also very grateful to our publishers Sara Crowley-Vigneau, Andrew Baird, Sally Daniell and Jemima Warren for giving us this opportunity and for their work in bringing the book to publication. Special thanks to our anonymous reviewers for their substantial and constructive advice.

Laboratoire de recherches sur les cultures anglophones – CNRS UMR 8225

Notes on Contributors

Agnès Alexandre-Collier is Professor of British Studies at the University of Burgundy (Dijon, France). She is the author of several books including *Anatomie des droites européennes*, with Xavier Jardin (2004); *Les habits neufs de David Cameron. Les conservateurs britanniques, 1990–2010* (2010) and *Les partis politiques en Grande-Bretagne*, with Emmanuelle Avril (2013).

Nicolas Bonnet is Professor of Italian Studies at the University of Burgundy.

Gilles Brachotte is associate professor in Communication Science at the University of Burgundy, member of the CIMEOS/3S research team (EA 4177) and teaches in the web design department of Dijon-Auxerre Technological Institute (IUT Dijon-Auxerre). He focuses on the way ICT is used in practice and more generally on social change resulting from adoption and integration of ICT in society, notably among young people, and in politics. His research brings together discursive, social, ergonomic and technical dimensions which are sources of meaning and contribute to complexifying the communication processes involved.

Françoise Coste is a graduate from the Ecole Normale Supérieure – Fontenay Saint Cloud and the University of Bordeaux, where she defended a PhD devoted to the Republican Party in the state of New York. She now teaches American political history at the University of Toulouse. Her research is centered on contemporary American politics and intellectual history and she will publish an ideological biography of Ronald Reagan in 2015 (Perrin Editions).

Alex Frame is associate professor in Communication Science at the Languages and Communication Faculty of the University of Burgundy. He graduated from the University of Oxford in 1998, before settling in France and completing his PhD in Communication Science at the University of Burgundy, in 2008. He recently co-edited *Communication and PR from a Cross-Cultural Standpoint: Practical and Methodological Issues* (2012).

Aurélie Godet is Senior Lecturer in US history at Paris Diderot University, Sorbonne Paris Cité. Her research so far has focused on the history of conservative movements in the United States. She wrote her doctoral thesis on the influence of the neoconservative intellectual Irving Kristol. In 2012 she published a book on the Tea Party movement entitled *Le Tea Party. Portrait d'une Amérique désorientée* (2012). She is now working on a political history of Mardi Gras in New Orleans.

Julia Heinemann graduated from the Ecole Normale Supérieure and is Research Fellow in political sociology at IRSEM (Institut de Recherche Strategique de l'Ecole Militaire) in Paris.

Laetitia Langlois is Senior Lecturer in British politics at the University of Angers, France. In 2010, she wrote a doctoral thesis entitled 'Edward Heath and the Conservative tradition: heir or moderniser?' and is currently working on the Conservative Party before Thatcher.

Gilles Leydier is Professor of British studies at the University of Toulon. He is the editor of the journal *L'Observatoire de la société britannique*. He is the author of several books and articles on British and Scottish politics, his recent publications including *Le Royaume-Uni à l'heure de la coalition* (2014), *Environmental Issues in political discourses in Britain and Ireland* (2013), *Le pouvoir politique britannique et sa représentation* (2012).

Alix Meyer, Assistant Professor at the University of Burgundy (Dijon, France), PhD in American Civilization from the University of Lyon 2, Fulbright Fellow at Princeton University in 2009–10.

Lionel Picard is a German teacher. He devoted his PhD at the University of Burgundy to the expellees in postwar Germany.

Saskia Richter is associate researcher in the Institute of Social Sciences at the University of Hildesheim. She holds a PhD in political science from the University of Göttingen. In 2010 she published the biography 'Die Aktivistin. Das Leben der Petra Kelly'. Her current research project is entitled 'Political Participation in Changing Societies' and asks how unconventional participation in Western democracies changes according to economic transformation.

Pauline Schnapper is Professor of British Studies at the University of Paris-Sorbonne Nouvelle and a junior member of the Institut Universitaire de France (IUF). She has published *British Political Parties and National Identity* (2011) and *Britain and the Crisis in the European Union* (forthcoming, Palgrave Macmillan, 2015).

Karine Tournier-Sol is Senior Lecturer in British politics at the University of Toulon, France. Her main research interests are in Britain's relations with the European Union, with a special focus on the UK Independence Party. Her most recent articles are: 'Will Farage's respectability drive destroy UKIP?' 27 February 2014, *Policy Network Observatory*, and 'Reworking the Eurosceptic and Conservative traditions into a populist narrative: UKIP's winning formula ?' *Journal of Common Market Studies*, vol. 53, n° 1, January 2015.

François Vergniolle de Chantal is Professor of American Government at Paris Diderot University (LARCA, Sorbonne Paris Cité). His research focuses on American political institutions (federalism, the presidency and Congress). His next book deals with the US Senate: *L'impossible présidence impériale. Le contrôle législatif aux Etats-Unis*, published by CNRS Edition in Paris. He is also the co-director of *Politique Américaine*, a journal on American politics published three times a year by *L'Harmattan*.

1
Introduction

Agnès Alexandre-Collier and François Vergniolle de Chantal

Leadership is a prime example of this iron law of political life: nothing meaningful can happen without someone in charge. The charismatic personality that Max Weber (1922) emphasized as one form of legitimacy is the core of democratic politics for better or worse. Leadership is thus the result of both necessity and opportunity. Structural changes and collective evolutions are necessary but never sufficient. The crucial element is the ability of leaders to use them. In *The Prince* (1513), Machiavelli wrote that 'fortuna' was the strongest ally of the leader. The politics of leadership is a constant reminder of this founding insight. Successful leadership results from the encounter between extraordinary circumstances and extraordinary (wo)men.

At the same time, political leadership, the very gist of politics, is a constant challenge to political science. It raises countless issues of fundamental value for the discipline – from legitimacy to agency, including charisma or electoral competition – but it remains on the margins of the field. This stands in stark contrast with the visibility of leadership as a general skill that can be taught and understood. American academia, for instance, has produced numerous books and articles intended for a general readership on its practice; in addition, so-called 'Leadership Schools' (usually associated with 'Public Policy' studies) loom large in the American educational field. Political science publications, however, are few and far between. James McGregor Burns' (1978) largely remains the standard analysis with its account of leadership as a relationship whose key is the discovery of shared purpose between followers and leaders.[1] Burns also made a distinction that still constitutes a dominant framework to account for what leadership is. The central distinction is between what he called 'transactional' and 'transforming' leadership. Transactional leadership takes place when 'one person takes the initiative in making contact with others for the purpose of an exchange of valued things'. This type of leadership is best described as the politics of exchange, in which, for example, a public official bargains jobs for votes. Transforming leadership, in contrast, has a moral dimension. It may be said to occur when 'one or more persons engage with each other in such a way that leaders and followers raise one another to higher levels of motivation and morality'. The transforming leader is one who, though initially impelled by the quest for individual recognition, ultimately advances collective purpose by being attuned to the aspirations of his or her followers. Burns also distinguished between leaders and 'power wielders' (Burns, 1978: 3–4). Leaders in some way satisfy the motives of their followers, whereas power-wielders are intent only on achieving their own purposes, whether or not these are shared by the people over whom they exert their power. Ever since these classic distinctions were made in the late 1970s, the gap between the increasing number of 'leadership guidebooks' and the relative lack of academic works in political science has been widening. This is all the more striking since the rise of executive power all over the world – including Western democracies – has been one of the most visible trends of the past decades. In Western Europe and in North America, the stability and strengthening of the executive branch has been the most striking feature of political development ever since the end of World War II. In the US, the 'imperial presidency' classically described by Arthur Schlesinger in his 1974 book is still very much the order of the day. G.W. Bush expanded executive powers so much that his two terms have been described as a revenge against Watergate and the subsequent weakening of the presidency (Schlesinger 1974, 2004; Rudalevige, 2009). Even though Obama's presidency currently illustrates the limits of executive powers in a context of divided government, Obama has nonetheless pursued the same goals as Bush. In Western Europe, most parliamentary democracies have succeeded in gaining the stability that they lacked prior to the war (Bale, 2013; Colomer, 2008). In 1958, France finally created a powerful and stable executive with a largely subordinated parliament as the price to pay. In Great Britain, despite the constitutional principle of parliamentary sovereignty, parliament is in no position to bring about the resignation of the government, thus making the Prime Minister the dominant force in British politics. As for the German chancellor, the 1949 Fundamental Law (*Grundgesetz*) pioneered a 'rationalization' of parliament that Germans have been living with ever since. Among the major European democracies, Italy is maybe the only exception here, even though prime ministers seem to have been gaining increasing powers since the early 1990s. In other words, the institutional trend toward executive-centered systems is somewhat similar among Western democracies. The emphasis on executives and personal leadership is thus shared by democracies on both sides of the Atlantic.

Considering this transnational trend, how can the relative lack of systematic analysis of political leadership be explained? For one thing, leadership is a black box that harks back to a traditional problem in social sciences: human agency. Unlike the 'hard' sciences, political science deals with conscious and reflective subjects, capable of acting differently under the same stimuli (Hay, 2002: 50). Agency thus injects an inherent indeterminacy and contingency that leadership embodies. Leaders are indeed actors that can refashion the context in which they find themselves, thus making it impossible to identify regularities that could satisfy political scientists. Alongside the opposition between agency and structure – or conduct and context – lies a lingering suspicion by many in the profession that was best captured by Jean Blondel: 'One reason why political leadership has not been systemati- cally analyzed is the *fear* which it has provoked among generations of liberal thinkers. Alongside a few "good" leaders, so many have been ruthless in controlling their subjects and in acquiring territories, usu- ally by force, that enthusiasm for leadership has been limited, to say the least. (…) The deeds of many 20th century leaders, both before and after the Second World War, did not help to modify the pessimis- tic view. Hence the widespread belief that leadership was essentially bad – a belief shared by many among the political elites of democratic countries, especially of those countries, on the Continent of Europe and in Latin America, where the population suffered particularly from the excesses of rulers' (Blondel in Foley, 2013: 17). Finally, the domination of so-called 'scientific' approaches in political science – from behaviorism in the 1950s to rational choice nowadays – has led many in the profession to look down on issues like leadership that smacked of 'old political science'. Thomas Carlyle wrote in 1841 that 'the history of the world (…) was the biography of great men'. James McGregor Burns also noted that traditional conceptions of leadership tend to be 'dominated by images of presidents and prime ministers speaking to the masses from on high' (Burns, 1978: 442). This classical conception paves the way for leadership studies that are merely a series of monographs or political biographies which say nothing about the regularities of political life and are based on the simplistic assumption that leadership is a top-down phenomenon.

As a consequence, Michael Foley is perfectly right when he notes that 'leaders were considered to be too variable; leadership was regarded as excessively concerned with the lure of agency over structure; its study was necessarily interpretative, variable, and unreliable in nature; and its corollary of followers smacked of properties that could not be construed as strictly rational' (Foley, 2013: 17).

This brief overview of the state of the debate is indicative of what has been called a 'tragedy' for political science (Ricci, 1984): by focusing on narrow attempts to understand politics 'scientifically', the discipline has lost sight of the 'big picture' and is unable – or maybe even unwilling – to tackle broader issues. Leadership being one of them, political scientists must tread carefully when approaching it. Classical views of leadership have been widely reduced, in terms of their influence, by social and cultural history as well as by other social sciences. Since Burns, it has become commonplace to say that leadership actually has very little to do with crude power and brutal domination. Leaders, in Burns' definition, induce followers to act in accord with the values and the motivations of both leaders and followers. It is a dynamic relationship that, at its best, finds leaders engaged in a process of raising the consciousness of followers, or at least engages both leaders and followers in a common enterprise. Leadership is meaningless without its democratic link with common purposes and collective needs.

According to this still-dominant definition, leadership is widely understood simply as a principal–agent theory: political leaders are 'agents' to whom authority is delegated in order to oversee tasks that advance the goals of their followers or 'principals'. Franklin Roosevelt supposedly said in 1931 that 'leadership can be successful only through the greatest amount of party harmony' (Roosevelt, 1947: 244). This perspective has been especially influential in studies of legislative leadership. But this view largely fails to account for many characteristics of political leadership, which is individually based and events-driven.

To fully grasp political leadership, a heavy dose of contextual analysis is always required as well as a detailed account of how an individual fits into this wider framework and succeeds in altering the balance (s)he inherited. Thus, neo-institutionalism, especially in its historical form, provides a suitable scientific framework here, acknowledging as it does the pervasive influence of institutions on leadership through rules, norms and other frameworks. Leaders are thus partly 'agents' in so far as they are deeply embedded in their cultural, social and political environments. In his 1993 book, Stephen Skowronek provided a classical framework for understanding presidential leadership in the US when he differentiated between articulation (presidents expanding the institutional and political arrangements they inherited), repudiation (presidents breaking with past legacies) and disjunction (presidents caught up in past legacies and unable to adjust). Such an insight, that emphasizes structures and timing over agency, used by Fred Greenstein in his analysis of presidential leadership (Greenstein, 2009 a & b), could be expanded to other types of leaders. The view presenting leaders as agents of their followers fits only one of Skowronek's categories, namely 'articulation'. History is indeed littered with examples of 'leaders' who were not merely expressing the views of their supporters, but were also 'builders' or 'architects' of something new: from de Gaulle in 1940 to Tony Blair in 1994 and Barack Obama nowadays, many political leaders have largely been active of efficient causes, forces effecting or facilitating a certain result. Leaders at times act independently of their followers, tending toward important institutional innovations, new political departures or in some cases both. 'Repudiation' thus appears to be leadership in its most advanced and positive form. If 'repudiation' is the main criterion for a successful leadership, then 'disjunction' would seem to imply a failed leadership.

Our aim in this book is indeed to offer a more thorough understanding of leadership by detecting when leaders act as causal agents (or 'actors') rather than as agents of their followers. Our concern will be about the major threat, posed by the fracturing of the relationship between leaders and followers, which leaders need to keep in mind when building up their leadership. There is no denying that political leaders will usually be more assertive and active regarding political situations in which followers are already in agreement with what they want. In such cases, however, the leader him/herself as such does not matter: what the followers want is much more important than who the leader is. Yet, in uncertain situations, causal leadership is seen as the most effective solution. This notion of uncertainty has spawned a substantial number of studies concerning theories of risk or uncertainty management. In the field of politics, most of these studies have been concerned with theorizing or providing quantitative models to limit risks and control uncertainty (see among others: Cioffi-Revilla, 1998; Schedler, 2013). We posit that this notion of uncertainty in politics can be understood in the following ways: when the political, economic and geopolitical contexts are impossible to decipher (*contextual uncertainty*) and when division and confusion among followers blur the messages sent to the leaders (*social uncertainty*). The view we articulate through case studies in this book may eventually emphasize uncertain configurations in which leaders themselves mattered as game-changers. Drawing on neo-institutionalism, we suggest that leaders can also be influential in political situations in which followers are uncertain or divided about what they want. Taking this approach, one could go on to argue that the complex yet solid environments in which leaders are embedded weigh more heavily on them than their unstable and uncertain followers, whether it be political institutions as such, or pressures exercised by media or party structures. Taking the lead under these conditions, however, involves great political risks. Leaders should thus be defined first and foremost as risk-takers. Next, division and uncertainty among followers become a condition providing potential leaders with opportunities to shape the views of their supporters at a certain moment when they know what they reject without organizing their views into a positive and coherent whole. This is when a leader's role becomes decisive.

This broad characterization says nothing, however, about the sequence of events and the reasons why some leaders actually cross the red line.[2] Of course, the diversity of contexts makes it impossible to identify a common thread running through cultures and centuries. It is, however, within the reach of social sciences to identify a configuration shared by most successful leaders. To single out the main characteristics of this configuration, we can pose four preliminary questions:

What makes a leader possible? Leadership matters most when past legacies are deemed insufficient to face new challenges and when the potential followership is still unsure of what the solutions could be. This is when the window of opportunity for a tentative leader is at its maximum. The general context makes 'efficient' leadership possible, meaning leadership as causal and independent agent.

What does a leader bring? A leader is not just a risk-taker in a context of division and uncertainty. (S)he is also a provider of stability. 'Repudiation' does not stand alone; it also implies an ability to formulate new and accepted common values for society. A leader is able to devise a new vision for his/her country, which explains why many have been decried by their opponents as being responsible for debasing the traditional order. Such accusations have always been sparked off by successful leaders, from Franklin Delanoe Roosevelt and Barack Obama as being somehow 'un-American' to George Washington or Charles de Gaulle as somehow 'terminating the Republic'.

What is a leader? Leading on from what we have just said, (s)he is both an innovator and a builder. But a leader is also a communicator. The link between followership and leadership is the core of this political dynamic in which one person raises the awareness of a section of public opinion and conveys a series of values and objectives that become part of the national consensus.

What causes a leader to fail? The first three questions point to what makes a successful leader. But how is failure to be accounted for? Together with the absence of a lasting legacy, a failed leader is first and foremost an isolated leader. Not only does leadership imply communication, but it also requires a certain empathy with civil society and public opinion. Unlike a dictator, whose personal power paradoxically cuts him off from the people, a leader is essentially a link between society and wider moral values.

Following on from these questions, we contend that a potential leader will rely differently on environments and structures in order to act independently of his/her followers at a specific point in time. Having no control over uncertainty, leaders will be tempted to depend on structures which provide a reassuring framework. What our chapters show is the extent to which leaders are embedded in their specific environment (institutions, media, parties) while trying constantly to change it with a view to connecting or reconnecting with followers. Successful leaders have thus an adversarial relation with their environment and can be described as game-changers, seeking to mould a new consensus and not merely replicate the existing order. *Game-changers,* however, are also inherently *stability-providers*, as exemplified by some of the contributions on American politics. In their respective pieces on the US Congress, Alix Meyer and François Vergniolle de Chantal show how much congressional leadership depends on the acceptance of institutional norms beyond the mere majority–minority arithmetic. Alix Meyer documents the way in which Speaker John Boehner has dealt with his Republican majority in the budget negotiations since 2010. He emphasizes the perils of congressional leadership with high expectations but limited means to fulfill them. François Vergniolle de Chantal focuses on the US Senate and relies mainly on procedural debates to cast the upper chamber as a paradoxical institution where the Majority Leadership finds numerous advantages in minority procedures such as filibusters or holds. Mostly 'leading from behind', the Majority Leader is nonetheless able to reform procedures, as illustrated by the limit on filibusters adopted during the fall of 2013. Leadership of the US Senate is thus highly risky and unrewarding, but far from impossible. Pauline Schnapper illustrates a similar sort of dynamics when recounting the British side of the run-up to the second Iraq war in 2002–3. In establishing a new doctrine for foreign military intervention, which contradicted the traditional 'realist' approach of British foreign policy and recon-nected it to its nineteenth-century liberal roots, Tony Blair was able to become a 'game-changer', twisting the usual functioning of institutions to reach his goal. But as the war proved a military disaster and support for it waned, Blair was then accused of increasing the 'presidentializa-tion' of British prime ministers, for which some of his predecessors had already been criticized and seen as contrary to the constitutional principle of collective responsibility. The current return to parliamen-tary action prior to military intervention overseas has not been given any legal sanction. Adapting this institutional perspective to the case of the devolved institutions in Scotland, Gilles Leydier suggests that the newly created Scottish institutions allow First Ministers to devise their leadership. Establishing it meant crossing a number of identified institutional hurdles within a complex environment involving their legitimacy within their own party, control of their political majority at Holyrood, communication with Scottish opinion and media, as well as a potentially problematic relationship with Westminster. On the whole, one of the most visible trends of Scottish politics since 1999 has been the rise of executive power. As both heads of government and party leaders, most First Ministers have sought to develop their core executive and extend their initially limited patronage power. But Alex Salmond has brought a new dimension to the office of Scottish First Minister. By giving a 'presidential' turn to the First Ministerial function, and thus pursuing the same 'presidentializing' agenda as Tony Blair, he has suc-ceeded in displaying management credibility and communication skills as well as in developing a dynamic relation with his followers, even giving the impression of refashioning the institutions to his advantage.

Yet, institutions are not the only means available to both sustain and constrain political leadership. The environment in which leaders operate also includes the media, the party, and civil society, three cat-egories extensively covered in this book. The fact that modern media offer near-unlimited access to the public has been amply demonstrated, at least since Franklin Roosevelt routinized his 'fireside chats' over the radio. Our book also highlights the part played by modern tools of communication, in France as well as in Italy. Some leaders, capitalizing on their image as 'communicators', build up a substantial part of their political base through the media, as seen in Italy with Silvio Berlusconi, while others are still trying to figure out how to use new means of communication – from Twitter to Facebook – to bring out their mes-sage. Nicolas Bonnet's chapter on recent Italian politics sets out to assess the impact of Berlusconi on the national stage, thus highlighting the specificities of a leadership based on impressive communication skills and near-constant media exposure. In their chapter, Gilles Brachotte and Alex Frame document the use by various French 'premières dames' (First Ladies) of Twitter as a new channel to convey the national political message of their presidential partners. Finally, Julia Heinemann adds a historical dimension to this analysis by discussing the relations between President de Gaulle and the media at the beginning of the Fifth Republic. She argues that de Gaulle constantly instrumentalized the media in order to strengthen his public image as the savior of the nation in times of crisis. The media not only acted as an additional tool to further increase the charismatic domination that lies at the heart of Gaullism, but also as an efficient weapon to mobilize public opinion in times of uncertainty.

The third environmental constraint explored in this book deals with leaders in relation to their party. Karine Tournier-Sol, Agnès Alexandre-Collier and Emmanuelle Avril touch on the partisan side of the issue in the context of contemporary British politics. Karine Tournier-Sol discusses the impact of the European debate on British politics from Margaret Thatcher to John Major. In her view, both leaders gradually toughened their European stance and policy which were characterized by a growing opposition to European integration. Yet, the major difference that emerges between them is their motivation for such radicalization. Margaret Thatcher hardened her position out of conviction – in keeping with her reputation as 'a conviction politician' – whereas John Major did so for party considerations, in an attempt to rally his Eurosceptics and maintain the unity of the Conservative Party which was then deeply affected by political infighting over Europe. Remaining in the UK context, Agnès Alexandre-Collier adopts a similar party perspective to consider internal changes in the present Conservative Party. She shows how Prime Minister David Cameron has capitalized on and expanded the organizational reforms, launched by William Hague in 1998, to try and reconnect with his followers. Combined with an extensive use of referenda, this new method of party management, which now includes the organization of open primaries for the selection of parliamentary candidates, has paved the way for a more populist approach to leadership. David Cameron is indeed yielding primarily to grassroots pressure, with party members now responsible for his staying in power and voters more likely to turn to the United Kingdom Independence Party (UKIP) if they feel that the Conservatives are failing to deliver on Europe. Similarly, Emmanuelle Avril questions the process of leaders' selection and democracy within the British Labour Party. She highlights the inherent tension between the expectations of party members, who tend to vote for candidates meeting the ideological criteria of the party, and the requirements of national politics, which are mainly focused on electability. Party leaders must thus navigate constantly between these two obstacles, hence the part played in politics by personality, which functions as a sort of adjustment variable.

Finally, three contributions address the issue of leadership originating from civil society. Aurélie Godet analyzes the Tea Party movement in the US and considers the claim that this is a 'leaderless', 'grassroots', and 'spontaneous' movement. She fully recognizes that 'leaderlessness' has certainly allowed the Tea Party to achieve national prominence. A low degree of operational leadership has paved the way for what she calls a 'frame resonance' that has kept the decentralized organization together. Yet, this centralization of intent and purpose is now blurred. The initial fiscal conservatism of the Tea Party is being replaced by moral conservatism, which may partly explain the difficulties of the Tea Party since 2011. The other two chapters take up the issue of non-partisan leadership in Germany. Lionel Picard studies the national movement fighting for the rights of displaced Germans after World War II (expellees) and Saskia Richter writes about Petra Kelly, the icon of the Peace Movement. In both cases, these 'grassroots connectors' often verge on populism in so far as they follow Pierre Rosanvallon's definition (2011) of this highly porous concept. According to this French historian and philosopher, populism is based on three forms of simplification: a simplification of the people – 'We the People' is always perfectly clear in the eyes of populist leaders, be it an ethnic group, a class, or a nation; a simplification of democracy – representation is a detour that allows for all sorts of manipulations; and, finally, a simplification of responsibilities in so far as the 'enemy' is, just like 'the people', perfectly identifiable. As already shown, Agnès Alexandre-Collier also draws attention to the populist risk when addressing David Cameron's moves.

The topics addressed in these chapters are complemented in two later chapters which take a step back and explain how a leader fails. The initial choice of leaders to depend on specific environments (institutions, media, parties and civil society) is not a precondition of their success in adapting to these environments. Through the different examples of American president Ronald Reagan and British prime minister Edward Heath, Françoise Coste and Laetitia Langlois examine two typical cases of 'disjunction' in which the failures of these leaders may have originated from their own choice to rely on structures into which they could not fit. Françoise Coste takes the example of one of the most revered leaders of the contemporary period, Ronald Reagan, and contrasts his public achievements with his relations with his staff. She underlines the gap between both records and concludes that Reagan's inability to lead his staff paved the way for the disasters of his second term. Laetitia Langlois points out that Heath's central problem, and central failure, was communication. Her article explores the key role of communication in the success or failure of a political leader. Heath's obstinate refusal to recognize the paramount importance of communication forged a gap between him and his party, and also between him and the nation, leaving him an isolated leader.

Our case studies draw an overall picture of leadership as a purely democratic phenomenon, which explains why the different chapters of this book all concern Western nations, and aim at proposing a wider understanding of what makes political leadership successful. More specifically, they try to assess the conditions surrounding leadership attempts and by doing so they emphasize first of all the part played by context (*contextual uncertainty*) and division among followers (*social uncertainty*). They then go on to evaluate the constant tensions within leaders' specific environments (institutions, media, parties and civil society) – what Schedler termed *institutional uncertainty* (2013) – since the success of leaders depends on them being both game-changers and stability-builders. Under these conditions, leadership can become a cause in itself and not be reduced to the mere consequence of a chain of previous events.

Notes

1 See Works Cited section for a brief overview of the academic literature on political leadership since Burns' book.
2 In this book, we do not touch on the psychological dimension of leadership. Many studies are devoted to the personal ways of exerting leadership, for instance in the field of presidential studies in the US with the standard analysis by James D. Barber, *The Presidential Character* (1972). The 'love of fame' so aptly named by Alexander Hamilton in the *Federalist Papers* will be considered sufficient here to understand personal motivations.

Works cited

Bale, T. (3rd edition 2013) *European Politics: A Comparative Introduction* (Basingstoke: Palgrave Macmillan)
Barber, J.D. (2008 [1972]) *The Presidential Character: Predicting Performance in the White House* (New York: Pearson), 4th ed.
Blondel, J. (1987) *Political Leadership: Towards A General Analysis* (Beverly Hills: Sage)

Blondel, J., Thiébault, J.-L. (eds) (2010) *Political Leadership, Parties and Citizens* (New York: Routledge)

Bryman, A., Collinson, D.L., Grint, K. Jackson, B., Uhl-Bien, M. (eds) (2011) *The Sage Handbook of Political Leadership* (London: Sage)

Burns, J. (1978) *Leadership* (New York: Harper & Row Publishers)

Burns, J. (2003) *Transforming Leadership* (New York: Grove Press)

Carlyle, T. (1995 [1841]) 'On Heroes, Hero-Worship, and the Heroic in History', in Carlyle, T. Selected Writings (NY: Penguin Classics), pp. 124–212

Cioffi-Revilla, C. (1998) *Politics and Uncertainty: Theory, Models and Applications* (Cambridge: Cambridge University Press)

Colomer, J. (3rd edition 2008) *Comparative European Politics: Political Institutions in Europe* (London: Routledge)

Elcock, H. (2001) *Political Leadership* (Northampton, Mass.: Edward Elgar)

Foley, M. (ed.) (2013) *Political Leadership: Themes, Contexts, and Critiques* (Oxford: Oxford University Press)

Gill, R. (2006) *Theory and Practice of Leadership* (London: Sage)

Goleman, D., Boyatsis, R.E., McKee, A. (2003) *The New Leaders: Transforming the Art of Leadership* (London: Time Warner)

Greenleaf, R.K. (2002) *A Journey into the Nature of Legitimate Power and Greatness* (Mahwah, NJ: Paulist Press)

Greenstein, F. (2009a) *Inventing the Job of President: Leadership Style from George Washington to Andrew Jackson* (Princeton, NJ: Princeton University Press)

Greenstein, F. (2009b) *The Presidential Difference: Leadership Style from FDR to Obama* (Princeton, NJ: Princeton University Press)

Grint, K. (2000) *The Arts of Leadership* (Oxford: Oxford University Press)

Gudkykunst, W.B. (2005) *Theorizing about Intercultural Communication* (Thousand Oaks, CA: Sage)

Hamilton, A., Jay, J., Madison, J. (2010 [1788]) *The Federalist: A Commentary on the Constitution of the United States*, with an introduction by Robert Scigliano (New York: Modern Library).

Hay, C. (2002) *Political Analysis* (London, Palgrave Macmillan)

Helms, L. (ed.) (2012) *Comparative Political Leadership* (Basingstoke: Palgrave Macmillan)

Jones, B.D. (ed.) (1989) *Leadership and Politics. New Perspectives in Political Science* (Lawrence, Kansas: Kansas University Press)

Kellerman, B. (ed.) (1984), *Leadership: Multidisciplinary Perspectives* (Englewood Cliffs, NJ: Prentice Hall)

Machiavelli, N. (2003 [1513]) *The Prince* (NY: Penguin Classics).

Masciulli, R., Molchanov, M.A., Knight, W.A. (eds) (2009) *The Ashgate Research Companion to Political Leadership* (Farnham: Ashgate)

Miroff, B. (2007) 'Leadership and American Political Development', Skowronek, S., Glassman, M., (eds) *Formative Acts. American Politics in the Making* (Philadelphia, PA: University of Pennsylvania Press), pp. 32–51

Northouse, P. (1997) *Leadership: Theory and Practice* (Thousand Oaks, CA: Sage)

Ricci, D.M. (1984) *The Tragedy of Political Science: Politics, Scholarship, and Democracy* (New Haven: Yale University Press)

Roosevelt, E. (ed.) (1947) *FDR: His Personal Letters, 1928–1945*, Vol. 1, 1947–1950 (New York: Duell, Sloane and Pearce)

Rosanvallon, P. (2011) 'A Reflection on Populism', *Books & Ideas* http://www. booksandideas.net/A-Reflection-on-Populism.html date accessed July 2014

Rudalevige, A. (2009) *The New Imperial Presidency: Renewing Presidential Power after Watergate* 3rd edition (Ann Arbor: University of Michigan Press)

Schedler, A. (2013) *The Politics of Uncertainty: Sustaining and Subverting Electoral Authoritarianism* (Oxford: Oxford University Press)

Schlesinger Jr., A.M. (2004 [1974]) *The Imperial Presidency* (Boston: Houghton Mifflin Co.)

Skowronek, S. (2nd ed. 1997 [1993]) *The Politics Presidents Make. Leadership from John Adams to Bill Clinton* (Cambridge, Mass.: Harvard University Press)

Weber, M. (2010 [1922]) *Economy and Society* (London: Routledge)

2
Is Senatorial Leadership even possible? The Deadlock of the American Upper Chamber

François Vergniolle de Chantal

Checks and balances, the founding principle of American institutions, are not only found in the constant inter-branch dialog. The same applies within each branch, and especially in Congress. The bicameral division was initially meant by the Founding Fathers as an internal check within the lawmaking process. The upper chamber, the great anchor of the republic according to James Madison, was supposed to be a council to the Executive. As such, it was one of the institutional barriers meant to control the vortex of demagoguery and instability that the lower chamber was always in danger of becoming.

Nowadays, the internal legislative check of the founding generation is still the order of the day even though the political dynamic is not the one envisioned in the late eighteenth century. The two chambers making up Congress often do check and balance each other, especially when each party controls one chamber. The reasons accounting for this mutual control are numerous and varied. From constituency size to different electoral constraints including diverging partisan balance, many political factors contribute to the complex relations between the two chambers. One is especially important though: the majoritarian decision-making process in the House of Representatives compared with the omnipresence of minority procedures in the Senate. Under specific conditions, the Speaker of the House may impose a partisan discipline on his troops while shutting out the minority from any meaningful action. In the Senate, however, a single senator can derail the entire legislative process thanks to a whole range of minority procedures such as the filibuster, the most (in)famous of them all. Highly unusual until the 1960s, the filibuster, or rather the threat of its use (known as a 'hold'), is now the norm (Wawro, 2011).

The leadership of the Senate is thus a risky, unrewarding and uncertain task. The Majority Leader is often unable to garner the necessary support to have a bill adopted or even considered on the floor. Despite the high expectations in him – no woman has ever held this position so far – the Majority Leader is formally weak. Unlike the Speaker of the House, he has no constitutional status and his powers are merely the results of twentieth-century practice. Being a *primus inter pares*, he can only bargain with his colleagues, which paves the way for highly uncertain outcomes. Senate leadership has thus been compared by former Majority Leaders to 'herding cats', 'pushing wet noodles' or 'keeping frogs in a wheelbarrow', a series of telling expressions that illustrate the constant frustrations inherent to the job.

The point of this chapter is to temper this usual assessment by highlighting that the omnipresence of minority procedures is also in line with majority interests. Even though Senate Leaders are caught up in a web of confusing procedures, conflicting past precedents and various partisan imperatives, they may at times rely on this uncertain environment to promote their specific goals. They typically do it through informal bargaining. They can also, however, act as game-changers, especially when their Caucus is divided (Strahan, 2007). If significant procedural changes are indeed few and far between, this does not imply that senatorial Leadership is impotent. In November 2013, the Senate profoundly altered the use of filibusters on presidential nominations and this was as big a decision as the creation of cloture votes in 1917, while the century in between was characterized by minor adjustments even though the larger political landscape experienced tremendous changes (social reforms of the 1930s and 1960s, Civil Rights, conservative backlash, etc.). The relative lack of successful senatorial reforms is indicative of the fact that the procedural specificities of the upper chamber are not only the result of minorities somehow hijacking the regular process; rather, they are also tolerated by the majority, in so far as minority procedures are a convenient tool for the majority. Indeed, divisions within the majority party, the prospect of soon becoming the minority, or the relations to the Presidency are considerations that temper the theoretical commitment of the majority party to a majoritarian decision-making process.

The historical development of leadership in the US Senate

In his famous 1960 book on presidential powers, Richard Neustadt explained that presidents could only act one way with Congress, through persuasion (Neustadt, 1990 [1960]). The same could be said about senatorial leadership. Historically, the Senate remained essentially unorganized[1] until Woodrow Wilson's presidency. Elected to the presidency after decades of near-complete Republican domination on the executive branch, Wilson considered he had gained a mandate to govern and consequently built on Theodore Roosevelt's achievements to turn the presidency into an institution designed to promote social changes. One of the main illustrations of that change was his relations to Congress. Not only did he initiate the tradition of addressing Congress for the State of the Union, but he also pressured Democratic majorities – in the 63rd Congress elected in 1912, Democrats had a slim majority in the Senate and dominated the House – into organizing themselves to facilitate the passage of the presidential agenda. The 'greatest deliberative body in the world', the US Senate, was the most impacted since the House already was largely organized in a majoritarian way.

Under presidential pressure, the Democratic majority created in 1913 a new position, that of Senate Majority Leader, meant to unify the Democratic majority (Hatcher, 2010). The newly created Leadership – under the aegis of John Kern (a Democrat from Indiana) – tried to organize floor deliberation, thus formalizing the process of Unanimous Consent Agreement (UCA) that had been sporadically implemented in the previous decades.[2] Three years later, after 'a few willful men' prevented a bill to arm merchant ships from being adopted, the Senate adopted the 'cloture', a provision to end filibusters (Rule XXII(2)) that was used to limit debate on the Treaty of Versailles. Its use remained largely unusual though in the 1920s and 1930s (Mayhew, 2003). The Senate Majority Leader, despite his lack of formal powers, could effectively manage the floor and have substantial legislation adopted when needed. The New Deal witnessed another important change. The Senate Majority Leader gained what is to this day his only official power, the 'right of first recognition': the Senate Majority Leader will always be the first to be recognized by the chair, which allows him to set the floor agenda by making motions, including the motion to proceed to the consideration of a measure, before any other senator can do so. A skillful Leader can thus shape the ensuing debate while minimizing disruption.

By mid-century, the main leadership components of today's Senate were thus in place. The rules made the Leadership a consensus-building tool. The main role of the Majority Leader was to craft a UCA to debate a bill after committee action.[3] This meant to get the approval of all senators – or at least a sufficient number to invoke cloture – on how to debate a bill on the floor (number and type of amendments, for instance); then, the Majority Leader used his right of first recognition to formally open the debate. In case of obstruction – generally confined to Civil Rights issues until the 1960s – the Majority Leader could ask for a cloture vote to end debate and get a final vote on the text. The Democratic Majority Leaders of the 1950s and 1960s (Lyndon Johnson, Texas, and Mike Mansfield, Montana) operated in a procedural vacuum that made it possible for them to develop their own personal style of leadership. If Johnson became famous for his ability to force his colleagues into action (Caro, 2002),[4] Mansfield adopted a more subtle tactic that relied on constant listening and accommodation. In both instances, the personal qualities of the Leaders mattered much more than their formal power. The normal mode of operation was informal. According to the rules, the Majority Leader only has one power, the right of first recognition. By international standard, this is incredibly weak, which raises the question: why has the US Senate stuck to such a lack of leadership rules? How was it even possible to organize the lawmaking process?

Part of the answer lies in the classic assessment made by Donald Matthews in his 1960 account of the Senate, *U.S. Senators and their World*. According to him, members of the upper house operated according to informal norms that regulated their behaviors, including seniority (the longer a member of the majority has served in the institution the higher up (s)he is in the hierarchy) and self-restraint in the use of minority obstruction. But this focus on norms has to be complemented by two other factors. First, the early procedural decisions in the Senate: Binder (1997a) largely documented the abolition of a previous question motion in 1806, its cumulative consequences and the ensuing procedural divergence with the House. The lack of a previous question motion – a common tool of all legislative chambers in the world to stop debate and proceed to a vote – proved crucial. Indeed, this initial choice by a Senate barely over 30 members paved the way for the current lack of discipline in the upper chamber. Second, the specificities of the US party system are also to be taken into account. Until the 1960s, American parties were divided to such an extent that their delegations in Congress were largely empty shells. Republicans had a substantial wing of moderates and even some progressives, whereas Democrats had a southern branch made up of explicitly racist and highly conservative members who used filibusters for race issues only. This meant that party discipline was basically nonexistent, especially on Civil Rights measures. A majority was almost always bipartisan, as witnessed during the New Deal and the Great Society. Taken together, procedural path-dependency, partisan and ideological mismatch, the light touch of effective Majority Leaders and informal norms of behaviors, were mutually supportive and combined to create the 'most exclusive club' described by William White in his 1957 journalistic account of the Senate, likened to a *Citadel*. To some, including White, the Senate was thus the prime example of a consensual, tradition-bound and stable institution; to others, the Senate was a stuffy venue, wholly disconnected from national trends and hijacked by Southern segregationists.

Going into the 1970s and 1980s, the Senate experienced profound mutations that were summarized by Barbara Sinclair in her 1989 book, *The Transformation of the US Senate*. She called that 'new Senate' a 'hyperpartisan and individualistic' chamber where values and practices inherited from the 1950s and 1960s were turned upside down. The norms of self-restraint and institutional pride gave way to a politicized and partisan chamber where the 'permanent campaign' (Blumenthal, 1982) was the obsession shared by all senators. They have become more extreme in their views and they never hesitate about using minority procedures to further their own particularistic objectives without any consideration for their leadership or larger policy objectives. The confluence between individualistic behavior and partisan polarization has proven to be extremely toxic. In 2006, Thomas E. Mann and Norman Ornstein called it 'the curse of the Senate' in *The Broken Branch*, a book criticizing the supine Congress of the Bush years. The senatorial politics of the 2000s and 2010s seem to be an echo chamber that amplifies the worst characteristics of American politics, namely individualism and extremism.

A leadership crisis?

Compared with the House, the contemporary Senate seems to be a legislative state of nature. Polarization has also impacted the lower chamber but its consequences have been quite different. Since the 104th Congress and Newt Gingrich's Speakership, centralization and strict majority-rule are the guiding principles of lawmaking in the House of Representatives. John Boehner is maybe the weakest of all Speakers since 1994 but his formal powers bear no comparison with the lone right of first recognition of Mitch McConnell in the Senate. The 'conditional party government' thesis articulated by D. Rohde in 1991 for the House of Representatives does not fit the Senate. The key proposition of Rohde is that polarized parties produce a lawmaking process that is centralized in majority party leaders. Indeed, polarization implies that most members of the party will trust strong central leaders to act on their behalf. Party Leaders are thus mainly followers of their troops. Franklin Roosevelt famously wrote in 1931 that 'Leadership can be successful only through the greatest amount of party harmony' (see Introduction), an insight shared by most theories of legislative decision-making, including Rohde's. But in the Senate, the ability of a minority to block changes in the rules and the inherent weakness of the chair (no constitutional status, no stability) have limited the powers of the majority party leadership. As a result, polarization of parties has not translated into rules that enhance the procedural advantages of the majority party and its leader.

This shows how wide a gap there is between party discipline and a shift to extremes. To that extent, the word 'polarization' is a misnomer that hides a major difference. In the House, both ideological extremism and party discipline have been mutually supportive at least until the rise of the Tea Party and the Leadership of John Boehner (see Alix Meyer's chapter in this volume). But the Senate illustrates the divergence between the two ever since the early 1990s. In a legislative body that empowers legislators with resources, both the Minority and Majority party leadership have few means to restrain fellow partisans. Even within a quite homogeneous party, there will be legislators whose personal views, home constituencies, and political ambitions will motivate them to pursue uncommon strategies that party leaders would not otherwise pursue. The party leadership will often find that floor strategies are driven by the day-to-day tactics of more extreme legislators. The Tea Party senators have often tried to promote their own views without any consideration for their leadership; for instance, during the numerous fiscal debates that have taken place since 2010. When Democrats were the Majority, until 2014, the same has applied, since Harry Reid had many difficulties keeping his party united during the healthcare debate. The rolling debate on immigration reform has also repeatedly shown that Senate Democrats do not speak in one voice. More generally, Senate Leaders cannot retain their position without the support of their colleagues, and they have few resources they can use to motivate compliant behavior. As a procedural matter, the Majority Leader always needs unanimous consent to conduct the normal business of the Senate and cannot afford to seriously alienate any of his colleagues. His institutional role is thus limited to bargaining and the preservation of good relations within his Caucus.

Leaders in the 'new Senate' have seemed to be passive bystanders in a chamber spinning out of control. Their common objective has been to try to accommodate their fellow senators as much as they could without radically altering the rules giving them so much legislative freedom. The fact is that the only significant change in Senate's history remains to this day the creation of cloture in 1917. The war context and the recent passage of the 17th Amendment instituting the direct election of senators were certainly decisive factors whose impact cannot be replicated nowadays. Since the early 1990s, the striking fact about minority procedures in the Senate is the lack of reform. The upper chamber formally adopted a rule change for the last time in 1986 when Rule XXII was amended to limit post-cloture debate to 30 hours. Between 1986 and the Fall of 2013, minority procedures remained unchanged. Besides, the Leadership came to tolerate new practices that were not even mentioned in the rules, such as 'holds', which are individual notifications of intent that a senator plans to filibuster a bill or a nomination. Instead of addressing the crucial issue of minority procedures, Leaders have constantly tried to avoid the subject.[5] They have rather developed forms of 'unorthodox lawmaking' (Sinclair, 2007 [1995]). Indeed, more polarized parties have accelerated procedural innovation. Thus, according to Steven Smith (2014), a pattern of obstruction and restriction similar to a 'parliamentary arms race' has pervaded the Senate, just like in the House during the 1980s. The deep partisan divide of the past two decades has intensified and broadened minority obstruction and majority reaction. With less resistance from within the party, each party has an incentive to score political points against the opposition. A cohesive minority party especially is able to block action; it has become the norm in the modern Senate. Thus, for today's generation of senators, the ability of a minority party, if it is fairly cohesive, to obstruct a majority party is the normal state of affairs. Senators began to assume that the other party would fully exploit its procedural options and prepared to do the same. The majority cannot assume that there will be a final vote on a bill or nomination; the minority cannot assume that opportunities to offer amendments will be preserved. This is what Steven Smith recently called the 'Senate Syndrome' (2014). Since the late 1980s, Majority Leaders have responded to minority obstruction with innovations in parliamentary tactics and new precedents but never frontally addressed the issue of minority procedures.

Procedural makeshift in a polarized Senate

The 'dysfunction' of the contemporary Senate is illustrated by the omnipresence of the filibuster threat. This is the main characteristic of today's Senate: the threat of a filibuster and not an actual – 'talking' – filibuster, the way Frank Capra famously showed in his 1939 movie, *Mr. Smith Goes to Washington*. Indeed, Leaders have condoned the rise of the so-called 'holds' since the 1970s. They are requests to the floor leader[6] that a measure not be considered on the floor until some condition is met. From the start, floor leaders kept confidential the identity of the senator placing a hold. At times, floor leaders may have used the secrecy to their advantage by privately addressing the concern of the senator or even using the hold as an excuse to delay floor action on a matter. But on the whole, holds became a serious problem for lawmaking in the Senate. During the 1970s and 1980s, repeated announcements by Majority Leaders that holds were not a right and could be ignored did not make much of a difference.[7] Leaders still wanted advance notice of problems, and senators appreciated the opportunity to exercise something approaching a personal veto (Smith, 1989). That is how holds gained their effectiveness as implicit threats to filibuster. The threats became more credible and the floor leaders' need for predictability increased as the number of actual filibusters increased. The holds thus became a defining feature of the Senate because Leaders started to take into account the mere notification of an individual senator's opposition to a given measure or nomination as a veto. This form of 'silent filibuster' is nowadays omnipresent, even though its secret nature has been recently reformed. In 2007 and 2011, the Senate officially addressed the issue. In 2007, an ethics reform bill was adopted that incorporated changes to holds. The new rule did not ban holds but rather was intended to make public the identity of senators placing holds under certain circumstances. But the process was convoluted and full of ambiguity. A new agreement was thus implemented in 2011, after Obama officially called for an end to holds on executive nominations in his 2010 State of the Union Address and a most embarrassing episode that occurred the same year when Richard Shelby (a Republican from Alabama) objected to Senate action on nearly 70 executive branch appointments because of his interest in acquiring an Air Force tanker project and an antiterrorism center for his state. As part of the 2011 agreement, the Senate's party leaders agreed to tighten the rule governing holds. Again, holds were not banned, but a disclosure requirement was imposed after two days. The debate on holds is a prime example of Leaders' ambiguous relations to minority procedures (Smith, 2014). Even though holds are obstacles to a proper unfolding of the lawmaking process, Leaders have reneged on any attempt to seriously temper holds.

No surprise then in the fact that the number of cloture votes has been steadily on the rise ever since holds started and no matter which party was in power. There was a first steep increase in cloture motions in the early 1970s, another in the 1990s, and yet another at the end of the first decade of the twenty-first century, after Republicans lost control of the chamber in 2006. In the 96th Congress (1979–80), the 'last great Senate' according to one observer (Shapiro, 2012), 18 cloture votes were taken; 45 such votes were taken during the 103rd Congress (1993–94), but 108 in the 110th Congress.[8] In the 113th Congress, cloture motions have skyrocketed: from 3 January 2013 through 4 August 2014, 190 cloture motions were filed. But this is only the tip of the iceberg. The expansion of minority rights over the past 20 years has been so pronounced that the minority party Leadership now refers to the upper chamber as the '60-vote Senate' – the necessary threshold to successfully invoke cloture and proceed to a vote.

Leaders have devised ways of circumventing minority obstruction. Cloture is one. It ends debate and allows for a final vote. But this is by no means the only one. The other major freedom of individual senators – next to the freedom of unlimited debate – is the freedom to amend a text on the floor. There is no 'germaneness' requirement governing floor debate, so that a single senator can derail the general debate by offering an amendment that has no connection whatsoever to the bill under consideration. Majority Leaders have been able to limit this freedom. Some statutory limitations have been created, for instance in the budget process since the 1974 Budget Act. It made the consideration of budget measures largely immune to filibusters and imposed strict germaneness rules to amendments. But these were the result of a larger confrontation between Congress and the Presidency. In the context of the Watergate scandal, Congress members garnered the necessary institutional patriotism to counter the budgetary moves decided by Nixon. In order to preserve their constitutional budgetary prerogatives against presidential 'impoundments' (unilateral presidential decisions not to spend the appropriations voted by Congress), Congress members created a new legislative framework that limited the individual powers of senators while protecting the legislative budget power. But the amendment process was limited in another way and this time it was an innovation by Majority Leaders. Trent Lott, a Republican senator from Mississippi and Majority Leader in the early 2000s, systematized the practice of 'filling the amendment tree', an innovation that was taken up afterwards by both Republican Bill Frist and Democrat Harry Reid (Smith, 2014). The Majority Leader can fill the 'amendment tree'[9] by virtue of his right of first recognition. By seeking recognition to offer a series of amendments, the Majority Leader can prevent other amendments from being offered, at least temporarily. At a minimum, filling the tree stalls the amendment process, thus providing the Leader with some control of the floor proceeding.

Building around minority obstruction to get results, Majority Leaders have been most cautious when formally dealing with minority rights. For instance, Harry Reid, the Democratic Majority Leader between 2006 and 2014, resisted demands for a bold move at the start of the 212th Congress in 2011 and instead negotiated an agreement with Republican Minority Leader Mitch McConnell. This 'gentlemen's agreement' was simply based on a common exercise in self-restraint. It was merely intended to smooth relations between the parties and avert a confrontation over formal changes in Senate rules.[10] Later, at the start of the 113th Congress, in January 2013, the Senate adopted modest procedural reforms: limiting the number of times that any one bill can be filibustered and limiting the time to debate a motion to take up a bill or to debate a minor nomination. The minority Republicans went along because they were given opportunities to offer amendments in return. Plus, these changes were supposed to be temporary, good only for the 113th Congress (2013–14), unless renewed by the Senate.

The modesty of these changes offers a striking contrast to the intensity of polarization. The question then becomes: why has Senate Leadership remained so passive when confronted with the rise of minority obstruction in a polarized context? A subsidiary to this first question is why a sudden reform in the Fall of 2013 was implemented which none of the Senate watchers anticipated.

Senatorial leadership and procedural reform

The only significant procedural reform in Senate's history was the creation of cloture in 1917. However, the external shocks that made it possible are – fortunately – not on the horizon nowadays. Under more routine circumstances, the upper chamber seems to be impossible to reform and forever tied in procedural knots. There are broadly two reasons accounting for this dead-end: procedural first and political second.

Senatorial rules can be formally amended in two ways, both of which are not unanimously agreed on by all senators (Smith, 2014).[11] The first one is the simplest: a majority vote to change the rules. But this raises a difficulty: the motion to proceed on a rules change is debatable, which means that it can be filibustered. In the current context, this implies that a rule change requires a 2/3 majority of voting senators, the super-majority required by Rule XXII.[12] The other option is more complicated and has been a rolling debate in senatorial circles since the late 1950s. It requires a ruling by the presiding officer of the Senate. It is based on the opinion of vice-president Nixon in 1957 in response to a parliamentary inquiry from Hubert Humphrey (a Democrat from Minnesota) about the rules under which the Senate was proceeding. According to Nixon's opinion,[13] a simple majority is plainly entitled to change the rules of the Senate at the start of each new Congress. In the mid-2000s, when the debate on confirmations was stuck, the Republican Majority Leader, Bill Frist, devised a 'constitutional option' – quickly dubbed 'nuclear option' in the media because of its wide-ranging implications on Senate governance – that would end obstruction on nominations. The scenario, as explained in a Law Review article written by a former Senate Republican leadership aide (Gold, Gupta, 2004), would work like this: in times of a unified government, a senator from the majority party would make a point of order that the Constitution implies an obligation on the Senate to vote on nominations, which means that a simple majority may invoke cloture on a nomination. The presiding officer, probably the vice-president for that occasion, would rule in favor of the point of order. The minority party would appeal the ruling, but a member of the majority party – presumably the Majority Leader himself – would be recognized by the chair to offer a motion to 'table' (meaning to 'discard') the appeal. Because it takes just a simple-majority vote to adopt the nondebatable motion to table, the appeal would be tabled and the presiding officer's ruling on the point of order would stand. Thus, simple-majority cloture for nominations would be instituted by a ruling of the chair backed by a simple majority of senators.[14]

The other set of reasons are political and electoral, starting with the fact that individual senators want to retain their prerogatives. It sounds like a real challenge to convince a supermajority of senators to weaken their powers within the institution. Just as obvious is the fact that senators anticipate an electoral swing and their resulting minority status. Since the 1980 election, the upper chamber has changed majorities more often than the House – in 1980, in 1986, in 1994, briefly between 2000 and 2001, in 2006 and again in 2014 – and the electoral vulnerability of senators compared to Representatives is a long-recognized fact of political science (Abramowitz, Segal, 1992; Krasno, 1994; Gronke, 2000). Nearly all senators nowadays have experienced a change in party control and are sensitized to its consequences (committee chairmanships and hearings, agenda control). This has consequences for the policy and electoral calculations of the parties. The prospect of a change in party control encourages the minority to withhold support for legislation in the hopes of having a stronger hand after the next election. It also may encourage the majority to push a larger agenda for fear of losing seats at the next election. Either way, obstructionism is encouraged (Smith, 2014). Additional electoral calculations and anticipations can easily be added to the mix. The Majority Leader can tolerate minority obstruction so as to avoid a disruption of his party's legislative agenda because of the divisions within the party. This may be especially the case with Democrats, whose moderate wing – currently known as 'Blue Dogs' – remains influential. Plus, even if there are ways for a majority to force a change in the rules, there are also costs that the minority can impose if the majority does so. In the context of most legislating, a fight over the rules is certainly too costly for the majority, as illustrated by the fight against nominations between 2003 and 2005. Moreover, a party that controls the presidency may find supermajority cloture to be an advantage or disadvantage depending on whether it wants to pass or block legislation. The filibuster can be used to block legislation that the president opposes. Since 2010, the ideological frenzy of the House Republicans – under pressure from Tea Party members – has systematically gone nowhere because the Senate would not budge. Clinton also benefited from this moderating effect of the upper chamber when Republican Majority Leader Bob Dole contributed to the moderation of ideological impulses coming from the lower chamber during the 104th Congress. As for the minority party, it quickly recognizes that it may not be held accountable for outcomes in a Senate 'controlled' by the other party and, considering the low approval ratings of Congress,[15] it can hope that frustration with Washington will cost electoral support for majority party senators. This is the calculation made by Republicans since 2010.

Both the complexity of rules and electoral anticipations from senators themselves thus seemed to make impossible any substantial readjustment of minority procedures. Until the Fall of 2013 that is. With the benefit of hindsight, it is possible to decipher the alignment of factors that made reform possible. First, the electoral configuration: the surprising outcome of the 2012 Senate elections, which increased the Democrats' majority from 53 to 55 seats, and the re-election of Democratic President Barack Obama encouraged the majority party to act on its agenda in the 113th Congress despite Republican obstruction. The Democrats correctly expected to lose seats in the 2014 elections and to suffer a loss of presidential influence in Obama's last two years in

office during the next Congress. Second, is the deterioration of the relations between Mitch McConnell and Harry Reid. By the Fall of 2011, the
'gentlemen's agreement' of the previous January had disintegrated. Reid
and the Democrats complained of a Republican obstruction as early as
the Spring of 2011; but after the collapse of the President's job bill in
the Fall, Reid publicly declared that the agreement had broken down. In
January 2013, Reid and McConnell came up with two minor procedural
changes that streamlined the process for bringing up a bill in the 113th
Congress and facilitated quick action on a motion to proceed. But these
were limited in scope and in duration. Until then, Reid had opposed
the reform-by-ruling approach advocated by Tom Udall (Democrat from
New Mexico) and Jeff Merkley (Democrat from Oregon); he had given
only the most token support for the general idea of reform (Smith,
2014). But on November 21, 2013, the Democratic Majority Leader
Harry Reid made a point of order on presidential nominations. In other
words, he raised an issue of parliamentary procedure by asking whether
or not the rules had been broken. His point was that the Senate could
close debate on the consideration of a presidential nomination, other
than to the Supreme Court, by a simple majority vote. This point of
order called upon the chair to make a ruling. Because Reid's point of
order was inconsistent with Senate Rule XXII, the cloture rule that
requires a three-fifths majority of all senators to close debate, the presiding officer ruled against Reid's point of order. Then, by a 48–52 vote,
the Senate failed to sustain the ruling of the chair, thereby adopting the
precedent that Reid requested.

   This was a momentous change. The precedent of 2013 is one of the
most important procedural developments in Senate history whose
impact is yet to be assessed, especially the way Republicans will be
reacting. Not only does the new threshold reshape the strategic calculations of presidents and senators involved in the nomination and confirmation process,[16] but it also shows that minority procedures are not
the insurmountable obstacle that analysts believed them to be. This is
explained by the fact that contrary to the usual assumptions made by
most theories of legislative leadership, Majority Leaders are not just the
agents of their principals. They are not merely expressing the will of their
Caucus or giving them what they want (in that case the preservation of
their individual powers). The theory of 'conditional agency framework'
proposed by Randall Strahan (2007) better fits the recent development
in senatorial politics. He emphasizes two elements that make it possible
for Leadership to matter. First, building on Richard Fenno's framework
(1973), the leader must have specific intensely held goals beyond

staying in office, such as power in the institution and 'good' public policy. Second, followers must be dissatisfied with the status quo but divided about how to change it. The 2013 decision is illustrative of this framework. Harry Reid, without being committed to procedural reform *per se*, was nonetheless aware of the constitutional duties of the Senate in the field of nominations, especially with a Democratic President. Nominations and confirmations are prime examples of checks and balances at work since all three powers are explicitly involved and the tensions within that crucial process have been running high since 2005. Here was a situation where the Senate as an institution was on the brink of defaulting on one of its key constitutional obligations. Second, the Democrats were not united in their assessment of the crisis on nominations. Apart from some leading proponents of reforms – mostly junior and recently elected – the rest of the Democratic Caucus is tepid at best when it comes to reform of minority procedures – Harry Reid himself being a good illustration here – because of electoral and political considerations. Taken together, there was in 2013 a window of opportunity to act decisively on minority procedures and Harry Reid, unlike Bill Frist in 2005, decided to do so, thus proving once more the only existing law of politics, namely that it is event-driven and individually-shaped.

Conclusion

Unlike the House, where the Speaker is largely the agent of his principal, a majority of the majority party as Dennis Hastert used to say, the US Senate illustrates how decisive the Leader can be, especially when uncertainty is on the rise. In the context of polarization and individualism, the Leadership has nonetheless succeeded in 'leading from behind' over the past 20 years. The relative lack of substantial procedural reform until 2013 actually exemplifies the extent to which Leadership control can successfully take informal paths. Senate Leadership, just like the presidential influence theorized by Neustadt (1960), is both omnipresent and largely invisible. The recent reform of filibusters on nominations also shows that Leaders can be assertive under certain circumstances – individual leadership, intensely held goals, and division of the followership. A red line seems to be crossed when institutional stalemate is so intense as to prevent the upper chamber from fulfilling its core executive functions. The dysfunctional nature of the nomination process since 2003 has proven to be the catalyst for procedural change. A larger factor at work to understand the recent reform is also that no assembly and no elected official can have a purely negative record. The contemporary

Senate has been a gigantic veto factory – including for major bills – and the two latest Congresses – the 112th and 113th – have been the most unproductive since the historic 80th 'Do-Nothing' Congress of 1946–48. This may have been the necessary shock for a long-expected streamlining of senatorial procedures by a determined Majority Leader, thus bringing the upper chamber closer to a properly working assembly.

Notes

1   The key to this lack of organization is to be found in the Constitution. It provides for a presiding officer, the vice-president, who may vote only when the Senate is equally divided (Article 1, section 3). The political separation of the Senate from its presiding officer has had a significant effect on the procedural development of the institution. Since the president of the Senate is not a senator, he very rarely participates in floor debates. He is usually replaced. Either by a president *pro tempore* – the senior senator of the majority party – or, as is most often the case, a junior member who takes up this chore as part of his 'apprenticeship' of Senate ways. He has mostly ministerial and ceremonial duties, even though ruling from the chair may occasionally prove decisive.

2   Thanks to a rule adopted in 1914 – Rule XII(4) – unanimous consent agreements were considered orders to the Senate to be enforced by the presiding officer. That is why they became the most frequently used tool of the majority leader for orchestrating floor activity.

3   Committees are weaker in the Senate than in the House. Rules make it thus easier to report a bill out of committee and to the floor in the upper chamber.

4   The Johnson 'Treatment' was captured by famous pictures of a face-to-face discussion between Lyndon Johnson and the chairman of the Foreign Relations Committee, Theodore F. Green, in 1957. These pictures are available on the *New York Times* website: http://www.afterimagegallery.com/nytjohnson.htm (accessed in August 2014). Two journalists, Evans Rowland and Robert Novak, described the 'Treatment' thus: 'The Treatment could last ten minutes or four hours. It came, enveloping its target, at the Johnson Ranch swimming pool, in one of Johnson's offices, in the Senate cloakroom, on the floor of the Senate itself – wherever Johnson might find a fellow Senator within his reach. Its tone could be supplication, accusation, cajolery, exuberance, scorn, tears, complaint and the hint of threat. It was all of these together. It ran the gamut of human emotions. Its velocity was breathtaking, and it was all in one direction. Interjections from the target were rare. Johnson anticipated them before they could be spoken. He moved in close, his face a scant millimeter from his target, his eyes widening and narrowing, his eyebrows rising and falling. From his pockets poured clippings, memos, statistics. Mimicry, humor, and the genius of analogy made The Treatment an almost hypnotic experience and rendered the target stunned and helpless' in *Lyndon Johnson: The Exercise of Power*, New York, New American Library, 1966, p.104.

5   Some individual senators are known to be in favor of reform. They regularly came up with reform proposals but none of them were ever taken up by the

Leadership and successfully voted on. Tom Harkin (Democrat from Iowa) has championed filibuster reform since the early 1990s. Recently, Tom Udall (Democrat from New Mexico) and Jeff Merkley (Democrat from Oregon) have been the lead reformers.

6 Senators place 'holds' requests via their party's leader. Thus members of the minority do not directly approach the Majority Leader. But both the Majority and Minority Leaders usually work together on the consideration of a given bill.

7 As early as 1973, Senator Robert Byrd (a Democrat from West Virginia who later became known for his defense of the Senate's values) complained about senators exploiting holds and creating problems for the majority leadership. By late 1982, Howard Baker was fed up and announced on the floor that he would no longer treat holds as binding. Bob Dole would say the same thing in the 1990s. The fact that the issue had to be addressed repetitively reflected the basic logic of the situation: floor leaders needed to plan floor sessions and clear legislation with their colleagues, which created an opportunity for individual and factional obstructionism.

8 The data is available on the Brookings website: http://www.brookings.edu/ blogs/brookings-now/posts/2013/11/chart-recent-history-of-senate-cloture-votes-to-end-filibusters (accessed in August 2014). Cloture votes are imperfect ways of measuring obstruction however. Many bills are never on the floor because of the anticipation of obstruction. This imperfect instrument remains the only tool to measure obstruction though.

9 The 'tree' is a diagram presenting the permissible amendments during a floor debate (Oleszek, 2011). Senate precedents identify the types of amendments that may be pending simultaneously during floor debate. These precedents stipulate that when an amendment to a bill is offered, it can be followed by a substitute amendment and a perfecting amendment to the first amendment. The original amendment is called 'first degree amendment' and the other two are 'amendments in the second degree'. No amendment in the third degree is allowed.

10 The negotiations were led by Rules Committee leaders Charles Schumer (Democrat from New York) and Lamar Alexander (Republican from Tennessee) and produced commitments from both leaders. The Republican Leader, Mitch McConnell, promised to only rarely filibuster a motion to proceed and to endorse a change in the rules banning secret holds. Harry Reid, the Democratic Leader, promised to protect minority-party opportunities to offer amendments. Both Leaders agreed to refuse to pursue the 'constitutional' option to reform (cf. below) in the 112th and 113th Congresses. Both Leaders also agreed to support legislation to reduce the number of executive branch positions subject to Senate confirmation (so as to avoid obstruction).

11 There remains genuine and deep disagreement among senators about how they can exercise their power to determine their own rules because the Constitution is silent about it (Article 1, section 5 merely provides that 'each house may determine the rules of its proceedings'). Both the House and Senate assume that a simple majority is implied to be the standard decision rule. Over the decades, the Senate has acquired 44 standing rules, many of which have been amended several times.

12 The rule also indicates that three-fifths of all elected senators is required to invoke cloture on all other matters. Democrats achieved two-thirds of

the seats only in the 88th and 89th Congresses (1963–66). But since 1980, when the Republicans won a Senate majority for the first time since the early 1950s, the mean size of the minority party has been nearly 46. Only for half a year in 2009, after the seating of Al Franken (Democrat from Minnesota) in July and before the special election of Republican Scott Brown (Massachusetts) in January 2010, did the majority party hold 60 seats – a three-fifths majority – in the Senate.

13 Indeed, his views did not have the force of a ruling in response to a point of order. It was merely advisory.

14 The great tactical advantage here is to succeed in changing the application of the rules, by a ruling of the presiding officer rather than by changing the standing rules. It avoids a filibuster on a resolution to change the rules, which would be difficult to circumvent under the Rule XXII requirement of a two-thirds majority for cloture on a measure that changes the standing rules.

15 It has hovered below 10 percent over the past few years. A recent Gallup poll (January 2014) showed that only 7 percent of Americans have 'quite a lot' or a 'great deal' of confidence in the country's legislative branch. This is the lowest approval of the past 40 years. When Gallup started measuring confidence toward Congress, in 1973, it stood at 42 per cent. See: http://www.usnews.com/news/blogs/ballot-2014/2014/06/19/poll-congressional-popularity-tanks (accessed August 2014).

16 So far the reform has sped up the confirmation of Obama's judicial nominees, especially in states with two Democratic Senators. See Burgess Everett, 'How Going Nuclear Unclogged the Senate', *Politico*, 22 August 2014: http://www.politico.com/story/2014/08/how-going-nuclear-unclogged-the-senate-110238.html (accessed August 2014).

Works cited

Abramowitz, A., Segal, J. (1992) *Senate Elections* (Ann Arbor: University of Michigan Press).

Binder, S. (2003) *Stalemate: Causes and Consequences of Legislative Gridlock* (Washington DC: Brookings Press).

Binder, S. (1997a) *Politics or Principle? Filibustering in the United States Senate* (Washington DC: Brookings Press).

Binder, S. (1997b) *Minority Rights, Majority Rule* (New York: Cambridge University Press).

Blumenthal, S. (1982) *The Permanent Campaign* (New York: Simon & Schuster).

Caro, R. (2002) *The Years of Lyndon Johnson: Master of the Senate* (New York: Vintage Books).

Fenno, R. (1973) *Congressmen in Committees* (Boston: Little, Brown).

Gold, M. (2004) *Senate Procedure and Practice* (Lanham: Rowman & Littlefield).

Gold, M., Gupta, D. (2004) 'The Constitutional Option to Change Senate Rules and Procedures: A Majoritarian Means to Overcome the Filibuster', *Harvard Journal of Law and Public Policy*, Vol.28, 205–72.

Gronke, P. (2000) *The Electorate, the Campaign, and the Office: A Unified Approach to Senate and House Elections* (Ann Arbor: University of Michigan Press).

Hatcher, A. (2010) *Majority Leadership in the US Congress: Balancing Constraints* (Amherst: Cambria Press).

Koger, G. (2010) *Filibustering: A Political History of Obstruction in the House and the Senate* (Chicago: University of Chicago Press).

Krasno, J. (1994) *Challengers, Competition, and Reelection: Comparing Senate and House Elections* (New Haven: Yale University Press).

Mann, T., Ornstein, N. (2006) *The Broken Branch* (Oxford & New York: Oxford University Press).

Matthews, D. (2nd ed. 1973) *U.S. Senators and Their World* (New York: Norton).

Mayhew, D. (2003) 'Supermajority Rule in the US Senate', *PS: Political Science and Politics*, Vol.36 (1), 31–6.

Monroe, N., Roberts, J., Rohde, D., (eds) (2008) *Why Not Parties? Party Effects in the United States Senate* (Chicago: University of Chicago Press).

Neustadt, R. (2nd ed. 1990) *Presidential Power and the Modern Presidents* (New York: Free Press).

Oleszek, W. (8th ed. 2011) *Congressional Procedures and the Policy Process* (Washington DC: CQ Press).

Rohde, D. (1991) *Parties and Leaders in the Postreform House* (Chicago: University of Chicago Press).

Shapiro, I. (2012) *The Last Great Senate* (New York: Public Affairs).

Sinclair, B. (1995, 3rd ed. 2007). *Unorthodox Lawmaking: New Legislative Processes in the US Congress.* (Washington DC, CQ Press).

Sinclair, B. (2006) *Party Wars: Polarization and the Politics of National Policy-Making* (Norman: University of Oklahoma Press).

Sinclair, B. (1989) *The Transformation of the US Senate* (Baltimore: Johns Hopkins University Press).

Smith, S. (2014) *The Senate Syndrome: The Evolution of Procedural Warfare in the Modern US Senate* (Norman: University of Oklahoma Press).

Smith, S. (2007) *Party Influence in Congress* (New York: Cambridge University Press).

Smith, S. (2005) 'Parties and Leadership in the Senate', in Quirk, P., Binder, S., (ed.) *The Legislative Branch.* (Oxford: Oxford University Press), pp. 255–78 .

Smith, S. (1989) *Call to Order: Floor Politics in the House and the Senate* (Washington DC: Brookings Press).

Strahan, R. (2007) *Leading Representatives: The Agency of Leaders in the Politics of the U.S. House* (Baltimore: Johns Hopkins University Press).

Taylor, A. (2013) *The Floor in Congressional Life* (Ann Arbor: University of Michigan Press).

Wawro, G. (2011) 'The Supermajority Senate', in Schickler, E., Lee, F., (eds) *The Oxford Handbook of the American Congress* (Oxford: Oxford University Press), pp.426–50.

Wawro, G., Schickler, E. (2006) *Filibuster: Obstruction and Lawmaking in the U.S. Senate* (Princeton: Princeton University Press).

White, W. (1957) *Citadel: The Story of the US Senate* (New York: Harper & Brothers).

3
The Office-Holder: John Boehner as Speaker of the US House of Representatives

Alix Meyer

Introduction

Congressional leadership is a peculiar category of leadership. First of all, because it is derivative. All members of Congress are elected in their own constituencies. They do not hold their office thanks to their leaders and they are not at their mercy. In fact, members of Congress elect leaders to further their own individual goals.[1] Second, congressional leadership is shaped by the dual mission of the institution. The US legislature is the locus of deliberation and decision-making by a collection of individuals who must represent the interests of their constituents. This led certain scholars to describe 'two congresses': an assembly of representatives and a lawmaking body (Davidson et al., 2009: 3). The tensions between these two congresses are embodied in the contradictory demands that members of Congress can make of their leaders.

To foster cooperation among the members of Congress, two institutions have emerged: political parties and the committee system. The institutional history of Capitol Hill is one of typical Madisonian pendulum swings of power between committee chairs and party leaders (Connelly, 2010: 236). To explain the relative rise and fall of congressional leaders, political scientists have developed a theory of 'conditional party government' (Rohde, 1991; Aldrich, 1995). The basic premise is that 'the impact of institutional context on leadership power and style is determined primarily by party strength. (...) The higher the degree of party unity or cohesion, the more power in both the formal and party systems can be concentrated in the hands of party leaders and the more leadership style will be oriented to command and task or goal attainment. The lower the degree of party unity or cohesion the more power in both the formal and party systems will be dispersed and the more the leadership style will be oriented to bargaining and the main-tenance of good relations.' (Cooper and Brady, 1981: 424)·The influence of the party is conditioned on the degree of ideological congruence of its members. Under this theory, in an era when US politics is dominated by partisan polarization (Abramowitz, 2010; McCarty et al., 2006), it would be logical to expect to see congressional leaders entrusted with important powers. Yet, an alternative understanding of the US Congress argues that partisan organization in the House and Senate are mostly irrelevant. What matters is the preference of the pivotal legislator on any given bill – that 218th vote in the House and 60th vote to end debate in the Senate (Krehbiel, 1998).

While they differ on the identity of the principal – the majority party or the numerical majority – both theories actually understand congressional leaders as their agents. Leaders in Congress are supposed to give their followers what they want. In that sense, for most political scientists: 'congressional leadership is mostly followership' (Strahan, 2007: 39). In contradistinction, Randall Strahan proposed a theory of 'Conditional Agency Framework'. According to him, the relationship between leaders and followers in Congress is non-linear. Leaders can actually assert their powers under two conditions. First, the leader must have specific intensely held goals beyond staying in office. Second, fol-lowers must be dissatisfied with the status quo but divided about how to change it. In such context, leaders can either convince or use rewards and punishment to achieve their own goals.

How does the experience of the current Speaker of the House fit these different models? To answer this question it will be necessary to start by reviewing the institutional tools that the leader of the House of Representatives can rely on before actually looking at three specific legislative case studies that shed light on how John Boehner tried, and often failed, to lead his majority.

The speakership

The office of Speaker is a constitutional office.[2] Its importance was made even clearer when the Presidential Succession Act of 1947[3] put the Speaker of the House third in line for the presidency. Still, in the early Congresses of the young American republic, the Speaker played only a very formal role in the proceedings. It was only through a long and protracted historical process that the House gave more responsibilities to its leaders notably under the speakerships of Henry Clay, Thomas Reed and Joseph ('Uncle Joe') Cannon.[4] After a revolt against 'Czar'

Cannon, the powers of the Speaker were curtailed for over half a century in a context where the majority was mired by ideological divisions. Consistent with the theories of conditional party government, the partisan realignment and polarization that accompanied the end of the Reagan years allowed for a revival of the speakership as witnessed under Newt Gingrich in the 104th Congress of 1995 and 1996 (Aldrich and Rohde, 1997). His successor, Dennis Hastert, displayed a less forceful style without surrendering any of his prerogatives (Cohen, 2001). When the Democratic party won back the majority of the House after the midterm elections of 2006, Nancy Pelosi became the first women to rise to the speakership. She proved very adept at wielding the powers of the office and is widely considered to have been a strong Speaker (Peters, 2010; Oleszek, 2011: 372).

Throughout the history of the House of Representatives, the powers that have been entrusted in the Speaker's chair have actually waxed and waned. Beyond the important and growing resources in money and staff at the leadership's disposal (Smith, 2007: 65) to help him in his role as representative of his party before the other branches of government and the media, the real source of his power has always been his, or her, influence on the committee assignment of his members. The majority party's true power is a function of its ability to control the agenda (Cox and McCubbins, 2005). In the US House of Representatives, the order of legislative business is actually set by the Rules Committee. The Speaker controls the Rules Committee by directly appointing all of the members for his party and its Chairman.[5] He can also exert his power to influence assignment of his party members to the other committees, a task officially devolved to the Republican Steering Committee. Nonetheless, the Speaker sits on the Steering Committee where his voice and vote carry particular clout. Finally, the Speaker is responsible for choosing the members of the majority that will sit on any conference committee that could be called to reconcile the differences between the House and Senate on a specific bill.

John Boehner as Speaker

Taken together, these powers represent the most obvious tools that the Speaker can use to exert his leadership. Their effectiveness depends on how much individual members value a specific committee assignment, a place at the leadership table and, or, any influence on legislating itself. In 2010, the problem for Speaker John Boehner was that he owed his gavel to the election of a large group of 86 Republican freshmen who, for the most part, did not seem interested either in a career on Capitol Hill or in passing laws. Instead, they had come to Washington to defy the establishment and roll back government. By promising to oppose and not propose new policies, these freshmen were going against some of the tenets of the traditional political theory on lawmakers. Indeed, scholars have long believed that elected officials had at least *some* policy goals to orient their actions in a constrained institutional context (Fenno, 1973; Mayhew, 1974 but also Neustadt, 1960 and Skrowrenek, 1993). The following developments will show that the consequences of their resolute opposition on the legislative process were quite problematic but, electorally speaking, their steadfastness would be rewarded. All but nine of the 86 freshmen were re-elected in 2012.

On 2 November 2010, the Democrats suffered a dramatic electoral defeat in the midterms. The party lost 63 House seats and the majority. As the 112th Congress opened in January 2011, the 241 House Republicans elected John Boehner as their Speaker. In more than two decades in the House, the Representative from the 8th district of Ohio has maintained a solidly conservative voting record.[6] First elected in 1990, he was already in the leadership team of Newt Gingrich in 1994 as Conference Chairman. During the years of Republican dominance in Congress, he saw his star fade as his long-term rival from Texas, Tom DeLay, ascended to a leading role as Majority Whip and then Majority Leader. In 2006, when Speaker Hastert stepped down, the law had caught up with Representative DeLay. John Boehner convinced his colleagues to choose him as their new Minority Leader. His long career did not really help his reputation among the more radical members of his party especially since it came with a history of cutting deals with the other side.[7] Even more damaging for the more fiscally intransigent Tea Party movement was his plea for his colleagues to vote in favor of the bank bailout in September 2008. Finally, his legendary tan and reputation as an avid golfer made him the perfect symbol of the very Republican establishment that the Tea Party promised to set straight.

In the 2010 campaign, Boehner and the House Republicans had proposed a 'Pledge to America'; a very direct echo to the 1994 'Contract with America'. After the election, the institutional setup was comparable. A young Democratic president in the middle of his first term was now faced with a determined Republican opposition which held the majority of the House. Unlike the situation under Newt Gingrich though, House Republicans did not feel beholden to their Speaker. The House Republicans of 1995 saw their Speaker as a great tactician whose vision and long-term efforts had finally led them out of the political wilderness that was the minority status. He had crafted a formidable and innovative electoral strategy that nationalized congressional elections to capitalize on the unpopularity of President Clinton and the Democratic Party. This time, many of them owed their seats to insurgent campaigns that defeated more traditional candidates in the Republican primaries. They had campaigned *against* the GOP (Grand Old Party). With the help and the funding of conservative outside groups such as Americans for Prosperity or Heritage Action, they came to Washington to purify their own party. To defeat the RINOs (Republicans in Name Only) whom they accused of being insufficiently conservatives, these groups wielded the threat of funding future primary opponents for the members of the Republican conference who would stray too far from their preferred path of systematic opposition. As he prepared to lead his troops against President Obama, John Boehner was thus in a comparatively weak position.

There are 435 members in the US House of Representatives; a majority is therefore 218 votes. Since the Republicans only numbered 241 in the House, John Boehner could theoretically only afford to lose 23 of his members on any given vote. As soon as more than 23 Republicans refused to follow his instructions, he would be forced to turn to the Democratic minority to supply him with the necessary votes. Thus, the division inside the majority party brought the House minority party back to unexpected relevance. John Boehner's speakership came to be dominated by his attempts to square the circle: his colleagues' maximalist ambitions seemed to push him toward the Democratic side of aisle but every move in that direction opened him to the charges that he was not a true conservative and endangered his position as leader. The Speaker of the House is elected by the House majority on the first day of every Congress. He owes his power to the support of his majority. One of the lessons from the Gingrich speakership is that once you lose that support, you can lose your job. A failed coup against Speaker Gingrich in 1997 eventually led him to step down in 1998 (Wolfensberger, 2001: 198). This precedent led his successor to be very wary of antagonizing his majority. In fact, Speaker Hastert's name came to be associated with a new unwritten rule of leadership in the House. According to this 'Hastert Rule', the Speaker should not allow a bill to be brought to the House floor for a vote if is not backed by a majority of his majority.[8] According to this idea, the role of the Speaker is to cater to the needs of the majority of his majority and that should make him very wary of relying on too many votes from across the aisle.

Leadership lessons from the budget battles

It is impossible to understand John Boehner's speakership without focusing on fiscal issues as they dominated the conversation in Washington[9] and as Republicans attempted to use the budget process to force the policy changes that they favored. They felt that they had no other choice. Indeed, House Republicans were proposing important policy changes from a position of institutional weakness. The situation was even worse than under the Clinton administration. This time they only controlled one chamber as the Democrats had kept their hold on the Senate. Since House and Senate are coequal partners in the legislative process, they would have to convince Senate Democrats to vote their bills. Even if they could do so in part, President Obama could veto any legislation that would contradict his political ambitions.

In the weak hand they were dealt, the budget stood out as a potential trump card. Unlike any other piece of legislation, the bills that fund the government absolutely have to be adopted every year before the beginning of the fiscal year on 1 October. Failure to do so forces the federal government to shut its doors for lack of legal authority to use the public treasury. House Republicans could therefore hope to use the leverage offered by a potential threat to shut down the government to extract policy concessions from the White House and Senate Democrats. The same logic led them to see the debt ceiling as another form of leverage. Like the budget bills, the debt ceiling vote is unavoidable. Should Congress fail to authorize the administration to borrow more funds, the US government would be forced to default on at least some of its financial obligations.[10] The threat of some partial government shutdown was thus compounded by the threat of a default that could trigger a worldwide financial panic as Treasury bonds play a central role in international exchanges. Focusing their efforts on these two areas where they could not be ignored by the Senate and the President, House Republicans embarked on a strategy that made them relevant but also threatened to make them potentially responsible for catastrophic outcomes should the other side refuse to blink.

Speaker Boehner found himself at the helm of a group of legislators determined to use the threat of a shutdown and potential harm to the full faith and credit of the United States to force the Obama administration to cut spending, reform entitlement and agree to roll back the Affordable Care Act. As their leader, John Boehner would be the one to negotiate with the White House and Senate Democrats where he would be caught between the imperious demands of his members and the reality of a situation where the other party could not be expected to simply roll over and abandon control of the government. The fighting took the form of several skirmishes but for the sake of clarity, it is preferable to concentrate on three particularly important episodes and what they reveal about the limits and opportunities of House leadership.

The Budget Control Act and the 'Madman theory' of leadership

When the new Republican House majority took control, they first set out to use continuing resolutions – temporary budgets that fund the operations of the US government up to a set date – to extract concessions from the Democratic majority in the Senate and the Democratic president. Three short-term continuing resolutions[11] were adopted in exchange for very limited spending cuts.[12] The most noteworthy aspect of these successive agreements is a dwindling level of support among House Republicans. On the vote for the first continuing resolution, only six Republicans voted no.[13] On the second continuing resolution, their numbers had swollen to 54.[14] On the third, 59 Republicans voted no.[15]

The drama surrounding the continuing resolutions was soon overshadowed by the negotiations around the debt ceiling. Under current law, the US Treasury could not have outstanding obligations beyond 14.3 trillion dollars. According to Treasury estimates, that 'ceiling' would have been breached in early August 2011. After having seen a growing proportion of his majority vote against the compromises he had brokered with the Senate and the President, Speaker Boehner knew he could not afford to give an inch. A portion of his majority had declared their intention to vote against any debt-ceiling hike (Collender, 2012). Yet, he also knew that refusing to raise the debt ceiling was not a realistic option given the catastrophic financial consequences. As a journalist put it, he was 'stuck between the Tea Party and a hard place' (Carey, 2011).

As a way out of this dilemma, John Boehner opened secret negotiations with President Obama around a 'Grand Bargain'. He proposed to tie the debt ceiling with a deal whereby the Democrats would allow substantial reforms in entitlement programs – Social Security, Medicare and Medicaid, which together represent the lion's share of future government spending and deficit. In exchange, Republicans would agree to some revenue increase. This ambitious plan was at the heart of several protracted discussions between the two leaders and their staffs over the summer.[16] After allegedly coming close to an agreement, the talks fell apart amid mutual recriminations. Republicans accused the President of having moved the goalposts while Democrats said the talks failed because the Speaker could not hold his majority. Convincing his Republican colleague to agree to augment federal revenues was always thought to be the hardest part. As the Speaker tried to get ahead of his caucus on this issue, he was undercut by his own Majority Leader Eric Cantor who refused to endorse the scheme.

Once his ambitious 'Grand Bargain' had failed, John Boehner proposed a different approach that he hoped would find more support among his troops: every dollar of increase in the debt ceiling should be matched by a dollar in spending cuts. After some finessing around the mechanisms and the calendar and the intervention of Senate Republicans this new 'Boehner Rule' was eventually enacted into law on 1 August 2011 as part of the Budget Control Act.[17] Despite this achievement for their Speaker, 66 Republicans voted no on that final bill and it passed only thanks to the help of 95 Democratic votes in favor.[18]

At the end of this fight, Speaker Boehner could claim to have extracted substantial concessions from the Democrats while maintaining the support of a majority of his majority. Yet his image as a leader was battered. At the height of the battle he had pressed his members to close ranks[19] but the tough talk failed to move enough of them to support his plan so that he would not have to go to the Democrats to cobble up a majority. His leadership team also proved willing to defy him on the issue.

The early reviews on this first big test of his speakership were not always kind[20] but those who insisted that one should 'pity John Boehner' (Milbank, 2012) might have failed to see how he actually managed to leverage the very volatile nature of his majority to improve his bargaining position with President Obama and Senate Democrats. Under a more positive reading of the events, it is possible to see how the intransigence of his majority allowed him to ask for more than the Democrats might have been willing to give had he been able to simply commit his majority to whatever deal he was personally willing to strike. In a manner somewhat similar to the famed 'Madman theory' of President Nixon in his negotiation with the North Vietnamese, Speaker Boehner tried to make the most of his troops' professed willingness to cut spending at any cost.[21] Likewise, the split in the leadership could have been choreographed to extract more concessions from a White House that seemed to be pushing for a deal. It is impossible to disentangle facts, motives, self-serving explanations and ex post facto rationalizations. What remains is that the House Republican majority convinced enough Democrats to vote along with them for a compromise that cut spending to levels they initially objected to. The intensity of his conference preferences allowed the Speaker to drive a hard bargain.

Leading the herd away from the (fiscal) cliff

While it proved effective, this tactic could only work as long as the Democrats felt they had enough to lose by not reaching a deal. The situation was somewhat reversed over what came to be called the 'Fiscal Cliff'. The Budget Control Act had created a complex set of triggers to implement the spending cuts. The most prominent instrument was sequestration: automatic across-the-board cuts to a variety of programs. The timing for the next round of sequester cuts coincided with the expiration of the Bush tax cuts. In effect, if Congress failed to act before January 1, 2013, the American people were set to see their taxes ratchet up significantly[22] while their government would see its funding automatically reduced.

This turned the status quo to the Democrats' advantage. Tax increases represented 4/5 of the overall package of deficit reduction with spending cuts the remaining fifth. Should nothing happen, Democrats would thus come closer to their legislative goal (higher taxes) while Republicans would be defeated on their number one policy ambition – keeping taxes low. Republicans supported reduced federal spending in theory but they deplored the fact that the cuts promised to target particularly Defense spending.

The options available to the Republican leader were quite limited. As often happens during election years and despite tentative negotiations, both sides hoped the voters would settle the dispute at the ballot box. The result proved disappointing for Republicans. They held on to their majority in the House but failed to capture the Senate and saw their presidential candidate lose by a substantial margin in the popular vote and the electoral college.[23] With the confirmation of divided government, the stage was set for a compromise that could not fail to displease the most radical Republicans.

While the final bill did not include most tax increases, it still promised to raise overall federal revenues by $632 billions over the next ten years while the sequester cuts were pushed back by a couple of months. Despite the alluring title, in the end only 85 Republicans voted for the American Taxpayer Relief Act.[24] The legislation was only sent to the Senate thanks to the vote of 172 Democrats. On this vote, John Boehner disregarded the 'Hastert Rule': only a minority of his majority chose to support this legislation. In fact, the situation was more complex.

Before this final vote could take place, the legislation had been brought to the House floor with the adoption of a special rule on which all but two House Republicans voted yes.[25] The majority willingly allowed the minority to pass this bill with minimal support. Members of the House GOP were loath to vote for any tax increase but they knew that failure to act would only cause even higher tax increases. As a way out of this dilemma, they simply chose to let the Democrats vote for the package so as not to leave any fingerprint.

The most conservative wing of the Republican Party was not happy with what was described as a 'surrender' (Montgomery and Helderman, 2013). The Speaker of the House does not usually cast a vote but John Boehner insisted on voting 'aye'. By throwing his lot with the minority of his majority he showed the limits of his leadership. Upon seeing the result of the November elections, the Speaker had tried to revive the elusive 'Grand Bargain' only to see the negotiations flounder once again (Bresnahan et al., 2013). Two weeks before the final vote, he gambled on a 'Plan B' of an alternative package of tax increases and spending cuts but, to his very public embarrassment, his members refused to even vote on his proposal (Kane et al., 2012). Once again, the negotiations were eventually concluded in the Senate and the House had to ratify what the other chamber and the President had agreed upon. The same dynamic would repeat itself in even more dramatic fashion over the government shutdown a few months later.

Government shutdown and its aftermath: teaching a leadership lesson

The American Taxpayer Relief Act was the last bill taken up by the 112th Congress. On the very next day, the 113th Congress opened. The Republicans were still in the majority but their numbers had been reduced to 233. Their first order of business was the election of the Speaker of the House. A group of radical conservative House Republicans had repeatedly criticized John Boehner's insufficient fortitude. They believed that they did not have to compromise and that if they resolutely held their ground, Senate Democrats and the President would have eventually caved. They were so outraged at the Speaker for letting Democrats raise taxes on his watch that they decided to foment an ill-fated coup against John Boehner (Sherman and Bresnahan, 2013). On January 3, Speaker Boehner was re-elected but a dozen of his most conservative members refused to vote for him (Weisman, 2013). With their smaller majority, House Republicans could only afford to lose fewer than 20 votes on any given legislation if they didn't want to appeal to Democratic votes. The task of John Boehner promised to be even more challenging than in the previous Congress. Disappointed with the election and the policy results, a growing share of his conference appeared determined to fight Democrats to the bitter end this time. At their traditional retreat to plot strategy, House leaders realized that their appeal to reason to avoid a government shutdown or a debt default were likely to fall on deaf ears the next time around.[26]

By the time the new fiscal year opened on 1 October 2013, House, Senate and President had not found an agreement on a continuing resolution. Both sides' calculations put them on a collision course. With the economy on the mend and a new lease on the White House, Democrats were less eager for a deal. On the campaign trail, President Obama had declared that his re-election would 'break the fever' (Leibovich, 2012) in the Republican ranks and force them to realize the unpopularity of their tactics and their policies. But instead, the confirmation of their majority status in the House emboldened conservatives. Despite the warnings from the polls, the right wing of the Republican party remained convinced that the blame for the government shutdown would fall on Democrats. After having been denied for two years, their wish for a government shutdown was finally granted. At the same time, the Treasury was again edging closer to the debt ceiling and so additional action would also be needed on that front before mid-October to prevent a government default.

Without the proper statutory authority to engage funds, most federal agencies had to shut their doors and all non-essential federal workers were furloughed until a new bill could be passed by both houses of Congress and signed by the President. The first government shutdown since 1996 eventually lasted for 16 days. House Republicans and their supporters in the Senate had entered the showdown determined to extract some concession from Democrats in exchange for allowing the government to reopen and raising the debt ceiling. Some continued to hope they could force a full repeal of the Affordable Care Act and they pushed their leadership to enlist in what was widely perceived to be a losing battle (Montgomery and Kane, 2013). In the end, the warning from Republican leaders was proven correct. The tactic failed dramatically. Republicans were largely held responsible for closing down the US government in an attempt to impose their policy preferences. The rising anger of the population convinced Senate Republicans to strike a deal that simply reopened the government and raised the debt ceiling without any concession from Democrats (Montgomery and

Helderman, 2013). The deal was then sent to the House where, once again, Republicans had to rely on the Democrats to pass the bill. 144 House Republicans voted against the Continuing Appropriations Act.[27] The majority of the majority again allowed a very important piece of legislation to be adopted with the votes of the minority and only 87 Republican votes.

The deal to reopen the government was temporary but it paved the way for new negotiations between the two parties for a longer term solution. Led by the chairs of the House and Senate Budget committees – Senator Patty Murray and Representative Paul Ryan – a bipartisan group of lawmakers found a compromise that became the Consolidated Appropriations Act. This final deal passed the House of Representatives with 166 Republicans joining 193 Democrats.[28] 64 Republicans voted against the bill.

The law that reopened the government had suspended the debt ceiling until 7 February 2014. As a coda to these budget battles, Congress had to adopt new legislation to raise the debt ceiling again. House Republicans tried to get some policy concessions in exchange but their efforts came to naught when they failed to agree on which ones (Cillizza, 2014). With two dozen House Republicans committed to voting against any debt ceiling hike, John Boehner tried in vain to find a policy that could unify his conference. Unable to corral 218 Republican votes, on 11 February, he had to rely on the same strange coalition of almost every Democrat and only 28 Republicans to prevent the US government from defaulting (Kane et al., 2014). Of course, the condition for Democratic support was that it would be a 'clean' bill – the debt ceiling was thus raised without any counterpart. John Boehner had again led his Republicans through another legislative defeat.

After the government shutdown, Speaker Boehner could have taunted his members with an 'I told you so.' Like a parent who wants to protect his children from getting into trouble, he repeatedly tried to prevent the most radical House Republicans from getting what they wanted but, in the end, he relented and let them make their own mistakes. Unable to convince them that their intransigence was counterproductive, his hold on the House was now limited to finding enough Republican votes to provide the Democrats with a majority.

Conclusion: John Boehner's leadership style

'When I looked up, I saw my colleagues going this way,' Boehner said of the shutdown. 'You learn that a leader without followers is simply a man taking a walk. So I said, 'If you want to go fight this fight, I'll go fight the fight with you.' But it was a very predictable disaster. (Bresnahan and Sherman, 2014)

In their classic survey of Speakers' different leadership styles, Joseph Cooper and David Brady reached the conclusion that 'institutional context rather than personal skill is the primary determinant of leadership power in the House.'(Cooper and Brady, 1981: 423)· If that is the case, John Boehner's predicament can be entirely explained by the existence of divided government, the lack of cohesion inside his party and the interplay between the two.[29] The split between a very conservative Tea Party wing and a somewhat less conservative 'establishment' has more to do with tactics than ideology but the effect on their leaders is the same. More importantly, with the rise of outside groups, there are now alternative sources of funding and other avenues for conservative rebels to get their message out. Intent on preserving their outsider credentials and professing a desire to dismantle the federal government rather than reform it, they are impervious to the usual incentives of the legislative game. They do not covet any specific committee assignment, they do not want to propose legislation or amendment. By refusing to take part in the legislative game they have become impervious to the traditional incentives that allow the system to function through the cohesion brought by the leadership. They have no use for the Republican organization and the Republican organization has no leverage on them.

Given these constraints, it should not be surprising that John Boehner only rarely tried to use the traditional toolbox of the Speaker to impose its will on his followers. Early in his speakership, he did try to punish some members whom he found too critical before himself reversing.[30] Again, after the 2012 election, he went on to punish four wayward members by reassigning them to different committees to very limited effect (Steinhauer, 2012). After the shutdown, he very publicly took aim at outside conservative groups for leading Republicans astray (Kane and O'Keefe, 2013). Beyond the ephemeral tough talk, the pattern of behavior that has emerged seems to be to let his majority work its will even when he knows it is futile and, once there is no other solution, to turn to the Democratic minority's vote and a small group of loyal moderates. The bipartisan alliance that allows the Speaker to reach the magic number of 218 votes could lead us to conclude on the triumph of pivotal politics.

Perhaps, it would be better to see in John Boehner's speakership a good example of legislative *realpolitik*. Returning to the 'Conditional

Agency Framework', we must conclude that John Boehner did not have intensely held goals beyond staying in office. Indeed, the recent example of the debt ceiling replicated the exact conditions for leadership with his followers unhappy with the status quo but unable to agree on what to do. John Boehner's refusal to wager his office for an improbable legislative victory raises a problem with this theory. Should we realistically expect leadership in Congress to come at the expense of maintenance in office? A critical vision of John Boehner's leadership has focused on his willingness to sacrifice his principles and his policy ambitions to hold on to the Speaker's gavel (House, 2013). A more positive appraisal presented his flexibility as a calming balm that allowed him to work around the self-destructive impulses of his conference (Scheiber, 2013; Douthat, 2103). Future historians will be better positioned to hand a more definitive verdict. What can be said is that John Boehner's leadership style has been dominated by his willingness to protect his members – even, or especially, from themselves.

Notes

1 Richard Fenno famously identified three goals: reelection, influence inside Congress, and public policy. (Fenno, 1973). David Mayhew preferred to reduce these to the one over-arching goal of getting reelected (Mayhew, 1974).
2 United States Constitution, Article 1, Section 2, clause 5 : 'The House of Representatives shall choose their Speaker'.
3 61 Stat. 380, 3 U.S.C.§19.
4 For a detailed history of these particular Speakers see Richard B. Cheney, *Kings of the Hill: Power and Personality in the House of Representatives* (New York: Continuum, 1983), chapters 1, 4 and 5.
5 See Rule 12 (b) (1) in House Republican Conference, *Rules of the House Republican Conference for the 113th Congress.*
6 There are different ways to try to gauge the relative ideological positioning of a member of Congress. A traditional instrument is the voting scorecards compiled by special interest groups who monitor certain specific votes and 'score' them according to their preferences. For example, the American Conservative Union gave John Boehner a lifetime score of 88% based on his whole voting record (https://votesmart.org/interest-group/1481/rating/6734). Another type of measure is offered by the pioneering work of political scientists Keith T. Poole and Howard Rosenthal who developed a spatial model of congressional voting that allows to rank legislators based on how they voted compared with their colleagues. Based on a sophisticated methodology, they are then able to assign for each member of Congress an ideal-point – a DW-NOMINATE score – on a scale that maps the ideological spectrum from very liberal (–1) to very conservative (+1). In the 209th Congress, John Boehner's DW-Nominate score of 0.677 placed him among the top 25% of his colleagues in the House Republican party. Since the

beginning of his congressional career he has had an average DW-NOMINATE score of 0.6222. For more explanations on DW-NOMINATE see Keith T. Poole and Howard Rosenthal, *Congress: A Political-Economic History of Roll Call Voting* (New York: Oxford University Press, 1997). All their data is available at http://voteview.com.

7 He famously collaborated with Democratic Senator Ted Kennedy on the 2003 'No Child Left Behind' education reform law.

8 Dennis Hastert actually referred to this 'rule' as a principle that he tried to abide by: 'My fifth principle is to please the majority of your majority. (...) The job of Speaker is not to expedite legislation that runs counter to the wishes of the majority of his majority.' 'The Changing Nature of the Speakership' (presented at the The Cannon Centenary Conference, Washington, D.C.: US Government Printing Office, 2003), 62. The other principles were 'Be a good listener'; 'Keep your word'; 'Respect the regular order'; 'Get the job done'; 'Focus on the House and nothing but the House'.

9 Among the various planks of the 'Pledge to America', fiscal issues held a prominent place. The Republican answer to the first two years of the Obama presidency was summarized in the slogan: 'Cut, Cap and Balance'. If elected, the new majority promised to cut current federal spending back to their 2008 levels, cap future spending and balance the budget in the long-term while refusing any new taxes. 'A Pledge to America,' 2010, 21–2, http://www.gop.gov/indepth/pledge/downloads#body.

10 This statutory authorization appeared in the 1939 in replacement of the past practice by which every round of US Treasury bonds had to be duly authorized by a specific law. This cumbersome mechanism was thus replaced by a global authorization to emit bonds up to a certain amount (Austin and Levit, 2014: 7). Because the overall amount of debt is a function of past decisions on spending and taxes, previous Congressional majorities sometimes included an automatic rise of the debt ceiling when they adopted the Budget resolution, the document that is supposed to set the country's fiscal policy. This process was known as the 'Gephardt Rule.' (Austin and Levit, 2014: 14). For more, see (Meyer, 2014).

11 Public Law 112-4 extended funding authority from 1 March 2011 to 15 March. Public Law 112-6 from 15 March to 8 April and Public Law 112-10 from 8 April to the end of the fiscal year – i.e. 30 September.

12 See for example this explanation by a budget expert: 'Most of the announced $4 billion in savings in the House GOP plan, which Senate Democrats at least initially signaled a willingness to accept, comes from cutting $2.8 billion in earmarks. But removing earmarks doesn't actually cut spending; it only shifts the decision about how to use the funds from the legislative branch to the executive branch. Getting rid of earmarks only reduces spending if the appropriation is cut by the same amount. At the time this column was being written, it was not at all clear if that would be the case.' (Collender, 2011)

13 Roll Call 154. Among the six were Representatives Michelle Bachmann of Minnesota, Steve King of Iowa, Ron Paul and Louie Gohmert of Texas.

14 Roll Call 179.

15 Roll Call 268.

16 For detailed reporting on the offers, counteroffers and the eventual break-down and outcome of the talks see (Corn, 2012: 303–49; Woodward, 2012; Kane, Bacon Jr, and Fahrenthold, 2011; Bai, 2012)

17 Public Law 112-25.

18 Roll Call 690.

19 The expression he used was more colorful. He invited them to 'get your ass in line' (Sherman, Bresnahan, 2011).

20 The admittedly adversarial anchor of the Rachel Maddow Show had a recurrent segment on how John Boehner was bad at his job. There were also other unflattering appraisals in the opinion sections of newspapers. For one example see Milbank, 2011.

21 The comparison was drawn by Kurt Andersen, 'The Madman Theory', *New York Times*, August 5, 2011, sec. Opinion, http://www.nytimes.com/2011/08/06/opinion/the-madman-theory.html.

22 A whole host of various taxes were to be affected. With the expiration of a temporary extension of the Bush tax cuts, income tax rates were set to return to the higher levels that prevailed during the Clinton administration. Likewise for the Estate tax and the tax on Capital Gains and dividends. At the same time, payroll tax rates would also return to their higher prevailing trend. Finally, additional taxes on the most wealthy Americans had been included as part of the Affordable Care Act to help pay for the expansion of health insurance coverage. Those would also kick in on 1 January. Finally, on the same day, a set of perennial tax extenders was set to expire and the Alternative Minimum Tax would suddenly hit millions of taxpayers if it failed to be 'patched' as it usually was.

23 President Obama was re-elected with 51.1% of the popular vote to Mitt Romney's 47.2% which translated into 332 to 206 votes in the Electoral College.

24 Public Law 112-240. Roll Call 659.

25 Roll Call 658 on H.Res 844.

26 'House Speaker John Boehner 'may need a shutdown just to get it out of their system', said a top GOP leadership adviser. 'We might need to do that for member-management purposes – so they have an endgame and can show their constituents they're fighting.' (VandeHei et al., 2013)

27 Roll Call 550.

28 Roll Call 21.

29 '(...) divided government has a negative effect on the approval of the speaker within his or her own party. Indeed, many of the difficulties Speaker John Boehner has encountered in trying to preside over the current House of Representatives have resulted from differences of opinion within his own party as conservatives have questioned his leadership' (Hassell, 2014: 127).

30 '"Look what he did to Flake," notes the ex-leadership aide, referring to how Arizona's Jeff Flake, mouthing off once too often about his Republican colleagues' taste for pork, found himself stripped of his seat on the Judiciary Committee. Flake isn't an isolated case. Just three months after becoming majority leader in 2006, Boehner warned members in a closed-door meeting that those who opposed his budget resolution could kiss their prime committee assignments goodbye; he even singled out Democrat-turned-Republican Walter B. Jones as someone who needed to

be "talked to" by colleagues.' (Cottle, 2009). Yet, in 2010, the same Jeff Flake was handed a seat on the coveted Appropriations Committee (Kane, Fahrenthold, 2013).

Works cited

Abramowitz, A.I. (2010) *The Disappearing Center: Engaged Citizens, Polarization, and American Democracy* (New Haven: Yale University Press).

Aldrich, J.H. (1995) *Why Parties?: The Origin and Transformation of Political Parties in America*, 1st ed. (Chicago: University of Chicago Press).

Aldrich, J.H., Rohde, D.W. (1997) 'The Transition to Republican Rule in the House: Implications for Theories of Congressional Politics', *Political Science Quarterly*, Vol. 112, n° 4, 541–67.

Andersen, K. (2011) 'The Madman Theory', *New York Times*, August 5, 2011, sec. Opinion. http://www.nytimes.com/2011/08/06/opinion/the-madman-theory.html.

D.A. Austin, M.R. Levit (2014), 'The Debt Limit: History and Recent Increases', *CRS Report*, RL31967, October 28. http://www.senate.gov/CRSReports/crs-publish.cfm?pid='0E%2C*P%5C%3F%3D%23%20%20%20%0A

Bai, M. (2012) 'The Game Is Called Chicken'. *New York Times –Magazine*, April 2012.

Bresnahan, J., Brown, C.B., Raju, M., Sherman, J. (2013) 'The Fiscal Cliff Deal That Almost Wasn't', *Politico*, January 2. http://www.politico.com/story/2013/01/the-fiscal-cliff-deal-that-almost-wasnt-85663.html, date accessed 12 June 2014.

Bresnahan, J., Sherman J. (2014), 'John Boehner, Unchained', *Politico*. January 28, http://www.politico.com/story/2014/01/john-boehner-unchained102687_Page2.html#ixzz2rlriocry, date accessed 12 June 2014.

Carey, N. (2011) 'Special Report: Stuck between the Tea Party and a Hard Place', *Reuters*, May 17.

Cheney, R.B. (1983) *Kings of the Hill: Power and Personality in the House of Representatives* (New York: Continuum).

Cillizza, C.(2014) 'John Boehner Gives Up. Again', *Washington Post*, February. http://www.washingtonpost.com/blogs/the-fix/wp/2014/02/11/john-boehner-gives-up-again/.

Cohen, R.E. (2001) 'Hastert's Hidden Hand', *National Journal*, January.

Collender, S. (2011) 'Why Not Try a Summit Instead of a Shutdown?'*Roll Call*, March 1, 2011, http://capitalgainsandgames.com/blog/stan-collender/2158/gop-should-push-budget-summit-instead-government-shutdown, date accessed 8 November, 2012.

Collender, S. (2012) 'The Tea Party and Me: A Very True Story', *Stan Collender's Capital Gains and Games*. http://capitalgainsandgames.com/blog/stan-collender/2184/tea-party-and-me-very-true-story, date accessed 8 November.

Connelly, W.F. (2010) *James Madison Rules America: The Constitutional Origins of Congressional Partisanship* (Lanham, Md: Rowman & Littlefield).

Cooper, J., Brady, D.W. (1981) 'Institutional Context and Leadership Style: The House from Cannon to Rayburn', *American Political Science Review*, Vol. 75, n° 2, 411–25.

Corn, D. (2012) *Showdown: The Inside Story of How Obama Battled the GOP to Set Up the 2012 Election* (New York: William Morrow Paperbacks).

Cottle, M. (2009) 'The Retro Man', *The New Republic*, 30 November.

Cox, G.W., McCubbin, M.D. (2005) *Setting the Agenda: Responsible Party Government in the U.S. House of Representatives* (Cambridge: Cambridge University Press).

Davidson, R.H., Oleszek W.J., Lee, F.E. (2009) *Congress And Its Members*, 12th ed. (Washington, D.C.: CQ Press).

Douthat, R. (2013) 'Boehner, American', *New York Times*, January 5.

Fenno, R. (1973) *Congressmen in Committees* (Boston: Little Brown).

Hassell, H.G.H. (2014) 'Public and Partisan Opinions of the Speaker of the House', *Congress & The Presidency*, Vol. 41, n° 1, 107–27.

House, B. (2013) 'John Boehner's Big Choice', *NJ Daily*, 13 November. http://www. nationaljournal.com/daily/will-anyone-remember-john-boehner-20131112.

House Republican Conference (2012) *Rules of the House Republican Conference for the 113th Congress*. http://www.gop.gov/113th-rules/, date accessed 12 June 2014. Joint Committee on Printing (2004) *The Cannon Century Conference: The Changing Nature of the Speakership*. (Washington, DC: U.S. Government Printing Office). http://www.gpo.gov/fdsys/pkg/CDOC-108hdoc204/pdf/CDOC-108hdoc204.pdf, date accessed 12 June 2014.

Kane, P., Costa R., O'Keefe E. (2014) 'House Passes "clean" Debt-Ceiling Bill, Ending Two-Week Showdown', *Washington Post*, February 12.

Kane, P., Bacon, P. Jr., Fahrenthold, D.A. (2011) 'Budget Battle Came down to 3 Men and Their Weaknesses', *Washington Post*, 11 April.

Kane, P., Fahrenthold, D.A. (2013) 'Boehner's Laid-Back Approach Is Considered Both Boon, Bane for House Republicans', *Washington Post*, 30 June.

Kane, P., O'Keefe, E. (2013) 'Boehner Attacks Tea Party Groups as House Approves Budget Deal', *Washington Post*, 13 December.

Kane, P., O'Keefe, E., Montgomery, L. (2012) 'How Boehner's Plan B for the 'Fiscal Cliff' Began and Fell Apart', *Washington Post*, 21 December.

Krehbiel, K. (1998) *Pivotal Politics: A Theory of U.S. Lawmaking* (Chicago: University of Chicago Press).

Leibovich M. (2012) 'Feel the Loathing on the Campaign Trail', *New York Times – Magazine*, August.

Mayhew, D. (1974) *Congress : The Electoral Connection* (New Haven: Yale University Press).

McCarty, N., Poole, K.T., Rosenthal, H. (2006) *Polarized America: The Dance of Ideology and Unequal Riches* (Cambridge: MIT Press).

Meyer, A. (2014) 'Le budget fédéral de l'ère Obama: politique de la chaise vide ou de la caisse vide?', *Politique Américaine*, n° 22, 154–78.

Milbank, D. (2011) 'John Boehner's No-Confidence Vote', *Washington Post*, July 29.

Milbank, D. (2012) 'Republican Leader Boehner May Be Ready to Bargain', *Washington Post*, 11 August.

Montgomery, L. Helderman, R.S. (2013a) 'Congress Approves 'Fiscal Cliff' Measure', *Washington Post*, 2 January.

Montgomery, L. Helderman, R.S. (2013b) 'Obama Signs Bill to Raise Debt Limit, Reopen Government', *Washington Post*, 17 October.

Montgomery L., Kane, P. (2013) 'Government Shutdown Moves Closer to Reality', *Washington Post*, 18 September.

Neustadt, R.E. (1960) *Presidential Power* (New York: Macmillan Publishing Company).

Oleszek, W. (2011) *Congressional Procedures and the Policy Process,* 8th ed. (Washington D.C.: CQ Press).

Peters, R.M. (2010) *Speaker Nancy Pelosi and the New American Politics* (Oxford & New York: Oxford University Press).

Poole, K.T., Rosenthal H. (1997) *Congress: A Political-Economic History of Roll Call Voting* (Oxford & New York: Oxford University Press).

Republicans in Congress (2010) *A Pledge to America,* http://www.gop.gov/indepth/pledge/downloads#body, date accessed 12 June 2014.

Rohde, D.W. (1991) *Parties and Leaders in the Postreform House,* 2nd ed. (Chicago: University of Chicago Press).

Scheiber, N. (2013) 'The Power of Orange', *The New Republic,* 5 March.

Sherman, J., Bresnahan, J. (2011) 'Boehner Tries to Tame GOP on Debt Ceiling Plan', *Politico,* 28 July. http://www.politico.com/news/stories/0711/60022.html, date accessed 12 June, 2014.

Sherman, J., Bresnahan, J. (2013) 'Conservatives Rebel against John Boehner', *Politico,* 3 January. http://www.politico.com/story/2013/01/conservatives-rebel-against-boehner-85749.html, date accessed 12 June 2014.

Skowronek, S. (1993) *The Politics Presidents Make* (Cambridge: Harvard University Press).

Steinhauer, S.J. (2012) 'Republicans Who Have Opposed Leadership See Committee Assignments Stripped', *New York Times – The Caucus,* 3 December. http://thecaucus.blogs.nytimes.com/2012/12/03/republicans-who-have-opposed-leadership-see-committee-assignments-stripped/, date accessed 12 June 2014.

Smith, S.S. (2007) *Party Influence in Congress* (Cambridge: Cambridge University Press).

Strahan, R. (2007) *Leading Representatives: The Agency of Leaders in the Politics of the U.S. House* (Baltimore: Johns Hopkins University Press).

VandeHei, J., Allen, M., Sherman, J. (2014) 'Double Trouble: House GOP Eyes Default, Shutdown', *Politico,* 13 January, 2013. http://dyn.politico.com/print-story.cfm?uuid=EC16A727-91B2-4C84-A4C4-1A5E703F4A9A, date accessed 12 June, 2014.

Weisman, J. (2013) 'Boehner Narrowly Holds On to Speaker's Post', *New York Times,* 3 January.

Wolfensberger, D.R. (2001) *Congress and the People: Deliberative Democracy on Trial* (Baltimore: Johns Hopkins University Press).

Woodward, B. (2012) *The Price of Politics* (New York: Simon & Schuster).

4
Tony Blair's Leadership Style in Foreign Policy: Hubris without Constraints?

Pauline Schnapper

Political leadership has traditionally been less analysed in the UK than in the United States, with its presidential system. Yet Tony Blair's style of leadership and decision-making in foreign policy have been probed more than most of his predecessors', with the possible exception of Margaret Thatcher, in the public debate as well as in the academic literature. No less than three official reports (Butler, Hutton, Chilcot, though still not published at the time of writing) have been partly devoted to his decision-making.[1] This is both because he successfully transformed the Labour party and reversed its electoral fortune in the 1990s and because of the controversies surrounding the way he took the decision to send British troops alongside Americans to invade Iraq in 2003. In establishing a new doctrine for foreign military intervention, which contradicted the traditional 'realist' approach of British foreign policy and reconnected it to its nineteenth century liberal roots, Blair was able to become a 'game-changer', in the sense, established in the introduction to this volume, that he twisted the usual functioning of institutions to reach his goal. But as the war proved a military disaster and its popularity waned, he was then accused of increasing the 'presidentialisation' of British Prime Ministers already blamed on some of his predecessors and seen as contrary to the constitutional principle of collective responsibility (Pryce, 1997; Crossman, 1963). His case has therefore been included in a long-running debate between 'prime ministerial' and 'Cabinet' government as evidence of the former (Hailsham, 1976; Foley, 2000).

The aim of this chapter is therefore two-fold – not just to analyse the nature of his leadership in war-time, which occupied a large amount of his time in office with no less than four military interventions – but also to look at the attitudes of other actors towards his leadership, and especially to establish whether the other parts of the British power structure played their constitutional role in these specific circumstances. In a first section, I discuss the nature of Blair's leadership in relation to traditional definitions of political leadership, especially Max Weber's, and show why I adopt instead the 'statecraft' or 'core executive' approach to understand the lack of checks on Blair's growing hubris. Then I will establish the nature of Blair's statecraft in foreign policy in the early years of his premiership with particular references to Sierra Leone and Kosovo. I then do not record the already well-documented way in which the fateful decision to attack Iraq was taken, but show the failures of the institutions that could have prevented the Prime Minister's leadership from turning into hubris, especially Cabinet and Parliament.

Charismatic leadership or statecraft?

As Blondel put it, political leadership is about power, domestically as well as possibly internationally (Blondel, 1987). A political leader is able to make others do a number of things that they might not have done otherwise. In the case of a national leader s/he can even direct members of the nation as a whole towards action – the extreme case being to lead them to war (Blondel, 1987: 3). In *Economy and Society* (1921) Max Weber famously distinguished between three types of authority. The first one was traditional authority, which came from long-established traditions and social patterns. The second one was the rational-legalistic authority, which was the modern form of authority derived from bureaucratic expertise and experience. Finally the third type was charismatic authority, derived from 'a certain quality of an individual personality by virtue of which he is considered and treated as endowed with supernatural, superhuman or exceptional forces or qualities' (quoted in Blondel, 1987: 55).

Could Tony Blair be considered as a 'charismatic' Prime Minister in the Weberian sense? The 'supernatural, superhuman' dimension described by Weber can hardly be applied to him, but charisma in the modern setting includes oratory qualities, presentational skills and marketing techniques. Blair's leadership was certainly based on an appeal to emotions and, in the case of his attempt to convince voters of the need to invade Iraq, on an almost religious or at least highly moralistic rhetoric of defending good versus evil – what Sampson called his 'pulpit style' (Sampson, 2004: 89). It is therefore not totally far-fetched to compare his leadership to the charismatic ideal-type. Dyson has identified three psychological features possessed by Blair which are also consistent with this model: a high belief in his ability to control events – what Hennessy quotes as the 'Tony wants' phenomenon (Hennessy, 2005: 6); limited conceptual complexity, meaning he was slow to perceive evidence that did not fit with his preconceptions; finally a need for control and power (Dyson, 2009: 30). Stephen Wall, who had worked with five different Prime Ministers, including Margaret Thatcher, said he was the one with the most self-assurance.[2] These psychological traits then translate into a highly centralised and personalised, 'presidential' leadership style and decision-making process, also dubbed 'sofa government' as it bypassed the normal channels of civil service and Cabinet (Riddell, 2001, Norton, 2008). Important decisions were taken by him with a small group of people involving a few ministers and advisers, rarely in the full Cabinet meetings which were often very short (Hennessy, 2005: 11–12, Bennister, 2012: 51–3). They were then 'sold' by the Prime Minister himself through a highly effective communications machine led by Alastair Campbell to both party and the public at large. This style was even more effective in foreign policy than domestic policy, as institutional constraints were fewer, at least until Iraq, and there was no Blair/ Brown feud in this area. As Blondel put it:

> The 'flight into foreign affairs' appears to have a somewhat 'cathartic' effect for leaders: they feel they can engage in 'high politics' without being encumbered by the daily trivia of ensuring the gradual implementation of their economic or social policy; they depend markedly less on the goodwill and competence of members of the government, the civil service and, indeed, the population. (Blondel, 1987: 77–8)

This is even more true in the British political system, where the Prime Minister enjoys a wide margin of manoeuvre. The Royal Prerogative confers on him the exercise of power which theoretically belongs to the monarch, especially in foreign policy, including the right to declare war and deploy forces, without requiring any parliamentary consent. Parliamentary scrutiny of the government action in these matters is often limited and inadequate (Burrall et al., 2006). But this Weberian approach, instructive as it is on some elements of personal style, is nevertheless limited for a thorough analysis of Blair's leadership. First, it ignores the political and institutional context in which leadership is exercised, in other words, focuses almost exclusively on agency to the detriment of structure, or rather the interaction between the leader and his/her environment (Elgie, 1995; Foley, 2000; Theakston, 2002). Also, it stresses the power of an individual to an extent which is problematic in a parliamentary system, where leadership is supposed to be plural and the Prime Minister *primus inter pares*. Indeed, as Heffernan put it,

> An actor such as the Prime Minister operates within structures, principally institutions and networks. These structures are affected by context, which is best described as political, economic and social environments. Clearly, actors, structures and contexts affect each other, just as networks affect outcomes and outcomes affect networks. All influence how the core executive operates and the policy outcomes it produces. As such, operating within structured contexts that constrain or enable their actions, prime ministers are never free to do everything they would wish (Heffernan, 2003: 349).

Even Blair, whatever his claims, had to take these institutions into account. Following Buller and James, themselves quoting Jim Bulpitt on Thatcher, I therefore wish to build on the concept of statecraft to describe Blair as a leader (Bulpitt, 1986). This means taking in the fact that in the UK the Prime Minister is not alone in taking decisions but part of a 'clique' or 'core executive' including senior party leaders, advisers and civil servants (Smith, 1999). Thereafter s/he needs the support of a majority in Parliament, which in theory acts as a check on prime ministerial power. It therefore requires an appraisal of what Bulpitt called the constraints of party management; the achievement of political argument hegemony; a winning electoral strategy; and an image of governing competence (Buller and James, 2008: 13). Tony Blair clearly achieved these goals – he established his leadership of the Labour party between 1994 and 1997; he won three general elections. He also arguably set a new hegemony of political/economic discourse in the post-Thatcherite 'Third Way' and reversed Labour's image of economic incompetence. In foreign policy, the striking fact about Blair's leadership, especially in the run up to the war in Iraq, was that he was exceptionally successful in imposing his will on Cabinet, Party and Parliament and therefore dealing with these constraints, but that the way he achieved this did not just break with the theoretical constitutional arrangements but also eventually led to disaster.

Blair's leadership in the early years

Blair's style of leadership, as briefly described above, worked well in the early years of his premiership, which reinforced his self-confidence. Not originally interested in foreign policy or military intervention, Blair was quickly drawn into international affairs and decided early on to send British troops to Kosovo following the breakdown of talks with Serbia in December 1998. Kosovo provided an opportunity for him to develop a clearer view of his foreign policy priorities, developed in his Chicago speech of April 1999. This became known as the doctrine of the international community, in which he described the interdependence of countries in a new globalised world and asserted conditions which made it legitimate to intervene militarily against dictators (Blair, 1999). In our perspective what is interesting about the speech is that it was drafted by Lawrence Freedman, a well-known academic, not by the usual channel of the Foreign Office which was largely by-passed. Hill reports that 'the Foreign Office had not been consulted and the final result produced some shock and anger in King Charles Street – not least among the senior legal advisers, whose territory it blithely invaded' (Hill, 2001: 344). Blair himself wrote:

> from the outset I was extraordinarily forward in advocating a military solution. I look back and can see that throughout, to the irritation of many of our allies *and the consternation of a large part of our system*, I was totally and unyieldingly for resolution, not pacification. (Blair, 2010: 227, emphasis added)

This appeared as a very personal decision, taken with a tight group of aides of whom only Jonathan Powell had a background in diplomacy. The Cabinet was informed rather than really involved (Riddell, 2001: 32). Blair prided himself on having convinced President Clinton to threaten to send troops on the ground when the air campaign seemed to be ineffective. Again, the way he described it says a lot about his decision- and policy-making:

> I then took a clear decision. I spoke to Alistair [Campbell] and Jonathan [Powell] and then called the close team together. I said: I am willing to lose the job on this, but we are going to go for broke. We are going to take even more of a fronting-up, out-there, leadership position and stake it all on winning. (Blair, 2010: 237)

The fact that it was a personal decision did not raise eyebrows at the time because the decision was not controversial and Blair got broad cross-party support in Parliament, especially from both opposition parties.[3] There was no formal vote in the House of Commons but a motion promoted by opponents to the war (mostly Labour) attracted only

11 votes.[4] By then Blair had become convinced that he was a leader not just at home but also internationally and that he could influence American power.

This view was reinforced in the following year when British troops were sent to Sierra Leone, a former British colony, on a much smaller operation to support UN troops and restore the elected president, Ahmed Tejan Kabbah. Operation Palliser was decided by Tony Blair, who does not allude to any discussion about it or Kosovo in Cabinet or Parliament in his *Memoirs* (Blair, 2010: 247). Again there was broad agreement, especially when the operation was successful.

Blair managed, during his first term, to both strengthen his very personal type of leadership at home, thanks to a large and quiescent majority in the House of Commons and a presidentialisation of decision-making in 10 Downing Street, and to project his leadership abroad through personal links with US President Bill Clinton and in the European Union (Riddell, 2003). In the latter case, being a 'leader in Europe' was an oft-repeated mantra from the 1997 Labour manifesto onwards. Blair tried, with mixed results, to forge bilateral relations with Chancellor Schröder, Presidents Chirac later Aznar and Berlusconi to advance his objectives, rather than to play by the collective rules. Having pledged to put an end to British isolation in Europe, he signed up to the Amsterdam and Nice treaties. He was able to push forward British interests in the EU, notably with the Lisbon agenda adopted in 2000, the Franco-British agreement on an autonomous European defence in 1998, and his professed aim to take Britain in the single currency. By 2001 Blair had to a large extent reversed his country's semi-detached status in the EU, though a big question mark remained over the single currency. His leadership was strongly established.

From leadership to hubris

Following the events of 9/11, Blair's belief in his own destiny to change the world only grew in parallel with his lack of respect for institutions. In the weeks that followed the attacks, he travelled around the world to rally allied countries around an American-led response, which was first a large-scale attack against the Taliban in Afghanistan – he was seen as what Riddell called 'Bush's Ambassador at Large' (Riddell, 2003: 161). His statesmanship was confirmed on the international stage while at home he had secured a second landslide in the May 2001 general election. Blair committed Britain to Afghanistan again with broad support from public opinion and Parliament. Iain Duncan Smith, the new leader of the Conservative Party praised the Prime Minister when Parliament was recalled, for 'responding to this crisis quickly and resolutely, and giving a lead to other nations that value freedom and democracy' and assured him of his party's full support 'for his immediate pledge to stand shoulder to shoulder with our strongest friends and allies in the United States'.[5]

Things started to change when the debate moved to Iraq and the domestic as well as European consensus broke down. The chronology of Blair's decision to follow (thinking he might be leading) the Americans in 2002 is now well documented in both primary and secondary sources (Blair, 2010; Riddell, 2003; Naughtie, 2004). But why were none of the normal constraints on personal power in the UK system effective?

In the months between September 2002 and March 2003, Tony Blair attempted to convince his Cabinet, Parliament and the public at large of the threat that Saddam Hussein posed in order to put an end to what he himself called his 'colossal' domestic isolation on Iraq (Blair, 2010: 412). This was done first by the publication by the Joint Intelligence Committee of the famous 'dossier' about Iraq's programme of weapons of mass destruction (WMD), which turned out later to have been based on dubious sources and about which there were allegations that it had been 'sexed up' by Alistair Campbell with an ambiguous claim that Iraq could deploy WMD in 45 minutes (athough that was refuted by the Hutton report (2004: p.153)). The second instrument was getting approval from the UN Security Council in a second resolution, which was crucial to get the Cabinet and Parliament to approve of military intervention. When this proved impossible, the Attorney General, Lord Goldsmith, provided short advice to Cabinet saying military intervention would be nevertheless legal.

What happened in Cabinet is now well sourced thanks to a number of memoirs and the different reports already mentioned (Cook, 2004; Short, 2004; Butler, 2004). On the one hand, Blair claims that the convention of collective responsibility was fully respected:

> One of the most bizarre things said about the build-up to war is that it was a kind of one-man mission, discussed with a few special advisers on the famous sofa in the den, with the Cabinet excluded. Actually, it was *the* topic at virtually every Cabinet meeting for nigh on six months, with not just me but Jack Straw [Foreign Secretary] and Geoff Hoon [Defence Secretary] briefing extensively, and everyone not just having the right to have their say, but saying it. (Blair, 2010: 428)

But Clare Short's account of these discussions differs markedly:

> there is a great difference between the Cabinet being updated each
> week on the events they are reading about in the press and any seri-
> ous discussion of the risks and the political, diplomatic and military
> options and the hammering out of an agreed strategy to handle the
> crisis. There was no such discussion and we now know from the Butler
> report that papers were prepared for Cabinet but never circulated, and
> that there was a review of UK strategy towards Iraq in March 2002
> which was not shared. This is Blair's style. (Short, 2004: 150)

Indeed, as the Butler report showed, quantity did not necessarily equate
to quality:

> Over the period from April 2002 to the start of military action, some
> 25 meetings attended by the small number of key Ministers, officials
> and military officers most closely involved provided the framework
> of discussion and decision-making within government. One inescap-
> able consequence of this was *to limit wider collective discussion and
> consideration by the Cabinet to the frequent but unscripted occasions
> when the Prime Minister, Foreign Secretary and Defence Secretary briefed
> the Cabinet orally.* Excellent quality papers were written by officials,
> but these were not discussed in Cabinet or in Cabinet Committee.
> *Without papers circulated in advance, it remains possible but is obvi-
> ously much more difficult for members of the Cabinet outside the small
> circle directly involved to bring their political judgement and experience to
> bear on the major decisions for which the Cabinet as a whole must carry
> responsibility.* The absence of papers on the Cabinet agenda so that
> Ministers could obtain briefings in advance from the Cabinet Office,
> their own departments or from the intelligence agencies plainly
> reduced their ability to prepare properly for such discussions. (Butler,
> 2004: §609–610, emphases added)

Things changed slightly once the war had started, with a more formal
War Cabinet (the Overseas Policy and Defence Committee) taking
over, but by then it was effectively too late (Bennister, 2012: 59). There
is nothing new about the decline of Cabinet as a decision-making
body. Crossman claimed in the 1960s that Cabinet had become part
of the dignified, not efficient, side of the constitution under Wilson
(Crossman, 1963). Cabinet was dismissed by Margaret Thatcher who
famously stated before coming to power: 'As Prime Minister I could

not waste time having internal arguments [in Cabinet]' (Hennessy, 2001: 308). But the presidentialisation under Blair went further and his Cabinet was even weaker than in the past (Norton, 2008). Alastair Campbell attended meetings, which was unprecedented for a Press secretary. Also Blair had a formidable rival inside Cabinet, Gordon Brown, who on the issue of Iraq was remarkably silent and subservient. As Chancellor and as Blair's former mentor, he had a powerful base in the government and in the party which could have constrained the Prime Minister (Heffernan, 2003). The framework of acute rivalry and competing centres of power in 10 and 11 Downing Street, well documented in domestic policy, did not apply to the crucial issue of peace and war (Rawnsley, 2010; Mandelson, 2010). At no point did Brown signal any reluctance to follow the path laid by Blair. Indeed at the Chilcot inquiry he described the decision to go to war as 'the right decision for the right reason'.[6] Other major figures like the Foreign Secretary (Jack Straw) and Defence Secretary (Geoff Hoon) also followed Blair without qualms, although it was revealed that in April 2002 Straw had warned Blair about the risks of war and he told the Chilcot inquiry in 2010 that he had 'very reluctantly' backed the war.[7] As for Hoon, he said the Attorney General's legal advice was conclusive and did not need to be debated in Cabinet.[8] Only two Cabinet members spoke out against the war and eventually resigned, Robin Cook (then Leader of the House of Commons) and Clare Short (Secretary of State for International Development).

The failure of the Cabinet to act as a core executive and hold Blair into account was the result of the centralisation of the Labour party in the 1994–97 period, reducing the power of other sources of authority like the National Executive Council (NEC). As a result, and in comparison with previous Labour administrations in the 1960s and 1970s, Cabinet members did not have the kind of power base that enabled them to stand up to the leader. It made the government more united than in the past but failed to limit the growing hubris of the Prime Minister. Nor was Blair's deliberate choice not to circulate papers new. Stephen Wall, his adviser on Europe, summed it up at the Chilcot enquiry:

You have to be quite brave I think if you are Secretary of State for Health or Education to intervene on a subject that's not your own subject. The advantage of having a document that sets out the issues is you have the basis for doing that. You don't feel an idiot putting up your hand saying 'How about so and so ?'. That was not lost under Tony Blair. That was lost under Margaret Thatcher, that habit of Cabinet papers.[9]

According to him, Blair was also afraid of leaks if he gave too much information to the Cabinet. But he added that Cabinet committees had met frequently under Major, whereas Blair had a preference for informal meetings on a bilateral or multilateral basis.

Blair's control of Parliament was equally effective on the Iraqi issue, at least until February 2003. During the first term, Blair and the whips had put much pressure on the parliamentary party to follow the line, again in order to break with the past, and as a result the number of rebellions was limited (Cowley and Stuart, 2008). Parliament was in recess during the summer of 2002, when Blair travelled to the US and agreed to support the Bush administration in the midst of public debates in the media. Charles Kennedy, then leader of the Liberal Democrats, was quoted as saying about Blair: 'He's been answering questions everywhere except from our elected representatives' (Sampson, 2004: 15). When MPs were recalled in September to debate the WMD dossier, they were shown it three hours before the debate. Tony Blair didn't have to ask Parliament for a vote on the invasion as it is a Royal Prerogative to declare war and deploy armed forces, but following the mass demonstration against the war in the streets of London, a debate was held on 26 February in the Commons, opened by Jack Straw.[10] Many views were heard, both in support of the government (including from the opposition front benches) and against it, mostly from the Liberal Democrat and Labour benches. That day, 121 Labour MPs voted against the motion presented by the government, which was more than a quarter of the parliamentary group. In the crucial second debate of 18 March, the figure rose to 139. This represented the largest parliamentary rebellion for over 150 years (Cowley and Stuart, 2008: 110). The final vote was 396 supporting the government against 217, with 15 Conservative MPs voting against the war. The crucial factor in this vote was therefore the votes of the Conservatives – without a large majority of them supporting the Blair government, war would not have taken place. The Conservative accepting the Blair rhetoric about the Iraqi threat and the need to support the Americans can be explained by a shared vision of what Gamble calls the 'anglosphere', with the special relationship becoming an end in itself, more important than a critical judgement on the government (Gamble, 2003).

Public opinion, in a representative democracy, is mediated through Parliament. Policy is not supposed to be influenced by social protest.

But leaders normally take account of voters' opinions if they can threaten their leadership. In the case of Iraq polls showed ambivalence during the winter of 2002–3 – on average, a small majority supporting war provided it was sanctioned by a second resolution of the UN Security Council.[11] When this proved impossible, over a million people marched on the streets of London on 15 February 2003 to oppose the war, which was unprecedented since the end of the Second World War. Because he had the legitimacy of a vote in Parliament, Blair was able to ignore the protest. The only lesson drawn by Blair was it 'remind[ed him] of [his] isolation and the responsibility for the decision [he] was about to make' (Blair, 2010: 414). Being isolated only made his leadership more necessary, it seemed, but it actually was the beginning of the end of his successful leadership. The empathy that he had been able to establish with public opinion about the need for military intervention was dwindling at the same time as his authority. The war became increasingly unpopular as it appeared that no weapons of mass destruction were found in Iraq, making Blair's main argument in favour of the war irrelevant. In political terms, he was never able to recover from the fatal decision, even though he remained in power until 2007.

Conclusion

The Blair case illustrates the complexity of modern leadership. This cannot be reduced to a personality, however powerful and charismatic. It needs to be based on a wider core executive which includes Cabinet, civil servants and an effective Parliament to check it. In foreign policy, Blair was able to enjoy an exceptionally favourable political context until 2003, where he was in full control of his party, of his Cabinet and basked in popularity with the public at large. He was able to impose his will on military intervention in Kosovo, Sierra Leone and Afghanistan and enjoy the rewards not just of national but also international leadership. He enjoyed unfettered control.

Prime Ministerial power in itself may not be a bad thing – things get done, there is unity at the helm. But when the context changed with Iraq and the decision became highly contentious, the normal structures surrounding the Prime Minister failed. Cabinet was weak, except for two members who resigned, Parliamentary approval was sustained by the main opposition party, blinded by its support for the special relationship with the United States. There was no effective check on the Prime Minister's power and authority even though the decision he was taking was highly contentious. It is therefore not just a leader, but the whole core executive, indeed the whole political structure which was found wanting. Lessons were learned, to some extent, by his successors. Gordon Brown promised to reform the Royal Prerogative to make it mandatory to have Parliament approval for the deployment of troops abroad, but did not fulfil his promise while he was Prime Minister (2007–10). His successor, David Cameron, asked for a vote from Parliament a day after starting military action in Libya on 21 March 2011 and got a majority supporting action. In August 2013, when intervention in the Syrian civil war was contemplated following the use of chemical weapons by the regime, he again asked for a vote in the House of Commons and did not get a majority supporting him, which cancelled all plans for intervention and weakened his leadership.[12] There is now a convention, but no statute, that military intervention should be backed by Parliament.

Notes

1 The author wishes to thank David L. Baker for his useful suggestions for this chapter.
2 Sir Stephen Wall, oral evidence to the Iraq Inquiry, 19 January 2011, http://www.iraqinquiry.org.uk/transcripts/oralevidence-bydate/110119.aspx.
3 House of Commons Parliamentary Debates, 23 March 1999, Vol. 328, col. 163.
4 http://news.bbc.co.uk/2/hi/uk_news/politics/323465.stm.
5 House of Comons Parliamentary Debates, 14 September 2001, vol. 372, col. 607.
6 http://www.iraqinquiry.org.uk/transcripts/oralevidence-bydate/100305.aspx 5 May 2010, accessed 28 May 2014.
7 'Iraq inquiry: Straw's warnings to Blair revealed', *Daily Telegraph*, 17 January 2010 and 'Straw says Iraq 'most difficult decision' in his life, BBC, 21 January 2010, available on http://news.bbc.co.uk/2/hi/8471511.stm.
8 'Iraq inquiry: 45-minute weapon claim 'new' to Hoon', BBC, 19 January 2010, available on http://news.bbc.co.uk/2/hi/8466828.stm.
9 Sir Stephen Wall, *op. cit.*
10 House of Commons Parliamentary Debates, 26 February 2003, Vol. 400, col. 265 and foll.
11 'Support for war falls to new low', *The Guardian*, 21 January 2003; see also YouGov polls on http://research.yougov.co.uk/news/iraq/, accessed 28 May 2014.
12 House of Comons Parliamentary Debates, 29 August 2013, vol. 566.

Works cited

Bennister, M. (2012) *Prime Ministers in Power: Political Leadership in Britain and Australia* (Basingstoke: Palgrave Macmillan).
Blair, T. (1999) Speech on the doctrine of the international community, Chicago, 23 March, available at http://www.britishpoliticalspeech.org/speech-archive.htm?speech=279, accessed 29 May 2014.

Blair, T. (2010) *A Journey* (London: Hutchinson).

Blondel, J. (1987) *Political Leadership: Towards a General Analysis* (London: Sage).

Buller, J. and James, T.S. (2008), 'Statecraft and the assessment of political leadership in Britain', Paper for the PSA Annual Conference, Swansea.

Bulpitt, J. (1986) 'The Discipline of the New Democracy: Mrs Thatcher's Domestic Statecraft', *Political Studies*, Vol. 34, n° 1, 19–39.

Burrall, S., Donnelly, B. and Weir, S. (2006) *Not in Our Name: Democracy and Foreign Policy in the UK* (London: Politico's).

Butler, L. (2004), *Review of Intelligence on Weapons of Mass Destruction* (London: Stationery Office, HC 898, available at www.archive2.official-documents. co.uk/document/deps/hc/.../898.pdf. Accessed 30 October 2012).

Cook, R. (2004) *The Point of Departure: Diaries from the Frontbench*, new ed., (London: Pocket Books).

Cowley, P. and Stuart, M. (2008) 'A Rebellious Decade: Backbench Rebellions under Tony Blair' in Matt Beech and Simon Lee (eds) *Ten Years of New Labour* (Basingstoke: Palgrave Macmillan), pp. 103–19.

Crossman, R. (1963) 'Introduction' in Walter Bagehot, *The English Constitution* (London: Fontana Press).

Dyson, S.B. (2009) *The Blair Identity: Leadership and Foreign Policy* (Manchester: Manchester University Press).

Elgie, R. (1995). *Political Leadership in Liberal Democracies* (London: Macmillan).

Foley, M. (2000) *The British Presidency* (Manchester: Manchester University Press).

Gamble, A. (2003) *Between Europe and America: The future of British politics.* Basingstoke: Palgrave Macmillan.

Hailsham, Lord (1976) 'Elective Dictatorship', *The Listener*, 496–500.

Heffernan, R. (2003) 'Prime Ministerial Dominance? The Core Executive in the UK', *British Journal of Politics and International Relations*, Vol. 5, n° 3, 347–72.

Hennessy, P. (2001) *Whitehall* (London: Pimlico).

Hennessy, P. (2005) 'Rulers and Servants of the State: The Blair Style of Government 1997–2004', *Parliamentary Affairs*, Vol. 58, n° 1, 6–16.

Hill, Christopher (2001) 'Foreign Policy' in Anthony Seldon (ed.), *The Blair Effect* (London: Little, Brown Company), pp. 331–53.

Hill, C. (2005) 'Putting the world to rights: Tony Blair's foreign policy mission' in Anthony Seldon and Dennis Kavanagh (eds) *The Blair Effect 2001–2005* (Cambridge: Cambridge University Press), pp. 384–409.

Hutton, L. (2004) *Report of the Inquiry into the Circumstances Surrounding the Death of Dr David Kelly*, available on
http://webarchive.nationalarchives.gov.uk/20090128221550/http://www.the-hutton-inquiry.org.uk/content/report/index.htm, accessed 17 September 2012.

Kavanagh, D. (2005) 'The Blair Premiership' in Anthony Seldon and Dennis Runciman (eds), *The Blair Effect 2001–2005* (Cambridge: Cambridge University Press), pp. 3–19.

Mandelson, P. (2010) *The Third Man* (London: HarperPress).

Naughtie, J. (2004) *The Accidental American: Tony Blair and the Presidency* (Basingstoke: Macmillan).

Norton, P. (2008) 'Tony Blair and the Office of Prime Minister' in Matt Beech and Simon Lee (eds), *Ten Years of New Labour* (Basingstoke: Palgrave Macmillan), pp. 89–102.

Pryce, S. (1997) *Presidentializing the Premiership* (Basingstoke: Macmillan).

Rawnsley, A. (2010) *The End of the Party: The Rise and Fall of New Labour* (London: Penguin).

Riddell, P. (2001) 'Blair as Prime Minister' in Anthony Seldon (ed.) *The Blair Effect* (London: Little, Brown Company), pp. 21–40.

Riddell, P. (2003) *Hug Them Close: Blair, Clinton and the 'Special Relationship'* (London: Politico's).

Runciman, W.G. (ed.) (2004) *Hutton and Butler: Lifting the Lid on the Workings of Power*, British Academy Occasional Paper, (Oxford: Oxford University Press).

Sampson, A. (2004) *Who Runs this Place? The Anatomy of Britain in the 21st Century* (London: Murray).

Short, C. (2004) *An Honourable Deception? New Labour, Iraq, and the Misuse of Power* (London: Simon & Schuster).

Smith, M.J. (ed.) (1999) *The Core Executive in Britain* (Basingstoke: Macmillan).

Theakston, K. (2002) 'Political Skills and Context in Prime Ministerial Leadership in Britain', *Politics and Policy*, Vol. 30, n° 2, June, 283–323.

5
From Dewar to Salmond: The Scottish First Ministers and the Establishment of their Leadership

Gilles Leydier

The implementation of the Devolution settlement in 1999[1] created a legislative body, the Scottish Parliament, as well as a separate political Executive, composed of a First Minister and a Cabinet, which comprises about two dozen senior and junior ministers. Although a great deal of research (Arter, 2004; Bogdanor, 2001; Bort and Harvie, 2005; Jeffery and Mitchell, 2009; McCrone, 2005, McLean, 2001; Mitchell, 2009; Paterson, 2000; Taylor, 1999; Trench, 2004; Trench, 2005) has been devoted to the functioning and achievements of the new Scottish Parliament, very few political comments have focused upon the executive power and the devolved ministers. More strikingly, the coverage and analysis of the position and achievements of the Scottish First Ministers since 1999 has been extremely limited.

This chapter aims at understanding political leadership in the original context of the newly created Scottish devolved institutions. It will focus on the conditions which have framed political leadership in Scotland since 1999, the way the First Ministers have gained and built their legitimacy and influence, faced challenges and constraints, interacted with their followership, dealt with public opinion and the media. Under which circumstances have Scottish politicians acceded to leadership position? To what extent have Scottish leaders been visible and efficient? What have they brought to the new Scottish institutional framework? Why have they failed or been successful? Stability providers, game-changers, communicators or 'grassroots-connectors': how have the Scottish First Ministers fitted into this leadership typology? In order to answer these questions this chapter provides an overview of the role and actions of the Scottish First Ministers since the start of the devolved institutions in 1999. It studies their political initiatives and assesses their performances, in order to explore the way the successive incumbents have embraced their function to establish a political leadership upon the Scottish stage. The analysis starts with a description of the place of the Scottish Executive and First Ministers within the framework of the newly devolved institutions, with an exploration of the political environment and the institutional limits and constraints upon them. It then focuses on the successive Scottish leaders' backgrounds, legitimacy and profiles. It finally moves to an evaluation of their record and legacy as political leaders, trying to outline a typology of their leadership style.

The Scottish leaders and the devolved institutions

The post of First Minister (FM) was created by the Scotland Act 1998. Under this settlement the FM is the leader of the Cabinet and primarily responsible for the formulation, development and presentation of Scottish government policy. Appointed by the Queen from among the Scottish Parliament, he is directly accountable to it for his actions and those of the wider government. He has the power to choose his ministers, who must be members of and nominated by the Scottish Parliament. In practice the First Minister has an almost free rein in order to appoint and dismiss the members of his team, and complete liberty to intervene in the policy fields according to his priorities. The First Minister is also assisted by a Deputy First Minister, a post which was originally created for the leader of the junior party in the prospect of a coalition government. The Scottish Cabinet operates in the Westminster style and on the principle of collective responsibility with weekly meetings and the assistance provided by the work of a small number of Cabinet committees.

Since 1999 Scotland has had five First Ministers as well as one acting First Minister. Labour leader Donald Dewar, the main architect of the Scotland Act, was the first FM from May 1999 until his sudden death in October 2000 (Alexander, 2005). Then Labour Henry McLeish occupied the post until he decided to resign in November 2001 over the accusations of office expense irregularities. He was succeeded by another Labour leader, Jack McConnell, who held the position of First Minister until his party came second at the May 2007 Scottish elections. Following the electoral success of his party, the SNP leader Alex Salmond became First Minister and remained in power seven and a half years – the longest-serving FM since the establisment of devolution – until he decided to resign from office following the referendum on Scottish independence. In November 2014, Salmond was replaced as leader of the SNP and First Minister by Nicola Sturgeon, the former Deputy First Minister. On three occasions, owing to Donald Dewar's sickness and then following Donald Dewar's death and Henry McLeish's resignation, the Liberal Democrat Deputy First Minister Jim Wallace has assumed the role of 'Acting' First Minister for a short period of time.

The office of First Minister was thus characterized by great instability during the first three years of devolution (Mitchell, 2003). Since 2002, however, McConnell (five and a half years as FM) and Salmond (seven years in office in May 2014) have managed to secure their position and establish their leadership on a long-term basis.

Constraints upon the leadership

From 1999 to 2007, with no single party holding an absolute majority in Parliament, devolution was characterized by coalition governments between Labour (the leading party at Holyrood) and the Liberal-Democrats. Under coalition[2] the Scottish Executive must negotiate a policy platform at the beginning of each parliamentary session. In 1999 the establishment of this programme was subject to rather difficult bargaining between the two coalition partners, notably over the questions of university fees, free personal care for the elderly and land reforms. In 2003 the negotiations between the two political parties were easier and shorter, but the Lib-Dems were in a stronger position to impose their policy priorities on Labour First Minister Jack McConnell, notably on the issue of the introduction of proportional representation in local government. Coalition management also implies that the First Minister has to work closely with the deputy FM in order to deliver the Executive Partnership's programme, both leaders being responsible for the policies engaged. Furthermore, the coalition allows the leader of the junior party to select its own ministers and give a veto over their dismissal. The power of appointment and dismissal of the FM is therefore reduced. On the whole, the political autonomy of the first three FMs has been constrained by the realities of coalition government (Parry, 2003).

Between 2007 and 2011 the scenario changed with the advent of a SNP-led minority government (Jones, 2007; Johns et al., 2010). Although the Scottish Executive was freed from coalition bargaining and recovered some flexibility in policy making, it had to find a majority of Members of the Scottish Parliament (MSPs) for each piece of legislation. For the new First Minister Alex Salmond the constraint upon his power was thus about the concessions he could make in order to have his programme approved by the Parliament while avoiding having to face a vote of confidence. From this perspective the vote of the first Budget of the new administration was crucial. While the Budget was initially defeated in the Scottish Parliament by a coalition of Labour, Lib-Dems and Green MSPs, the Scottish Executive did not resign and Salmond demonstrated his leadership skills by calling a media briefing, directly challenging the opposition by threatening to call for new elections. Eventually after a week a new Budget deal was agreed and passed in Parliament with the support of both Labour and the Liberal-Democrats and the authority of the new FM upon the Scottish political stage was firmly established for the following months (Hassan, 2009). Meanwhile, during his first term as FM, Salmond was also able to propose consensual policies – such as the removal of tuition fees, the defence of the national health service or the protection of universal benefits or free care for the elderly that could be accepted by a majority of MSPs whatever their political obedience.

After 2011 the absolute majority gained by the SNP at the Scottish elections enabled FM Alex Salmond to have free rein to promote his priorities and consolidate his leadership (Curtice, 2011).

Relations with London

In addition to the Scottish situation, the UK political context has also been of some importance for the political autonomy of the First Minister and the assertion of his authority. Between 1999 and 2007 the successive Labour-dominated coalitions and Labour-led Executives in Scotland coincided with New Labour governments and Tony Blair's premiership in London. There have been close links between Labour ministers in London and Edinburgh, the presence of several important Scottish ministers in the UK government, such as Gordon Brown, Robin Cook or Alastair Darling, facilitating these connections (Hassan, 2004). In practice, Scottish ministers often had to refer to their London counterparts or contemplate what the Labour Party leadership in the centre would think of their initiatives.

Because of his previous experience as a long-serving Westminster MP and member of the Labour Cabinet between 1997 and 1999, Donald Dewar was naturally at ease in that context and dealing with the London leadership when he became First Minister (McLean, 2001). However, he embarked on a turf war with the first post-devolution Scotland Secretary within the London government, John Reid. Henry McLeish for his part could also rely on his experience as a Westminster

MP and on his London networks established as a Minister of State for the Scottish Office from 1997 to 1999 (McLeish, 2004).

As for Jack McConnell, he was a political outsider to Westminster lacking the networks of contacts in London and the FM least dependent on London for his position (Davidson, 2005). Nevertheless he chose to align as much as possible with London and stick to the New Labour government, as was the case when he decided to put the issue of the 'ned culture' (anti-social behaviour) at the forefront of the Scottish political agenda. Even when Scottish policies diverged from those implemented in England, as in public-system provision for instance, McConnell kept a low profile and refused to play up the issue in front of London, contrary to the situation at the same moment in Wales, where First Minister Rhodri Morgan openly capitalized on traditional 'Old Labour' values, claiming to put 'clear red water' between him and Blair (Keating, 2010: 145).

In 2007 the situation changed with different parties being in charge at the two executive levels. The establishment of an SNP government in Edinburgh was a major test for the devolution settlement. Although many observers had anticipated regular internal conflicts and a possible breakdown of the system in the context of divided party control, informal links and a working collaboration were gradually established between ministers in Edinburgh and in London. At the First Minister level Alex Salmond worked hand in hand with the London government on issues of British importance such as the Glasgow Airport terrorist attack in 2007 or the tenth anniversary of the foot-and-mouth crisis in 2011. However, on regular occasions there were real arguments between the Scottish Executive and Westminster, on topics such as energy policy and the removal of Trident submarines for Treasury funding. During the financial crisis Alex Salmond expressed a clear divergence about the solution implemented by Gordon Brown in order to save the Scottish banks HBOS and RBS. But the high-profile row between Salmond and London concerned the future of the convicted Lockerbie bomber Abdelbaset al-Megrahi – who was later released by the Scottish government on compassionate grounds on account of his terminal illness in the face of huge criticism from the US and others. Since 2010 with David Cameron in charge in London, Salmond has often 'played the Scottish card' in order to resist Westminster cuts, and the renewed legitimacy provided by his electoral triumph at the 2011 elections enabled him to directly challenge the British Prime Minister in the negotiations around the terms of the 2014 Scottish independence referendum (Torrance, 2012).

Taking policy initiatives

In order to assert their authority upon the Scottish political stage, the successive First Ministers have used their office in order to put their stamp on Scottish politics by promoting specific and/or symbolic policy initiatives.

At the beginning of his term Henry McLeish decided to put the emphasis on the issue of free health care for the elderly, a social measure that should be funded by the Scottish Executive. Although the idea was rather popular among Scottish opinion, it was very controversial within Scottish and British politics. Notably the previous FM Donald Dewar, the majority of the members of McLeish's Cabinet including his Health Minister and the majority of the Labour MSPs as well as the Labour government in London, were all favourable to the idea that the state should finance health-care costs for elderly people through means testing. But McLeish decided to do otherwise on this prominent welfare issue. By doing so he distanced himself from his predecessor and asserted his leadership within the Executive as a whole (Lynch, 2006: 427). He also demonstrated the autonomy of Scottish policy towards the UK government in front of Scottish opinion and could claim it as the major achievement of his term.

During his term in office FM Jack McConnell also chose to pursue distinctive flagship policies. He first made a personal political mark by promoting 'environment justice' as a cross-cutting issue influencing the work of the whole Executive. In addition he promoted a series of symbolic initiatives intended to strike the opinion and/or change its behaviour. There was first 'One Scotland–Many Cultures', a campaign designed to tackle the on-going problems of racism and sectarianism within Scottish society; then the 'Fresh Talent initiative' aimed at arresting Scotland's demographic decline and attracting young and skilled immigrants to come to live and work in Scotland; last but not least, there was the campaign to ban smoking in Scottish public places, an initiative that gave Scotland the leadership within the United Kingdom and which can be considered as McConnell's most far-reaching achievement (Macdonnel, 2009).

For Alex Salmond his accession to the post of First Minister in 2007 was soon followed by a spectacular gesture aimed at changing the name of the 'Scottish Executive' into that of 'Scottish Government'. That move had been previously tried by Henry MacLeish in 2001 but quickly stopped by Labour at Westminster. There was again some resistance to the initiative from opponents in London as well as in some Scottish media. But Salmond stayed firm and the symbolic change was soon implemented. At the same time the FM decided to drastically cut down the size of the Cabinet from 12 to six members, a way to demonstrate his willingness to put his term on the bases of coherent and efficient governance rather than political bargaining.

A few weeks after his accession to the FM post Alex Salmond unveiled the Independence White Paper and launched a 'National Conversation' with the Scottish people on Scotland's constitutional future (Scottish Government, 2007). For the new First Minister that was an opportunity not only to maintain his party push for independence – the SNP's raison d'être – but also to set Scotland's political agenda and take the Scottish – as well as British – leadership on the key issue of the future of devolution for the years to come. Since 2007 Salmond has managed to keep the lead on the constitutional debate while adapting to the electoral realities of Scottish politics and the preferences of Scottish opinion (Harvey and Lynch, 2011): first by supporting from the start the idea of a multi-option referendum including the choice of 'enhanced devolution'; then two years later by promoting 'fiscal autonomy' in Scotland while offering the possibility of 'devolution max', the most popular constitutional option within the Scottish opinion; later by giving up the idea of delivering a referendum in 2010 while disconnecting the issue of Scotland's constitutional future from the 2011 Holyrood election campaign; and eventually by using his new enhanced position following the 2011 elections to impose the referendum of 2014 on the issue of Scottish independence.

Scottish leaders in the international environment

In order to assert their leadership the different First Ministers have tried to give their office some international visibility, by promoting Scotland abroad and developing a role in European and external affairs (Scottish Executive, 2004a and b).

First Ministers McLeish and McConnell were particularly active in personally promoting 'Tartan Day' in New York and the United States. After 2007 Salmond downplayed this controversial celebration criticized for giving a stereotyped image of Scotland based on outdated 'tartanry'; however, he continued to promote Scotland abroad – this time more as a modern and serious nation – through the concept of the 'Scottish Week'.

McLeish and McConnell have also been keen to develop a diaspora strategy as the Scottish Executive launched the wider networks 'Global

Scots' and 'Global Friends of Scotland', in order to identify expatriates who could help investment and/or development. Inspired by the success of the Irish experience this strategy encouraging the Scottish diaspora to invest in or return to Scotland was continued after 2007 by the SNP with 2009 being declared the year of 'Homecoming'.

Concerning European matters Labour First Ministers have sought to make the Scottish Executive sign cooperation agreements with European regions such as Catalonia, Tuscany, Bavaria, North-Rhein Westphalia or Flanders, and to develop economic partnerships with Nordic countries on common concerns or with new EU incomers such as Estonia or the Czech Republic on European structural fund matters. In 2001 McLeish signed the Declaration of Flanders with the 'constitutional regions' of Europe, calling for recognition of their position within the European Union. Throughout his term McConnell was personally involved in the Conference of Presidents of Regional Legislative Assemblies of Europe and was President of RegLeg (European regions with legislative powers) for one year, hosting Regleg's fifth annual meeting in Edinburgh in November 2004.

From a more global perspective in line with his commitment to put the emphasis on environmental policy McConnell attended the World Summit on Sustainable Development in Johannesburg in 2002, subsequently developing an economic link between Scotland and the South African region of Eastern Cape. Throughout his term McConnell also demonstrated a constant interest for Malawi, forging development programmes with this underdeveloped country historically linked with Scotland. Eventually McConnell played a prominent role in securing the hosting of the 2014 Commonwealth Games for Glasgow (Macdonell, 2009: 236).

On the whole the Scottish First Ministers and their Executives have progressively implemented a 'paradiplomacy', based on the forging of international links and partnerships mainly in the economic, commercial and cultural fields. After 2007 with the SNP in office the emphasis continued to be on a strategy of economic promotion, trade development and inward investment. However, it can be argued that there has been a shift towards the emergence of a more political 'proto-diplomacy', with Scotland no longer promoted as a European region or a sub-state government but as a nation-state in the making (Keating, 2010: 161–4). Thus for instance the existing links with German Länder were minimized while those with Catalonia or Flanders – two highly autonomous regional components engaged like Scotland in the process of nation-building – were highlighted. Managing to wrap himself in head-of-state's clothes First Minister Alex Salmond has put Scotland on a par with small independent states in northern Europe, praising the example of the 'arc of prosperity' (until Ireland and Iceland happened to be seriously affected by the financial crisis of 2008) or promoting the Norwegian model. There was also more open competition between the First Minister and the London government in the struggle for attracting foreign investments, as exemplified by the case of China, a country for which Salmond has demonstrated a special interest, paying three personal visits there since 2007.

Political legitimacy and styles of leadership

Each of the four successive Scottish First Ministers has occupied the position with his own political legitimacy, personality and leadership style.

The first incumbent, Donald Dewar, was very popular and uncontested at the beginning of his term, his position as the first First Minister in a devolved Parliament looking almost like a matter of historical inevitability (McLean, 2001). Highly respected within his own party and Scottish politics as one of the key men who kept the devolution cause alive in Labour circles over the previous decades and the one who eventually brought back a Scottish Parliament three centuries after its dissolution, his commitment to the devolution cause has gained him the label of 'Father of the Parliament' or – more – 'Father of the Scottish nation' (Alexander, 2005). In his first speech for the opening of the new institutions he caught the mood brilliantly (Paterson, 2000). But that initial iconic status was soon challenged by the numerous problems of his new administration, embroiled in the access-to-ministers scandal, the spiraling cost of the Holyrood building, the row over the repeal of Section 28 on homosexuality or the exam results fiasco. Dewar had to face harsh criticisms from sections of the Scottish press who had decided devolution was a mess and achieving nothing. Although his integrity, decency and fairness were never contested in public opinion and despite the fact that he remained close to his followers and could rely on his party's backing, Dewar failed to be convincing with regard to the fact that, had he been the right man to deliver devolution, he was the right one to run Scotland. Reasonable, moderate, supremely cautious, not confrontational, working in a collegiate style, he was something of a reluctant leader, suspected of lacking the 'messianic zeal' and authority over his team. In fact, being mainly preoccupied by the setting up of the new institutions, Dewar had little time to sponsor a personal policy area or to establish the power of the Executive facing the stronger legitimacy of the Scottish Parliament. Acting as a link and a buffer between Edinburgh and London he also devoted much time finding a breathing space and a workable relationship with the Secretary of State for Scotland, a position he had occupied before 1999 and from which he seemed to find it difficult to distance himself as First Minister.

When he became First Minister in October 2000, Dewar's successor Henry McLeish could rely on his background as a Westminster MP and as devolution minister in the Scottish Office before 1999, as well as his experience as a holder of a prominent ministerial post within the Scottish Executive after May 1999. Considered as Gordon Brown's 'protégé', he was seen as a safe pair of hands and backed by the Labour leadership in London to take over the reins following Dewar's death. But like Dewar before him, McLeish had to share the position of Scottish Labour leader with the Secretary of State for Scotland – at this time Helen Liddell – as well as to manage the new Executive in the context of a coalition government with the Liberal-Democrats. The rather confused situation over the status of the First Minister within the Scottish Labour Party – with one leader for the Scottish elections, and another leader for the British ones – affected McLeish's power and authority, especially as, unlike Dewar – he had not faced a Scottish election as Scottish leader (Lynch, 2006: 431). As a natural conciliator McLeish adapted to the electoral reality by taking up the policies which seemed to have majority support in the Scottish Parliament, like free personal care for the elderly and putting a distinctive Scottish stamp on policies. But he failed to establish the authority of the Executive before Parliament as well his own over the Labour Party in Scotland (Hassan and Warhurst, 2002). His inability to control rebellion within his own ranks proved lethal to the First Minister when he got caught in the row over his Westminster constituency expenses. His inability to resolve 'Officegate' in the eyes of the public and the media, describing his actions as 'a muddle, not a fiddle' led to his quick fall after only one year in office (Macdonell, 2009: 63–72).

Contrary to McLeish, McConnell was in a stronger political position within the Scottish Labour Party when he became First Minister, having used his years working in Labour's Scottish headquarters to build a network of supporters in order to prepare for a leadership contest at some future date. He also had demonstrated his ambitions by challenging McLeish for the post of FM in 2000, gaining the support of most Labour backbenchers during the leadership contest. McConnell did provide stability for the Scottish Labour Party when he became leader, his grip on his own supporters being also eased by the decreased importance of the Secretary of State for Scotland within the London government after 2003. McLeish was really eager to assert his authority upon the Scottish Executive, beginning with a purge of prominent members of the Dewar and McLeish Cabinets and their replacement by his own supporters when establishing his first team. Having no Westminster connections but significant experience in the previous Executives as a former Finance Minister and then Education, Europe and External Affairs Minister, McConnell constantly sought to readjust the balance of power within the devolved institutions in favour of the Executive, as demonstrated by the unilateral decision to ban smoking in enclosed public places imposed by the FM in October 2004 (Bort and Harvie, 2005). He also extended the reach of the Executive within Parliament by creating the posts of Ministerial Parliamentary Aides (MPAs) and by being personally involved in the selection of members and chairs of parliamentary committees, all of whose initiatives contributed to a useful extension of his patronage power (Keating and Carney, 2006). Furthermore, McConnell also wanted to bind the Scottish bureaucracy closer to his Executive and answerable only to him, although it has remained part of the UK public service. On the whole McConnell managed to develop a core Executive in Scotland and expand his own support mechanisms within it (Lynch, 2006: 435).

If McConnell demonstrated political shrewdness and authority in extending the role and resources of the office of First Minister, he had more difficulty in imposing himself as a 'national leader' in Scottish opinion. His modest credo about 'doing less, better', as well as his absence of proposals on the constitutional debate about Scotland's future, failed to capture the people's imagination and fuelled the criticisms about his 'lack of vision' and his 'New Labour conformism'. His absence of personal charisma, which had been already striking during the 2003 elections when his 'recognition factor' was rather low and comparable with the one of marginal left-wing activist Tommy Sheridan, had later to suffer from the comparison with SNP's leader Alex Salmond after 2004. During the 2007 legislative campaign, although the Labour Party and the SNP were neck and neck in the polls, 43 per cent of the Scottish opinion was claiming that Salmond would make the best FM, against only 23 per cent supporting McConnell.

Alex Salmond's charismatic leadership

According to the classical Weberian definition, charismatic authority can be described as a power legitimized by a leader's exceptional personal qualities, which creates a strong personal relationship between the leader and the political environment and inspires loyalty and obedience from followers. To what extent does Alex Salmond's domination over the Scottish political stage over the last ten years or so fit into that leadership category?

Before becoming First Minister Alex Salmond had managed to build up a strong leadership within his own party as well as a high profile in London where he relentlessly promoted the nationalist case at Westminster and in numerous broadcast political programmes (Lynch, 2002). By the time of the 2007 Holyrood elections he had clearly become a major electoral asset for the SNP, with the polls showing him to be far more popular than the incumbent First Minister, Jack McConnell. This prompted the SNP to emphasize the contrast between the party leaders, a strategy that culminated in the party using 'Alex Salmond for First Minister' instead of 'SNP' as the main party identifier on the regional ballot paper (Murray and Crawford, 2010).

Following the result of the 2007 election Salmond's first coup was the decision to go for a minority government, calculating that by seizing the machinery of power while maintaining party integrity, he could consolidate the SNP's advantage (Harvie, 2008). The decision illustrates the profile of Salmond as a risk-taker, a feature that he had the opportunity to demonstrate on later occasions, notably on the course towards the independence referendum, his major gamble.

When in power Salmond and his minority government promoted an agenda based on competence, consensus and change. They produced evidence of their capacity to govern within the constraints of the devolution settlement, to make some difference on significant issues, such as transport, health, education, energy or the economy, and to implement a social contract faithful to the values of Scottish opinion (Leydier, 2009). At the same time they put forward a vision of the future for Scotland and managed to keep the constitutional debate alive, by focusing on the opportunities that further steps in the devolution process would provide for Scottish interests (Harvey and Lynch, 2011). Thus the renamed Scottish government positioned itself as an efficient alternative to the previous coalition within the present constitutional settlement as well as the best embodiment of the dynamics of devolution.

As head of the Executive Salmond could rely on an astonishing loyalty from his followers, with not a sign of dissent inside the SNP where his supremacy had been unchallenged since 2004. Within the devolved institutions and under the constraint of a minority government he displayed at the same time authority, tactical sense, pragmatism and an ability to exploit opportunities, demonstrating his leadership skills on numerous occasions: by using the threat of a vote of confidence throughout the first three years of his term in order to get his policies approved by a majority of MSPs; by showing the capacity to adapt to the situation when he decided to change the referendum agenda in 2010; or by proving his resilience and ability to take difficult decisions in the case of the release of the Lockerbie bomber. Salmond also behaved as a British leader, taking opportunity of the existence of the British–Irish Council, developing relationships with Cardiff, Belfast and Dublin, claiming a seat in the party leaders' TV debates and proposing a 'Lib–Lab–Nat' coalition at Westminster during the 2010 general election campaign.

Long before his accession to the position of First Minister, Alex Salmond has been acclaimed by the Scottish media altogether not only as an efficient and talented politician, but also as a charismatic and magnetic leader, capable of capturing people's imagination and inspiring fervour (Torrance, 2010). Salmond's charismatic domination over the Scottish stage, fuelled by his communication skills, media performances and presidential style campaigns, has found in the position of First Minister an ideal environment in which to flourish. As the Scottish government leader, he developed a stirring, hope-inspiring narrative towards the Scottish population, employing sometimes messianic accents to evoke Scotland's potential – such as, for instance, in the field of renewable energy – and future. In a Gaullist posture he often managed to put himself above party politics. Eventually his active proto-diplomacy promoting Scotland as a nation-state in the making also contributed to making him largely identified with Scotland and achieving a head-of-state's status, a dimension that even David Cameron, when trying to debunk him as 'El Presidente Salmondo' (Torrance, 2011: 28), was implicitly forced to admit.

Salmond's personal aura and statesmanship played a large part in the electoral triumph of the SNP during the 2011 Holyrood election, which turned into a personality contest and a presidential race (Whitaker, 2010). From 2007 to 2011, whatever the fortunes of his party, Salmond had benefited from permanent net positive ratings in the polls and on polling day, 52 per cent of the Scottish electorate thought Salmond would make the best FM, against 33 per cent supporting one of the four alternative possibilities and only 17 per cent supporting his main rival Ian Gray (Curtice, 2011). Salmond's charismatic domination over the Scottish political scene had reached an unprecedented height (Denver, 2011).

Conclusion

This chapter has identified a number of constraints in examining the role and functions of Scottish First Ministers. Since 1999, successive First Ministers have struggled to put their stamp upon Scottish politics within the framework of the newly devolved institutions. The initial constitutional settlement was largely favourable to the Scottish Parliament, considered as the democratic embodiment of Scottish society and the main source of legitimacy for Scottish policies. Successive FMs had thus to reverse the balance of power between the Executive and legislative powers, as well as to impose their grip within a Cabinet system of government. The establishment of their leadership had to go through a number of identified institutional hurdles and within a complex and multi-level environment involving their internal legitimacy within their own party, the control of their political majority at Holyrood, the communication with Scottish opinion and media as well as a potentially problematic relationship with the London government. On the whole one of the most visible trends of Scottish politics since 1999 has been the rise of Executive power, and the affirmation of its leader, in the British model and following recent trends in contemporary democracies (Blick and Jones, 2010; Foley, 2001).

By reference to the initial typology suggested in this volume, successive Scottish FMs can be mostly seen as game-changers, creating then strengthening the newly established Scottish Executive in search of legitimacy. The first two FMs were in post for short periods of time, the first one at a time of transition during the early months of devolution. Three out of the four FMs occupied their position in a context of coalition governments and of similar majorities in London. The fourth FM had to deal with a situation of a minority government before eventually obtaining an absolute majority, in both cases with a diverging majority in charge at Westminster. If Dewar was the architect of the new institutions and had little time to develop the office of FM, the following leaders have tried to establish their power and increase their resources, largely building on the arrangements they inherited. As heads of government as well as party leaders, they have notably sought to take distance with collective responsibility within their Cabinet, develop their core Executive, extend their initially limited patronage power, increase their grip on policy making, promote specific flagship policies and establish their visibility on the European and international stage. McConnell was particularly active and innovative in establishing the Scottish FM power within the devolved institutions in the specific context of a coalition government.

Salmond has brought a new dimension to the office of Scottish First Minister. If, like Dewar before him, he could rely on a strong partisan and popular legitimacy before taking the position, he managed to display management credibility as well as developing dynamic relations with his followers and Scottish opinion when becoming FM. His aptitude for communicating a strong and positive narrative, his uncontested authority within his own camp and his capacity to exploit the Scottish card when dealing with London, have all brought the conditions for an effective leadership in Scotland, despite the restrictive context of a minority government. Eventually Salmond's personal charismatic domination over the Scottish political stage has made the First Ministerial position turn presidential, a situation which has been reinforced since 2011 in the unprecedented context of a one-party majority government. A risk-taker or a game-changer, Salmond has also been able to incorporate the other facets of political leadership. A great communicator with a strong public image, he has managed to connect with civil society and extend his support above his traditional party followers. And the unparalleled length of his mandate together with the exceptional political conditions of his second term have eventually provided greater stability and visibility to the position of the Scottish First Minister.

Notes

1 The 1998 Scotland Act established a Scottish Parliament of 129 members (MSPs) – 73 elected by first-past-the-post for individual constituencies and 56 elected proportionally from party lists in regional constituencies, all elected for a fixed four-year term with high hurdles against dissolution at any time. The Scottish Parliament was given extensive powers of primary legislation in 'devolved areas' such as education and training, housing and planning, health, social work, law and order, economic development and transport, local government, the administration of the European structural funds as well as limited fiscal powers confined to the possibility of varying the British rate of income tax by up to 3p in the pound. Meanwhile the Westminster Parliament was keeping the 'reserved powers' in the main fields of defence, foreign affairs, social security, fiscal and monetary policy, employment relations, immigration, energy, nuclear safety and the constitution. Besides a Scottish Executive was established, led by a First Minister chosen among the MSPs and submitted by the Presiding Officer to the Queen for formal appointment. The first Scottish Parliament elections took place in May 1999 (Forman, 2002: 89)

2 Coalition government was made almost inevitable by the importance of proportional representation within the electoral system. The first Scottish Parliament elections in 1999 resulted in the election of 56 Labour, 35 SNP, 18 Conservative, 17 Liberal-Democrats, 1 Socialist, 1 Independent and 1 Green MSPs. Although being the leading party with 39% of the votes, the Scottish Labour Party had to conclude an alliance with the Lib-Dems in order to secure a majority in the first Holyrood Parliament. The following elections in 2003 resulted in an even more diversified representation (the 'rainbow Parliament'), with the Labour Party losing 7 seats, and an electoral coalition between Labour (50 MSPs) and the Lib-Dems (17 MSPs) being necessary again in order to reach the majority of 65 MSPs at Holyrood.

Works cited

Alexander, W. (ed.) (2005) *Donald Dewar: Scotland's First Minister* (Edinburgh: Mainstream).

Arter, D. (2004) *The Scottish Parliament: A Scandinavian-style Assembly* (London: Frank Cass).

Blick, A., Jones, G. (2010), *Premiership* (London: Imprint Academic).

Bogdanor, V. (2001) *Devolution in the United Kingdom* (Oxford: Oxford University Press).

Bort, E., Harvie, C. (2005) 'After the albatross: a new start for the Scottish Parliament?', *Scottish Affairs*, Vol. 50, 26–38.

Curtice, J. (2011) 'The 2011 Scottish election: records tumble, barriers breached', *Scottish Affairs*, Vol. 76, 51–73.

Davidson, L. (2005) *Lucky Jack: Scotland's First Minister* (Edinburgh: Black & White Publishing).

Denver, D. (2011) 'Another historic moment: the Scottish Parliament elections 2011, *Scottish Affairs*, Vol. 76, 33–50.

Foley, M. (2001) *The British Presidency* (Manchester: Manchester University Press).

Forman, F.N. (2002) *Constitutional change in the United Kingdom*, The Constitution Unit (London: Routledge).

Harvey, M., Lynch, P. (2011) 'Inside the National Conversation: the SNP Government and the Politics of Independence 2007–2010, *Scottish Affairs* 80, 91–116.

Harvie, C. (2008) 'A year with Salmond', *Scottish Affairs*, Vol. 65, 38–46.

Hassan, G. (ed.) (2004) *The Scottish Labour Party* (Edinburgh: Edinburgh University Press).

Hassan, G. (ed.) (2009) *The Modern SNP from Protest to Power* (Edinburgh: Edinburgh University Press).

Hassan, G., Warhurst, C. (eds.) (2002) *Anatomy of the New Scotland: Power, Influence and Change* (Edinburgh: Mainstream).

Jeffery, C., Mitchell, J. (eds) (2009) *The Scottish Parliament 1999–2009: The First decade* Edinburgh: Luath Press/Hansard Society.

Johns, R., Mitchell, J., Denver, D., Pattie, C. (2010) *Voting for a Scottish government: the Scottish Parliament elections of 2007* (Manchester: Manchester University Press).

Jones, P. (2007) 'The Smooth Wooing: the SNP's Victory in the 2007 Scottish Parliament Elections', *Scottish Affairs*, Vol. 60, 6–23.

Keating, M. (2010) *The Government of Scotland* (Edinburgh: Edinburgh University Press).

Keating, M., Carney, P. (2006) 'A new elite? Politicians and civil servants in Scotland after devolution', *Parliamentary Affairs*, Vol. 59, n° 1, 1–17.

Leydier, G. (2011) 'Devolution: the next stakes', in Finding, S., Jones, M., Cauvet, P. (eds.), *Unfinished business, governance and the four nations: devolution in the UK* (Bordeaux: Presses Universitaires de Bordeaux).

Lynch, P. (2002) *The History of the Scottish National Party* (Cardiff: Welsh Academic Press).

Lynch, P. (2006) 'Governing Devolution: understanding the office of FM in Scotland and Wales', *Parliamentary affairs*, Vol. 59, n° 3, 420–436.

Macdonell, H. (2009) *Unchartered Territory. The Story of Scottish Devolution, 1999–2009* (London: Politico's).

McCrone, D. (2005) 'A Parliament for a People: Holyrood in an Understated Nation', *Scottish Affairs*, Vol. 50, 1–26.

McLean, R. (2001) 'Gallant crusader or cautious persuader? Donald Dewar's role in securing Scotland's Parliament', *Scottish Affairs*, Vol. 34, 1–10.

McLeish, H. (2004) *Scotland First: Truth and Consequences* (Edinburgh: Mainstream).

Mitchell, J. (2003) 'Third Year, Third First Minister', *in* Hazell, R. (ed.), *The State of the Nations* (Exeter: Imprint Academic).

Mitchell, J. (2009) *Devolution in the United Kingdom* (Manchester: Manchester University Press).

Murray, L., Crawford, E. (2010) *The role of charismatic leadership in a nationalist movement – A Case Study*. University of the West of Scotland, unpublished paper.

Parry, R. (2003) 'The Scottish Executive and the challenges of complex policy making', *The Political Quarterly*, Vol. 74, n° 4, 450–458.

Paterson, L. (2000) 'Scottish democracy and Scottish utopias: the first year of the Scottish Parliament', *Scottish Affairs*, Vol. 33, 45–61.

Scottish Executive (2004a) *European Strategy* (Edinburgh: Scottish Executive).

Scottish Executive (2004b) *International Strategy* (Edinburgh: Scottish Executive).

Scottish Government (2007) *Choosing Scotland's Future. A National Conversation. Independence and Responsibility in the Modern World*, Edinburgh: Scottish Government.

Taylor, B. (1999), *The Scottish Parliament* (Edinburgh: Polygon).

Torrance, D. (2010), *Salmond against the Odds* (Edinburgh: Birlinn).

Torrance, D. (2011) 'A tale of two elections', *Scottish Affairs*, Vol. 76, 10–32.

Torrance, D. (2012) 'Better together or Yes Scotland? Year one in the battle of Britain, *Scottish Affairs*, Vol. 80, 62–90.

Trench, A. (ed.) (2004) *Has Devolution made a difference? The State of the Nations* (Exeter: Imprint Academic).

Trench, A. (ed.) (2005) *The Dynamics of Devolution. The State of the Nations* (Exeter: Imprint Academic).

Whitaker, A. (2010) 'Holyrood elections will be a battle of leaders', *The Scotsman*, 14 October 2010.

6
Political leadership and the instrumentalization of the media: General de Gaulle between politics and the military (1958–1962)

Julia Heinemann

Introduction

Decision-making and authority-producing political leaders need support. Their modes of action, power relations and manners of governance are intrinsically linked to the questions of how to ensure support and how to cope with possible divisions. Both of these require effective use of the media. This applies not only to current leaders, forced to operate in an environment characterized by multimedia ensembles, but also to more historical political leaders. General De Gaulle can be considered as one of the most striking examples: The analysis of the General's life through the prism of his media relations shows indeed that their instrumentalization was of increasing importance, especially between 1958 and 1962, the period this contribution focuses on. In view of this, media were not only used to reach out to the population and the military, but significantly contributed to the construction of the leader's legitimacy.

1958 marks De Gaulle's return to power in the midst of the 'Algerian crisis' which began in 1954 (Jauffret, 2007: 77–81),[1] ended in 1962 and was not officially called the 'Algerian War' in France until 1999.[2] During this period, the French military were fighting against the nationalist National Liberation Front (FLN – Front de Libération Nationale) and its armed wing, the National Liberation Army (ALN – Armée de Libération Nationale), in the French counties (*départements*) in North Africa. General De Gaulle, who assumed the highest state functions after 1958, had to establish himself as the Head of State on the one hand, and as the manager of quite a complex situation in Algeria and metropolitan France on the other. The former military man, who had become a politician thenceforward, found himself between the political and the military sphere. Instead of contenting

82

himself with his political role, he rather chose to present himself as an integral part of the political scene as well as the military milieu, in particular when he donned his officer's uniform in moments of profound crisis.

These crises resulted from political change of course, which was progressively introduced: the Algerian policy undertaken by De Gaulle after his return to power in 1958 became more and more incompatible with the aspirations of many officers. After having supported the official attachment to French Algeria, the General actually considered a policy of self-determination and, finally, independence. In his speeches in 1958, De Gaulle was still referring to an attachment to French Algeria. In March 1959, he already recognized 'the new personality of Algeria' and made his audience understand that 'no doors will be closed'. In September 1959, he explicitly mentioned the right to self-determination, a further step towards the possibility of independence, and outlined his idea of an 'Algerian Algeria' one year later. Facing this new policy of disengagement, the military, who wanted to maintain Algeria as French territory, progressively opted for another camp different from the Head of State and Chief of Staff. It was precisely this choice that caused frictions and tensions and which finally led to a real rebellion against the political power that manifested itself through the 'week of the barricades' in 1960 (Stora, 2005: 19–20; Pervillé, 1993: 216–17),[3] the putsch of the generals in 1961 (Vaïsse, 2011; Pervillé, 2006)[4] and the formation of the Organisation of the Secret Army (OAS) (Dard, 1999 and 2005).[5]

During these crises, De Gaulle exploited different media in order to consolidate and reinforce, as well as legitimize his leadership. Therefore, the first part of this analysis of the instrumentalization of media between 1958 and 1962 explores the overall relations between De Gaulle and the media. The second section specifically analyses his self-presentation between politics and the military. The third part examines the rebellion, which was caused by the political change within the military institution by scrutinizing how his self-presentation was distorted by those who plotted against him by using the media in another way.

General De Gaulle and the media

Since long before the Algerian War, De Gaulle and the radio were almost inextricably linked. It is impossible to relate the General's life without taking into consideration this means of communication. De Gaulle's special relationship with the radio evolved throughout the Second World War, during which De Gaulle became the 'General micro' (Jeanneney, 2001: 239),[6] as the National Socialist propaganda called him, not least because of his famous 'Appeal of 18 June', a speech on the BBC in 1940, and the following broadcasts promoting 'Free France'. However, in order to explore his relationship with the radio, it is helpful to take a closer look at his opinions of the press and of other media.

In his *Memoirs of Hope*, De Gaulle asserted that he 'took the tone of the master of the hour in front of the press' (De Gaulle, 1970: 26). According to one of his biographers, Jean Lacouture, he had 'an eye for glancing through newspapers, photographing the headings, the layout of the pages, to get to the heart of the matter'. 'Nothing was more important to him than the reading of newspapers – the French, Parisian and regional press, as well as the foreign papers'. De Gaulle 'loved the fragrance of fresh ink and paper, hated anonymous press reviews [...] He became extremely impatient when newspapers were late while he was travelling'. As Lacouture relates: 'The General usually got up at 7:30 am – had a very light breakfast, washed, and spent about an hour reading the morning press – office at 9:30 am – synthesis of the press (again...)'. At 3 pm, he read *Le Monde* and leafed through *Paris-Presse* (Lacouture, 1986: pp.19–21). However, this passion for the press rather originated from his distrustful attitude towards the journalists and their work. In 1963, during an interview with his Minister of Information, Alain Peyrefitte, De Gaulle reportedly stated that 'the attitude of the press [...] has something unbelievable, like a system of denigration and falsification. The press is a hostile citadel' (Peyrefitte, 1997: 193).

De Gaulle's views of the press are inextricably linked to his experiences gained throughout the Second World War during which he had to deal with the collaborationist press as well as an international press, which often criticized him harshly. What was De Gaulle's most serious problem with the press? He was not able to control it easily. Thus it seems almost self-evident that the General 'preferred' more direct communication, especially by radio and later by television.

With his return to power in 1958, De Gaulle also recovered the right to access to the airwaves and thereby overcame the period called 'the crossing of the desert', which was not only of a personal and political but also of a mediatized nature (Wächter, 2006: 206; Kauffer, 2006: 23; Lacouture, 1985: 400). Enabled by the state monopoly on a French radio broadcasting service (Almeida, Delporte, 2010; Chupin et al., 2009: 61; Eck, 2001: 46–8)[7] that constantly worked for 'an increasingly governmental information' (Tudesq, 1994) on the one hand, and technical progress which made radios less bulky and easier to transport on the other, De Gaulle delivered several radio speeches[8] which were not only listened to by a civilian audience but also by many members of the military personnel in Algeria. To ensure a 'massive' use of and audience for the transistor radio, the French army was regularly encouraged to buy these radios and to listen to the broadcastings of the Radio of Algiers [Radio d'Alger] or the Voice of the Bled [Voix du Bled] in advertisements published in the internal magazine, *Le Bled* (Médard, 2005: 814).[9]

While the use of radio by De Gaulle is obviously related to his memory of the Second World War during which he had reportedly 'learned a lot about the radio', the use of television seems to be consistent with his desire to control and 'watch over "his" television' (Foulon, 1994: 23). To the politician René Capitant, De Gaulle reportedly said: '"You know, Capitant, I am not under any illusions. The political parties made me come back because they did not know how to get rid of the Algerian affair. But as soon as I have helped them to get rid of the Algerian affair, they will do the same as in 1946, they will force me to leave". Then he stopped and continued: "Maybe not this time, Capitant, because I had no television in 1946"' (Plantey, 1994: 61).

The 'mass media', namely the press, the radio and the television, did not only play a significant role in the General's schedule – from the newspaper reading in the morning until the evening enriched with television and sometimes cinema (Lacouture, 1986, vol. 3: 22) – but they were also important means for De Gaulle to put himself in the limelight as a political leader. Like his contemporaries, he had to learn to adapt to the media in order to become more and more competent to communicate by these channels. Thus, during his first televised address on 13 June 1958, he was still wearing his black glasses and reading his text lying in front of him, but in his speech on 27 June 1958, a mere two weeks later, things were already very different: he seemed much more relaxed, his eyes looked straight into the camera and the text had been learnt by heart (Bourdon, 1994: 54). Apparently, a metamorphosis had taken place, and it was initiated by one of the pioneers of advertising in France, Marcel Bleustein-Blanchet. He had seen De Gaulle's first speech on the television and was actually so horrified that he called De Gaulle's aide-de-camp to alert him. Thereupon Bleustein-Blanchet taught him first and foremost that it was 'necessary to look straight in the eyes', meaning the camera, 'in a personal way' (Bourdon, 1994: 55).

Nevertheless, this man who spent a lot of time with the different types of mass communication was no less regular a user of direct communication. His visits to Algeria attracted widespread public attention. However, these trips to North Africa responded not only to his desire to 'take the pulse of the army' (Argoud, 1974: 179) but also to his will to convince the armed forces in personal meetings of the wisdom of his political choices. On these occasions, he not only presented himself as the political leader but also as the military chief, not least because he put on his officer's uniform, not only in 1958 during his first official visit to Algiers but also on the occasion of his televised speech during the putsch in April 1961. In this context, the wearing of the uniform can be seen as a kind of non-verbal communication which symbolizes a whole set of imaginary connotations referring to De Gaulle at the time of Free France [France Libre] and the memory of the promise to which it had been linked since 1940.

De Gaulle's (self-) presentation between politics and the military

It was indeed this memory of the General having saved France and having ensured that it emerged victorious from the Second World War (rather than a country having collaborated with Nazi Germany and, therefore, having lost the war) that was promoted by a real network of civilians and members of the military when the situation in Algeria and in metropolitan France was worsening during the course of 1958. De Gaulle's followers did their best to convince the population in the North African *départements* and in large sections of the political circles that only the General was able to resolve the crisis. They campaigned for his return to power and used photographs and posters, as well as postcards, to spread his image. In June 1958, General Raoul Salan recommended that these postcards should be 'disseminated as widely as possible, and particularly among the troops'.[10]

Numerous representations of De Gaulle bore a specific symbol, which was added to the General's portrait: The Cross of Lorraine [Croix de Lorraine] and/or the 'V' representing victory. These presentations recall the period of the French Resistance [Résistance] and Free France [France Libre] during which the General established himself as the 'saviour of the nation' (Schmale, 2000: 366) who solved the crisis 'alone and deprived of everything' (Gallo, 1998: 474). This symbolism can be found on thousands of tricolour leaflets and flyers which were printed by the Fifth Offices [Cinquièmes Bureaux], the part of the military institution in charge of media relations, which means responsible for any kind of propaganda.[11] Moreover, these symbols similarly adorned the 'information pamphlets' [*Bulletins d'Information*], which also included the General's portrait, the 'V' for victory and the Cross of Lorraine.[12] The design of other means of communication was quite similar. Thus, the internal magazines used the same symbols and combined them with direct quotations from

De Gaulle: for instance, the front page of the twenty-seventh edition of the newspaper *Aurès Nemencha* sports a huge red 'V' pointing to the appeal of the General before the referendum in 1958 like an arrow: 'On behalf of France, I am asking you with all my heart to answer "yes"'.[13]

With the help of communication and advertising experts, in particular those around Bleustein-Blanchet, the use of the media for political purposes was increasingly professionalized (Bleustein-Blanchet, 1988). When De Gaulle returned to power, his own communication efforts were relayed by the military in North Africa, who disseminated his statements faithfully on the ground. Furthermore, this did not only apply to military publications but also to civilian newspapers in Algeria, which followed the logic of De Gaulle's policy in similar ways. For instance, in June 1958, when they placed high hopes on the General's return to power, the newspapers *L'Echo d'Alger* and *Les Réalités* published extensive extracts from De Gaulle's speech and exalted this 'historic day for French Algeria'.[14] By contrast, during the months following the official announcement of the project of possible self-determination for the Algerian people and on the occasion of several acute crises – such as the week of the barricades or the putsch of the generals – the same newspapers dedicated their columns predominantly to military news, on-going machinations and the evolutions of the resistance *against* the Gaullist project of future Algerian independence. For instance, on 24 April 1961, the *Dépêche quotidienne d'Algérie* dedicated its front page to the 'alliances all over Algeria where complete calm reigns', *L'Echo d'Alger* to the arrival of Salan and the intensification of the 'fight against the rebellion', whereas the press in metropolitan France, for instance *Libération* and *Le Monde*, prioritized information about the generals having planned the putsch as well as all those who had refused to rally. By doing so, the Algerian-based colonial newspapers favoured the point of view of a certain part of the army and distorted the reliable and faithful transmission and communication of the General's project and his self-presentation in and by the media.

Rebellions and distortion of the intended message

While De Gaulle's speeches were transmitted and reproduced without any modification and without any elaboration, accentuation or highlighting in 1959 – for example his address on 16 September 1959[15] – their communication and publication in North Africa was guided, distorted or garbled when the political and military circumstances prompted a part of the army to distance itself from the position of the

Head of State. Concerning this matter, it is instructive to take a closer look at the transmission of the General's speech on 29 January 1960,[16] while taking into account the political context of the barricades that were erected in January 1960. The simple typographical presentation of the speech guides the transmission of De Gaulle's address and its resulting representations in and by the media. General Faure, who later actively supported the putsch, signed a version of the speech, which tries to highlight all of the elements that may lead to the belief that De Gaulle was to remain attached to French Algeria.[17]

It is therefore essential to distinguish between the presentation and self-presentation of and by De Gaulle and his loyal entourage and the media products, which were realized by the army (but also by what can be called the 'lobby of the settlers') in North Africa. The political change of course caused disappointment and frustration among part of the army *in situ* and generated more and more tension. De Gaulle, whose famous speech 'I have understood you' ['Je vous ai compris'] from June 1958 was not only aimed at people living in the French *départements* in North Africa, but also at the military. Afterwards, he gradually became and presented himself as what may be called an 'enlightened de-colonialist' by referring more and more explicitly to the possibility of Algerian independence.

After having realized that most of the members of the military personnel who were responsible for media relations and the communication of his policy were actually supporting the fight to maintain a French Algeria, De Gaulle took several decisions in order to reduce their influence and to prevent their communication counter-attacks.[18] Within 18 months following his return to power, the Fifth Offices [*Cinquièmes Bureaux*] in charge of communication lost their influence[19] and were finally dissolved in 1960 – to the great chagrin of their leading supporters. The officers who did not resign after the failed barricades and the putsch were replaced or repatriated. De Gaulle tried a kind of 'purification', 'cleansing' or 'purging' of the media and communication activities of the military in Algeria, replaced the editor-in-chief of the internal military paper *Le Bled* and closed down the Cinematographic Section of the French Army in Algiers.

Nonetheless, the most extreme opponents of De Gaulle's policy – predominantly the military but also civilians – used the existing communication apparatus like the newspaper *Bled* or created their own means of distribution. In addition to leaflets and posters which were actually created with the help of printing devices belonging to the army, and which were substantially designed for the military as the target audience, the Organisation of the Secret Army (OAS) even produced a clandestine magazine *Les Centurions*, which was 'reserved for the officers and executives' and in which De Gaulle's quotations were used and instrumentalized for the purposes of the OAS propaganda.[20]

Conclusion

The analysis of the use of the media by a political leader such as Charles De Gaulle has shown that it is necessary to take into account the intended, programmed and planned communication as well as the finished media products which may significantly differ from the initial ones, depending on the context, either political, social or military. The different ways of using the media should therefore always be contextualized, first and foremost because divisions among followers or even opponents can decisively alter the communication and its efforts. As De Gaulle's example during the Algerian War shows, his efforts to exploit the media and his government's media policy aimed at instrumentalizing the media for their purposes were somehow foiled by the military's use of the media in North Africa. In this sense, the leader's opponents challenged the leadership which relied on the media-constructed legitimization on precisely the same level, that is, the media level.

During and after the Second World War, De Gaulle and his entourage succeeded in imposing a meticulously constructed image of the 'saviour'. In the context of the Algerian War, he succeeded again by convincing numerous members of the military and settlers in North Africa to support his policy. This network managed to portray him as the only one able to solve the Algerian crisis in May 1958, just as in 1940 when he 'prophetically' proclaimed Free France in London and afterwards succeeded in elevating France to one of the victorious powers among the Allies. In 1958, he was once again successful and distinguished himself as the only possible 'saviour'. His legitimacy derived first of all from the Gaullist legacy and tradition as a saviour in times of crisis and, secondly, from his own personality and his capacity to instrumentalize his image by taking advantage of his charisma and his oratorical talents, and by managing to adapt quickly to new media such as television. Thirdly, legitimacy came from the fact that he successfully transformed his return to power in a rational and primarily legal accession to supreme power, whereas the analysis of the process shows that it was quite similar to a genuine *coup d'état*.

These three sources of legitimacy correspond to the three ideal types of legitimate domination described by Max Weber in *Economy and Society [Wirtschaft und Gesellschaft]*: the 'traditional' domination, the 'charismatic' domination and the 'rational-legal' domination (Weber, 1978: 325). Considering that the use and instrumentalization of the media as well as the courtship of the media constitute another source of a political leader's legitimacy, it may be useful to scrutinize the existence – or not – of any kind of 'media domination' in order to improve the understanding of political leadership in general.

Notes

1 Although most historians date the beginning of the Algerian war to 1954, the first uprisings took place in Sétif, Guelma and Kherrata in May 1945. The French army violently put down these revolts. Therefore, some authors raised the question if the beginning of the Algerian war can be dated back to 1945.
2 In France, the Algerian War was officially called 'operations to maintain order', 'the events in Algeria' or 'pacification' *Cf.* Michel Debré's speech to the National Assembly, 2 February 1960, available at http://www.assem blee-nationale.fr/histoire/michel-debre/discours/02021960.asp (accessed 6 February 2014). In 1999, the years between 1954 and 1962 were officially recognized as a 'war'. *Cf.* Law n° 99–882 of 18 October 1999, JORF 244, 20 October 1999, 15647.
3 After De Gaulle's speech about Algeria's self-determination, most Europeans living in the North African *départements* felt unsafe. The week of the barricades in Algiers began on 24 January 1960 and lasted until 1 February. On 29 February, De Gaulle condemned the rioters and spoke directly to the military inviting them to obey him.
4 The putsch was led by the generals Challe, Zeller, Jouhaud and Salan in order to keep Algeria French. Although they had been successful in winning over some military in the run-up to the putsch, the *coup d'état* failed.
5 In an attempt to prevent Algeria's secession from French governance, the *Organisation Armée Secrète* (OAS) fought to maintain Algeria French.
6 De Gaulle's nickname given by the National-Socialist propaganda. A poster bearing this nickname shows De Gaulle behind a huge microphone.
7 An ordinance from 3 March 1945 permanently instituted the state's monopoly on the French Radio Broadcasting Service [Radiodiffusion française, RDF] created in 1941 by the Vichy authorities.
8 These speeches were also broadcast on television. The reason why this phenomenon is not scrutinized here lies in the very limited number of television sets among the military in Algeria. (By contrast, more and more households were equipped with a television in metropolitan France: in 1958, 8% were equipped; by 1960, one million.)
9 The paper *Le Bled* appeared in December 1955 with two issues per month, later once a week. In 1958, it was changed to *Bled* and became *Bled 5/5* in 1961 when it merged with the monthly journal *5/5 Forces françaises*. It reached a circulation of 350,000.
10 Note with the list of the recipients and the quantity of the postcards, signed by General Salan, Algiers, 16 June 1958. The total number on the fourth page stipulates 247,000 copies. *Cf.* Archives: *Service Historique de la Défense* (SHD), Vincennes, France, 1 H 1117.

11 For instance, note signed by Salan on 3 August 1958, including a list with a total number of leaflets of 250,000. *Cf.* Archives: *Service Historique de la Défense* (SHD), Vincennes, France, 1 H 1117.

12 *Cf.* Archives of the Fifth Office [Cinquième Bureau] stating that 40,000 were issued on 20 July 1958 by terrestrial transmission. *Cf.* Archives: *Service Historique de la Défense* (SHD), Vincennes, France, 1 H 2503.

13 Strange detail: De Gaulle's quotation is dated 4 September 1958 and therefore does not comply with the period during which the newspaper was edited according to its front page; July–August 1958. *Cf.* Archives: *Service Historique de la Défense* (SHD), Vincennes, France, 1 H 1118.

14 Quotation in *L'Echo d'Alger* from 5 June 1958. On 22 June 1958, the newspaper *Les Réalités* dedicated its front page to a photograph of the general and quotations from his speech. *Cf.* Archives: *Service Historique de la Défense* (SHD), Vincennes, France, 1 H 1118.

15 De Gaulle's speech on 16 September 1959 and accompanying letter [Bordereau d'envoi]. *Cf.* Archives: *Service Historique de la Défense* (SHD), Vincennes, France, 1 H 1123.

16 De Gaulle's speech on 29 January 1960 and accompanying letter [Bordereau d'envoi]. *Cf.* Archives: *Service Historique de la Défense* (SHD), Vincennes, France, 1 H 4396.

17 To give an example: the words 'Algérie' and 'the most French solution' are typographically highlighted (large-, bold- and italic-written). *Cf.* Archives: *Service Historique de la Défense* (SHD), Vincennes, France, 1 H 4396.

18 This Gaullist policy of what can be called the 'repatriation of media activities' in order to improve their control, stemmed from the desire to de-politicize the army which had become too political, according to De Gaulle. As Jean Planchais writes, in De Gaulle's opinion, the army 'has to be an instrument without any personal political thought' (Planchais, 1967: 355).

19 One of the first signs of this diminishing of influence is linked to the decision taken at the top of the state, to transform the 'Service d'Action Psychologique et d'Information du Ministère' into the 'Service d'Information et d'Etudes du Ministère des Armées' (SIEMA). Notes d'Information sur l'action psychologique du mois de décembre 1958, *cf.* Archives: *Service Historique de la Défense* (SHD), Vincennes, France, 10 T 516.

20 Some copies of *Les Centurions* can be consulted at the Archives *Service historique de la Défense* in Vincennes, France, 1 H 1737. To give an example: in edition number 8, which is not dated [number 2 is from 20 August 1961], De Gaulle's words are instrumentalized and used to 'prove' that the Gaullist policy of self-determination is 'completely illegal'. It should be noted that the OAS also – illegally – broadcast by radio and television in Algiers.

Works cited

Argoud, A. (1974) *La Décadence, l'Imposture et la Tragédie* (Paris: Fayard).

Bleustein-Blanchet, M. (1988) *Mémoires d'un lion* (Paris, Perrin).

Bourdon, J. (1994) *Haute fidélité. Pouvoir et télévision. 1935–1994* (Paris: Seuil).

Chupin, I., Hubé, N., Kaciaf, N. (2009) *Histoire politique et économique des médias en France* (Paris: Flammarion).

D'Almeida, F., Delporte, C. (2010 [2003]) *Histoire des médias en France de la Grande Guerre à nos jours* (Paris: Flammarion).

Dard, O. (2005) *Voyage au cœur de l'OAS* (Paris: Perrin).

Dard, O. (1999) 'L'armée française face à l'organisation armée secrète (O.A.S.)' in Forcade, O., Duhamel, É., Vial, P. (eds) *Militaires en République. 1870–1962. Les officiers, le pouvoir et la vie publique en France* (Paris: Publications de la Sorbonne), p. 687–99.

De Gaulle, Charles (1970) *Mémoires d'espoir I* (Paris: Plon).

Eck, H. (2001 [1999]) 'La radiodiffusion française (RDF-RTF)' in Jeanneney, J.-N., (ed.) *L'écho du siècle. Dictionnaire historique de la radio et la télévision France* (Paris and Issy-les-Moulineaux: Hachette and Arte), pp. 46–8.

Foulon, C.-L. (1994) 'A Londres et à Alger. De la 'Force française' au gouvernement provisoire, l'information et son contrôle (1940–1946)' in Plantey, A. (ed.) *De Gaulle et les Médias* (Paris: Plon and Fondation Charles de Gaulle), pp. 20–6.

Gallo, M. (1998) *De Gaulle. L'appel du destin* (Paris: Robert Laffont).

Jauffret, J.-C. (2007) '1945, L'insurrection du Nord-Constantinois' in Rioux, J.-P. (ed.) *Dictionnaire de la France coloniale* (Paris: Flammarion), pp. 77–81.

Jeanneney, J.-N. (2001 [1996]), *Une histoire des médias des origines à nos jours* (Paris and Issy-les-Moulineaux: Hachette and Arte).

Kauffer, R. (2006) 'L'opération Résurrection: la Ve République naît d'un coup d'État' in Faligot, R., Guisnel, J., (eds) *Histoire secrète de la Ve République* (Paris: La Découverte).

Lacouture, J. (1986) *De Gaulle. 3. Le souverain. 1959–1970* (Paris: Seuil).

Lacouture, J. (1985) *De Gaulle. 2. Le politique. 1944–1959* (Paris: Seuil).

Médard, F. (2005) 'La presse militaire pendant la guerre d'Algérie (1954–1962), vue à travers la *Revue de Défense nationale*, la *Revue militaire d'information* et *Le Bled*' in Coutau-Bégarie, H. (ed.) *Les médias et la guerre* (Paris: Commission française d'histoire militaire), pp. 811–33.

Pervillé, G. (2006) 'Putsch des généraux' in Andrieu, C., Braud, P., Piketty, G. (eds) *Dictionnaire de Gaulle* (Paris: Laffont), pp. 976–8.

Pervillé, G. (1993) *De l'Empire français à la décolonisation* (Paris: Hachette).

Peyrefitte, A. (1997) *C'était de Gaulle*, Volume 2 'La France reprend sa place dans le monde' (Paris: Fayard).

Planchais, J. (1967) *Une Histoire politique de l'armée. Tome II 1940–1967. De de Gaulle à De Gaulle* (Paris: Seuil).

Plantey, A. (1994) (ed.) *De Gaulle et les Médias* (Paris: Plon and Fondation Charles de Gaulle).

Schmale, W. (2000) *Geschichte Frankreichs* (Stuttgart: Eugen Ulmer).

Stora, B. (2005) *Les mots de la guerre d'Algérie* (Toulouse: Presses universitaires du Mirail).

Tudesq, A.-J. (1994) 'La radio et la télévision: instruments du pouvoir en concurrence? La radio et la télévision en 1958' in Plantey, A. (ed.) *De Gaulle et les Médias* (Paris: Plon and Fondation Charles de Gaulle), pp. 76–97.

Vaïsse, M. (2011) *Comment de Gaulle fit échouer le putsch d'Alger* (Brussels: André Versaille).

Wächter, M. (2006) *Der Mythos des Gaullismus. Heldenkult, Geschichtspolitik und Ideologie 1940 bis 1958* (Göttingen: Walstein).

Weber, M. (1978 [1922]) *Economy and Society. An outline of interpretive sociology* (Berkeley: University of California Press).

7
Silvio's Party

Nicolas Bonnet

Introduction

Italy is going through a new crisis in its party system comparable in many respects to the one that brought down the First Republic at the beginning of the 1990s. On 12 November 2011, against the background of a global economic and financial crisis that hit the southern countries in the euro zone particularly severely, with Italy according to the experts threatened with bankruptcy in the same way as Greece and Portugal, Silvio Berlusconi, under pressure from Brussels and the financial markets, was forced to tender his resignation as Italy's Prime minister. A few days later, the President of the Republic, Giorgio Napolitano, appointed Professor Mario Monti who quickly put together a government of political and financial experts. The Monti administration immediately imposed a raft of austerity measures that, after only a few months, had the effect of restoring Italy's credibility in the international financial markets. At the end of 2012, after some hesitation, emboldened by his initial success, Monti announced that he would lead a centrist coalition in snap parliamentary elections held on 24 and 25 February 2013. However, the strong medicine Italians had been forced to swallow to restore the health of the state's finances seriously undermined the popularity of the man who had entered office as 'Super Mario', and the *'Con Monti per l'Italia'* list, far from carrying off the anticipated victory suffered a drop in support that was seen as an outright rejection.[1] With neither of the two grand coalitions of Italy's bipolar system able to claim outright victory – the center left being only marginally ahead of the center right[2] – the true victor was Beppe Grillo's 5 *Star* protest movement. After impressive results in municipal and regional by-elections in 2012,[3] the *'Grillini'* entered Parliament in spectacular fashion in the

February 2013 legislative elections by taking 23.5 per cent of seats in the Senate and 25.5 per cent in the Chamber of Deputies.[4] On 28 April 2013, Monti's successor, the Democratic Party vice-secretary, Enrico Letta, formed a grand coalition government which continued to pursue the reformist agenda imposed by Brussels until the new party secretary,[5] Matteo Renzi, through back-room maneuvering, secured Letta's resignation and took over from him on 17 February 2014, becoming at the age of 39 Italy's youngest ever Prime Minister. Renzi has enjoyed exceptional popularity since entering office, and the Democrats' excellent results in the 25 May European elections (40.81 per cent) has given his nomination a degree of democratic legitimacy. But it seems safe to predict this honeymoon period will not last since Renzi has little choice but to pursue the policy of austerity introduced by his predecessors.

Even if the future remains uncertain, it seems an appropriate moment to take provisional stock of the 'Berlusconi years'. What are the specific leadership qualities of the man who has dominated the Italian political stage for the best part of the last 20 years? And how far did the breakup of the old party system and the transition from – what has become known as – the *First* to the *Second Republic* favor his emergence at the beginning of the 1990s? The Berlusconi phenomenon can only be properly understood by studying and analyzing its archaeology; the key to Berlusconi's political engagement lies in the obscure and murky origins of his dazzling career as a captain of industry, and his close links with the corrupt ruling class that has adopted him. By embodying the fusion of party, business and the state, Berlusconi has introduced (as this chapter tries to show) a new style of leadership. In terms of the typology presented in the introduction to this volume, he is simultaneously the ideal-type and the caricature of the 'communicator'.

The beginnings of the business-firm party

Berlusconi emerged in the early 1970s as one of Italy's leading property developers. Investing significant capital of – to say the least – uncertain origin[6] in vast development projects, he built several urban complexes ('Milano 2' followed by 'Milano 3') in the Milan suburbs and created a cable-television channel Telemilano exclusively for the residents of his new housing schemes. In 1979, soon after becoming president of the Fininvest Group, he turned Telemilano into Canale 5. Profiting from the absence of anti-trust legislation, he acquired Italia 1 from the giant industrial publishing group Rusconi in 1982 and then, in 1984, bought Rete4 from another publisher, Mondadori. As a result, by the mid-1980s, and with the backing of the then Prime Minister, Bettino Craxi, Berlusconi found himself at the head of a veritable media empire capable of competing with public service television. The 1990 'Mammi Law' effectively approved the RAI-Fininvest duopoly by limiting to three the number of channels controlled by the same group.

Facilitated by the collapse of the party system in the wake of 'Operation Clean Hand', Berlusconi's entry into politics in 1994 produced a nexus of political, economic and media power unique in the western world (Stille, 2007, 2012: 17). In this sense, the phenomenon of Berlusconi-ism represents a radical and potentially irreversible 'deformation' of Italian democracy (Genovese, 2011). It is doubtful whether one can talk of an authentic political vocation in Berlusconi's case, since circumstances, at least in the beginning, have played a much more influential part than personal ambition in the entrepreneur's decision to found a new party. Several factors led Berlusconi into politics in the early 1990s. First, the business tycoon was worried that Mediaset's heavy losses might bring down the entire group; secondly, he was aware that the left were set to win the elections for the first time and had reason to fear that once in power it would introduce new anti-trust laws aimed at breaking up his media empire; but above all he was afraid that the posse of judges leading 'Operation Clean Hand' would discover, in the course of investigating the opaque administration of his holding company, the existence of his secret foreign bank accounts (Bionda and Porcedda, 2013).

The party Berlusconi created in the space of a few months at the end of 1993 was a business-firm party (Hopkin and Paolucci, 1999). Berlusconi selected the future leaders of Forza Italia from his inner circle of business partners. Perhaps for the first time ever, a political party was conceived along the lines of an industrial product and launched according to the laws of marketing (Latella, 2009). If the old governing class appeared to be completely out of touch with social reality, Berlusconi, by contrast, soon showed he had his finger firmly on the country's pulse. Leaving nothing to chance, his communications strategy was exclusively centered on a methodical analysis of opinion polls and surveys (Reda, 2011: 141–2). As Amadori stresses, within the context of an emerging 'opinion-based democracy', the systematic use of opinion polls allowed the party's communications experts (all graduates of Mediaset) to reverse the conventional strategy: the task was not so much to make attractive to voters an already worked-out program, but rather to construct one calculated to appeal to their expectations, with the aim of guaranteeing electoral success (Amadori, 2004: 96).

The party's ideological philosophy contains nothing very new: a predictable synthesis of economic liberalism and anti-communism (five years after the fall of the Berlin wall and the transformation of the Italian Communist Party into the Social Democratic Party, Berlusconi, in his political speeches, continued to identify his main left-wing adversary with the old collectivist party), the common inheritance of all conservative groupings. But, with all his communications experience, Berlusconi knew how to make the product he wanted to sell attractive to voters. He succeeded in selling his dream of a new economic miracle because he represented the epitome of the *self-made man*: someone who had started with nothing and now stood at the head of a vast industrial empire. If he was not the first to have rejected the 'double-speak' of the *politichese*, he clearly belonged to a new breed of populist politician able to excite mass audiences with a brand of rhetoric taking its metaphors from the sports arena. The new leader is the owner of A.C. Milan, one of Italy's most successful soccer clubs – a major asset in a country where football matches are quasi-religious collective rites. As Lazar reminds us, the matches of the *Nazionale* represent important moments of national cohesion (Romano et al., 2001: 97). Berlusconi describes his political engagement as if it was a competitive sport (he has decided 'to enter the field', etc.) and, by doing so, creates a sort of *tifoseria*, or fan hysteria, among his political supporters. 'Forza Italia' or 'Go on, Italy!' (one hardly needs reminding) is the battle cry of fans of the Italian national team. Above all, Berlusconi has known how to create for himself and exploit the image of a dynamic winner, an irresistible charmer with the gift of eternal youth.[7] But Forza Italia's success is explained above all by the absence of any credible rival on the political right. The break-up of the Christian Democrats after a hegemony lasting more than 40 years left its moderate electorate with nowhere to go, and it was precisely this vacuum in the system that Berlusconi's party would fill in a matter of months (Fella and Ruzza, 2011). In 1994, the leaders of Italy's left-wing parties looked on this new kind of adversary with a mixture of contempt and irony, as one who did not fit any of the conventional categories of professional politician, and who was therefore unclassifiable; even Umberto Bossi, leader of the Northern League, with his extreme language and anti-system rhetoric, could be identified with the traditional image of the populist orator. In short, no one really took this *dilettante* seriously.

But Berlusconi's strength was his ability to systematically exploit the latest forms of communication, in the face of – and in contrast to – a political left that had difficulty adapting to the codes of a media system it tended to distrust, mainly because it was still very much under the influence of the thesis emanating from the Frankfurt School that identifies the mass media as an instrument of alienation (a comparison of the formal style of Achille Occhetto in his televised speeches in the 1980s with the ease with which Matteo Renzi performs before the television cameras today shows just how far things have advanced in the last 20 years). The new electoral-majority law, which was passed in 1993 and marked the transition from the First to the Second Republic, made this adaptation essential. The collegial leadership model that still prevailed on the left at the end of the 1980s is simply no longer workable: the majority system necessitates the formation of grand coalitions that can only be led by charismatic individuals able to unite the different tendencies of which they are made up. An indication of what the personalization of politics might look like came with the introduction of directly elected mayors in 1993, which also marked the first appearance of 'personal parties' in Italy (Calise, 2010: 63). But the parliamentary elections in March 1994 were the first national elections in which the phenomenon of the personalization of party leaders was really significant in Italy. The new rules forced different parties to come together to form coalitions capable of winning power. Berlusconi chose as his principal allies two groupings outside the old, discredited system: the Northern League (the federalist movement led by Umberto Bossi) and the National Alliance (the post-fascist party led by Gianfranco Fini). In the 1994 elections, the center-right coalition led by Berlusconi triumphed. And although the defection of the Northern League meant that Berlusconi was only in office for five months, he was re-elected in 2001 for a full term as part of the same coalition (from June 2001 to May 2006) and again following early elections on 13 and 14 April 2008, until the financial crisis forced him to resign on 12 November 2011.

The limits of videocracy

It is often claimed that Berlusconi-ism is synonymous with videocracy, and that Berlusconi was able to operate a disguised dictatorship thanks to his media empire (Ginsborg, 2005). As Marc Lazar in particular has remarked, this claim is over-simplistic, since it is questionable whether the media can ever have a profound and lasting effect on public opinion (Lazar, 2006). In fact, if nearly 84 per cent of Italians questioned in 2011 in a survey of viewing and listening habits said that television was their principal source of news information, only 21 per cent considered it to be 'the most unbiased and independent source'.[8] If control of the media was all that was needed to win and stay in power, it is not clear why Berlusconi should have been defeated in 1996 and 2006. Besides, it is surely significant that in both these elections the victorious center-left coalition was led by the distinctly un-telegenic Romano Prodi. Evidently, the control of the audio-visual media and manipulation of their codes do not provide an unconditional guarantee of electoral success, as representatives of both center-right and center-left parties are ready to admit: the former, in order to play down the anomaly that Berlusconi represents; the latter, to disguise their failure to deal with the problem of conflicts of interests when they were in a position to do so.[9] Nevertheless, even if the influence of television has been overstated, it can still be sufficiently significant, according to the experts, to influence voters' intentions by between 3 to 6 per cent – enough to prove decisive when the gap separating the competing coalitions is so tight (Polidori, 2011: 11).

Control of the media unquestionably allows a leader to make direct contact with the nation, and occasionally to exercise considerable influence on public opinion. Nevertheless, it is a gross distortion to suggest that, when in power, Berlusconi was in control of the quasi totality of the peninsula's media and consequently able to manipulate public opinion as he pleased. Even if one questions the loyalty of Berlusconi and his allies to democratic and republican values, and has legitimate worries about the authoritarian bent the Prime Minister sought to give the executive during his different terms of office,[10] it is still hard to argue convincingly that the necessary conditions were ever in place to turn the parliamentary republic into a totalitarian regime. For one thing, the center-right's takeover of the public service television channels was never absolute, if only because the old *lotizzazione* system, under which they were shared out among the main political parties,[11] was never done away with.[12] Consequently, whatever the make-up of the ruling majority, the third channel remained under the control of the main party on the left: the Democratic Party. Even on the second channel, dominated like the first mainly by the center-right coalition after Berlusconi's return to office in 2008–11, the left managed to keep hold of certain important slots[13] for long periods. As for the Mediaset channels, they have without question contributed greatly to the dumbing down of popular taste over the past 30 years, and it would be hard to overestimate the part played by Berlusconian commercial television in the gradual cultural transformation of society by the imposition on millions of Italians of a value system based solely on consumerism and hedonistic individualism (Polidori, 2011). The media sub-culture that as a result of the growth of commercial television now permeates large segments of the population is clearly one of the secrets of the success of Berlusconi-ism. As Nanni Moretti laments in his film *Il Caimano*

(2006), 'Berlusconi won hands down twenty, thirty years ago; he has brainwashed us with his televisions'.

Even so, it would be wrong to think that since entering politics Berlusconi has managed to turn his three channels into propaganda tools without meeting any resistance. Even if he was able to organize in only a few months the launch of Forza Italia by mobilizing all the resources of his media empire, and prepare the way for his first electoral victory in 1994,[14] the fact is that *il Cavaliere* was forced in subsequent years to acknowledge certain institutional constraints. Italy does, in fact, have some effective safeguards protecting it from the worst excesses of Berlusconi's videocracy; notably AGCOM (the equivalent of OFCOM in Great Britain and the CSA in France), which was set up in 1997 to ensure that all audio-visual companies respect the principle of pluralism.[15] For example, the authority imposed a heavy fine on the public service first channel for the blatant politicization of its news editorials after Berlusconi's re-election in 2008. It is also worth noting that this politicization led to audience ratings dropping appreciably, showing that the strategy had been counterproductive.[16]

Besides, the days of the RAI-Mediaset duopoly are over. Not only has Cairo Communication's La7 succeeded in carving a place for itself alongside the Mediaset channels, but a new player has emerged in the last ten years to upset the old balance of power in the shape of Rupert Murdoch.[17] Murdoch has established a hegemony in subscription satellite television and has at last succeeded in acquiring the lion's share of the advertising market at the expense of the commercial terrestrial channels. Although the pair were initially close, this competition led to the gradual deterioration of relations between Murdoch and Berlusconi. Following its victory in 2008, the center-right majority government adopted a series of measures deliberately targeting the Australian American magnate's media interests with the aim of undermining his position. For five years, Murdoch and Berlusconi indulged in a merciless struggle for domination. Unsurprisingly, the confrontation took the form of a communications war. However, in 2013, the crisis facing the television sector drove the two rivals to put aside their differences and join forces in order to fend off competition from the new media, and the Internet in particular.[18]

It seems reasonable to believe that the role of television in forming public opinion is destined to decline. The supporters of cyberdemocracy are busy undermining the foundations of the videocracy. The success of Movimento 5 Stelle, which in only a few years has become Italy's second biggest political party, is symptomatic of an irreversible evolutionary process: the rapid expansion of the new information technology and the growth of the Internet have supplanted the old mass media. Berlusconi, father of the commercially-driven new television, is a twentieth-century man with little or no influence over the twenty-first-century media.

Sarkoberlusconi-ism

It is possible to question the aptness of Pierre Musso's concept 'sarkoberlusconi-ism', according to which Berlusconi and Sarkozy embody two complementary archetypes: on the one hand, the entrepreneur using his media empire to propel himself onto the political stage; and, on the other, the politician forging pacts with the media and business worlds to advance his career and increase his power. According to Musso, not only does sarkoberlusconi-ism represent an excessive personalization of power, upsetting the existing powerbalance and the functioning of government institutions by concentrating power in the hands of the head of the executive, but the ideology and language of the two men have many traits in common, two of which stand out in particular: a tendency to present the entrepreneurial-managerial model as the only viable way of reviving a moribund socio-economic system, and the attempt to appropriate the cultural and spiritual values of the Roman Catholic Church in order to be seen as the champions of a specifically *Latin* neoliberalism, the counterpart of Anglo-Saxon neoliberalism (Musso, 2008, 2009).

But, in the first place, it must be remembered that the personalization of power is a phenomenon affecting every western democracy, and that France and Italy are not unique in this regard. As Manin has explained, the 'democracy of the parties' has been supplanted by a 'democracy of the people', characterized by the personalization of party leaders and the emergence of a politico-media elite (Manin, 1995). Berlusconi and Sarkozy are the pure expression of this new form of democracy. They have an equal mastery of the codes of communication, and the rhetoric each uses has many common traits. Nevertheless, even if Berlusconi is always surrounded by advisers such as the journalist Giuliano Ferrara, he has never had recourse, unlike Sarkozy, to genuine spin doctors, preferring to trust his own instincts (Stringa, 2009: 67–8) – which no doubt explains his undeniably original style as well as his countless verbal blunders and diplomatic gaffes.

If the personalization of power is now a general phenomenon in western democracies, it is evident that the Italian parliamentary system lends itself less readily than the French semi-presidential system to this development. For example, if Sarkozy can legitimately be accused of having interfered with the institutions of the Fifth Republic, this is hardly comparable, as Sofia Venturi in particular has underlined, with the interference the Italian Parliament was subjected to as a result of the strengthening of the executive's powers during Berlusconi's years in power (Venturi, 2012: 144–5). If, in France, the expansion of the President's powers at the expense of those of the Prime Minster (by the introduction in 2002 of the five-year presidential term) has altered the balance of power at the heart of the executive, it has not really threatened the integrity of the system – and one can add in passing that Sarkozy's successor at the Elysée, François Hollande, despite promises made during the election to return to a more conventional style of presidency, behaves in his turn like a 'super-president'. In Italy, on the other hand, the consolidation of the Prime Minister's powers turned the parliamentary system of government into a thinly disguised *de facto* presidential system (Calise, 2005). Having declared himself in favor of the semi-presidentialism of France's Fifth Republic, Berlusconi sought to turn Italy into a populist democracy.

Clearly, the pragmatism professed in equal measure by Berlusconi and Sarkozy is inspired by managerial and entrepreneurial models, while the 'performance-based culture' espoused by the latter would not be disowned by the former; in fact, it is only an updated version of the 'principle of accountability'.[19] Moreover, the entrepreneurial model seems now to have gained universal acceptance, and it is probably no coincidence in this context that the new leader of the Democratic Party, Matteo Renzi, who became Prime Minister in February 2014, and is nicknamed the 'scrap merchant' because of his determination to rid the party of its old ex-Communist Party leaders, is seen by many on the left as a 'closet' Berlusconian. His ambitious administrative reform program aimed at grouping public services together is sufficient proof of this.

To what extent does the neoliberalism championed by Berlusconi and Sarkozy in their respective countries have, as Musso claims, a distinctive Catholic-Latin character distinguishing it from Anglo-Saxon neoliberal ideology? If the pro-Americanism which has earned Sarkozy the sarcastic sobriquet 'the American', marks a break with Gaullist tradition (it should be remembered that he was one of the few leading lights of the UMP to back the intervention in Iraq), that of Berlusconi, by contrast, is consistent with Italy's postwar pro-Atlantic Alliance tradition of pledging unfailing support to the United States (a tradition Bettino Craxi attempted to break with in the 1980s by pursuing a more autonomous foreign policy, notably with regard to the Palestinian question, so creating some tension between the two countries) (Achilli, 1989). The fact that Berlusconi has shown himself in favor of Turkey joining the European Union while Sarkozy has always been resolutely opposed, would suggest that the latter, unlike the former, is more concerned with the views of domestic voters than with pleasing the United States.

As far as the two leaders' positions *vis-à-vis* the Catholic Church are concerned, if Sarkozy's covert advances towards Christian spiritual and moral values has been received in some quarters of French society as a violation of the Republican principle of secularism as enshrined in the 1905 law, Berlusconi's acknowledgement of the Church's authority is totally in keeping with the traditions of the Christian Democrats, to whom he has attempted to demonstrate his affiliation by repeatedly citing De Gasperi's name. Although Catholicism may have ceased to be the official religion of Italy in 1984 with the promulgation of the new concordat, it would be an exaggeration to talk of a total separation between Church and state or claim that the latter is always neutral in religious matters. With regard to Sarkozy, it would certainly be going too far to interpret what was purely a strategy to capture the Catholic vote as an attempt to undermine the foundations of Republican secularism – not least because Sarkozy has often stressed his attachment to secularism, notably in his discussions with the leaders of France's Islamic community. Indeed, this in itself has led to accusations of inconsistency. If Sarkozy's professions of religious faith were more an election ploy than a genuine attack on Republican secular values, those voiced by Berlusconi are increasingly in flagrant contradiction with his dissolute life-style and the innumerable sexual and business scandals with which his name has become inescapably linked, causing embarrassment to the Church and inciting a virulent polemic between the Catholic press and Berlusconi's newspapers. One should add that, in turning the fight against rising immigration into an issue of national priority, both leaders have shown their contempt for the Church's social doctrine and, by so doing, have soured relations with its hierarchy.

But in spite of the undeniable parallels that exist between the two men, there is one essential difference: if Sarkozy-ism represents a classic example of the complicity between the political and media elite and the inner circles of the financial and economic world (the links between the former French President and major industrialists such as Bouygues, Bolloré and the Bettencourt family are now common knowledge), Berlusconi-ism is more simply a blatant case of conflicting interests unprecedented in a major democracy. In this respect, Sarkozy has more in common with a politician like Craxi who backed Berlusconi in the 1980s and received support in return, rather than with Berlusconi himself who went into politics at the beginning of the 1980s specifically to defend his own business interests.

As Giachetti points out, using politics to serve private rather than public ends is not without historical precedent; but Berlusconi has tended to use politics to help his own interests rather than the interests of the entrepreneurial class in general (Giachetti, 2010: 88). This explains why Sarkozy enjoyed the support of the MEDEF for the full term of his presidency, while CONFINDUSTRIA, though initially sympathetic to Berlusconi in so far as it saw him as providing an effective defense against the center left, never gave the business tycoon its unconditional backing, and eventually disassociated itself from him completely.

Another essential difference between the two leaders is illustrated by the fact that even if Sarkozy was able to gain temporary control of the UMP and to use it as a springboard into the Elysée Palace (Haegel, 2012), his leadership represents only a brief episode in the existence of the Gaullist party, while the party formed by Berlusconi in 1994 is so closely linked with its leader that it is now uncertain whether it will survive him. Far from being accidental, this identification of the party with the man is fundamental, as the quasi-surreal words of the 2008 electoral campaign anthem testify: 'Meno male che Silvio c'é!' ('Happily, Silvio is here!'). The fusion of Forza Italia with the Alleanza Nazionale in 2009 was, according to Gianfranco Fini, a fool's bargain, since Berlusconi, seeing Popolo della Libertà as his own creation, clearly intended to exercise the same absolute control over it that he had exercised over his old party.[20]

As the example of Sarkozy illustrates still more clearly than that of Berlusconi, the excessive personalization of power and 'hyper-presidentialism' (favored by the quasi-monarchical institutions of the Fifth Republic along whose lines the Italian right would like to remodel the 1948 constitution) exposes a charismatic leader, should his policies fail, to a drop in popularity even more spectacular than the level of infatuation that first brought him into power. What the examples of Berlusconi and Sarkozy both illustrate is that 'hyper-presidentialism' can only prosper where the institutional terrain is right for it.

Berlusconi's legacy

Berlusconi-ism emerged in the context of what the sociologist Zygmunt Bauman has called the 'second' or 'liquid modernity'. This is the result of the decay or 'deliquescence' of the solid 'first modernity' institutions, such as political parties and trade unions, and the emergence of 'individualized societies' in which citizens no longer come together to form stable structures, but instead join fragile, ephemeral networks that are continually forming and dissolving (Bauman, 2000). In this fluid world in which the Church, political parties and trade unions have lost their traditional function and where (as in all Mediterranean countries) the only institution offering any resistance is the family, not only have the clear divisions between social classes disappeared, since each individual defines his or herself according to their own needs, but there are also no longer any lasting shared values, no more group projects, and even the concept of 'the public interest' has been emptied of meaning.

The right-wing journalist Marcello Veneziani, who had been one of *il Cavaliere*'s most fervent supporters at the start of his political career, quickly shook off his early illusions and by 2000 was already criticizing Berlusconi-ism as the triumph of personalities over ideas and the transformation of politics into media entertainment (Veneziani, 2005: 125–6). Contrary to those who think Berlusconi-ism has profoundly transformed – for better or worse – the political culture of Italy, Marcello Veneziani now maintains that the liberal revolution that *il Cavaliere* seemed to be in a position to deliver by uniting around his charismatic personality the different factions on the right hasn't happened, and that his real achievements are actually very modest. In the last analysis, according to the essayist, Berlusconi-ism has revealed itself to be nothing more than a personalized version of the old centrist politics: a sort of 'ego-centrism' (Veneziani, 2012).

In fact, the project for liberal reform that was central to Forza Italia's first legislative program gradually disappeared from its subsequent lists of priorities (Campus, 2006: 147; Ventura, 2012: 99). If Berlusconi has failed to achieve the kind of conservative revolution carried out by Margaret Thatcher in the United Kingdom, this can be explained in part by the nature of his electorate: in the north, this is made up largely of small business owners and the self-employed; whereas in the southern regions, where the economy is heavily reliant on state subsidies, his voters are mostly public-service workers employed by the welfare state (Diamanti, 2003). In the end, Berlusconi neither carried out the federal reforms demanded by the Northern League, nor (despite attempting to exercise power in a quasi-monarchical fashion) the reform of government along the presidential republican lines for which right-wing nationalists had clamored. Through each of his mandates, his overriding concern has been to get laws passed that can only be described as *ad personam* or (to make use of a barbarism that has become a journalistic cliché) *ad aziendam*; in other words, *for the family business*.

The last word?

Leader of the center-right coalition and four times Prime Minister between 1994 and 2011, Berlusconi has survived longer than any other postwar head of government in Italy. Forced to resign in November 2011 after losing a vote of confidence in Parliament, *il Cavaliere* announced on October 24, 2012 that he would not be standing for election as Prime Minister and that it was time to hand over the reins to someone else. With this in mind, he officially designated Angelino Alfano (appointed secretary-general of the party on 27 July 2011) as his successor as head of Popolo della Libertà until the election of a new leader could be organized. By now Berlusconi's image seemed to have been irreparably damaged by a succession of business and sex scandals in which he was involved. On 20 October he was sentenced to four years imprisonment prior to appeal for tax evasion in connection with Mediaset, and banned from holding public office for five years. A comeback in such circumstances looked improbable. In spite of this, Alfano, Berlusconi's heir apparent, announced in December 2012 that *il Cavaliere* had gone back on his decision and would stand in the parliamentary elections to be held on the 24 and 25 February 2013. To everyone's surprise, Berlusconi's coalition was only narrowly beaten (by 300,000 votes) by the list of center-left candidates led by Pier Luigi Bersani (elected secretary of the Democratic Party in 2009) which, lacking an absolute majority in the Senate, was unable to form a government. After protracted negotiations, the President of the Republic Giorgio Napolitano (re-elected on 20 April) asked Enrico Letta, vice-secretary of the party, to form a grand coalition government of ministers drawn from the Democratic Party and Popolo della Libertà. Elected for the first time to the Senate, Berlusconi clearly intended to continue leading the center-right coalition. Following poor results in the June 2013 local elections, the ageing leader, no doubt hoping to find a new lease of life, announced his intention to re-launch Forza Italia. Meanwhile, the Court of Cassation upheld the judgment of the Appeal Court, and Berlusconi was sentenced on 1 August 2013 to four years imprisonment for tax evasion – a term later reduced to one year. On 26 November, the Senate voted by a large majority to depose Berlusconi as a direct result of this final legal judgment.

But have some commentators been too hasty in judging Berlusconi's political career to be definitely over? During the national assembly of Popolo della Libertà on 16 November 2014, Berlusconi in reaction to the party's split into 'loyalists' and 'reformers' (the latter contesting his leadership), officially announced the re-birth of Forza Italia. The 50 or so secessionists, for their part, grouped together under the label

Nuovo Centrodestra. Early in 2014, a survey of voter intentions in the forthcoming parliamentary elections put the Partito Democratico and Movimento 5 Stelle in front with 30 per cent and 24 per cent respectively; Forza Italia, with just over 20 per cent, maintained its position as the most popular center-right party; while Angelino Alfano's Nuovo Centrodestra managed less than 4 per cent.[21] Moreover, in spite of imprudently exclaiming 'game over!' at the announcement of Berlusconi's deposition in November 2013, Matteo Renzi, the leader of Partito Democratico, has shown no hesitation in mapping out with him a project for constitutional reform and a new electoral law soon to go before Parliament. The fact that the new secretary of the Democratic Party, nominated Prime Minister in February 2014, does not consider Berlusconi as being irredeemably disqualified after his conviction for tax evasion, has not gone down well with public opinion. It remains to be seen if the fact that a sizeable fraction of the population is still willing to trust him is enough to rehabilitate the disgraced hero. It is certain that the six to nine million Italians prepared to vote for Berlusconi no longer really believe he can deliver the economic metamorphosis he promised in 1994, 2001 and again in 2008; nevertheless, after experiencing an appreciable rise in rates and taxes since 2011, many hope he will introduce policies to ease the tax burden, as he has in the past. In a country where 80 per cent of the electorate are owner-occupiers, the pledge (promptly fulfilled) to abolish property rates on principal residences proved an election winner in 2008. Re-introduced by Mario Monti, this highly unpopular tax was abolished again in 2013 by the government of Enrico Letta under pressure from Berlusconi's supporters. Nevertheless, a property tax under a different name was re-introduced at the beginning of 2014. Clearly, Berlusconi has at his disposal a valuable asset that he will undoubtedly know how to exploit in the next election campaign. If every home-owner dreams of being exempt from property tax, not all of them stop to think about the harmful consequences such a measure would have for Italy's national debt (Brussels forecasts that Italy's debt will reach 135.2 per cent of its GDP in 2014) – but Silvio's people would like the dream to continue.

Notes

1 In the 2013 legislative elections the centrist coalition totaled only 10.5% of votes in the Chamber of Deputies (Monti's Scelta Civica – Civic Choice – party accounted for 8.3%), and 9.1% in the Senate.
2 The center-left and center-right coalitions polled respectively 29.5% and 29.1% in the Chamber of Deputies and 31.6% and 30.7% in the Senate: a 'goal-less draw' that made the formation of a government problematical.

3 The main beneficiaries of the defeat of the conservative forces in the municipal elections on 20 and 21 May were not the Democratic Party and its allies,
who themselves suffered a major setback, but the protest movement Five
Star, led by the eccentric comedian Beppe Grillo who, refusing to have his
campaign expenses paid for out of public funds like other Italian politicians
but knowing how to use the Internet and social networks effectively, carried
off an unprecedented victory by taking the city of Parma as well as many
smaller towns in the north. In addition, the movement obtained excellent
results in the early regional elections in Sicily on 28 October 2012 when its
candidates took 18% of the vote – admittedly against the background of
record abstentions, with only 47.4% of those eligible voting.

4 The experience of exercising power represents an important test for the
movement, which must now show that it is capable of moving from protest
to constructive action. Does the Five Star phenomenon point to the emergence
of a new kind of participative democracy or, after shaking up the existing oli-
garchies and questioning the legitimacy of the system, will it, like the Northern
League, be absorbed into that system, adopting its worst practices along the
way? Whatever happens, the movement is centered round the charismatic
personality of its leader, and in this respect exhibits one of the principal
characteristics of present day political groups.

5 In the Democratic Party primaries held on 13 September 2012 Pier Luigi
Bersani won by a clear margin; but Renzi polled 68% in the December 2013
primaries, becoming the new party leader.

6 In 1972, the Christian Democrat mayor of Palermo, Vito Ciancimino, whose
links with the Cosa Nostra are public knowledge (he was arrested in 1984
for colluding the mafia bosses Totò Riina and Bernardo Provenzano) carried
out a vast money-laundering operation which involved investing a billion
and a half lire in the Milano 2 construction sites (Veltri, Travaglio, 2001).
On 9 May 2014, the Appeal Court upheld the conviction and a seven-year
prison sentence given to Marcello dell'Ultri, co-founder of Forza Italia and
Berlusconi's right-hand man, for 'acting in complicity with a criminal
organization'.

7 As Belpoliti mischievously suggests (referring to Kantorowicz's well-known
theory of the king's two bodies in *Monarchy by Divine Right*), the body of
that postmodern monarch, Berlusconi, endlessly remodelled with the help
of plastic surgery, realizes on a purely subjective level the improbable fusion of
the sovereign's material and perishable body with his symbolic and incorrupt-
ible being (Belpoliti, 2009).

8 http://www.demos.it/a00662.php (accessed 7 July 2014).

9 If the political class as a whole has consistently failed to tackle the problem
of conflicts of interest, this is no doubt due to its symbiotic relations with
the world of finance and business; no party, left or right, has proved to be
an exception to the rule. This quasi-umbilical bond is revealed whenever a
politico-financial scandal hits the news, such as the 'hidden derivatives' at
the Banco Monte dei Paschi di Siena, with its close links to the Democratic
Party, which came to light during the general election campaign in January
2013. This explains why the center-left, despite expressing some half-hearted
desire for reform, preferred to maintain the status quo when it was in power
between 1996–2001 and 2006–8. For his part, Berlusconi has used his terms
of office to get *ad personam* laws through Parliament in order to legitimize

his own anomalous position. The law passed on 13 July 2004, which sets out the rules and standards for resolving conflicts of interest, merely obliged any entrepreneur called to public office to appoint in his place authorized representatives without stipulating any restrictions. As the president of Fininvest is Berlusconi's own daughter, Berlusconi continues to maintain indirect control over this family holding. According to the American journal *Forbes*, in 2013 Berlusconi was the seventh richest man in Italy, with an estimated fortune of $6.2 billion, http://www.forbes.com/profile/silvio-berlusconi/.

10 It will suffice here to recall the strained and sometimes hostile relations between Berlusconi and successive Presidents of the Republic, from Scalfaro to Napolitano, that became apparent whenever the latter refused to sign his decrees. Similarly, Berlusconi never gave up questioning the legitimacy of the decisions of the constitutional court, which he simply regarded as a 'mouthpiece of the left'. But he reserved his most violent attacks for the magistrature, controlled according to him by 'red togas'.

11 Before the collapse at the beginning of the 1990s of what has become known as the First Republic, the three channels were controlled by the main political parties: RAI 1 (created in 1954) by the Christian Democrats, RAI 2 (created in 1961) by the Socialist Party, and RAI 3 (1979) by the Communist Party.

12 In 1993, following the shake-up brought about by 'Operation Clean Hand', a committee made up of five members appointed by the presidents of the upper and lower chambers was set up with the purpose of ending the *lottizzazione* system. In spite of this, RAI has never managed to become truly independent and remains under the tight control of the different political groups.

13 Notably the program *Annozero*, presented by Michele Santoro from September 2006 to June 2011.

14 Since the 'Garante delle telecomunicazioni' prohibits the media from publishing or broadcasting electoral messages during the official election campaign, the propaganda blitz took place in the pre-election period. (Poli, 2001: 63).

15 The Naples-based 'Autorità per le garanzie nelle comunicazioni', or AGCOM, came into being on 31 July 1997 (the Mallanico law, n° 249). This body, replacing the old 'Garante per le radiodiffusione e l'editoria' set up in the eighties, is made up of eight commissioners elected by the two chambers. The chairman is appointed by the Italian President on the recommendation of the Prime Minister. In other words, it is a relatively independent body whose role is to ensure that the rules designed to prevent monopolies in the media and communications industry are not infringed, and that diversity in news presentation is respected. The 'Par Condicio' (inscribed in law no. 28, 22 February 2000) lays down the principle that the different political parties, irrespective of their electoral weight, must have equal access to television channels, and be subject to the same conditions. The time given to politicians on television is rigorously measured and the impartiality of news reports carefully monitored. Even the order in which different political positions are presented is strictly regulated.

16 Until Berlusconi's come-back in 2008, only two channels broadcast blatantly partisan news programs: the third public service channel, RAI 3; and

Mediaset's third channel, RETE 4 – the second with a bias towards the center-right, the first with a bias to the center-left. On the other hand, the two most popular news programs, broadcast by RAI 1 and CANALE 5, were relatively balanced in their reporting. However, the situation changed in 2009 when the journalist – and close associate of Berlusconi – Augusto Minzolini became the head of TGI's editorial board. Following his appointment, the news on the public service's first channel became a clone of the RETE 4 program. After issuing repeated warnings to the progam's managers, AGCOM fined the RAI 1 and RETE 4 news programs 100,000 euros (the heaviest sanction possible) for violating the 'Par Condicio'. In December 2001, the largely discredited Minzolini was replaced by Alberto Maccari.

17 In the space of just a few years, the satellite television channels of the Australian American tycoon have become phenomenally successful, while Mediaset Premium, launched in 2005, has still to get off the ground. In 2008, Sky Italia's revenues from advertising overtook those of Mediaset. By 2011, Murdoch's satellite channels had almost five million subscribers. However the group has been hit by the economic crisis of 2012 and the number of subscribers had fallen by 51,000 by the end of March 2013.

18 http://espresso.repubblica.it/affari/2013/04/11/news/b-e-murdoch-scoppia-la-pace-1.5308 (accessed 21 June 2014).

19 In so far as he has always asserted his readiness to assume responsibility for his actions, Berlusconi must be credited with introducing the principle of 'accountability' into Italian politics, even turning it into a theatrical event on occasion. For instance, while appearing on Bruno Vespa's television program *Porta a Porta* on 8 May 2001, five days before the parliamentary election, Berlusconi, taking his inspiration from the 'contract with America' that had been the centerpiece of the Republicans' 1994 manifesto, signed his 'contract with the Italian people', promising never to stand again if at least four of his five election pledges were not kept.

20 Like Cronus, Berlusconi has a tendency to devour his own children: once regarded as heirs apparent, Gianfranco Fini and Angelino Alfano not only failed to succeed him as head of the party after standing in his shadow for so long, but also paid dearly for their disloyalty when their respective scissions came to nothing. The latest candidate to succeed Berlusconi, Giovanni Toti, has spent his entire career as a Mediaset journalist, and was only appointed a Forza Italia counsellor as a reward for his unflinching subservience to the party chief.

21 http://www.sondaitalia.com/2014/02/sondaggio-emg-per-tgla7-cresce.html (accessed 21 June 2014).

Works cited

Achilli, M. (1989) *I socialisti tra Israele e Palestina (dal 1982 ai giorni nostri)* (Milano: Marzorati).

Amadori, A. (2004) *Mi consenta. Metafore, messaggi e simboli Come Silvio Berlusconi ha conquistato il consenso degli italiani,* 2nd edn (Milano: Libri Scheiwiller).

Bauman, Z. (2000) *Liquid modernity* (Cambridge: Polity Press).

Belpoliti, M. (2009) *Il corpo del capo* (Parma: Guanda).

Bionda, P., Porcedda, C. (2013) *Il Cavaliere nero. Il tesoro nascosto di Silvio Berlusconi* (Milano: Chiarelettere).
Calise, M. (2005) 'Presidentialisation, Italian Style' in Poguntke, T., Webb, P. (eds) *The Presidenzialisation of Politics: A Comparative Study of Modern Democracies* (Oxford: Oxford University Press), pp. 88–106.
Calise, M. (2010) *Il partito personale: I due corpi del leader* (Roma-Bari: Laterza).
Campus, D. (2006) *L'antipolitica al governo: De Gaulle, Reagan, Berlusconi* (Bologna: Mulino).
Diamanti, I. (2003) *Bianco, rosso, verde e...azzurro: mappe e colori dell'Italia politica* (Bologna: Mulino).
Fella, S., Ruzza, C. (2011) *Reinventing the Italian Right: Territorial politics, populism and 'post-fascism'* (London: Routledge).
Genovese, R. (2011) *Che cos'è il berlusconismo ? La democrazia deformata e il caso italiano* (Roma: Manifestolibri).
Giachetti, D. (2010) *Berlusconi e il berlusconismo* (Varese: Edizioni Arterigere).
Ginsborg P. (2005) *Silvio Berlusconi: Television, Power and Patrimony* (London: Verso Books).
Haegel, F. (2012) *Les droites en fusion: Transformations de l'UMP* (Paris: Presses de Sciences Po).
Hopkin, J., Paolucci, C. (1999) 'The business firm model of party organisation; cases from Spain and Italy', *European Journal of Political Research*, Vol. 35, n° 3, 305–39.
Latella, M. (2009) *Come si conquista un paese: I sei mesi in cui Berlusconi ha cambiato l'Italia* (Milano: Rizzoli).
Lazar, M. (2006) *L'Italie à la dérive* (Paris: Perrin).
Manin, B. (1995) *Principes du gouvernement représentatif* (Paris: Flammarion).
Musso, P. (2008) *Le Sarkoberlusconisme* (La Tour-d'Aigues: L'Aube).
Musso, P. (2009) *Télé-politique: Le sarkoberlusconisme à l'écran* (La Tour-d'Aigues, L'Aube).
Poli, E. (2001) *Forza Italia: Strutture, leadership e radicamento territoriale* (Bologna: Il Mulino).
Polidori, E.G. (2011) *Berlusconi e la fabbrica del popolo* (Reggio-Emilia: Aliberti).
Reda, V. (2011) *I sondaggi dei presidenti* (Milano: Università Bocconi Editore).
Romano, S., Lazar, M., Canonica, M. (2011) *L'Italia desunita* (Milano: Longanesi)
Stille, A. (2007) *Sack of Rome: Media + Money + Celebrity = Power = Silvio Berlusconi* (London: Penguin).
Stille, A. (2012) *Citizen Berlusconi Il Cavalier Miracolo: La vita, le imprese, la politica*, 2nd edn (Milano: Garzanti).
Stringa, P. (2009) *Lo spin doctoring: strategie di comunicazione politica* (Roma: Carocci).
Veltri, E., Travaglio, M. (2001) *L'odore dei soldi* (Roma: Editori Riuniti).
Venturi, S. (2012) *Il racconto del capo: Berlusconi e Sarkozy* (Bari, Laterza).
Veneziani, M. (2005) *La sconfitta delle idee*, 2nd edn (Roma-Bari: Laterza).
Veneziani, M. (2012) *La rivoluzione conservatrice in Italia: Dalla nascita dell'ideologia italiana alla fine del berlusconismo* (Milano: SugarCo).

8
Leader of my Heart! Use of Twitter by Leaders' Partners during Election Campaigns

Alex Frame and Gilles Brachotte

The first decade of the twenty-first century has witnessed the emergence of 'new' media technologies which have contributed to reshaping the relationships between politicians, journalists and the general public in Western democracies and around the world (Fox and Ramos, 2012; Lilleker and Jackson, 2013). After diverse early attempts in several countries to harness these new tools during election periods, their use by Barack Obama's campaign team in the 2008 US presidential elections is often cited as one of the first examples in which they appeared to contribute positively to mobilising sympathisers and party activists around the campaign (Thimm, 2011). In the subsequent 2010 UK general election and the 2012 French and US presidential elections, explored in this chapter, all major parties exploited web-based tools, including Facebook and Twitter accounts, websites, blogs and dedicated online platforms used to coordinate local campaign actions.

Alongside the official party tools, many individual candidates and virtually all major party/political leaders had their own dedicated social media accounts through which they could communicate. In social terms, this evolution seems to be linked to a broader trend towards the 'personalisation' of politics and political communication, notably that of political leaders (Seiler, 2002). Social media may (naively) be seen by politicians and voters as a direct, im-*media*-te, 'horse's mouth' channel through which politicians and party leaders can voice their ideas and opinions directly to voters. Moreover, such tools can also be associated with the 'intimization' of politics (Stanyer, 2013: 14),[1] notably in the light of social representations of the use of Facebook and Twitter among adolescents to publicly display what can often be considered intimate details. Politicians' tweets or posts on Facebook can thus be framed as part of a more global self-presentation strategy (Goffman, 1959), sometimes including information from the private/personal/intimate sphere[2] (Frame, 2012; Frame and Brachotte, 2013).

In the case of party leaders, personalisation or intimization strategies can also be associated at times with a bid to appear 'normal' – to borrow a term frequently used by François Hollande during the 2012 French presidential election. David Cameron has notably been said to adopt this strategy, in the light of his innumerable media appearances (Craig, 2014), and notably when he refers to his family or domestic situation (Alexandre-Collier, 2010: 122). In the video posted on his video blog 'Webcameron', on Election Day in 2010, for example, he addresses his audience in his shirt sleeves, standing in a kitchen, exhorting them to go out and vote.[3] Other campaign videos on Cameron's blog feature his wife Samantha, who, we have argued elsewhere (Brachotte and Frame 2011), can be seen to contribute to strengthening this domestic image of the political leader who is also a father and a husband. Indeed, although the figure of 'First Lady' has long been mediatised, Stanyer (2013: 11) notes that in both the US and the UK, leaders' wives are under increasing media scrutiny. The same is true of France, as noted by Constance Vergara (2012) in her interview-based review of the evolving role of First Lady in that country. Christiane Restier-Melleray (2002: 124) further highlights the importance of the role played by leaders' companions in this process of intimization, suggesting that they often serve to underscore the leaders' private virtues, while portraying them as 'ordinary' (married) people.

The authors of this chapter consider that the popularity but also the perceived legitimacy of modern leaders in Western democracies is very often directly related to their own personal skills as communicators, but equally that their image, notably in the context of election campaigns, also depends on the way that their wives/partners[4] contribute to portraying them. These presentations, notably through social media channels, which might portray a leader as particularly virtuous, for example, may be seen to contribute to his/her 'cult of personality'. This might seem compatible with a communication strategy to present a 'charismatic leader' in Weber's sense of 'charismatic authority' (Weber, 1947 [1922]). However, insisting on the leader's 'ordinariness' or normality might actually have the opposite effect, since charismatic leaders are 'set apart from ordinary men and treated as endowed with supernatural, superhuman, or at least specifically exceptional powers or qualities. These are such as are not accessible to the ordinary person, but are regarded as of divine origin or as exemplary, and on the basis of them the individual concerned is treated as a leader' (Weber, 1947 [1922]: 157).

This chapter examines the co-construction of the image of leader by the leaders' partners, by looking at the way in which one particular social media channel, Twitter, was used by partners during the 2010 general elections in the UK and the 2012 presidential elections in France and the US. It focuses on the way partners present themselves as spouses, parents, citizens, admirers or defenders of 'their' candidates and the extent to which their tweets can be interpreted as efforts to bridge the symbolic, social and political gaps between leaders, followers and voters.

Corpus and methodology

The global corpus, covering the three countries and elections, includes the (potential) Twitter activity of 13 leaders' partners over a given period of time leading up to each election. The British corpus covers the official election campaign of one month (6 March–6 April 2010). It includes the wives of the three major party leaders: Sarah Brown, Samantha Cameron and Myriam González Durántez, wife of Liberal Democrat leader Nick Clegg. The French corpus also corresponds to the dates of the official two-month presidential election campaign (19 February – 20 April 2012). It includes the partners of the five largest parties: Carla Bruni-Sarkozy, wife of the President in office; Valérie Trierweiler, partner of the Socialist candidate François Hollande; Louis Aliot, partner of Marine Le Pen, candidate for the Front National party; Elisabeth Bayrou, wife of centrist François Bayrou; plus the wife of Jean-Luc Mélenchon, representing the Front de Gauche. In the US, the corpus includes the Twitter accounts of Michelle Obama and the wives of the last four remaining Republican candidates seeking nomination by their party, in the nine months between the Iowa Caucuses (6 February 2012) and Election Day (6 November 2012): Cally Gingrich, Carol Paul, Ann Romney and Karen Santorum. The tweets captured from the selected official accounts were subjected to content analysis, both to define recurrent words and themes and to identify the use of different operators in use on Twitter (http://; #, @, RT), enabling us to characterize the 'Twitter styles' (Dang-Anh et al., 2012) of different users.

Political contexts, uses and non-uses of Twitter

The partners studied showed very different strategies and practices on Twitter, ranging from non-use (for over half of the sample) to intensive use for others. Table 8.1 shows the number of tweets during the period and the number of followers at the end of the period for each partner.

Table 8.1   Activity on Twitter during election campaigns

Partner	N° of Tweets Posted	Corpus Dates	Followers (approx.)
Aliot	221	19 February–	1,500
Bayrou	0	20 April 2012	0
Bruni-Sarkozy	0		0
Mélenchon	0		0
Trierweiler	42		30,000
Brown	359	6 March–	1,100,000
Cameron	0	6 April 2010	0
González Durántez	0		0
Gingrich	472 (267)[5]	6 February–	10,000 (8,500)
Obama	82 (576)[6]	6 November 2012	2,170,000
Paul	0		0
Romney	56		170,000
Santorum	0		0

Note: Compiled by the authors.

Use of Twitter by partners seems to be linked to a variety of factors, including their own professional activity, the electoral campaign itself, and the place of Twitter in the wider national media context. In May 2010, around 8 percent of UK citizens had a Twitter account, a figure which had risen to around a third in 2012 (over 23 million accounts). Around a third of US citizens also had an account in the first half of 2012 (around 107 million accounts), whereas at the same period in France the proportion of users was still close to the 2010 British figure of 8 percent (just over 5 million accounts).[7] It can be surmised that there was less popular pressure for leaders' partners to have their own Twitter account in the UK in 2010 and in France in 2012 than in the US at this time.

Individual reasons for not opening an account do appear to vary, however. In France, declarations from François Bayrou and Jean-Luc Mélenchon and the almost total absence of their spouses and families from the media seem linked to a desire to protect their private lives. This is traditionally accepted in France, especially from leaders who have only very slim hopes of becoming President. Indeed, Louis Aliot's presence on Twitter may well have less to do with his being Marine Le Pen's partner, than with his own political role as Vice-President of Front National. He airs his own political opinions through this account, retweets Mme Le Pen, but does not indulge in any references to the domestic sphere.

The two favourites for the position of 'Première Dame' are under much more intense media pressure, though once again their strategies also differ. Valérie Trierweiler set up her own Twitter account one month before the socialist primaries, in September 2011. As a political journalist for the magazine *Paris Match* and the television channel Direct 8, Trierweiler had become involved emotionally with François Hollande for several years, before he and Ségolène Royale officially ended their relationship. Trierweiler came to the front of the media stage during the election campaign itself. Her professional identity dominates, to a certain extent, her use of Twitter during the campaign, even though she also makes several references to her partner in her tweets.[8] She also tends to use Twitter defensively to react to or ironize about criticism she has received during the campaign.

Carla Bruni-Sarkozy had had a highly publicized relationship with Nicolas Sarkozy shortly after he entered office, before the couple married far from the cameras in February 2008, inside the Élysée palace. In the run-up to the election, Sarkozy appears to have changed tack and sought to shift media attention away from the private sphere. Although their relationship continued to fuel the gossip press in France and elsewhere, Bruni-Sarkozy was very careful not to communicate outside the Élysée's official channels (including her own official website). She had no official Twitter account, and the only tweet she sent during the election period was from her husband's official Twitter account: *'J'emprunte momentanément le compte de mon mari pour vous saluer, chers followers. Merci pour votre soutien! Carla'.*[9]

Sarah Brown, wife of the incumbent Prime Minister, could not be in a more different situation to her French counterpart. A PR professional, Sarah Brown had been dubbed 'high priestess of Twitter' by the *Daily Mail*.[10] She posted over 12 tweets a day on average from her *SarahBrown10*[11] account which had over a million followers during the period studied, i.e. over 20 times more than any of the official UK political party accounts. In the face of such a powerful presence, it is possibly not surprising that neither of the other partners had a Twitter account at this time. Miriam González Durántez, of Spanish nationality, clearly sought to position herself apart from her two rivals, explaining that she could not put her career on hold to accompany her husband during the campaign.[12] She was much less present in the media and also less likely to become 'First Lady', given the configuration of the British political landscape. Indeed, Sam Cameron was generally presented in the media and elsewhere as Sarah Brown's main rival, and her absence from Twitter appears to be a strategic choice in keeping with her husband's global communication strategy. Indeed, not only did both Sam and David Cameron use the Webcameron video blog to talk directly to voters, stage their intimacy and show the 'wings' of the campaign (Brachotte and Frame, 2011), the choice to boycott Twitter was one Cameron had to some degree inflicted upon himself in July 2009. During an interview with Christian O'Connell on Absolute Radio, he joked that *'too many twits might make a twat'*.[13]

In the US, in 2012, the Republican candidates' wives were all present at their husbands' sides in accordance with presidential tradition. However, Carol Paul and Karen Santorum, both absent from Twitter, were also the least publicly visible partners. Callista Gingrich had been using Twitter since April 2009, and tweeted regularly in accordance with her own and her husband's political activities during the period studied, though only around half as frequently once her husband had withdrawn from the race for nomination. Her number of followers in comparison with her rivals is possibly also a reflection of a proportionally low level of public interest during the primaries, since the number of followers of the other accounts rose more sharply in the later months of the campaign. In contrast, Ann Romney's Twitter account was only set up on 12 April 2012, well into the campaign itself, after she had been accused by Democrat strategist Hilary Rosen of having 'never worked a day in her life'.[14] The ensuing debate about 'stay-at-home Mums' attracted many supporters to the newly created Facebook and Twitter accounts set up by the Romney campaign team, including the Facebook page 'Mums with Mitt'. Despite only 13 messages being posted in the first 19 days of its existence, Ann Romney's Twitter account had attracted around five times as many followers as that of Cally Gingrich in that time. Its popularity continued to grow during the final six months of the campaign. Michele Obama's Twitter account was also only set up on 12 January 2012, though it had attracted 750,000 followers in the first three months, and well over 2 million on Election Day. The account was explicitly run by the Obama campaign staff, though just over 14 percent of tweets sent during the period were signed personally by Michelle Obama.

Political tweets

It is possibly an unsurprising result that the vast majority of tweets sent from these accounts can be interpreted as having a more or less explicit political purpose or message, given the identities of the account holders. However, it is interesting to note that there appear to be different ways and degrees of being political. On one extreme, Louis Aliot and Sarah Brown both use their accounts to overtly promote their (partners') parties: '*@halenmo Labour is the party that does support all kinds of families, and believes in fairness. here is the link http://www.labour.org.uk*'.[15] This is true also of many messages posted by the campaign team to Michele Obama's account, which overtly support Obama and the Democrat position. In signed messages, where this is the case, a more personal note can often be detected: '*I am so proud of how Barack has represented us on the world stage for the past four years. Tonight he shined on the debate stage, too. –mo*'.[16]

This personal, admirational tone is also used to varying degrees by Sarah Brown, Ann Romney and Cally Gingrich, alongside more routine messages recounting various stopovers on the campaign trail: '*Had a wonderful time at #CPAC yesterday with @newtgingrich. Read more about our day here: http://www.newt.org/callistas-canvas/callista-gingrich-cpac-2012*'.[17] Gingrich uses this style particularly often, and it is not uncommon to find variations on the theme: '*looking forward to travelling to X with my husband*', followed several hours later by '*had a wonderful time in X with my husband*'. Although all of the individuals followed tend to retweet messages from their partners, in the case of Valérie Trierweiler, possibly because of her professional identity and because she was not actually married to François Hollande, references to her companion in her own tweets were to remain more veiled, often employing a collusive tone: '*je vous donne rendez/vous à 19 heures sur radio hollande pour 20 minutes d'entretiens avec Pierre Lescure.#FH2012*'[18] or: '*Le changement – de chaîne – c'est maintenant! On se branche sur #Direct8, pour la dernière d'itinéraires*'.[19]

However, tweets expressing political affiliation are not the only or even the most common types of tweet to be found. In general terms, the majority of tweets are about other subjects, even though these can also very often be seen to contribute to creating a certain (political) image of the partners.

Tweeting for the female electorate

One of the common points to all of the female partners in the study is the role of ambassador they seem to play on 'women's issues', possibly in an attempt to gain support for a partner who is less credible or legitimate on such issues. Ann Romney's first tweet: '*I made a choice to stay home and raise five boys. Believe me, it was hard work*'[20] is an understandable reaction in the context that led to her account being set up (*supra*). Interestingly, 13 of her 23 first tweets, sent up until the end of May, refer directly to her role of mother or grandmother. Subsequent references to motherhood are less frequent, as Romney seems to adopt the technique of other female partners, widening her scope to women's issues in general. Alongside Romney, Michelle Obama and Sarah Brown can also be seen to comment on family issues. Independently of tweets about their own families (*infra*), Obama also reacts to the scandal provoked by Hilary Rosen's criticisms of Ann Romney: '*Every mother works hard, and every woman deserves to be respected. –mo*'[21] and Brown chooses to mention a visit to a family-oriented community centre: '*visited Atherton Sure Start Centre – so many activities for babies, children, mums & dads, and a youth club – just a joy to be there*'.[22] As well as being on the traditional Labour agenda, the interest and sympathy for families expressed by Sarah Brown may be aimed at compensating for her husband's less easy and convincing manner on such questions.

Other tweets are more overtly committed to defending or celebrating women's rights, for example from Michelle Obama: '*Generations of Americans marched and organized for women's rights. This Women's History Month, let's honor them with our service. –mo*'.[23] Similar kinds of messages are sent by Sarah Brown, on political activism for the female vote: '*Emmeline Pankhurst trending on Twitter. Let's remember the sacrifices the suffragettes made so we could exercise our right to vote.*'[24] or celebrating the female condition: '*http://twitpic.com/1evx4e – attending the Celebrating Women: Past, Present and Future, conference at Neasden Temple today*'.[25] Cally Gingrich's tweets are generally fewer calls to defend women's or mothers' rights, but generally underline the fact that she is representing her husband at meetings of women's associations: '*Great crowd at the Republican Women's Luncheon today at Food City in Kingsport, TN! http://instagram/p/HzViV1IJ4t/*'.[26] She does however launch a call to join a women's association supporting her husband: '*Join our Women with Newt coalition today and help us rebuild the America that we love. http://www.newt.org/coalitions/women/ #withnewt*'.[27] Finally, Valérie Trierweiler refers explicitly to women only once in a tweet sent on Women's Day: '*#forumElle. En tant que femme: heureuse et convaincue de l'engagement de @fhollande sur les questions des femmes. Notamment sur les violences*'.[28] She does lend her support to humanitarian and other causes, but these are not associated exclusively with women.

Another popular type of message linked to the female condition concerns women's health, including breast cancer and childbirth. Ann Romney tweets: '*It was inspiring to walk alongside so many wonderful women united to beat breast cancer. #prettyinpink pic.twitter.com/3UiaYeQd*'.[29]

Michelle Obama underlines the impact of her husband's health reforms for women: *'Thanks to Obamacare, insurance companies will no longer be able to charge women more than men for the same plan. http://OFA.BO/ owm4Uy'*[30] or *'Obamacare has expanded access to breast cancer screenings, helping patients and survivors get the care they need.pic.twitter.com/tQT dOT27'*.[31] Tweets of this kind are slightly rarer from Sarah Brown, and often include global rather than just women's health issues, but she does send a series of tweets on the theme of maternal mortality during the month observed: *'Serra Sippel of @genderhealth Blogs on Maternal Mortality Decrease. She says good news, but not 'Mission Accomplished' http://bit. ly/8ZCdPa'*[32] and *'Today is National Safe Motherhood Day in India – a big boost to the maternal mortality campaign and @WRAGLOBAL'*.[33] Ann Romney also refers to her own past health problems and the support given to her by her partner at that time: *'Routine check-ups are the key to early detection. I had my check-up yesterday, and am celebrating three years of being cancer-free'*.[34] or *'Today is World MS Day. Mitt's support when I was diagnosed got me through the most trying time of my life http://mi.tt/ L3g5vD'*.[35]

Tweeting in the private sphere

Such references to personal health issues can be considered to belong to the private sphere, exploited here in a bid for compassion or sympathy, and to show Romney as a strong, caring father figure. Although relatively unsurprising in a UK/US context,[36] it would be much harder to imagine such tweets in French political communication, in the same way that the tweet relayed by Cally Gingrich from her husband's account, concerning a rival's sick child would doubtless be considered by a French audience as a shocking intrusion into the private sphere: *'@CallyGingrich and I have @RickSantorum and family in our prayers since their daughter bella is back in the hospital'*.[37] Indeed, there are no references to the private sphere in Aliot's or Trierweiler's tweets, except when the latter calls for her journalist colleagues to respect this: *'Quel choc de se découvrir à la Une de son propre journal. Colère de découvrir l'utilisation de photos sans mon accord ni même être prévenue'*.[38]

Elements from the private sphere are thus much more widely evoked in the English-speaking tweets, possibly in response to higher media demand for such information. The strategy adopted appears to combine a desire to portray the partner as exemplary in his private life, through the roles of husband and father, while casting him in a domestic sphere to which followers can relate.

This strategy implies that the partner herself be cast in the role of 'traditional' spouse, which can appear slightly inconsistent with the calls for equal rights referred to previously (*supra*). Thus Sarah Brown, the successful career woman and co-founder of her own PR firm, cultivates a persona on Twitter who exchanges cooking recipes with her followers: '*RT @judithoreilly I tried out your recipes for lamb and crumble last night. They get my vote. http://bit.ly/9Hz9Cn [SO PLEASED!]*'.[39] She also mentions in passing how much she loves supermarkets (in general of course – no particular brand preferences!): '*@msjodavies I love pretty much every supermarket – I know not everyone likes a supermarket shop but I really really do*'.[40] The strategy seems to consist in showing the Labour leader's wife as an 'ordinary' person, who is happy to share with her million followers her complex about not having straight toes, or the fact that she stained her skirt by sitting on a pen: '*2nd mishap of the campaign for me after #feettweet: discover my favourite skirt has huge inkblot on the back from sitting on a pen #bottblot*'.[41] Brown is careful only to give such intimate details about herself, always showing her husband in a positive light and in a position as strong leader. If he had been the one to stain himself, she would most certainly not have tweeted about it. She plays the role of his 'ordinary', accessible 'other half', encouraging followers to identify with him through her.

In the US corpus, certain tweets also highlight the 'everyday behaviour' of the couples in the presidential contest. This is absent from Cally Gingrich's tweets, but true to a certain extent of Michelle Obama and Ann Romney, though generally less towards the end of the campaign. Obama uses a confidential tone to her followers: '*It was great to sit down for dinner with a few new friends last night. My date had a great time, too. –mo*',[42] or writes public messages for her husband: '*I wonder how Al Green ended up on our playlist, @BarackObama! –mo*'.[43]

Despite the fact that there are fewer self-references, family appears to be foregrounded to a greater extent in Obama and Romney's tweets than in those of Brown. They both celebrate various family birthdays and anniversaries. From Obama: '*Happy Fourth! What makes this day even more special is that it's the day our first child was born. Happy birthday, Malia! We love you. –mo*';[44] '*Happy 20th anniversary, Barack. Thank you for being an incredible partner, friend, and father every day. I love you! –mo*';[45] including the dog's: '*It's a big 4th birthday for Bo! He's getting some extra treats today. –mo*'.[46] From Romney: '*Thank You Matt! Love You RT @Matt_Romney Happy Birthday @AnnDRomney! Wish we could celebrate with you today mom, but see you soon!*'.[47] Mother's Day and Grandmother's Day are also celebrated: '*RT @joshromney @AnnDRomney, where r u? I need to*

*know where to send annual #MothersDay coupon book with promises to clean
my room, do dishes'*;[48] *'I want to wish a very happy Mother's Day to all of
the moms out there, especially mine. She's my rock every single day. Love you,
mom. –mo'.*[49] Ann Romney also talks about her grandchildren and even
posts photos of them to her Twitter account: *'Grandchildren 17 and 18
are here – congratulations @TRomney and Jen! We can't wait to meet David
and William'.*[50]

Conclusion

The conclusions drawn from this study can be tentative at best. Not
only was the approach a limited qualitative one relying on interpretation of a very small number of accounts, but the exclusive focus on
Twitter elides everything else being said through other media channels
and gives a very partial picture of the partners' communication during
the election campaigns, in which Twitter remained a fairly minor communication tool. While that does not invalidate its choice as an object
of study, further cross-media research taking into account notably the
communication strategies of those partners who chose to communicate
to different channels, could provide some interesting points of comparison. Despite these limits, the study does appear to bring to light certain
practices which could be interesting to study in more detail during
subsequent campaigns.

Whether they express themselves through Twitter or other channels,
partners of potential national political leaders face considerable pressure
from the media and often from their parties to play a role in their partners' campaigns. If they accept to sacrifice their own voice and views to
this political role, their unique position gives them a forum from which
they can contribute singularly to their partner's image, as Christiane
Restier-Melleray (2002: 124) points out. This was most evident in the
three accounts with the largest numbers of followers: those of Sarah
Brown, Michelle Obama and Ann Romney. These three women all give
a positive image of their partners, underlining their moral integrity
and family values and referring explicitly to their husbands' strength
and to their mutual/family love and support. More than her American
counterparts, Sarah Brown also tweets banal details of the everyday life
she shares with the Prime Minister, playing the role of the traditional
housewife and encouraging her followers to identify with her. This strategy, if taken at face value by her audience, appears to avoid some of the
risks associated with politicians who try themselves to give the image of
being 'normal' people. By making herself seem 'ordinary', Sarah Brown

helps others identify with her husband, without revealing potentially belittling details about him and without him needing to risk media and public scorn through artificial attempts to promote his own 'normality'.

Could the role of the partner described here thus be a way for political communicators to exploit the trend for personification of politics (Stanyer, 2013) while allowing the leader him/herself to retain a degree of distance compatible with the image of a charismatic leader? To what extent does the admiration expressed by the partner offset the 'normality' also portrayed and which might detract from the leader's perceived charisma? To answer such questions, more extensive research would be required. Indeed, the fact that the 'normality' described here is, in many cases, quite clearly staged may paradoxically contribute to the idea that in reality, the leader is *not* normal, since they are obliged to adopt artifices to prove that they are!

More generally, by tweeting about women's issues, and notably by confirming their partners' support for them, the four English and American women seem to be aiming at a wider female electorate to which their husbands are maybe less able to appeal. This is a key difference with the French corpus, where even Valérie Trierweiler seems to speak as much from her own point of view as from that of her partner. Although the corpus is evidently too small and idiosyncratic to be a source of any meaningful national comparisons, the absence of the private sphere from the French tweets appears coherent with the idea that the distinction between public and private in France is still widely accepted by public opinion, despite recent signs of evolution (Stanyer, 2013: 1–2). Independently of the gossip press's appetite for speculation about politicians' private lives, coverage in France still remains limited for legal, but also cultural, reasons. Although Nicolas Sarkozy appeared to want to venture into this area during the first part of his presidential term, famously visiting Disneyland with Carla Bruni, the criticism he received, or that directed at Hervé Morin when the latter shot a video in his own kitchen, suggests that French society is not yet ready to sacrifice this founding principle of the notion of *la citoyenneté*. Can this be interpreted as a sign that the French reject the idea of 'normality' in their leaders, incompatible with the hierarchical distance between politicians and their electorate? If Sarkozy seems to correspond to the ideal of 'charismatic leader', he was beaten by a rival who marketed himself as *'un president normal'*, yet François Hollande's lack of perceived charisma is arguably one of the keys to his unpopularity three years on. Daniel-Louis Seiler (2002: 163) has noted that countries which seem to disapprove of media coverage of politicians' private lives are generally more tolerant towards immoral behaviour on their part. He suggests that the difference lies in national cultural and religious heritage. Whereas English-language media coverage of politician's private lives might be criticized by the French for a lack of respect for the individual, in many English-speaking and Northern European traditionally Protestant societies, writes Seiler, voters see this as a necessary form of transparency. For them, politicians are first and foremost individuals, whose moral behaviour in the public sphere will likely reflect that of the private sphere. As elected representatives of the people, if they are to serve and represent the people well, politicians must be beyond reproach, and voters have a 'right to know'. From a French and, argues Seiler, more globally a Southern European point of view, marked by a Roman Catholic heritage, politicians are seen as individuals who have a right to live their private lives as they choose, as long as it does not interfere with the way they exercise in the public sphere. This distinction between public and private runs deep into the social pact underlying the French Fifth Republic, justifying the division between the Church and the state, among other things.[51]

Indeed, it should not be neglected that the question of the relationship between leaders and followers, addressed by all the contributions to this book, is inextricably linked not only to specific political circumstances and contexts, but also to the cultural heritage of the party and the society in question. As this chapter has pointed out, use of Twitter by the partners of political leaders was linked to a variety of factors, including their own professional identity and activity, their marital status, the relative likelihood of their partners being elected, the individual image of the latter and the specific communication strategies they adopted during their campaigns. However, the party identity, the wider media context and the cultural norms, practices and representations surrounding the distinction between private and public all also contributed to the way each partner sought to help their candidate construct their particular image of leader.

Notes

1 James Stanyer defines intimization as: 'a revelatory process which involves the publicizing of information and imagery from what we might ordinarily understand as a politician's personal life – broadly defined' (2013, 14). As the author points out, intimization can correspond to both 'flows of non-scandalous personal information and imagery consensually co-disclosed in the media and scandalous information' and 'imagery gathered and publicized in the public realm without a politician's consent' (2013, 17).

2 John Corner (2003, 73) distinguishes (i) public/popular, (ii) political and (iii) private spheres, but Stanyer (2013, 13) prefers 'personal' to private, suggesting that, once disclosed, the information in question is no longer strictly 'private'. Notwithstanding this objection, the terminology adopted here is that of Corner, since it is the sphere which can be considered 'private', rather than the information.

3 Video posted on 10.06.2010. Accessed on 15.01.2014. Available at: http://www.conservatives.com/Video/Webcameron.aspx?id=220cb871-b6cf-4f89-87b6-f30d99f87d8c.

4 For the sake of clarity and simplicity, the term 'partners' will be used throughout this chapter, to cover the wives and other female and male partners included in the study.

5 Figures in brackets are valid for 2 May 2010, when Newt Gingrich officially withdrew from the race for Republican nomination.

6 Figures in brackets correspond to tweets signed 'mo', indicating, according to the account profile, that they were sent by Michelle Obama herself, rather than by Obama campaign team staff.

7 Sources: http://blog.sysomos.com/2010/01/14/exploring-the-use-of-twitter-around-the-world/, http://wallblog.co.uk/2012/04/19/how-big-is-twitter-in-2012-infographic/ for the UK and the US; http://www.lemondeinformatique.fr/actualites/lire-la-france-compte-5-2-millions-de-comptes-twitter-47622.html for France. Pages accessed on 15.01.2012.

8 Trierweiller's highly controversial tweet, shortly after becoming First Lady, which went against both Hollande and the Socialist Party line to support a dissident socialist candidate running against Ségolène Royale during the June 2012 parliamentary elections, led her to later become much more cautious in her use of the medium, while sparking a national debate about the role and freedom of speech of an (unmarried) First Lady who happened to be a political journalist.

9 *'I am briefly borrowing my husband's account to say hello, dear followers. Thank you for your support. Carla.'* (Our translation).

10 http://www.dailymail.co.uk/debate/article-1264068/JAN-MOIR-War-wives-How-did-Sarah-Brown-SamCam-compare-fashion-stakes.html (accessed on 15.01.14).

11 When her husband left office, the account's name was changed to 'SarahBrownUK'. It still had over 1,180,000 followers in April 2012.

12 http://www.telegraph.co.uk/news/election-2010/7558842/Election-2010-the-battle-of-the-leaders-wives.html (accessed on 15.01.14).

13 http://www.youtube.com/watch?v=d3Mrfut-FSw (accessed on 15.01.14). After becoming Prime Minister and apologizing for this 'gaffe', Cameron finally opened his official Twitter account in October 2012.

14 http://usatoday30.usatoday.com/news/politics/story/2012-04-12/ann-romney-hilary-rosen-work/54235706/1 (accessed on 15.01.14).

15 Tweeted on 02.03.10.

16 Tweeted on 23.10.12.

17 Tweeted on 11.02.12.

18 *'Meet me at 7pm on hollande radio for 20 minutes of interviews with Pierre Lescure.#FH2012'* (our translation). Tweeted on 01.05.12.

19 *'Time to change – channels! Turn over to* Direct 8 *for the last episode of* Itinéraires' (our translation). Tweeted on 06.04.12.

20 Tweeted on 11.04.12.
21 Tweeted on 12.04.12.
22 Tweeted on 15.04.10.
23 Tweeted on 08.03.12.
24 Tweeted on 06.05.10.
25 Tweeted on 11.04.10.
26 Tweeted on 05.03.12.
27 Tweeted on 11.03.12.
28 Tweeted on 08.03.12. '*#forumElle. As a woman: happy and convinced about @fhollande's commitment to women's issues. Especially on violence*' (our translation).
29 Tweeted on 20.10.12.
30 Tweeted on 19.10.12.
31 Tweeted on 13.10.12.
32 Tweeted on 20.04.10.
33 Tweeted on 11.04.10.
34 Tweeted on 21.08.12.
35 Tweeted on 30.05.12.
36 In the British context, both Cameron and Brown have lost children and this information has been relayed by the media.
37 Tweeted on 06.04.10.
38 '*What a shock to discover oneself on the front of one's own magazine. Angry to discover that the photos were used without my permission or prior knowledge*' (our translation). Tweeted on 08.03.12.
39 Tweeted on 20.04.10.
40 Tweeted on 17.04.10.
41 Tweeted on 19.04.10.
42 Tweeted on 09.03.12.
43 Tweeted on 12.02.12.
44 Tweeted on 04.07.12.
45 Tweeted on 03.10.12.
46 Tweeted on 09.10.12.
47 Tweeted on 17.04.12.
48 Tweeted on 11.05.12.
49 Tweeted on 13.05.12.
50 Tweeted on 04.05.12.
51 The 2011 sexual scandal involving Dominique Strauss-Kahn came to light in the US, despite the fact that his behaviour had allegedly previously been public knowledge in political circles in France. Revelations about François Hollande's 'affair' with a Parisian actress in January 2014 were similarly brushed aside as 'private matters' by the President at a subsequent press conference.

Works cited

Alexandre-Collier, A. (2010) *Les habits neufs de David Cameron* (Paris: Presses de Sciences Po).

Brachotte, G. and Frame, A. (2011) 'Appropriation et usages des TIC chez des "leaders" politiques en France et en Grande-Bretagne: pratiques et discours'.

In F. Liénard and S. Zlitni (eds), *La communication électronique, enjeux de langues*, 65–76 (Limoges: Lambert-Lucas).

Corner, J. (2003) 'Mediated Persona and Political Culture'. In J. Corner and D. Pels (eds) *Media and the Restyling of Politics: Consumerism, Celebrity and Cynicism*, 67–84 (London: Sage).

Craig, G. (2014) '"A walking, talking news factory": David Cameron, performance politics, and everyday life'. Conference paper presented at MeCCSA 2014 'Media and the Margins', University of Bournemouth, 8–10 January 2014.

Dang-Anh, M. Einspänner, J. and Thimm C. (2012) 'Mediatisierung und Medialität in Social Media: Das Diskurssystem "Twitter". *Sprache und Kommunikation im technischen Zeitalter: Wieviel Internet (v) erträgt unsere Gesellschaft?* 2: 68.

Fox, R.L. and Ramos, J. (eds) (2012) *iPolitics: citizens, elections, and governing in the new media era* (Cambridge University Press).

Frame, A. (2012) 'Too many Twits? Réseaux sociaux et mise en scène de l'intimité par les candidats aux élections législatives britanniques en 2010'. In S. Crinquand and P. Bravo (eds), *L'intime à ses frontières*, 77–91 (Cortil-Wodon: E.M.E).

Frame, A. and Brachotte, G. (2013) 'Les campagnes des compagnes: Mise en scène de la vie publique et privée'. In F. Liénard and S. Zlitni (eds) *La communication électronique en questions*, 387–402 (Bern: Peter Lang AG).

Goffman, E. (1959) *The Presentation of Self in Everyday Life* (New York: Doubleday).

Lilleker, D. and Jackson, D. (2013) *Political Campaigning, Elections and the Internet: Comparing the US, UK, France and Germany* (London: Routledge).

Restier-Melleray, C. (2002) 'Les formes d'interventions journalistiques dans l'évocation de l'intimité'. In P. Baudry, C. Sorbets, and A. Vitalis (eds) *La vie privée à l'heure des médias*, 123–8 (Presses Universitaires de Bordeaux).

Seiler, D.-L. (2002) 'L'usage politique de la vie privée des hommes politiques en démocratie'. In P. Baudry, C. Sorbets, and A. Vitalis (eds) *La vie privée à l'heure des médias*, 149–65 (Presses Universitaires de Bordeaux).

Stanyer, J. (2013) *Intimate Politics: Publicity, Privacy and the Personal Lives of Politicians in Media Saturated Democracies* (Cambridge: Polity Press).

Thimm, C. (2011) 'The Visuals of Online Politics: Barack Obama's Web Campaign'. In: V. Depkat, and M. Zwingenberg (eds) *Visual Cultures – Transatlantic Perspectives*, 185–203. (Publications of the Bavarian American Academy, n°12).

Vergara, C. (2012) *Valérie, Carla, Cécilia, Bernadette et les autres, en campagne* (Paris: Tallandier).

Weber, M. (1947 [1922]) *The Theory of Social and Economic Organization*. Translated by A.M. Henderson and Talcott Parsons (New York: Oxford University Press).

9
Leadership and the European Debate from Margaret Thatcher to John Major

Karine Tournier-Sol

For a long time, the study of political leadership has aroused little interest in the UK (Foley, 2000: 244) – reflecting the traditional view of the Prime Minister as first among Cabinet equals and hence dependent on the Cabinet, but also on the governing party and on Parliament. This view of the premiership, which is based on the collective nature of the British political system, tends to dismiss personal leadership as being somewhat irrelevant to political life. Political studies have therefore mainly focused on the office of Prime Minister, assessing the performance of successive premiers, with few comparisons with and little interest in individual leaders and the impact of personal leadership on policy-making (Theakston, 2002: 283). However, the Thatcher era undoubtedly marked a turning-point in the study of political leadership in Britain. The unquestionable influence of Thatcher's strong leadership style on policy-making drew attention to the role of personal leadership and revived the interest of political scientists (Foley, 2002: 5).

This chapter explores political leadership in the light of the theoretical framework provided by works of reference and contributes to this book's attempt to analyse the dynamic relationship between the leader and his/her followers. It focuses on the premierships of Margaret Thatcher and John Major, trying to assess the influence of their respective leaderships on the particular sphere of European policy. Political leadership and the European issue played a decisive part in both their premierships, albeit in different ways, as will be demonstrated below.

The first part analyses and compares the leadership styles of Margaret Thatcher and John Major, considering the influence of these particular approaches on the decision-making processes favoured by both Prime Ministers. European policy being the main focus here, their respective visions of Europe will also be examined, with consideration given to questions concerning the role of personal leadership and the agency of the two political leaders. The second part will study the impact of political leadership on European policy-making – at the European level but also at national and party levels. As leadership appears inextricably linked to the European issue for both Margaret Thatcher and John Major, the relationship between the leader and his/her followers will be analysed and differentiated. How did political leadership and Europe interact under Thatcher and Major? How do both Prime Ministers fit within the typology provided by the authors in the introduction to this book?

Divergent leadership styles, converging European visions

First of all, the leadership styles of Margaret Thatcher and John Major were diametrically opposed. Margaret Thatcher was a conviction politician characterised by strong leadership and determination, as epitomised in the appellation 'the Iron Lady'. She came to power with a radical political agenda; she broke with the consensus which had prevailed since the Second World War in British political life, establishing a new political order – which makes her akin to the 'Reconstruction' leader identified by Stephen Skowronek in his typology of American presidents (Skowronek, 1997). Not only was Margaret Thatcher a charismatic leader as defined by Max Weber (Weber, 2004: 133–45), she was also a 'transforming leader' according to the theoretical framework provided by James Burns: 'Such leadership occurs when one or more person *engage* with others in such a way that leaders and followers raise one another to higher levels of motivation and morality' (Burns, 1979: 20). As a political leader, Margaret Thatcher acted as a causal agent and inspired a substantial number of followers with her political vision – Thatcherism well outlasted her premiership.

Succeeding Margaret Thatcher in power placed John Major in the position of what Skowronek describes as a leader of 'articulation': he inherited a resilient set of political beliefs – Thatcherism – and his role was to expand this new political order. When John Major came to power, he was perceived as the heir to Margaret Thatcher. Yet, though not departing from his predecessor in terms of substance, he was determined from the outset to break with her leadership style – which had eventually alienated her from her government and party. The context is worth underlining here: the party which Major inherited was still under shock from the eviction of its leader. He had presented himself as the leader of reconciliation. In terms of leadership style, John Major was deliberately the antithesis of his predecessor – a conciliator championing consensus as a strategy to ensure cohesion. Major consistently acted as the agent of his followers. He was a 'transactional leader' as defined by Burns, with a more traditional vision of leadership based upon negotiation and exchange. He had a collective approach to government and Cabinet – a typical illustration of classic 'Cabinet government', whereas Margaret Thatcher embodied Prime Ministerial government in the recurrent debate going on in Britain since the 1960s (Crossman, 1964; Mackintosh, 1968) concerning the increasing power of the Prime Minister at the expense of the Cabinet.

The accession to power of John Major was then supposed to mark the return to more 'normal' practice of British politics after the Thatcher era which was perceived as an exception, a 'temporary aberration' (Foley, 2000: 20) in terms of political leadership. Nevertheless, as demonstrated by Michael Foley, this impression could not be further from the truth: first, because the Thatcher years coincided with the emergence of a leadership dimension in British politics which goes well beyond the personality of Margaret Thatcher – 'a dimension (...) which has established the meaning and value of leadership as a political issue in its own right' (Foley, 2000: 25). Since the 1980s, a strong dynamic has been at work to which the mass media and opinion polling have contributed and which has set leadership as a key criterion of political evaluation. Foley describes this process as 'a systemic shift' (Foley, 2000, 25). Second, Margaret Thatcher redefined political leadership altogether by providing 'graphic evidence that one person could make a dramatic difference and that a gifted politician with drive, skill and conviction could be pivotal in changing the policy and position of government in society. Thatcher not only exposed the developing politics of leadership but explored its possibilities and enlarged its potential' (Foley, 2000: 249). That is why 'the Thatcher phenomenon proved to be a precedent of exceptional potency' (Foley, 2000: 22) with which John Major would be constantly compared throughout his premiership. Leadership thus turned out to be a pivotal and decisive factor, a key criterion in the Thatcher and Major years – though lack of leadership was mostly an issue for the latter.

Contrasting leadership styles resulted in distinctive decision-making processes. Whereas Margaret Thatcher used different strategies to bypass Cabinet, John Major endeavoured to gain its support through a less assertive and more collegiate approach. It was not only a question of personality and temperament: it was also a political strategy intended to engage the collective responsibility of the Cabinet. Actually, Major applied such tactics, which he may have developed when he was a whip in his early years at Westminster, to his whole parliamentary group. The Conservative leader probably thereby sought to avoid the intra-governmental dissent of the late Thatcher years and the increasing isolation of the Iron Lady which had led to her downfall. John Major regularly used this strategy in European policy-making with the aim of defusing any risk of internal strife in the Conservative Party, as the end of the Thatcher years had demonstrated how explosive the European issue could turn out to be.

Thus, in November 1991, before the Maastricht summit, the Prime Minister decided to hold a debate in the House of Commons in order to gain approval for his negotiating stance and thereby rally the support of his government and party. Similarly, when he came back from the Netherlands, he submitted the conditions he had obtained to another vote in the Commons. His strategy came to fruition in May 1992 during the second reading of the bill to ratify the Maastricht Treaty: the Conservative leader then presented the ratification as the mere continuity of the process which had been validated by the House of Commons every step of the way. The MPs therefore had no other option but to vote in favour of the ratification of a Treaty they had implicitly already endorsed. This was typical of Major's political leadership: collective decision-making as a tactic to ensure cohesion – a whip-inspired approach.

By contrast, the decision-making process at work under Margaret Thatcher was completely different. She would usually set up informal meetings gathering like-minded people to make decisions which would then be announced to the Cabinet. This strategy allowed her to get her own way without having to deal with diverging views. As Hugo Young wrote as early as 1980: 'Disagreements are not resolved so much as effaced, by doing major business outside the Cabinet itself. Small groups abound, not only for the efficient dispatch of marginal business, but so as to ensure that like-minded men work together towards the big policies on which they agree' (Young, *Sunday Times*, 27 April 1980). Thatcher also made good use of her power of appointment to assert her authority within her government. It is important to bear in mind that when Thatcher became Prime Minister in 1979, she only had minority support in her own Cabinet and government. Gradually, through successive reshuffles, she shifted the balance of power to her advantage in the Cabinet and surrounded herself with her supporters, such as Norman Tebbit or Nigel Lawson – 'is he one of us?' being the test phrase to select the members of the very exclusive Thatcher's club

(Young, 1990: xiii). According to Anthony King, she 'has probably been more concerned than any other post-war Prime Minister with promoting her own supporters inside the government and with ensuring that the departments of government that matter to her (...) are manned exclusively by those who share her views' (King, 1985: 132). Margaret Thatcher's strategy consisted in controlling everything so as to have her policies implemented.

As time went by, her leadership style became more and more authoritarian and generated increasing tensions in the very inner circle of her most faithful supporters, particularly on the European issue. This was notably the case concerning the long-standing question of the entry of the pound in the Exchange Rate Mechanism (ERM) of the European Monetary System (EMS). From 1985 to 1989, tensions kept growing between the Prime Minister, the Chancellor of the Exchequer Nigel Lawson and the Foreign Secretary Geoffrey Howe – both convinced Thatcherites by any standard. Although the Cabinet, government and the majority of the Conservative parliamentary group were in favour of joining the ERM, Margaret Thatcher hardened her position. She was adamant and refused to rally the majority view even among her most faithful supporters: she would not act as the agent of her followers. The authoritarianism she demonstrated to impose her views was to have dramatic consequences on her leadership, as discussed below.

European policy being the main focus in this chapter, Margaret Thatcher and John Major's respective visions of Europe need to be clarified and compared, as part of an exploration of the role of personal leadership and the agency of the two political leaders. Were their contrasting leadership styles also mirrored in the substance of their European vision – was there change or continuity in that sphere?

In her first years as Prime Minister, Margaret Thatcher consistently presented herself as pro-European. Yet, from the start, her European vision was characterised by pragmatism rather than enthusiasm, and was basically a minimalist one. She regarded the European Economic Community (EEC) as a large market to which the liberal economic principles she was applying in her own country should be extended – hence the decisive role of the UK in the advent of the single market, albeit at the cost of significant concessions. Even when she confronted her European partners during the budgetary dispute, she regularly reasserted her European credentials so as not to alienate pro-European Conservative MPs. But the Thatcher era was to coincide with an acceleration of European integration under the initiative of Jacques Delors, who was far too federalist in the eyes of the British Prime Minister: the

President of the European Commission advocated economic, social and political integration – which was simply unacceptable for Margaret Thatcher. The Conservative leader therefore reacted by delivering the Bruges speech on 20 September 1988, which marked a turning-point in her European approach. In response to the integrationist stance embodied by Delors within the Community, she offered an alternative vision of a Europe of nation states. In fact, what she advocated was a Thatcherisation of Europe – nothing new in substance, but the style and tone had definitely changed. Through this speech she clearly sent a message, not only to her European partners, but also to the members of her own government and civil service who wanted to force her into a European integration which she strongly rejected. The Bruges speech is commonly seen as the founding speech of Euroscepticism and is a reference for all British Eurosceptics. Margaret Thatcher therefore clearly stood out as an influential leader and a causal agent: she refused to act as the mere agent of her followers and positioned herself as a game-changer over Europe. From then on, she became an inspiration for all British Eurosceptics. In the process, she did not hesitate to take political risks – which eventually were to cause her downfall.

When John Major succeeded Margaret Thatcher in November 1990, the relations between the UK and the EEC had therefore become increasingly strained. By consistently resisting further integration, the Iron Lady had eventually alienated her European partners. Major was fully aware of this fact and explicitly stressed the need for a change of attitude: 'My aims for Britain in the Community can be simply stated. I want us to be where we belong – at the very heart of Europe, working with our partners in building the future. This is a challenge we take up with enthusiasm' (Cooke, 1992: 30). He intended to collaborate and co-operate with his European counterparts and to re-establish construc-tive dialogue. However, although the tone had definitely softened, in substance the British position showed no real change.

Three years later, the situation had radically altered. In the mean-time, the ratification of the Maastricht Treaty had severely divided the Conservative Party, threatening the very survival of the Major government. On 16 September 1992 – Black Wednesday – the pound had been forced to withdraw from the ERM. This was undoubtedly the turning-point of John Major's premiership which accounted for a radi-cal change in his European stance. Not only had he grown disillusioned by his experience at the European negotiating table (Major, 1999: 581), but his leadership had been deeply undermined by the Maastricht epi-sode. Consequently, the European vision he set out in *The Economist* in September 1993 marked a decisive break with his initial approach: enthusiasm and optimism had been replaced by scepticism. John Major hardened his position and tone towards his European partners – just as Thatcher had done when delivering the Bruges speech. Their visions now looked quite similar in style as well as in substance. Though differing greatly in their political leadership, Margaret Thatcher and John Major eventually ended up with a similar approach to European integration, albeit for distinctive reasons: Margaret Thatcher grew more radical out of conviction. She acted as a causal agent and a game-changer, whereas John Major was forced to take on such a stance by the political context, more specifically by the internal strife in his party which led him to act as the agent of his followers. He was blamed for subordinating the British national interest to party management – for acting less as a national leader than as a Chief whip only concerned with his party's unity, as discussed below.

But how did political leadership influence European policy-making in practice, whether at the European level or at national and party levels? How did political leadership and the European issue interact under Thatcher and Major?

Political leadership at work: European policy-making in practice

Barring a few exceptions, European policy-making under Margaret Thatcher and John Major was characterised by recurrent hostility and opposition towards Britain's European partners. The Thatcher era started with the question of Britain's contribution to the EEC budget – the British Budgetary Question (BBQ), also revealingly referred to outside the UK as the 'Bloody British Question'. The Conservative Prime Minister demanded to be given 'Britain's own money back' – which irritated her partners who preferred to talk about 'the Community's own resources'. The budgetary dispute lasted for five years during which European integration was close to paralysis, and was finally settled by the 1984 Fontainebleau agreement. This episode was exploited by Margaret Thatcher on two levels: first, the popular aspect of this battle was very clear for the Prime Minister who took advantage of it to increase her own popularity in Britain. The rhetoric of the *juste retour* then turned out to be 'an electoral bonus' (Gilmour, 1992: 259). The nationalist crusade fought by Thatcher in Brussels was proving as popular in Britain as the EEC was growing unpopular. But it also paid off in terms of party strategy as it certainly helped Margaret Thatcher to strengthen her position in her own party and government at a time when she was still in a minority position (George, 1989: 23). The budgetary dispute therefore allowed her to satisfy the right-wing of the party, where her core support lay, without alienating the left-wing and the pro-Europeans. Even though the latter may have been annoyed by Thatcher's tone and style, all agreed that she was right in substance. The Conservative leader skilfully mixed nationalism and Europeanism in her discourse: 'In Europe, we have shown that it is possible to combine a vigorous defence of our own interests with a deep commitment to the idea and to the ideals of the Community' (Cooke, 1989: 119). The budgetary question was not divisive for the Conservative Party because it did not question British membership of the EEC nor its pro-European stance at the time. Here Margaret Thatcher acted as the agent of her followers, thereby emphasising the dynamic relationship at work between leaders and the led.

While the budgetary episode was unquestionably marked by conflicting relations between Britain and the EEC, it was followed by a much more constructive approach to European integration on the part of the Thatcher government on the subject of the single market, which it contributed to initiating. The fact is that this project perfectly fitted in with the Thatcherite ideology as it represented an extension on a European scale of the liberal economic policy applied by the British Prime Minister at the national level. The UK therefore adopted a co-operative attitude towards the Community and accepted significant concessions in order to make the single market possible – concessions which Margaret Thatcher referred to as 'the price to pay' in her memoirs (Thatcher, 1993: 553). However, the Conservative leader seems to have underestimated the supranational nature of the Single European Act (SEA), which also contained an explicit reference to Economic and Monetary Union (EMU) the Prime Minister could not prevent and which later on contributed to justifying a deepening of European integration that Margaret Thatcher was to fight with strength. Apart from this positive episode, the relations between Britain and its European partners were mostly strained and characterised by a negative approach on the part of the Conservative leader, who remained on the defensive regarding European integration.

As already stated, John Major's accession to power was followed by a significant improvement of the relationships between the UK and the EC. However, it was more a change of style than a change of substance, as demonstrated by the opt-outs negotiated by Major at Maastricht – on the single currency but also on the social chapter. Yet, the ratification process of the Maastricht Treaty brought about deep divisions within the Conservative Party and put an end to John Major's constructive approach to the European Union (EU) – not only in his discourse as discussed above, but also in his actions on the European stage. The British leader went from conciliation to confrontation, echoing his predecessor's attitude. There are many examples of this: in March 1994, he opposed the raising of the blocking minority required by the enlargement of the EU to new member-states. Major was adamant and decided to turn this into a test of strength, until eventually he was forced to retreat. He had taken political risks in order to reassert his leadership over his deeply divided party but the situation had backfired and he was left humiliated, vulnerable to leadership speculation once again. A few months later, in June 1994, the British Prime Minister opposed his veto to the election of Jean-Luc Dehaene at the head of the European Commission, not only to protest against the 'French–German diktat' (Major, 1999: 594) but also because the candidate was too federalist for the British government. Lastly, in 1996, during the BSE ('mad cow disease') crisis, the Major government opted for an obstruction policy, blocking all EU decisions requiring unanimity, in protest against the ban on British beef. In fact, despite John Major's initial attempt to distance himself from his predecessor on the European issue, his premiership was characterised by continuity with the Thatcher years.

The radical change in John Major's approach to Europe was accompanied by an instrumentalisation of the European issue for partisan political purposes (Tournier-Sol, 2009: 85–99). Indeed, the eurosceptic turn taken by the Conservative leader aimed at rallying the very support of those in the party which the Maastricht ratification process had alienated. John Major thereby strove to contain the internal splits which were threatening to tear his party apart. Accordingly, he was blamed for subordinating the relationship between Britain and the EU to party management and for putting party unity before the national interest – he was a 'Chief whip *manqué*' (Kavanagh and Seldon, 1994: 48), 'a managerial leader and political tactician for whom holding the party together was virtually an end in itself' (Dorey, 1999: xv). This is quite symptomatic of John Major's political leadership: the Conservative leader acted as an agent of his followers in his own party for the sake of its – and his – own survival. Party cohesion was his utmost priority, with leadership a major factor.

However, conflicts were not limited to the European stage and also arose within the party and government during the end of the Thatcher era and the whole of Major's premiership. Those internal conflicts

affected their respective leaderships to which they were also inextricably linked, albeit differently – thereby shedding an instructive light on
the role of political leadership.

The Maastricht ratification severely damaged the leadership of John
Major, who had to face a rebellion in his party ranks. The Conservative
majority in the House of Commons had been reduced to 21 after the
1992 general election, thereby making the Major government very vulnerable to the euro-rebels by giving them disproportionate influence
during the ratification process (Baker et al., 1993; Alexandre-Collier,
2009). Although this episode undoubtedly undermined Major's leadership, the success of the ratification can also be considered as a considerable achievement in itself given the internal rifts in the Conservative
Party – an achievement which John Major can take full credit for and
which rests on his tactical skills as a political leader (Bogdanor, 2010:
174–5). The ratification process showed the Conservative leader taking
political risks, which were to have lasting consequences on his leadership. This episode was all the more decisive in his premiership that it
was also the founding element of his European policy after that.

Actually, John Major's post-Maastricht European policy is directly
linked to the question of leadership. Unity and authority are the two
key criteria dictating his European policy. They account for Major's
apparent ambivalence, giving coherence to actions which may sometimes look contradictory. Indeed, while John Major was yielding to his
Eurosceptics on the European stage, he confronted them at home within
his own party. Thus, in November 1994, the whip was withdrawn from
eight Conservative MPs for failing to support the government on a vote
of confidence related to the financing of the EU. However, this sanction proved counter-productive as it turned the whipless rebels almost
into quasi-heroic figures who had the courage of their convictions; it
also gave them disproportionate publicity as they toured the country
to promote Euroscepticism like 'a travelling circus' (Major, 1999: 603).
Their readmission five months later only came to emphasise the weakness of John Major's position and leadership – a leadership which was
consistently questioned throughout his premiership, including in his
own party and government. Faced with persistent rumours of a mounting leadership challenge, in June 1995 Major resorted to tactics again:
he resigned the leadership of the Conservative Party, forcing an early
contest and inviting his critics to 'put up or shut up' (Major, 1999: 612).
This bold move was intended to reassert Major's authority over his
deeply divided party. Paradoxically, his position of weakness caused him

to display the very determination and leadership which he was blamed for lacking. Unsurprisingly, John Major won the leadership contest against the Eurosceptic John Redwood. Although this re-election did not succeed in resolving the internal divisions on Europe, it proved that John Major was still the best leader to contain them and to maintain some unity in the party.

In a further effort to ease the tensions within the Conservative Party, in June 1996 Major made a radical U-turn and finally decided to endorse the principle of a referendum on the single currency – an idea which he had been strongly rejecting so far. Once again this decision was motivated by party considerations: the general election was due to be held the following year and the Conservative leader thereby sought to rally the support of his Eurosceptics in an attempt to contain the divisions and mitigate their damaging effect on election prospects (Lynch and Whitaker, 2013: 336). John Major was also responding to James Goldsmith's Referendum Party which intended to field candidates in all the constituencies where none of the other candidates would commit to a referendum on the single currency – a major threat to the Conservative vote which alarmed many MPs who were afraid it would cause them to lose their seats.

The European issue had therefore a decisive impact on John Major's leadership which it consistently undermined. It also had a critical influence on Margaret Thatcher's leadership though in a very different manner. The internal dissent in her government on sterling's entry into the ERM brought about a governmental crisis – a major conflict at the top of the executive between the Prime Minister and two of her Secretaries of State, namely Nigel Lawson at the Exchequer and Geoffrey Howe at the Foreign Office. The authoritarianism demonstrated by Margaret Thatcher as a means to impose her views only exacerbated tensions which reached a climax in June 1989 before the European Council in Madrid. The two ministers threatened Margaret Thatcher with their resignation if she did not make a statement in favour of sterling joining the ERM in Madrid. Thatcher had no other choice but to give in under pressure from her senior ministers. But one month later she hit back by moving Geoffrey Howe from the Foreign Office to the leadership of the House of Commons. Shortly afterwards, the resignation of Nigel Lawson – a convinced Thatcherite – on the question of the ERM provoked a major governmental crisis focusing on Thatcher's strong leadership style. Margaret Thatcher refused to be the agent of her followers which led her to take political risks. Weakened and isolated in her government, the Prime Minister finally yielded to her new Chancellor of the Exchequer, John Major, and agreed to the entry of sterling into the ERM on 5 October 1990. Yet the crisis was still far from over and tensions grew between Thatcher and Howe on Europe, until Howe eventually left the government. The resignation speech he delivered in the House of Commons in November 1990 was hugely damaging to Margaret Thatcher's leadership. It triggered a process which was to provoke her downfall, with political leadership and Europe as decisive elements.

Conclusion

The European issue was therefore inextricably linked to the leadership of both Margaret Thatcher and John Major; it proved decisive in each case, albeit for different reasons. Even though their respective leadership styles were completely antithetical, a striking continuity can be discerned in terms of their approaches to European policy-making. Both gradually hardened their initial position, not only in their political discourse but also in their actions – whether on the European or domestic stages. They demonstrated an increasing, if not systematic, opposition to European integration. Yet, this continuity must not conceal a fundamental difference between the two Conservative leaders, namely their motivations: John Major was mainly concerned with party considerations and consistently endeavoured to rally the support of his Eurosceptics so as to maintain the unity of the Conservative Party, whereas Margaret Thatcher took a eurosceptic turn out of conviction, even verging on Europhobia after she left power. This contrast is a reflection of their respective leadership styles. Margaret Thatcher acted as a causal agent, establishing a new political order. As a political leader, she definitely made a difference: she was what Alexandre-Collier and Vergniolle de Chantal describe as 'a game-changer' in their typology, and she did not content herself with being the mere agent of her followers – the downside of this being that she ended up being isolated and autocratic which eventually led to her downfall. From the start, John Major deliberately positioned himself as the antithesis of his predecessor: he was a leader of conciliation, an agent of his followers whose tactical skills allowed him to make it through his premiership despite the internal strife threatening the very survival of his party – and therefore his very survival as a leader. His constant efforts to reconnect with his party basis after the Maastricht episode make him a 'grassroots-connector' type of leader as defined in the introduction to this book.

Yet, the apparent contrast between Margaret Thatcher's strong leadership and John Major's assumed lack of leadership hardly conceals another key factor at work here: the political context. The end of the Thatcher era and the whole of John Major's premiership coincided with an acceleration of European integration which both Prime Ministers strongly rejected. There appear the limits of political leadership, Europe being a climax of uncertainty, the very issue which poisoned their respective leaderships, albeit in different ways.

References

Alexandre-Collier, A. (2009) 'John Major vs. the 'bastards' ou la puissance de la mobilisation eurosceptique contre le traité de Maastricht', in J.P. Fons (ed.), *Les années John Major 1990–1997* (Observatoire de la société britannique, no. 7).

Baker, D., Gamble, A. and Ludlam, S. (1994) 'The Parliamentary Siege of Maastricht 1993: Conservative Divisions and British Ratification', *Parliamentary Affairs*, 47:1, 37–60.

Bogdanor, V. (2010) *From New Jerusalem to New Labour: British Prime Ministers from Attlee to Blair* (Basingstoke: Palgrave Macmillan).

Burns, J.M. (1979) *Leadership* (New York: Harper Perennial).

Cooke, A.B. (1989) *Margaret Thatcher: The Revival of Britain, Speeches on Home and European Affairs 1975–1988* (London: Aurum Press).

Cooke, A.B. (1992) *John Major: Selected Speeches during his First Year as Prime Minister* (London: Conservative Party).

Crossman, R. (1964) 'Introduction' to Walter Bagehot, *The English Constitution* (London: Watts).

Dorey, P. (ed.) (1999) *The Major Premiership* (Basingstoke: Macmillan).

Foley, M. (2000) *The British Presidency* (Manchester: Manchester University Press).

Foley, M. (2002) *John Major, Tony Blair and a conflict of leadership: Collision course* (Manchester: Manchester University Press).

George, S. (1989) *Nationalism, Liberalism and the National Interest: Britain, France and the EEC* (Glasgow: Strathclyde papers on government and politics, no. 67).

Gilmour, I. (1992) *Dancing with dogma: Britain under Thatcherism* (London: Simon and Schuster).

Kavanagh, D. and Seldon A. (eds) (1994) *The Major Effect* (London: Macmillan).

King, A. (1985) *The British Prime Minister* 2nd edn (Durham: Duke University Press).

Lynch P., Whitaker, R. (2013) 'Where There is Discord, Can They Bring Harmony? Managing Intra-Party Dissent on European Integration in the Conservative Party', *British Journal of Politics and International Relations*, 15:3, 317–39.

Mackintosh, J.P. (1968) *The British Cabinet*, 2nd edn (London: Methuen).

Major, J. (1999) *The Autobiography* (London: HarperCollins).

Skowronek, S. (1997) *The Politics Presidents Make: Leadership from John Adams to Bill Clinton*, rev. edn (Harvard: Harvard University Press).

Thatcher, M. (1993) *The Downing Street Years* (London: HarperCollins).

Theakston, K. (2002) 'Political Skills and Context in Prime Ministerial Leadership in Britain', *Politics and Policy*, 30:2, 283–323.

Tournier-Sol, K. (2009) 'John Major et l'Europe, ou l'enjeu européen au service de l'intérêt partisan', in J.P. Fons (ed.), *Les années John Major 1990–1997* (Observatoire de la société britannique, no. 7).

Weber, M., Whimster, S. (2004) *The Essential Weber: A Reader* (London: Routledge).

Young, H. (1990) *One of Us: A Biography of Margaret Thatcher*, rev. edn (London: Pan Books/Macmillan).

10
The Temptation of Populism in David Cameron's Leadership Style

Agnès Alexandre-Collier

It may seem unusual to associate the widely-used concept of populism with the leadership of the British Prime Minister, David Cameron. Populism is, however, open to various interpretations and definitions and so easy to manipulate that it could apply to almost anything. Moreover, populism has so often been used to describe movements and groups critical of representative democracy, generating a 'malaise' (Mény and Surel, 2002: 21) or a 'threat' to democracy (Mudde and Kaltwasser, 2012), that it is has become difficult to conceive it as a new political practice in the hands of democratic governments. To accept what would appear to be a counter-natural association between populism and democracy, it is necessary to move beyond the endless debate on the meaning of populism and locate the word in present academic research on the rise of populism in Western democracies (Mény and Surel, 2002; Mudde and Kaltwasser, 2012). Examining the case of David Cameron's leadership provides both a specific context and a basic framework for analysis (Mudde and Kaltwasser, 2012).

Based on the EU referendum debate in Britain, from a call for a referendum on the Maastricht treaty in the 1990s to the current referendum debate on Britain's EU membership, this chapter will look at how the whole EU debate exerts pressure on – and also explains – the temptation of populism for David Cameron. His new style of leadership has been widely discussed elsewhere (Denham and O'Hara, 2007; Evans, 2008; Bale, 2009; Heppell, 2013b; Heffernan, 2014). In this chapter, it should be understood both as a strategy for governmentality and a method of party management. On a governmental level, the referendum has become a major instrument of this new practice. Since the 1990s, the extensive use of direct democracy in such a representative government has produced a paradox which the current Prime Minister has not failed to exploit in the face of the mounting public divisions on European integration and the rise of the United Kingdom Independence Party (UKIP), thus changing the relation with his followers, i.e. party members and voters. As far as party organization goes, Cameron's method of management also demonstrates a new style of leadership which takes more account of social environmental pressures, following Katz and Mair's 'cartel party' thesis (1995, 1997). The organizational reforms introduced in 1998 have provided successive Conservative leaders with an opportunity to give party members more direct access to decision-making inside the party. After 2005, David Cameron, among others, capitalized on internal democratization and the widening of the electorate, a strategy which resulted paradoxically in strengthening his leadership of the party. Therefore, given Pierre Rosanvallon's (2011) definition of populism mentioned in the introduction to this volume, David Cameron may be classified among 'grassroots-connectors' running the risk of lapsing into populism in his ambition to reconnect with the people at all costs.

Populism as a communicative strategy

The case of David Cameron's new style of leadership has often been raised elsewhere. To most scholars, his style has been primarily considered as part of a communicative strategy to popularize his image and 'detoxify' the brand of his party (Alexandre-Collier, 2010; Bale, 2011). In this framework, even though a relationship is established between rhetoric and political strategy (Higgins, 2013: 58), populism remains essentially a rhetorical device. Cameron's rhetoric, which was motivated by the 'emergent political and social circumstances' of the economic crisis (Higgins, 2013: 63), centred mainly on the message of the 'Big Society' which was particularly expedient as a means of displacing power from the elite to the people. Making the case for 'a massive, radical redistribution of power', Cameron argued that

> we should start by pushing political power down as far as possible. Politicians will have to change their attitude – big time. Politicians, and the senior civil servants and advisers who work for them, instinctively hoard power because they think that's the way to get things done. Well we're going to have to kill that instinct: and believe me, I know how hard that's going to be. It will require a serious culture change among ministers, among Whitehall officials – and beyond. With every decision government makes, it should ask a

series of simple questions: does this give power to people, or take it away? Could we let individuals, neighbourhoods and communities take control? How far can we push power down? (*The Guardian*, 25 May 2009)

Demonstrating that the 'Big Society' operates as a vehicle for empowerment, Higgins thus defines populism as a 'rhetoric of empowerment' (Higgins, 2013: 68). In that respect, populism is nothing more than a somewhat cosmetic device to reconnect with ordinary people. The purpose of our argument here is to move beyond the rhetorical dimension of David Cameron's style of leadership as Prime Minister and leader of the Conservative Party in order to look at how populism has come to characterize both his practice of government and his mode of party management.

Populism as a strategy for governmentality

Beyond the restricted framework of political communication, populism should be examined in a broader perspective. In this chapter, we suggest that David Cameron's style of leadership is also a compelling case regarding the use of populism as a political strategy. Drawing on Michael Higgins' application of Michel Foucault's concept of governmentality to Cameron's populist rhetoric, it is necessary to go further and look at the way populism serves not only as a communicative strategy but also as a specific practice of government, with the referendum as its main technical device. Starting from a general definition of populism, suggesting a special connection between the leader and the 'people', populism could be defined, as Peter Mair argued, as a 'a political style characterised by the promotion of a particular kind of link between political leaders and the electorate, a link structured around a loose and opportunistic appeal to "the people" in order to win' (Mair in Mény and Surel, 2002: 84). As Mudde suggested, such a definition could apply to any kind of electoralist strategy which resorts on occasions to demagogy or opportunism in order to broaden its appeal. What is actually contained in the notion of populism in the general sense of the word is a moral conception of politics and society. It can be viewed therefore as 'a thin-centred ideology that considers society to be ultimately separated into two homogeneous and antagonistic groups, "the pure people" and the "corrupt élite" and which argues that politics should be an expression of the *volonté générale* of the people' (Mudde, 2007: 23). Consequently, it could be argued that populism, in supporting popular sovereignty and majority rule, is fundamentally opposed to representation (Taggart, 2002). Yet, one can also understand populism as a tendency for representative democracies to appeal directly to the electorate beyond the sphere of their political representatives. This assumption would be in line with the general definition of populism as a political style. The notion of populism as containing the underlying assumption of political corruption triggers instead a feeling of suspicion towards political representatives. They become suspected of sometimes unproven flaws and unacceptable behaviour. In this perspective, democracy is viewed as an ideal world in which moral standards prevail. Representative democracy 'in practice' is, however, necessarily imperfect because human imperfection makes it impossible for its representatives to reach this ideal. Hence an inevitable trend towards a populist style of politics which also expresses a form of political cynicism. If representatives are essentially unable to reach the standards of behaviour that are expected of them, leaders may want to find new ways of bypassing them in order to appeal directly to the people. The main instruments of direct democracy, i.e. procedures that allow citizens to raise issues on the decision-making agenda without the mediation of parliamentary actors (Setälä and Schiller, 2009: 4), are therefore referendums.

In a country like the United Kingdom, whose democracy was built on the principle of parliamentary sovereignty, the referendum was long viewed as, in Margaret Thatcher's words, the 'weapon of dictators', a weapon strategically used by leaders who could thus manipulate public opinion and undermine the legitimacy of representatives often for 'plebiscitary motivations' (Morel, 2001). Yet motivations are diverse. Taxonomies of elite motives for initiating referendums have indeed been numerous (Bjørklund, 1982; Morel, 2001; Qvortrup, 2006; Rahat, 2009). Among the three goals identified by Rahat, two cases of government-initiated referendums were found in the UK. The June 1975 referendum on whether or not Britain should stay in the European Common Market, was considered as an isolated and exceptional experience, a desperate solution for a Prime Minister, Harold Wilson, who was unable to unite his party on the issue. The motive of *avoidance* – resulting from the fear that a decision might lead to a split within a unit whose cohesion the initiators and supporters of the referendum wish to sustain (Rahat, 2009:99) – is difficult to deny. However, when Tony Blair organized two referendums on the devolution of powers to Scotland and Wales on 11 and 18 September 1997, this decision was no longer motivated by a general mood of despair generated by the fear of division, but rather by the *addition* of a decision-making forum to legitimize the decision and/or empower the initiator of the referendum (Rahat, 2009: 99), a motivation indicating perhaps even a different conception of democracy. The notion of empowerment, which was also at the heart of the New Labour agenda, involved bringing people closer to their centres of power. Thus together with a whole package of constitutional reforms, this device was part of the strategy of creating proximity between the people and their representatives and revamping a link which, as the new government argued, had been eroded. Yet, in doing so, Prime Minister Tony Blair was seeking a means of legitimizing a decision which had already been included in the 1997 New Labour manifesto and of empowering his own leadership. The 1997 referendum can therefore easily be classified as 'plebiscitary' (Morel, 2001) or 'strategic' (Qvortrup, 2006). From a broader perspective, New Labour opened up a new cycle with Britain's parliamentary democracy no longer being viewed as incompatible with tools of direct democracy.

The EU referendum debate as an opportunity structure for populism

In this context, the EU debate which has divided public opinion and generated intra-party dissent (Lynch and Whitaker, 2013b) offers an ideal opportunity structure. With politicians mobilizing on either side of the debate regardless of party preferences, the referendum has become a major weapon in the hands of leaders to rally public opinion which feels excluded from decision-making on this specific issue. With the Cabinet itself divided on the euro, New Labour's referendum pledge from 1997 onwards to join the single currency became a motto, at least until 9/11 changed the government's priorities. It was also used by the Conservative Party which was becoming increasingly Eurosceptic as an effect of their opposition status and also perhaps as a mechanical reaction to Tony Blair's more pro-European vision. At the 2010 general election, the return to office of the Conservatives, in coalition with the Liberal Democrats, allowed them to attempt to promote a unified Eurosceptic agenda (Heppell, 2013a), in spite of the Liberal Democrats' pro-European stance. Liberal Democrats themselves kept relatively silent in the wake of the economic crisis of the eurozone which provided the Eurosceptics with further arguments. With the two parties of the coalition government in disagreement on the European issue, letting the people decide was seen as the best solution to avoid party divisions and protect the coalition government. Thus, David Cameron's pledge in January 2013 to organize a referendum on British membership of the

European Union if the Conservative Party is re-elected in May 2015, appears at first sight as an illustration of the *avoidance* motive identified by Rahat. But, as will be developed later, the rapid development of Euroscepticism in his parliamentary party has also compelled Cameron to make this announcement in order to further legitimize his decision and empower his leadership, and hence the possibility of classifying his motivation as the *addition* of another decision-making mechanism to the existing one (Rahat, 2009: 102). In any case, both interpretations fit with the argument of a 'direct democracy' cycle opened up by New Labour and perpetuated by the current coalition government.

From the mid-1990s, cynicism towards politicians has grown and leaders of the major parties have been searching for means of restoring confidence among the electorate/people. For the major parties in Britain, the prevailing argument was that British parliamentary democracy could even be enhanced by the sporadic practice of direct democracy. Empowering voters could therefore help rebuild the tacit contract with their representatives. For the Conservative Party in particular, the new use of the referendum was a response both to party divisions and to the rise of public Euroscepticism. In addition, the growing threat represented by the rise of small parties such as UKIP justified this populist shift (Ford and Goodwin, 2014). Launched in 1993 as a single-issue pressure group to oppose the ratification of the Maastricht treaty, UKIP first put up candidates in the 1994 European election. Following the demise of the Referendum Party, founded by Franco-British millionaire James Goldsmith to campaign for a referendum on the treaty, UKIP has gradually occupied its own space in the political spectrum, becoming the only united Eurosceptic party in British politics. It gained increasing popularity in European Parliament (EP) elections, progressing from three seats in 1999 to 24 in 2014. Since 2012, UKIP has come second in a series of by-elections in constituencies such as Rotherham on 29 November 2012 or Eastleigh on 28 February 2013 when the UKIP candidate, Diane James, won 27.8% of the votes. And in 2014, UKIP gained its first two MPs with Douglas Carswell and Mark Reckless who had defected from the Conservative Party and were re-elected for UKIP in by-elections. In 2013, UKIP claimed to be the third party in Britain as regards voting intentions, ahead of the Liberal Democrats.

With the Conservative Party failing to display a unified Eurosceptic platform, UKIP, with the help of newcomers in the 1990s such as Conservative MP Roger Knapman, has come to represent a major threat for the Tories, attracting voters among traditional Tory supporters. While opposing the EU for undermining national sovereignty and criticizing

EU institutions for being excessively bureaucratic and anathema to British parliamentary principles, UKIP gradually broadened the scope of its agenda (Ford and Goodwin, 2014) and ceased to focus on the defence of British parliamentary sovereignty in order to promote the extensive use of direct democracy. In diversifying its agenda beyond the one issue of Europe, UKIP also operated a shift from parliamentary to popular sovereignism. Under the leadership of Nigel Farage, UKIP has developed various proposals, mostly based on the extensive use of referendums and the development of local democracy. UKIP has devised a strategy whereby sovereignty should rest with the nation as embodied by the people. In addition, UKIP nourished resentment against traditional politicians seen as contemptuous of the people and often corrupt, encouraging voters to 'sod the lot' – as suggested by their electoral slogan in May 2010 aimed at the leaders of the three main parties – and vote for UKIP instead.

Populism as a style of party management

Shifting power

Scientific literature on party change has been particularly enriched by the 'cartel party' thesis which addressed the recent transformations of political parties in advanced democracies with acute relevance. Challenging the thesis of inexorable party decline, especially in terms of party membership and party dealignment (Dalton and Wattenberg, 2002), political parties as symbiotically connected with the state have become increasingly able to control their environment and respond to political changes and shocks (Katz and Mair, 1995, 1997). With the development of the cartel party, the goals of politics become self-referential, professional and technocratic, with the view that politics is increasingly depoliticized. The election campaigns conducted by cartel parties are capital-intensive, professionalized and centralized. More importantly, within the party, the distinction between members and non-members becomes blurred (Katz and Mair, 1995). The collapse of the boundary between members and non-members explains party leaders' growing need to address the wider electorate in what has come to be seen as a more populist style of leadership. In addition, the growing pressure of environmental changes has forced party leaders to adapt and find solutions. These environmental changes can concern the wider framework of social change and be heavily context-dependent. Among the various processes identified by Katz and Mair, growing professionalization has been noted, together with changes in the approaches to campaign activity and financial resources. But more importantly in the case of the Conservative Party examined here, internal democratization has generated a shift in the party's balance of power (Bale and Turner, 2012) by which the leader has paradoxically gained more power. This democratization process has become a common feature among parties. It has led to a dual process of inclusiveness and centralization by which parties have empowered their members who are thus given the opportunity to decide on important issues, while centralizing the decision process and consequently minimizing the power of organizational subunits within the party (Scarrow, 2005: 6). Democratization thus creates a vicious circle whereby more participation does not necessarily entail more influence (Avril, 2013: 3), democratization even meaning 'decapitation' (Katz, 2001 cited in Scarrow, 2005: 5) or 'emasculation' (Webb, 2000). Hence the strong reservations expressed by Hopkin when using the term 'democratization' because, he argues, as long as party leaderships are able to regulate and condition this process, members' choices will remain constrained (Hopkin, 2001: 358).

As a response to successive electoral defeats, which can be considered as major environmental changes (Bale and Turner, 2012: 3), the Conservative Party seems to have drawn inspiration from New Labour's *Partnership in Power* (1997) which promoted democratization in the form of enlarging consultation with the multiplication of policy forums and introducing the principle of OMOV (One Member One Vote) in the electoral college to elect leaders and the National Executive Committee (Avril, 2013: 3). New Labour then extended organizational reforms in 2010 (*Partnership into Power*) with the introduction of deliberation procedures. Having lost the 1997 general election, the Conservatives undertook organizational reforms summarized in a document entitled *Fresh Future*. Under a new codified constitution, the official argument was to draw together the three components of party organization (voluntary, professional and parliamentary) into a unified structure. In addition, members were to be consulted through internal referendums and the leader is now elected by both MPs and party members who also vote by postal ballot. Thus, in displaying this objective, the new leadership of William Hague indicated a shift towards a more populist style of party management since the 1998 organizational reforms officially resulted in relocating decision-making in the hands of the party grass-roots or, as Higgins put it, 'taking power from bureaucratic apparatchiks to return it to the ordinary populace' (Higgins, 2013: 58).

While electoral defeat was indeed a major environmental driver of change, the EU debate provides another significant opportunity. In the UK, the combined effects of devolution and EU integration were to create a multi-level structure which also exerts significant pressure on party change. Alongside the impact of Europeanization (Poguntke, 2007) on national parties, the national debate generated by issues such as the Maastricht treaty or the current referendum proposal on EU membership have created an environment which has favoured and even galvanized Cameron's populist style of party management. While government action has now integrated the referendum as a regular procedure, party management is also influenced by the impact of the EU debate. To some extent, the Maastricht episode planted the seeds of this transformation by changing the nature of the relationship between MPs and their leader, giving each the opportunity to bypass confrontation with the other by relying on the grass-roots instead.

Reducing parliamentary pressure

Prior to the 1998 reforms, the Conservative Party's centre of gravity was dominated by the parliamentary component. Priority was given to MPs in the election of the Conservative leader and the survival of the leader depended solely on backbenchers. The rules for Conservative leadership contests had been introduced for the first such election, in 1965, and modified in 1975. In accordance with the rules, there was a series of ballots, conducted by the 1922 Committee, i.e. the Conservative backbench organization. To win the contest in the first round, a candidate needed to have a margin of victory over the runner-up of 15 per cent of the total electorate. The latter rule had been changed in the 1975 review, having previously required a majority equal to 15 per cent of those voting. This procedure gave overwhelming importance to MPs in the selection of a leader who needed above all their loyalty and confidence to stay in power. In addition, MPs benefited from the extensive support of their local associations.

Again the European debate provided an expedient for MPs to rely on popular support, voters and party members all together. In the wake of the Maastricht debate, the so-called Maastricht rebels who refused to comply with their leader's instructions to ratify the treaty, devised strategies to mobilize public opinion. The number of extra-parliamentary organizations opposed to the Maastricht treaty – including the Bruges Group, Conservatives Against a Federal Europe, the European Foundation launched by Bill Cash, or UKIP, previously mentioned and initially created in 1993 as a single issue pressure group by Alan Sked, an academic at the London School of Economics – increased dramatically between 1992 and 1997 (Alexandre-Collier, 2002). On the whole, some

20 associations were formed and continued to proliferate at least until the mid-2000s. Eurosceptic MPs also relied on other resources available, namely Rupert Murdoch's press which provided the rebels with the best medium to convey their message. On the other hand, MPs were highly dependent on their local associations, giving priority to their constituents sometimes at the expense of national party leaders. Before 1998, local associations were largely autonomous, with little interference from Central Office, and some MPs had clearly made their reputation locally, enjoying local notability, which also explains the extent of the anti-Maastricht rebellion. MPs knew that they could always count on their local associations, particularly in the event of tensions with leaders in Parliament.

The call for a referendum became a consensual motto among Eurosceptic rebels. Yet, at the time, their motivation for a referendum is what Rahat termed *contradiction*: a minority blocking a majority decision or promoting a policy or reform that the majority in government and/or Parliament rejects (Rahat, 2009: 99). In the case of Eurosceptic rebels, their attempt was clearly promotional. The Maastricht episode increased the visibility of Eurosceptic MPs and more generally crystallized the influence of the parliamentary component in the party structure at the expense of leadership. The extra confidence provided by public support stimulated their motivations and strengthened their actions. One Eurosceptic MP, Michael Carttiss, recalled:

> I wanted a referendum nationally, of course, but I did my own in the sense that I gave my constituents the opportunity to talk to me on the phone over two periods, to say 'yes, they wanted a referendum' or 'no, they didn't want a referendum', 'yes, they supported Maastricht' or 'no they didn't'. (...) But when I lost the whip over refusing to vote for increasing the British contribution to the EU budget, then I got enormous support in my constituency and in my local association. (Interview, 13 June 1995)

Owing to local support, whips' pressures turned out to have little effect on some MPs (among rebels' testimonies, see for example Gorman, 1993). As a result, when John Major resigned from the party leadership in June 1995, asking his MPs to submit unconditionally to his authority, this was viewed as an awkward decision which contributed to strengthening the MPs' self-confidence and independence from the party (see chapter by Tournier-Sol in this volume). Consequently, John Major's failure to negotiate, facing them with a single alternative 'put up or shut up' can be interpreted as a misunderstanding of the basic rules of the game and of the importance of the parliamentary party (Alderman, 1996). Tensions between John Major and MPs also undermined the silent pact of confidence between the leader and his backbenchers, which David Cameron therefore set out to restore after his election. But in doing so, he actually introduced a measure which was felt by back-benchers as deliberately undermining their status and independence. On 19 May 2010, shortly after the formation of the coalition govern-ment, David Cameron suggested modifying the composition of the 1992 Committee to involve ministers in the recommendation-forming process. On 20 May 2010, Committee members voted to approve the change, with 168 votes in favour and 118 against. Apart from the offi-cial argument which was to give more coherence to the party, especially in its participation in a coalition government, Cameron's intention was to put an end to the confrontational climate that had deteriorated since Major's Premiership. What Cameron apparently called the 'them and us culture' (*The Guardian*, 24 May 2010) had come to affect the link between the Conservative leader and his MPs. This rhetoric can be viewed as part of a populist attempt at morally separating the elite and the people, with the leader deliberately placing himself on the side of the 'pure people' as opposed to the others who are thus implicitly portrayed as the enemies.

Empowering party members and voters

To some extent, the 1998 organizational reforms, in enabling the leader to rely on the grass-roots, could be seen as a strategy to further reduce the pressure exerted by MPs on party leadership. This new populist style of party management was illustrated by numerous examples, ranging from the election of David Cameron as leader of the party in December 2005 to the Totnes open primary in 2009. The leadership contest was a blatant illustration of this clear shift in the balance of power within the party. Following the new election rules enabling members to vote on a short-list of two, decided upon by the parliamentary party, the election of David Cameron divided the parliamentary party but was ultimately sanctioned by party members. The first round of voting among MPs took place on 18 October and Kenneth Clarke was eliminated (38 votes) leaving David Davis (62 votes), David Cameron (56 votes) and Liam Fox (42 votes) to go through to the second ballot on 20 October. MPs failed to reach a consensus and David Cameron only managed to rally a little over a quarter of the parliamentary party. In the second ballot, Liam Fox was eliminated (51 votes), leaving David Cameron (90 votes) and David Davis (57 votes) to go through to the members' postal ballot. The ballot, whose result was declared on 6 December 2005, saw David Cameron win 68 per cent of votes (134,446) to Davis's 32 per cent (64,398) (Heppell, 2008). In addition, the organization of the Totnes Conservative open primary in 2009 provides another revealing example. For the first time, registered voters, regardless of their party affiliation, were invited to select the Conservative candidate in a constituency-wide postal ballot. The A-list introduced by Conservative Central Office after December 2005 at David Cameron's request with a view to selecting more female candidates was also a means for the leadership of getting a firmer grip on the future intake of Conservative MPs. This partly explains the generational renewal often noted in the parliamentary party after 2010. But, above all, it empowered members and voters, once again undermining the influence of MPs. Yet, as Bale and Turner put it, the reality was different and certainly not that of a radical power shift towards the grass-roots: 'power has shifted upwards towards the party leadership (seen as a collective rather than as an individual – the latter, after all, has always been preeminent), and downwards towards individual members and away from activists, as well as some blurring of the boundary between members and non-members' (Bale and Turner, 2012: 9).

Once again the EU debate can be identified as a major 'environmental' pressure on David Cameron's proclivity to populism within his party organization, a temptation which the previous leader William Hague also experienced. As the initiator of the 'Fresh Future' reforms, Hague decided to test the relevance of multiplying internal referendums by organizing one on the European single currency. It was eventually rejected by 84.4 per cent of the Conservative members who took part in the vote on 5 October 1998. The very nature of the EU debate in British politics therefore operates as a national incentive for populism. It was argued, for example, that Cameron's election as leader in 2005 was also facilitated by his commitment to pull Conservative MEPs out of the European People's Party–European Democrats (EPP–ED) group in the European Parliament, thus gaining the support of some Eurosceptic MPs (Lynch and Whitaker, 2008; Lynch, 2012: 74–5). In October 2011, the parliamentary rebellion of 81 Conservative MPs calling for a referendum on Britain's membership of the EU, following a petition introduced by David Nuttall, a newly elected Conservative MP, and based on e-petitions from the public gathering 100,000 signatures, resurrected the trauma of Conservative factions (Gamble, 2012: 468; Gifford, 2014: 521; Lynch and Whitaker, 2013b). The increasing popularity of UKIP has also been stimulated by the efforts of Rupert Murdoch's popular press to galvanize public Euroscepticism. At the same time, following in the wake of Maastricht, the Conservative Party leadership has progressively externalized the EU debate or abandoned it to extra-parliamentary groups which mobilized on the question of a referendum on the future of the UK in the EU (FitzGibbon, 2013; Gifford, 2014: 520) well before David Cameron officially announced that a referendum would be held. With UKIP benefiting from several defections of Conservative MPs (Roger Knapman, Bob Spink,...) and peers (Lord Pearson of Rannoch, Lord Willoughby de Broke) and from the votes of traditional Tory voters switching to UKIP, Cameron's populism also looks like a desperate strategy to gain new voters after his failure to win an overall majority of seats at the 2010 general election (Lynch and Whitaker, 2013a).

Conclusion

David Cameron's referendum pledge on EU membership is an interesting indicator of his new populist style. At first sight, the use of this device seems motivated by the need to uphold the unity of his party and his government and to neutralize the issue which has always been one of the most divisive in British contemporary politics. More generally, referendum pledges, first on the euro then on EU membership, have become a leitmotiv of British governments since New Labour's election. With Euroscepticism spreading in Britain, public opinion and political parties as a whole – including pro-European ones – have made increasing demands for a referendum; hence the view that Cameron's response is simply a means of further legitimizing a decision that the majority of British people already seem to support.

Yet, looking more closely at David Cameron's announcement in January 2013, one needs to analyse this decision not as an isolated gesture but as part of a series of reforms, at both government and party organization levels, which point to a shift towards a populist style of leadership in terms of governmental practice and party management. This broader picture allows us to suggest that in this specific context, the referendum device, combined with organizational reforms in the party, such as changes in the leadership election procedure and the organization of open primaries, serves as an instrument of self-empowerment. Indeed, the circumstances of Cameron's election as party leader in December 2005, in which he failed to gain the support of more than a quarter of MPs in the first ballot, together with the circumstances of the 2010 general election in which the Conservative Party did not obtain an overall majority of seats, already exposed the vulnerability of his position. In addition, eschewing controversial decisions and turning to the people for further ratification can be viewed as a sign of weakness (Setälä and Schiller, 2009: 112). Indeed, Cameron's own survival, both as party leader and Prime Minister, is conditional upon popular reactions and decisions, especially on Europe, with party members now being responsible for him staying in power and voters more likely to turn to UKIP if they feel that the Conservatives fail to deliver on Europe. MPs are therefore freer now to represent their constituents' views which have in any case always been more Eurosceptic than those of Conservative politicians. In these circumstances, David Cameron seems to have no other choice but to yield to grass-roots pressure. Cameron's room for manoeuvre is admittedly limited by the institutional constraints of coalition government, with EU partners and Liberal Democrats forcing him to look in the opposite direction. The threat of the next general election in May 2015 also helps explain why he has become more receptive to popular opinion. Yet for Cameron the temptation of populism is not only the result of constraints. It is also a matter of choice. If people only perceive this decision as a strategy, then Cameron's calculation may turn out to be dangerous for him, because it risks being further interpreted as part of the cynical game that brings citizens to lose trust in politicians, as Rahat would argue (Setälä and Schiller, 2009: 215). The temptation of populism can therefore create a vicious circle in which David Cameron, by wishing to reconnect with the people, runs the risk of turning them against him.

Works cited

Alderman, K. (1996) 'The Conservative Party Leadership Election of 1995', *Parliamentary Affairs*, Vol. 49, n° 2, 316–32.

Alexandre-Collier, A. (2002) *La Grande-Bretagne eurosceptique. L'Europe dans le débat politique britannique* (Nantes: Editions du Temps).

Alexandre-Collier, A. (2010) *Les habits neufs de David Cameron. Les conservateurs britanniques* (Paris: Presses de Sciences Po).

Avril, E. (2013) 'The Evolution of Decision-Making in the British Labour Party: From Grassroots to Netroots?', in E. Avril and C. Zumello (eds) *New Technologies, Organizational Change and Governance* (Basingstoke: Palgrave Macmillan), pp. 102–16.

Bale, T. (2009) 'Cometh the hour, cometh the Dave: How far is the conservative party's revival all down to David Cameron', *Political Quarterly*, Vol. 18, n° 2, 222–32.

Bale, T. (2011) *The Conservative Party: From Thatcher to Cameron* (London: Polity).

Bale, T. and Turner, E. (2012) 'Modernisation in small steps? Comparing the organisational reforms of the British Conservative Party and the German CDU', PSA Paper.

Bjørklund, T. (1982) 'The demand for referendum: when does it arise and when does it succeed?', *Scandinavian Political Studies*, 5, 237–59.

Dalton, R.J., Wattenberg, M.P. (2002) *Parties without Partisans. Political Change in Advanced Industrial Democracies* (Oxford: Oxford University Press).

Denham, A., O'Hara, K. (2007) 'Cameron's "mandate": Democracy, legitimacy and conservative leadership', *Parliamentary Affairs*, Vol. 60, n° 3, 409–23.

Evans, S. (2008) 'Consigning its past to history? David Cameron and the Conservative party', *Parliamentary Affairs*, Vol. 62, n° 2, 291–314.

Fitzgibbon, J. (2013) 'Citizens Against Europe? Civil Society and Eurosceptic Protest in Ireland, the United Kingdom and Denmark', *Journal of Common Market Studies*, Vol. 51, n° 1, 105–22.

Ford, R., Goodwin, R. (2014) *Revolt on the Right. Explaining support for the radical right in Britain* (London and New York: Routledge).

Gamble, A. (2012) 'Better off Out? Britain and Europe, *Political Quarterly*, Vol. 83, n° 3, 468–77.

Gifford, C. (2014) 'The People Against Europe: The Eurosceptic Challenge to the United Kingdom's Coalition Government', *Journal of Common Market Studies*, Vol. 52, n° 3, 512–28.

Gorman, T. (1993) *The Bastards: Dirty Tricks and the Challenge to Europe* (London: Pan Books, Sidgwick and Jackson).

Heffernan, R. (2014) 'UK party leaders as "preeminent", but can also be "predominant": Cameron and the Conservatives, 2005–2010', *British Politics*, Vol. 9, n° 1, 51–67.

Heppell, T. (2008) *Choosing the Tory Leader: Conservative Party Leadership Elections from Heath to Cameron* (London: I.B. Tauris).

Heppell, T. (2013a) 'Cameron and Liberal Conservatism: Attitudes within the Parliamentary Conservative Party and Conservative Ministers', *British Journal of Politics and International Relations*, Vol. 15, n° 3, 340–61.

Heppell, T. (2013b) 'The Conservative party leadership of David Cameron: Heresthetics and the realignment of British politics', *British Politics*, Vol. 8, n° 3, 260–84.

Higgins, M. (2013) 'Governmentality, populism and empowerment. David Cameron's rhetoric of the big society', in R. Scullion, R. Gerodimos, D. Jackson and D.G. Lilleker (eds) *The Media, Participation and Empowerment* (Abingdon: Routledge).

Hopkin, Jonathan (2001) 'Bring the Members Back in? Candidate Selection in Britain and Spain', *Party Politics*, Vol. 7, n° 3, 343–61.

Katz, R.S. (2001) 'The Problem of Candidate Selection and Models of Party Democracy', *Party Politics* 7.

Katz, R.S., Mair, P. (1995) 'Changing Models of Party Organization and Party Democracy: The Emergence of the Cartel Party', *Party Politics*, Vol. 1, n° 1, 5–28.

Katz, R.S., Mair, P. (1997) 'Party Organisation, Party Democracy and the Emergence of the Cartel Party', in P. Mair, *Party System Change: Approaches and Interpretations* (Oxford: Oxford University Press), pp. 93–119.

Lynch, P. (2012) 'European Policy', in T. Heppell and D. Seawright (eds), *Cameron and the Conservatives. The Transition to Coalition Government* (Basingstoke: Palgrave Macmillan).

Lynch, P., Whitaker, R. (2008) 'A Loveless Marriage. The Conservatives and the European People's Party', *Parliamentary Affairs*, Vol. 61, n° 1, 31–51.

Lynch, P., Whitaker, R. (2013a) 'Rivalry on the right: The Conservatives, the UK Independence Party (UKIP) and the EU issue', *British Politics*, Vol. 8, n° 3, 285–312.

Lynch, P., Whitaker, R. (2013b) 'Where there is Discord, Can they Bring Harmony? Managing Intra-party Dissent on European Integration in the Conservative Party', *British Journal of Politics and International Relations*, Vol. 15, 317–39.

Mény, Y., Surel, Y. (eds) (2002) *Democracies and the Populist Challenge* (Basingstoke: Palgrave).

Morel, L. (2001) 'The rise of government-initiated referendums in consolidated democracies', in M. Mendelsohn and A. Parkin, *Referendum Democracy* (Basingstoke: Palgrave).

Mudde, C. (2007) *Populist Radical Right Parties in Europe* (Cambridge: Cambridge University Press).

Mudde, C., Kaltwasser, C.R. (eds) (2012) *Populism in Europe and the Americas. Threat or Corrective for Democracy* (Cambridge: Cambridge University Press).

Poguntke, T. *et al.* (2007) *The Europeanization of National Political Parties. Power and Organizational Adaptation* (London: Routledge).

Qvortrup, M. (2006) 'Democracy by delegation: The decision to hold a referendum in the United Kingdom', *Representation*, Vol. 42, 59–72.

Rahat, G. (2009) 'Elite motives for initiating referendums', in M. Setälä and T. Schiller (eds) *Referendums and Representative Democracy: Responsiveness, Accountability and Deliberation* (London: Routledge, ECPR Studies).

Rosanvallon, P. (2011) 'A Reflection on Populism', *Books and Ideas* http://www.booksandideas.net/A-Reflection-on-Populism.html, date accessed July 2014.

Scarrow, S. (2005) *Implementing Intra-Party Democracy* (National Democratic Institute for International Affairs: Series: Political Parties and Democracy: Theoretical and Practical Perspectives).

Setälä, M., Schiller, T. (eds) (2009) *Referendums and Representative Democracy: Responsiveness, Accountability and Deliberation* (London: Routledge, ECPR Studies).

Taggart, P. (2000) *Populism* (Buckingham: Open University Press).

Webb, P. (1994) 'Party Organizational Change in Britain: The Iron Law of Centralization?', in R.S. Katz and P. Mair (eds) *How Parties Organize: Change and Adaptation in Party Organizations in Western Democracies* (London: Sage), pp. 109–33.

11
Leadership Elections and Democracy in the British Labour Party

Emmanuelle Avril

The stark contrast between the marathon race to succeed Gordon Brown after he stood down as Labour Party leader in May 2010 and the bypassing of the Electoral College to appoint Brown in 2007, both of which triggered heated debates about the victor's authority and legitimacy as Labour Party leader, provide an interesting entry point into Labour Party leadership elections. Ed Miliband's subsequent struggle to counter his 'Old Labour' image with little legitimacy within his own party, followed by a complete overhaul of leadership election rules on 1 March 2014, also highlight the paramount importance of processes on perceptions of leaders. If we track the series of constitutional changes in the Labour Party since the 1980s, we see that leadership elections have increasingly been underpinned by a double imperative: on the one hand the need to choose a credible party leader and potential Prime Minister, and on the other the need to meet the requirements of internal democracy. This highlights the fundamental tension at work in any organisation between outcome and process and even more so in a political party committed, at least in theory, to the egalitarian principle: the Labour Party was created at the turn of the twentieth century as a coalition of various groups, among which trade unions played a major part, and as a result adopted a federal structure whereby the various stakeholders of the party were represented in the decision-making bodies, especially at the annual conference, the supreme authority in the Party.

The analysis of the selection of party leaders raises a number of interrelated organisational issues: first, the technical aspects, which have to do with the formal structures of the organisation and the distribution of power within it, and, second, the qualitative issues, to do with specific individuals, in particular party leaders, and their personal leadership qualities. As the founding fathers of political science (Moisei

Ostrogorski, Robert Michels and Max Weber) as well as more recent studies of party organisation (by Maurice Duverger, Samuel Eldersveld, Otto Kirchheimer and Angelo Panebianco) have shown, the ways in which leaders are selected reflect the nature of the relationship between the grassroots and the party leadership. In Labour's case this reveals a tension between the idea of a democratic party whose structure ought to reflect its egalitarian stance and that of a party of government which needs to focus on efficiency and winning elections. This second consideration raises issues of leadership, to do with the perception of the personal qualities of a leader, with the party leader projecting the party's image to the voters through the media who thereby assume a pivotal role in constructing political reputations. Tony Blair's performance as leader of the Labour Party and as Prime Minister, and the striking contrast it offers with his successors Gordon Brown and Ed Miliband, comes as a challenge to those who consider that personal leadership only plays a minor role in politics.

Political leadership as a concept is as essential as it is elusive. It is regarded in many disciplines as central to the understanding of political processes and outcomes – as once illustrated by the work of Machiavelli – and is a recurring issue in studies of political parties. Yet, as is pointed out in the introduction to this volume, relatively little emphasis has been placed on the modes of production and exercise of power in political organisations. Colin Hay thus defines the contours of an emerging 'new political science of British Politics', characterised by a 'post-disciplinary outlook' and, among other things, 'a desire to emphasize how institutions and ideas mediate the political process' (Hay, 2003: 184). There is a case, therefore, for analysing the roles played by party leaders in relation to the nature and structure of their organisations, in particular the interaction between modes of selection and leadership styles, a dimension on which there is no consensus.[1] The focus of this chapter is an evaluation, through the example of Labour leadership elections, of the relationship between internal democracy and party image, more specifically the impact of processes on leader image.

From elite ballot to mass participation

Modes of elections

At the outset it must be noted that, owing to the Labour Party's origins and its federal structure, the position of leader is a relatively recent concept in this organisation. Until the late 1970s the Labour leader was the leader of the parliamentary and not of the whole party. In fact, the title of 'Chairman and Leader of the Parliamentary Labour Party' was only created in 1922 and was only constitutionally acknowledged as 'Leader of the Labour Party' in 1979 and given an electoral constituency of the whole party two years later. From 1922 to 1981, the Labour Party leader was elected exclusively by Labour MPs, with the Parliamentary Labour Party (PLP) enjoying a 'semi-detached' situation in the party (Minkin, 1991: 376).

The issue of changing the leadership election rules emerged in the 1970s and first reached the annual conference agenda in 1972, and from then on was the subject of repeated conference resolutions (Russell, 2005: 36; on the left's struggle to gain prominence in the Labour Party see Kogan and Kogan, 1982). Specific options for change failed to be adopted and the status quo was retained until the 1980 annual conference narrowly passed a resolution to 'extend the franchise for the election of the leader' but without any specific mechanism being adopted. The left wing of the party settled for the idea of an Electoral College while the right favoured extending the franchise to the whole membership, an option they saw as more moderate although most in fact favoured the status quo, i.e. a vote by the parliamentary party alone.

On 24 January 1981, the Labour Party held a special conference at Wembley to determine the structure of the Electoral College. After a series of votes eliminated other possible methods the debates led to the unlikely result of an Electoral College in which the trade unions weighed more than the parliamentary party. The leader was to be elected by an Electoral College containing three elements: Affiliated Organisations (mostly trade unions, but also socialist societies) held 40 per cent of the vote; the PLP 30 per cent of the vote, and the Constituency Labour Parties 30 per cent. This was the formula used from 1981 until 1993. In 1993, a rebalancing of the sections was introduced, so that the leader has since been elected by an Electoral College comprising the three elements mentioned above but in equal proportions (each with one-third of the vote) (see Table 11.1). It must be stressed, however, that the three sections could never be thought of as having equal weight considering the fact that the PLP section only comprises a few hundred voters as against hundreds of thousands in the CLP section and several million in the affiliated organisations' section: an MP's vote therefore carries much more weight than that of an individual member, and even more so that of a trade unionist, in influencing the outcome of the contest.[2] In addition, MPs were often able to cast their vote in two or even all three sections, as an MP, a constituency party member and as a trade unionist.

Another change introduced in 1993 was the requirement that constituency parties, trade unions and other affiliated organisations actually ballot their members, and that their share of the vote then be allocated in accordance with the results of that ballot, thereby doing away with the system of delegatory democracy. John Smith, Neil Kinnock's successor, had wanted a much more radical reform in the shape of full individual voting of the membership – referred to as One-Member-One-Vote, or OMOV – but, because of opposition from the trade unions and

Table 11.1   Labour Party contests 1983–2007

1983–92 contest				
October 1983 ballot	*Affiliated*	*Constituencies*	*PLP*	*Total*
Neil Kinnock	29.042	27.452	14.778	71.272
Roy Hattersley	10.878	0.577	7.833	19.288
Eric Heffer	0.046	1.971	4.286	6.303
Peter Shore	0.033	0	3.103	3.137
October 1988 ballot	*Affiliated*	*Constituencies*	*PLP*	*Total*
Neil Kinnock	39.660	24.128	24.842	88.630
Tony Benn	0.340	5.872	5.158	11.370
July 1992 ballot	*Affiliated*	*Constituencies*	*PLP*	*Total*
John Smith	38.518	29.311	23.187	91.016
Bryan Gould	1.482	0.689	6.813	8.984

The figures represent the percentage of the total vote scored in each section

1994 contest (new structure)				
July 1994 ballot	*Affiliated*	*Constituencies*	*PLP*	*Total*
Tony Blair	52.3	58.2	60.5	57.0
John Prescott	28.4	24.4	19.6	24.1
Margaret Beckett	19.3	17.4	19.9	18.9

2007 contest
July 2007
Gordon Brown   Elected unopposed

The figures represent the percentage of the vote in each section of the College

Note: Adapted from House of Commons note on Leadership elections.[3]

lukewarm support from the CLPs, he had to settle for the rebalancing of the sections and the reform of the mode of voting in the constituencies and trade union sections. In the new system, which was used for the election of Tony Blair in 1994, trade unions were required to ballot those of their members eligible to vote (those paying the political levy in addition to their union membership fee). The system of delegatory democracy was also discarded within the CLP section so that members of the party were sent individual postal ballot papers which were then counted nationally, in a system of direct democracy.

The 2010 contest was triggered by Gordon Brown's resignation as Prime Minister and Labour Party leader on 11 May when it became clear that the Labour Party would not form a coalition government with the Liberal Democrats following the 'hung' result of the general election of 6 May. The 12.5 per cent nomination rule meant that leadership contenders had to be backed by 33 MPs to be eligible to enter the contest. Nominations opened on 24 May and closed at 12.30 on 9 June. The voting itself took place between 16 August and 22 September with the winner being announced on the first day of the party's conference in Manchester on 25 September. Deputy Leader Harriet Harman acted as leader during that period. The surprise was created by Ed Miliband who decided to challenge his brother, the favourite and the first to declare his intention to stand on 12 May. With five candidates among whom left-winger Diane Abbott (nominated by senior figures of the party including fellow contestant David Miliband to save the party from the embarrassing spectacle of an entirely white and male contest, John McDonnell pulling out on the morning of 9 June in the hope his 16 nominations would back her) and the biblical duel between the Miliband brothers, the long-drawn contest managed to grip the imagination of commentators. There were endless calculations about the effect the alternative voting system would have on the results and early on some were already predicting that second and third preferences might favour the younger Miliband, who won on the fourth round by a razor-thin margin with 50.65 per cent of the vote while his brother secured 49.35 per cent (see Table 11.2).

The contentious nature of Ed Miliband's election as leader in 2010 (Jobson and Wikham-Jones, 2011, consider that the leadership contest did not meet the criteria of a 'free and fair' election), as well as trends of falling participation and declining membership affecting all parties, recently prompted the party leadership to conduct an internal review, led by Ray Collins, on procedures, in a bid to reconnect the party with turned off voters. The recommendations, which were approved by a

Table 11.2 Labour Party 2010 contest

Summary of voting by round				

Section 1 – PLP; Section 2 – Constituencies; Section 3 – Affiliates

Round by round	Round 1	Round 2	Round 3	Round 4
ABBOTT, Diane	7.42	0	0	0
BALLS, Ed	11.79	13.23	16.02	0
BURNHAM, Andy	8.68	10.41	0	0
MILIBAND, David	37.78	38.89	42.72	49.35
MILIBAND, Ed	34.33	37.47	41.26	50.65

First Preferences	Section 1%	Section 2%	Section 3%	Total
ABBOTT, Diane	0.877	2.447	4.093	7.42
BALLS, Ed	5.013	3.371	3.411	11.79
BURNHAM, Andy	3.008	2.849	2.825	8.68
MILIBAND, David	13.910	14.688	9.182	37.78
MILIBAND, Ed	10.526	9.978	13.821	34.33
Total	33.333	33.333	33.333	100

2nd Round	%	%	%	Total %
ABBOTT, Diane	0	0	0	0
BALLS, Ed	5.177	3.829	4.224	13.23
BURNHAM, Andy	3.030	3.298	4.078	10.41
MILIBAND, David	14.015	15.076	9.799	38.89
MILIBAND, Ed	11.111	11.130	15.231	37.47
Total	33.333	33.333	33.333	100

3rd Round	%	%	%	Total %
ABBOTT, Diane	0	0	0	0
BALLS, Ed	5.429	4.823	5.766	16.02
BURNHAM, Andy	0	0	0	0
MILIBAND, David	15.783	16.076	10.861	42.72
MILIBAND, Ed	12.121	12.434	16.706	41.26
Total	33.333	33.333	33.333	100

4th Round	%	%	%	Total %
ABBOTT, Diane	0	0	0	0
BALLS, Ed	0	0	0	0
BURNHAM, Andy	0	0	0	0
MILIBAND, David	17.812	18.135	13.400	49.35
MILIBAND, Ed	15.522	15.198	19.934	50.65
Total	33.333	33.333	33.333	100

Note: Adapted from the Labour Party website.[4]

wide majority of delegates (86 per cent) at a special conference held on 1 March 2014 in the Excel Centre in London's Docklands, include the abandonment of the Electoral College and the adoption in its place of full OMOV for leadership elections (Collins, 2014: 8). The reform thus puts an end to multiple voting in leadership elections with a view to fully democratising the process. The reforms present the paradox of 'Red Ed' completing the task which John Smith had started a little over two decades earlier. In his speech at the special conference, Ed Miliband stated that the rule changes represented 'the biggest transfer of power in the history of our party to our members and supporters'. The reform agenda was couched by its advocates as the chance to rebuild Labour as a mass party at a time when all main political parties are losing members.

Overall, therefore, the series of reforms to the Labour leader's mode of election have established a general pattern of increased membership influence and greater integration of the parliamentary party into the party's overall formal structure. This is in keeping with a general trend among Western political parties for which all-member ballots have become the norm (Quinn, 2012). In fact Labour was the only one of the three main British parties which did not give the final say to individual party members. More importantly, the debate over the method of balloting and the push for the adoption of an individual structure in place of the collective one goes to the heart of Labour's origins, since the party was first set up as an 'indirect' party (Punnett, 2006). Disputes about the composition of the Electoral College illustrated the power struggles between the different constituencies of the party and reflected the federal origins and structure. Despite claims to the contrary in the Collins report, which insists upon the fact Labour is to remain a federal party, the promotion of OMOV clearly goes against the original commitment to collective affiliation (Minkin, 2014: 776). This raises a number of issues.

Issues of internal democracy

In general terms, the debate on leadership election rules opposes those for whom internal democracy is a fundamental requirement and those according to whom the practical effects of internally democratic procedures may have a detrimental effect on the organisation. Even though, since the late twentieth century, the intra-party democracy ideal has come to dominate all the main British political parties, as illustrated by the 1998 Conservative *Fresh Future* reforms, the ideological basis for adopting internally democratic procedures is still a source of division.

Advocates of intra-party democracy may take the pragmatic view that internal democracy is conducive to the selection of more able leaders and therefore to election victory, or take a more principled stance according to which a party using internally democratic procedures will 'strengthen democratic culture generally', making intra-party democracy desirable *per se* (Scarrow, 2005: 9). The debate over leadership election rules saw a clash between two competing views of democracy, since OMOV could be seen either as a logical extension of democracy or as a mode of election which would risk enfranchising 'armchair members' (i.e. inactive members).

As stated above, the move to adopt an Electoral College for the election of the leader was part of a train of reforms in the years 1979–81 initiated by the party's left.[5] Tony Benn and the members of the Campaign for Labour Party Democracy were deeply resentful of the way in which the Labour governments of 1974–79 had handled the economy, which it saw as having betrayed Labour's core supporters. They wanted to bring the PLP under control as well as revive grassroots democracy.[6] The idea behind the constitutional change was to deprive the parliamentary party of the exclusive right to choose the party leader and to give a greater say to the extra parliamentary party, in particular the party's grassroots. The overall effect of the reforms adopted at the Wembley conference was a redistribution of power towards activists and trade unions, which triggered the defection of the group of MPs who went on to form the Social Democratic Party. The modernisers' view of these events construes them as responsible for Labour's 18 wilderness years (although it must be noted that left-winger Michael Foot had won the leadership in 1980 under the old system).

With the introduction of OMOV, most decisions were now to be taken by the membership at large through individual postal or telephone voting rather than by delegates after debate in meetings among the more active members. The overall strategy, it would seem, was to 'empower' ordinary members more likely to endorse the leadership's policies (Webb, 2000: 208) in an attempt to create 'a new source of inactivist (hence 'moderate') support for the leadership in the shape of a wider membership who could be directly consulted through postal votes' (Panitch and Leys, 1997: 224). Such dilution of the constituency parties' power was based on the premise that activists held radical views and would be hostile to modernising reforms (this view of party activists as dangerous radicals is challenged in Avril, 2007 as well as Seyd and Whiteley, 1992). The idea being that the 'disaggregated members' would be unlikely to seriously challenge the leadership (Mair, 1994: 16).[7]

Therefore the tremendous widening of the franchise and the extension of new democratic rights to individual members under New Labour need to be understood in the context of the modernising reforms and set against the overall centralisation of power in the party (Avril, 2013).

It then becomes clear that the intention in extending the franchise was not to risk losing control of the process but to bypass both the activists and the parliamentary party. In fact, some have said that if it had still been the prerogative of Labour MPs to choose their own leader 'it is by no means certain that in 1994 they would have elected Tony Blair' (McSmith, 1997: 293). The paradox of the Electoral College which elected Tony Blair is that it adopted a formula which was apparently closer than any other to a democratic process, in which the decision was no longer the preserve of the parliamentary party, giving a say to ordinary members, but in which the membership's vote in the College was more akin to a referendum than to collective decision-making as the voting would be influenced not by discussion with fellow party members at local meetings, but by the national debate played out in the media.

Ironically therefore, although the move to adopt the Electoral College was initially seen as a way to democratise the party and bring the leadership under control, the new procedures have in fact broadened the authority of the leader. The change in the method of selecting the Labour Party leader, from an elite parliamentary ballot to a mass participatory Electoral College had been intended by the left to enhance the accountability of the incumbent party leader to the wider Labour movement but has had in fact the exact reverse effect of increasing the leader's autonomy, while the move to adopt OMOV has in reality shifted power back to the MPs, mainly because nomination rules prevent the grassroots from instigating a contest (as in the Conservative Party, the PLP retains the sole right to nominate candidates (Quinn, 2004)). Therefore the strategy of the left has clearly failed.

In this respect the March 2014 reforms can be interpreted as a continuation of this trend. Under the new rules, even if OMOV guarantees that double voting is now impossible, MPs retain their power to shortlist candidates. The Collins report states that 'nominations for the post of leader or deputy leader of the party must, in all circumstances, be supported by 15 per cent of the Commons members of the PLP to be valid' (Collins, 2014: 9). This confirms the evolution of the party towards the plebiscitary party model, where decision-making processes institute a direct relationship between the leadership and grassroots members in a more participatory fashion. The new 'registered supporters', a category of individuals who are not already party members or members of an affiliated organisation, but may take part in elections by registering with the party as a supporter, provided they 'declare their support for Labour values, provide the party with personal contact details, be on the electoral roll and pay the party a fee' (Collins, 2014: 8), is trumpeted as a way to further empower the party grassroots. However the changes need to be understood in the context of the party's relationship with the unions and the impact of this relationship in the media and public opinion.

The Party, the unions and the media

Reforming the Trade Union Link

The role of the trade unions in Labour Party decision-making processes is rooted in the Labour Party's history, which started its life in 1900 as the Labour Representation Committee. The Trade Union Link became an issue in the 1960s and 1970s, when unions came to be portrayed in the media as 'the enemy within' following several waves of strikes. Thus when the Electoral College was first adopted, this was greeted very negatively in the press and almost universally interpreted as a victory for the trade unions. Opponents stressed that power would now be wielded by a handful of unaccountable union barons.

Indeed, under the first Electoral College system, from 1981 to 1993, it was often the case that both the trade unions and constituency parties paid little attention to the views of their members as to the choice of party leader. Executive committees would decide whom they wished to support and then throw their entire voting power behind their chosen candidate. Although it must be remembered that the move to adopt the Electoral College meant that the trade unions became involved in elections that had been hitherto the prerogative of the parliamentary party and that they came to use procedures which had not been intended for such functions (Minkin, 1991: 334), there seemed to be a strong argument for changing a system in which the decision-making process was controlled by an unrepresentative minority.

The modernisation of the Labour Party was initiated by Neil Kinnock and his team, in an attempt to reverse the growing influence of trade unions and constituency parties on policy and candidate selection and therefore shift power back to the leadership. Organisational reform was given a new boost following the 1992 election defeat which was interpreted by the modernisers as a result of perceived excessive union influence, especially because the union block vote allowed union leaders to control decision-making both at conference (where they held 90 per cent of the vote) and in leadership elections (where they held 40 per cent of the vote). The 1992 leadership contest following Neil Kinnock's resignation confirmed this public view when it appeared that Bill Morris, General Secretary of the T&GWU, and John Edmonds, General Secretary of the GMB, held the key in the choice for Labour's new leader. The Trade Union Link[8] became the central issue in the media coverage of John Smith's election. The fact that his overwhelming victory (90.9 per cent against Bryan Gould's 9.1 per cent) was exaggerated by the block vote (a practice against which he had spoken frequently) meant that reform of the Electoral College had become a priority for a party that had come to think of itself as unelectable. The matter of the Electoral College had become part and parcel of a complete overhaul of the age-old Trade Union Link (Webb, 1994). In the end, the change adopted in 1993 was the most moderate option. The 1993 procedural change and the adoption of OMOV (the unions' vote share at conference was also reduced to 50 per cent) was therefore not the watershed it has come to be described as in New Labour mythology (Wickham-Jones, 2014), but more the closing of a long-running dispute.

The manner of Ed Miliband's victory over his brother David in 2010 rekindled the debate about the trade unions determining the results, with one shadow cabinet member describing the way in which the unions had won it for the younger Miliband as a Gothic horror (Wintour, 2010). The failure of Ed Miliband to secure a majority of the votes in both the parliamentary and constituencies sections seemed to cast doubt on his legitimacy as the leader of a party whose membership and parliamentary party did not choose him as their first choice, a fact that has allowed the Conservatives and the Conservative supporting press to wield the 'Red Ed' moniker at the new leader and opponents within the party to warn against a return to Labour's darkest hour. Even though the role of the trade unions in ensuring Ed Miliband's victory has been somewhat exaggerated by his political and media opponents (for a full discussion of the operation of the Electoral College in this election see Pemberton and Wickham-Jones, 2012), since Ed Miliband's victory resulted just as much from a very efficient second preferences strategy (Dorey and Denham, 2011), with Ed Balls's second preferences, in particular, proving to be crucial in the final round, and was therefore an effect of the alternative vote system, arguments stressing the historical origin of the link and the stabilising effect of the unions remain largely immaterial in the face of Ed Miliband's perceived illegitimacy.

This problem was compounded by the 2013 scandal in Falkirk, Scotland, where union activists from UNITE were accused of packing the local party with new members in an attempt to control the selection process for the parliamentary candidate ahead of the next election, with some members being apparently unaware that they were supposed to have joined the party. After the party headquarters called in the police to investigate, Ed Miliband declared that he would take action and clean up the Trade Union Link. The new rules adopted on 1 March 2014, beyond the introduction of the OMOV system for leadership elections, bring an end to the automatic affiliation of union members, a move which is bound to have a massive impact on the historic link between Labour and the unions, although the Collins report clearly states that the federal structure of the party is left untouched (the unions continue to have 'a collective constitutional role inside party structures, but on a more transparent basis' (Collins, 2014: 7)).

Even though the reforms are expected to eventually lead to cuts in affiliation funding, the unions have not wanted to be seen to be threatening Labour's finances a year before the general election. UNITE general secretary McCluskey declared that he welcomed the move for trade unionists to have a more direct affiliation with Labour, explaining that it was part of UNITE's political strategy to get more of their members engaged with Labour at grassroots level. It must be stressed that new members will be asked immediately if they want to affiliate, but that there will be a five-year period for consultation with existing union members. Crucially, the change has received very positive press coverage. Even if the delivery of the reform package is likely to be very different from the idealistic vision outlined at the March 2014 special conference, the change was hailed in the media as Miliband's 'Clause IV' moment and a 'historic' victory.

Projecting the right image

Because leadership elections have become PR battles which take place in full view of the public, the point of extending the franchise was not just a technical issue but also one of image. The fact that this internal decision – but one of national magnitude – attracts so much media attention made it crucial to increase the leader's legitimacy at the time when there was greater focus on him/her. What was at stake was the need to project the image of a democratic party, a party no longer dominated by the unions (on the impact of media scrutiny on internal debates see for example Faucher-King and Treille, 2003).

Nevertheless, even though the modernisers' political victory did not in fact mean that Labour could no longer be influenced by the union leaders, especially as a series of amalgamations have concentrated trade union power into fewer hands (Kettle, 2009),[9] it removed – for a time – the stigma of seeming to be in thrall to the unions. The desired effect seemed to have been achieved when the BBC described the 1994 ballot, the first time the party's leadership was decided by a secret ballot of all four million Labour Party members and union levy payers, without block voting, as 'the most democratic process ever used by a British political party' (BBC, 2005). Similarly today, Ed Miliband's allies make the case for reform of the link with the unions on grounds of the perceived level of internal democracy: 'At heart, this isn't primarily an argument about Labour's link with the trade unions; it is primarily about Labour's link with democracy, and whether our internal governance is democratic' (King, 2013).

At a first level, however, the OMOV rule meant that millions of trade union and ordinary members had to be contacted and this gave the media an unprecedented role as people who were unfamiliar with the party were getting their impressions from the media coverage. This has led commentators to state that, in effect, in 1994 'the media took the place filled by the union barons' in immediately identifying a frontrunner (Alderman and Carter, 1995: 452), tipping Tony Blair as the next leader in waiting. Overall, Tony Blair made 482 appearances in national newspaper reports during the weeks prior to the official campaign, dwarfing Gordon Brown's 182 (Franklin and Larsen, 1994). At a second level, as explained earlier, party leaders used to be elected by delegates at a special conference. With the adoption of OMOV the voting was now organised by individual postal or telephone voting (a strategy which was later extended to elections to the National Executive Committee). In such set-up, what influences the voters the most are no longer the views of their fellow party members, but whatever literature is sent to their homes and, even more importantly, the media coverage of candidates, both of which are heavily controlled by the leadership (Wring, 2005: 133). With the adoption of a full OMOV system, the same will apply to future leadership elections, with contests likely to be played out in the media on an even larger scale. The paradox of OMOV and the adoption of more open, transparent, and seemingly more democratic processes is that the public profile of candidates is now of paramount importance, illustrating the growing influence of celebrity status in internal party elections.

Even though differences of opinion among scholars reflect the problems faced in identifying what should count as leadership effects,[10] a change in leadership can also have a crucial impact upon the popularity of a political party. Despite Peter Mandelson's claim that 'New Labour is not about faces, it is about policies', nobody would question the fact that Tony Blair was a major political asset for the Labour Party (Evans and Andersen, 2005)[11] particularly in 1997 and 2001, nor that Gordon Brown's perceived lack of leadership qualities have adversely affected his party once his image had been damaged by the prevarications over the calling of a general election in the autumn of 2007. More to the point here, political leadership also affects the party internally. The significant rise in membership experienced by Labour in the years following the election of Blair as party leader in 1994 illustrates the importance of his personal leadership qualities in transforming the party. Although there is no consensus among academics about the impact of leader evaluation on voters' choice, appraisals of leaders' personal qualities undeniably matter, and even if the governance of a political party can never be explained by personality or charisma alone, individual leaders 'inhabit' the formal structures and procedures in ways which may contribute to shaping them.

Harold Lasswell's pioneering work on political psychology established the increased importance of personality (Lasswell, 1948), a trend confirmed by the emergence of modern political communication. The drastic changes in British society over the past 50 years make it impossible to ignore the impact of personality, as filtered through the lens of the media.[12] Studies conducted by David Butler and Donald Stokes in the 1970s and then by Ivor Crewe in the 1980s indicated that the rise of television exposure turned party leaders into highly visible figures. The growing focus on the leader and concomitant centralisation of power within the party result from the rise of the media's influence, a trait Pippa Norris has called the 'modern' campaign, defined as 'coordinated national and regional strategies with communications designed by specialists skilled in advertising, marketing, and polling' (Norris, 2002: 138). There is a consensus among most political analysts that, with the growth of media coverage from the postwar years onwards, political leadership now assumes a far greater importance in accounting for the electoral fortunes of political parties.

The growing emphasis on leaders rather than parties is clear even in a parliamentary system like Britain's where it is the party which is elected, not the Prime Minister. A view has developed that British general election campaigns have become presidential, with leader appraisal becoming the key component of election success.[13] Political parties therefore market their leaders in a way designed to appeal to the electorate (Denver, 1997; Foley, 2002), which raises the question of what constitutes 'personality' in such contexts.[14] Tony Blair's poll ratings would indeed seem to show a rise in the importance of perceptions of leadership (Lees-Marshment, 2001: 184). His main asset was to cut a media-friendly figure, so much so that he might have been 'a product of computer-aided design' (King, 1998: 201). Market intelligence gathered by the Labour Party modernisers showed that the voters wanted strong leadership and a sense of direction. Therefore Tony Blair, both by virtue of his politics and his personal qualities – he was seen as young, modern and purposeful – was a key element in designing New Labour. Gordon Brown, in contrast, was marketed as a 'safe pair of hands', who shared Blair's politics but who was soon seen as lacking in leadership qualities. David Denver quotes a Mori poll showing that 33 per cent of the voters agreed that Blair has 'a lot of personality' and the same proportion that he was a 'capable' leader (as opposed to 5 per cent and 19 per cent for John Major). Blair's personality provided an ideal combination which helped him come across to the public magically as likeable and competent (Denver, 1998: 42). He displayed at once a proficiency in political communication, political skills, policy vision, and emotional intelligence. As Andy McSmith puts it, 'all the tasks that a modern politician is required to do, Blair does well' (McSmith, 1997: 293).

With a leader such as Tony Blair, who put forward an 'instinctive' view of leadership as 'the only one worth having' (Blair, 2003), it is not surprising that the structures should have evolved towards a more populist, plebiscitary nature. Members were required to place their trust in a leader who asserted his ability to deliver an election victory. The trade-off may have been a decrease in the 'loyalty' to leaders traditionally shown in the Labour Party (Drucker, 1979),[15] both because new members (who joined in the mid- and late 1990s) did not fully espouse the Labour Party culture and were quick to move on, and because Tony Blair never pretended to be steeped in such a culture in the first place. The contract with more traditional members was on efficiency terms: a pragmatic acceptance of a non-Labour figure at the head of the party in exchange for electoral success. At the time of writing, hindsight is still insufficient to fully grasp the impact of Ed Miliband's style of leadership, a style which he readily admits is not 'charismatic'. Even though there is room for saying that a 'non-celebrity' leader is more suited to a period of austerity, with just over a year to go before the next general election, there is still a feeling that he has yet to grow into his role and polls show him trailing behind the other main party leaders in the leadership traits, including among Labour Party supporters. The March 2014 reform package is an attempt by Miliband to take a stand and imprint his mark on his party. Interestingly, however, his dismal personal ratings do not seem to badly affect the party's image.[16]

However striking the differences in the personal qualities of recent Labour leaders, the significance of personality must therefore not be overstated. There is a case for saying that the particular traits and behaviour displayed by individual leaders do not actually overweigh the substance of politics. In a study of Labour members' image of party leaders, Patrick Seyd and Paul Whiteley were surprised to discover that differences in perception between Neil Kinnock and Tony Blair (Blair was seen as a strong leader but slightly less likeable and caring than Kinnock) were in fact very slight (Seyd and Whiteley, 2002: 144). It may therefore be argued that it was the mode of election which really served to emphasise the differences between Brown and Blair where there was an obvious continuity of policy. It was mostly his mode of appointment which called Brown's authority into question. In the same way, Ed Miliband's legitimacy as leader was compromised from the start by his failure to get a majority of votes in the parliamentary and constituencies sections. We might never know how his brother David would have performed in his place. In such a close-run race, a lot of effort was made to stress the discrepancy between the brothers although commentators were often at pains to clearly differentiate them. Despite a number of obvious differences in the two brothers' personalities, they shared more similarities than differences, so that the focus on the 'soap opera' of this very public fraternal rift paradoxically served to highlight the primacy of content over packaging.

Conclusion

This chapter has shown that organisational structure is thus just as important as personality in understanding the logic of leadership, since the way in which tasks and benefits are distributed within a party may account for the emergence of a particular type of leadership. The developments following Brown's succession vindicated those who had warned that a leadership coronation which sought to bypass the Electoral College would damage the party. To have deprived the members of a choice of party leader was a risky strategy, as Tony Blair's strength as a leader had been largely derived from the legitimacy conferred on him by his mode of election. This shows that internal democracy is not a superfluous time-wasting device; involvement in a democratic choice binds voters to the result. Brown's dismal support among members[17] and the incessant talk of plotting against him was the price to pay for disregarding the very basic rule. In a way, the fact that the finger could once more be pointed at the unions for the election of Ed Miliband – in what was the first competitive leadership election since 1994 – can ironically be interpreted as a return to a healthier state of affairs.

But what was really distinctive about the 2010 leadership election was that on this occasion, contrary to all previous elections where the favourite had always won the contest,[18] both the selection rules and the leadership campaign itself seem to have had a significant effect on the outcome (Dorey and Denham, 2011). Even if the victory of 'Red Ed' over his more moderate brother could fit into the narrative of the adoption of the Electoral College as a victory of the left, overall the Electoral College has seemed to produce the opposite effects from those sought by its early supporters: not strengthening democracy inside the party but rather leading to the election of the two most autocratic leaders in Labour Party history (Heppell, 2010: 76–8, 2012). This can in part be attributed to the unintended effects of procedural reforms, as popularised by Robert K. Merton in the 1930s, just as the Conservatives first experienced after reforming their leadership election procedures, with the election of a series of lack lustre leaders.[19] Although one would expect all-member ballots to be more likely to lead to the election of more radical leaders, Stark (1996) and Quinn (2012) have argued that, on the contrary, members make their choice using the same criteria of party unity and electoral appeal as parliamentary elites.[20] Therefore the democratisation of leadership election rules may not have an identifiable impact on the type of leader who will emerge. Nevertheless a future leadership election under the newly adopted OMOV system is likely to further tip the balance towards a media personality contest, making the outcome even more unpredictable.

Notes

1 For example Leonard Stark concludes his analysis of party leadership contests on the idea that leadership selection rules rarely affect who stands for party leadership or who wins the contests (Stark, 1996).
2 Calculations show that in the 2010 contest the vote of one MP was worth the votes of nearly 608 party members and 12,915 affiliated members ('How Much is your Labour Leadership vote worth?', *New Statesman*. Available

at http://www.newstatesman.com/blogs/the-staggers/2010/08/vote-worth-labour-mps-members [accessed 02/07/2014].

3 Richard Kelly, Mary Durkin and Paul Lester (2010). House of Commons note on Leadership Elections, *Labour Party, Standard Note: SN/PC/3938*.

4 See http://www2.labour.org.uk/votes-by-round [accessed 02/07/2014].

5 The left managed to push through conference the mandatory reselection of MPs (to strengthen the link between the party in office and the party on ground); the adoption of the Electoral College for leadership elections (this would make it easier to 'hold the leader to account'); the principle that the election manifesto would be decided by the NEC only (to stop the PLP watering-down policies – but this reform was defeated).

6 'CLPD was formed in 1973 by a group of rank-and-file activists, with support from about ten Labour MPs. The main motivation for the Campaign was the record of the Labour governments in the sixties and the way that Annual Conference decisions were continually ignored on key domestic and international issues. CLPD's first demand was therefore for mandatory reselection of MPs so that they would be under pressure to carry out Conference policies. CLPD also sought to make the Leader accountable through election by an Electoral college involving MPs, CLPs and TUs. Hitherto Labour leaders were elected by MPs alone.' From CLPD website: http://home.freeuk.net/clpd/history.htm [accessed 02/07/2014].

7 Even though the relative success of the Grassroots Alliance shows an attempt to aggregate the members and counteract the effect of the reform. The Grassroots Alliance, created in 1998, presents itself as 'a body of democratic socialist groups and newspapers across the centre and left of the Labour Party, has promoted candidates who stand up for the rights of ordinary members'. http://www.clga.org.uk/ [accessed 02/07/2014].

8 The Trade Union Link refers to the formal link between trade unions and the Labour Party. The current relationship between trade unions and the Labour Party is rooted in the history of the labour movement. It was the actions of the trade unions, organising to ensure a political voice for working people in Parliament, which led to the formation of the Labour Party. (Adapted from the Unite website: http://www.unitetheunion.com.)

9 *Guardian* columnist Martin Kettle stresses that the amalgamations give 'today's five big barons unique sway over the choice of leader.' He goes on to emphasize that since a mere 8% of union members voted in the 2007 deputy leadership contest, 'historically small numbers can shape the outcome.'

10 In particular the necessary separation of partisanship from leader appraisal if one is to identify their distinct impact (Bartle and Crewe, 2002). For an evaluation of perceptions of leaders on electoral outcome, see also Mughan, 2000; Bean and Mughan, 1989: Crewe and King, 1999; Curtice and Holmberg, 2005. In this latest study, Curtice and Holmberg come to the conclusion that the impact of leaders is 'variable' and 'unpredictable'.

11 Geoffrey Evans and Robert Andersen's analysis (2005) show that perceptions of Blair had far stronger effects on voting for Labour than perceptions of either of the two other leaders in 2005.

12 For an up-to-date comparative analysis of changes in the social structure, the diminished role played by class and religious affiliation, and the growing significance of personality in political leadership see Blondel and Thiebault, 2009.

13 David Denver concludes on the impact of party leaders on electoral outcome that 'party leaders affect voting behaviour and hence election results only when there is a large difference in how they are regarded by the voters'. Therefore, 'to avoid significant electoral damage all that parties have to do is select a leader who is not patently unpopular or perceived to be lacking in competence' (Denver, 1989: 93). However, in a more recent study, Geoffrey Evans and Robert Andersen test the importance of leader appraisals on voting in the 2005 British election. Their main conclusion is that 'leader effects are far more important than a wide range of issues, social background and even, though to a far lesser degree, party identification' (Evans and Andersen, 2005: 836).

14 Anthony King sums up the four attributes which can be said to define a political leader's personality and personal characteristics: physical appearance, native intelligence, character or temperament, and political style (King, 2002: 8).

15 See Henry Drucker's famous exposition of the Labour Party's 'ethos' (1979).

16 According to an Ipsos MORI poll published in September 2013, Ed Miliband had negative ratings even among Labour supporters (52% were dissatisfied with his performance), his lowest rating among his own supporters since he became leader, although the party enjoyed a three point lead over the Conservatives in terms of voting intentions.

17 On 7 May 2008, a Populus poll for *The Times* showed a dramatic collapse of confidence in Gordon Brown's leadership with 55% of Labour voters saying they wanted Gordon Brown to resign.

18 From Wilson in 1963 to Blair in 1994, neither the selection rules in operation at the time, nor the campaigns undertaken by the candidates and their supporters, significantly affected, let alone changed, the result (Stark, 1996).

19 On the counter-productive consequences of party management under Blair see in particular Avril (2007) and Minkin (2014).

20 Quinn (2012) draws on Stark (1996) to define the three criteria which a choice of leader is based on: acceptability, electability and competence.

Works cited

Alderman, K., Carter, N. (1995) 'The Labour Leadership and Deputy Leadership Elections of 1994', *Parliamentary Affairs*, Vol. 48, n° 3, 438–55.

Avril, E. (2007) *Du Labour au New Labour: Le changement vu de l'intérieur* (Villeneuve d'Ascq: Presses Universitaires du Septentrion).

Avril, E. (2013) 'The Evolution of Decision-Making in the British Labour Party: From Grassroots to Netroots ?'. In Avril, E., Zumello, C. (eds) *New Technologies, Organizational Change and Governance* (Basingstoke: Palgrave Macmillan), pp. 102–16.

Bartle, J., Crewe, I. (2002) 'The impact of party leaders in Britain: Strong assumptions, weak evidence'. In King, A. (ed.) *Leaders' Personalities and the Outcomes of Democratic Elections* (Oxford: Oxford University Press).

BBC News (2005, 21 July) 'On This Day 1950–2005: 21 July 1994: Labour Chooses Blair'. Retrieved from http://news.bbc.co.uk/onthisday/hi/dates/stories/july/21/newsid_2515000/2515825.stm [accessed 02/07/2014].

Bean, C., Mughan, A. (1989) 'Leadership Effects in Parliamentary Elections in Australia and Britain', *American Political Science Review*, 83, 1165–79.

Blair, T. (2003, 30 September) Speech to the Labour Party Annual Conference.

Blondel, J., Thiebault, J.-L. (eds) (2009) *Political Leadership, Parties and Citizens: The Personalisation of Leadership* (London: Routledge).

Collins, R. (2014) *Building A One Nation Labour Party. The Collins Review into Labour Party* Reform (London: The Labour Party).

Crewe, I., King, A. (1999) 'Did Major win? Did Kinnock lose? Leadership effects in the 1992 election'. In Heath, A., Jowell, R., Curtice, J., Taylor, B. (eds) *Labour's Last Chance? The 1992 Election and Beyond* (Aldershot: Dartmouth).

Curtice, J., Holmberg, S. (2005) 'Party Leaders and Party Choice'. In Thomassen, J. (ed.) *The European Voter* (Oxford University Press), pp. 235–51.

Denver, D. (1989) *Elections and Voting Behaviour in Britain* (Deddington: Philip Allan).

Denver, D. (1997) 'Elections and Voting Behaviour'. In Robins, L.J., Jones, B. (eds) *Half a Century of British Politics* (Manchester: Manchester University Press), pp.128–43.

Denver, D. (1998) 'The Government that Could Do No Right'. In King, A. (ed.) *New Labour Triumphs: Labour At the Polls* (London: Chatham House).

Dorey, P., Denham, A. (2011) 'O brother where art thou?' The Labour Leadership of 2010, *British Politics*, Vol. 6, n°3, 286–316.

Drucker, H.M. (1979) *Doctrine and Ethos in the Labour Party* (London; Boston: Allen & Unwin).

Evans, G., Andersen, R. (2005) 'The Impact of Party Leaders: How Blair Lost Labour Votes', *Parliamentary Affairs*, Vol. 58, n° 4, 818–36.

Faucher-King, F., Treille, E. (2003) 'Managing Intra-party Democracy: Comparing the French Socialist and British Labour Party Conferences', *French Politics*, Vol. 1, n° 1, 61–82.

Foley, M. (2002) *John Major, Tony Blair and the Conflict of Leadership: Collision Course* (Manchester: Manchester University Press).

Franklin, B., Larsen, G. (1994) 'Kingmaking in the Labour Leadership Contest', *British Journalism Review*, Vol. 5, n° 4, 63–70.

Hay, C. (2003) 'How to Study the Labour Party? Contextual, Analytical and Theoretical Issues.' In Callaghan, J., Fielding, S., Ludlam, S. (eds) *Interpreting the Labour Party, Approaches to Labour Politics and History* (Manchester: Manchester University Press), pp. 182–94.

Heppell, T. (2010) 'Labour Leadership Elections from Wilson to Brown: Ideological Factions and Succession Planning Strategies', *Representation*, Vol. 46, n° 1, 69–79.

Heppell, T. (2012) *Choosing the Labour Leader. Labour Party Leadership Elections from Wilson to Brown* (London: Tauris Academic Studies).

Jobson, R., Wickham-Jones, M. (2011). 'Reinventing the block vote? Trade unions and the 2010 Labour party leadership election', *British Politics*, 6, 317–44.

Kettle, M. (2009, 7 May). 'A Leader Picked by Unions is an Explosive Trap for Labour', *The Guardian*. Retrieved from http://www.theguardian.com/commentis free/2009/may/07/tradeunions-labour [accessed 02/07/2014].

King, A. (1998). 'Why Labour Won – At Last'. In King, A. (ed.), *New Labour Triumphs: Labour At the Polls* (London: Chatham House).

King, A. (2002) *Leaders' Personalities and the Outcome of Democratic Elections* (Oxford: Oxford University Press).

King, O. (2013, 24 July) 'Ed Miliband's trade union reforms are essential to building a fairer society', *New Statesman*. Retrieved from http://www.newstatesman. com/staggers/2013/07/ed-milibands-trade-union-reforms-are-essential-to-building-fairer-society [accessed 02/07/2014].

Kogan, D., Kogan, M. (1982) *The Battle for the Labour Party* (London: Kogan Page).

Lasswell, H.D. (1948) *Power and Personality* (New York: W.W. Norton & Co).

Lees-Marshment, J. (2001). *Political Parties and British Political Parties: The Party's Just Begun* (Manchester: Manchester University Press).

Mair, P. (1994) 'Party Organizations: from Civil Society to State'. In Katz, R., Mair, P. (eds) *How Parties Organize: Change and Adaptation in Party Organizations in Western Democracies* (London: Sage).

McSmith, A. (1997) *Faces of Labour: the Inside Story* (London: Verso).

Minkin, L. (1991) *The Contentious Alliance: Trade Unions and the Labour Party* (Edinburgh: Edinburgh University Press).

Minkin, L. (2014) *The Blair Supremacy. A Study in the Politics of Labour's Party Management* (Manchester: Manchester University Press).

Mughan, A. (2000) *Media and the Presidentialization of Parliamentary Elections* (Basingstoke: Palgrave).

Norris, P. (2002) 'Campaign Communication'. In Leduc, L., Niemi, R.G. (eds) *Comparing Democracies 2: New Challenges in the Study of Elections and Voting* (London: Sage).

Panitch, L., Leys, C. (1997) *The End of Parliamentary Socialism* (London: Verso).

Pemberton, H., Wickham-Jones, M. (2012) 'Brothers all? The Operation of the Electoral College in the 2010 Labour Leadership Contest', *Parliamentary Affairs*, 66, 708–31.

Punnett M. (2006) 'Selecting the Party Leader in Britain: A Limited Participatory Revolution', *European Journal of Political Research*, Vol. 24, n° 3, 257–76.

Quinn, T. (2004) 'Electing the Leader: The British Labour Party's Electoral College', *British Journal of Politics and International Relations*, Vol. 6, n° 3, 333–52.

Quinn, T. (2012) *Electing and Ejecting Party Leaders in Britain* (Basingstoke: Palgrave Macmillan).

Russell, M. (2005) *Building New Labour: The Politics of Party Organisation* (Basingstoke: Palgrave Macmillan).

Scarrow, S. (2005) 'Political Parties and Democracy: Theoretical and Practical perspectives', *National Democratic Institute for International Affairs*, Implementing *Intra-Party Democracy*, 2005, p.9. Retrieved from http://www.ndi.org/files/1951_polpart_scarrow_110105.pdf [accessed 02/07/2014].

Seyd, P., Whiteley, P. (1992) *Labour's Grass Roots: The Politics of Party Membership* (Oxford: Clarendon Press).

Seyd, P., Whiteley, P. (2002) *New Labour's Grassroots: The Transformation of the Labour Party Membership* (Basingstoke: Palgrave Macmillan).

Stark, L. (1996) *Choosing a Leader: Party Leadership Contests in Britain from Macmillan to Blair* (New York: Saint Martin's Press).

Webb, P. (1994) 'Reforming the Labour Party-Trade Union Link: An Assessment', *Journal of Elections, Public Opinion & Parties*, Vol. 4, n° 1, 1–14.

Webb, P. (2000) *The Modern Party System* (London: Sage).

Wickham-Jones, M. (2014) 'Introducing OMOV: The Labour Party-Trade Union Review Group and the 1994 Leadership Contest', *British Journal of Industrial Relations*, Vol. 52, n° 1, 33–56.

Wintour, P. (2010, 27 September) 'Ed Miliband pledges to lead Labour from the front – but will David follow?', *The Guardian*. Retrieved from http://www.guardian.co.uk/politics/2010/sep/26/ed-miliband-david-labour-leader [accessed 02/07/2014].

Wring, D. (2005) *The Politics of Marketing the Labour Party* (Basingstoke: Palgrave Macmillan).

12
The (Seeming) Power of (Seemingly) Leaderless Organizations: The Tea Party Movement as a Case Study

Aurélie Godet

Introduction

In 2009, as newly elected President Barack Obama started to implement the Democratic agenda for economic recovery and healthcare reform, a right-wing populist movement that claimed to be 'mad as hell' (Rasmussen and Schoen, 2010) emerged in vigorous opposition to expanded government. Since then, the Tea Party has never been long out of the headlines, and its triumphs and travails have provided scholars with considerable food for thought (Formisano, 2012; Godet, 2012; Horwitz, 2013; Huret, 2014; Kabaservice, 2012; Lepore, 2010; Libby, 2013; Skocpol and Williamson, 2012; Parker and Barreto, 2013; Van Dyke and Meyer, 2014).

Available empirical evidence, however, shows that Tea Party activity has been declining sharply since 2010. A 2011 report from ThinkProgress examined the total number of events across the country listed on the Tea Party Patriots (TPP) and Americans for Prosperity (AFP) websites each month between January 2010 and September 2011. It then compared the number of Tea Parties that occurred in 2010 with the number that took place in the first seven months of 2011. The results were startling. Fewer than half the number of Tea Party Patriots events took place in the first seven months of 2011 compared with the same time period in 2010 (Keyes, 2011). A more recent survey by the Pew Research Center showed that negative views of the Tea Party among the general public have nearly doubled since 2010, reaching an all-time high in October 2013 (49 per cent). Only 19 per cent of Americans now say they agree with the Tea Party movement, down from 27 per cent in November 2010 (Pew Research Center, 2013a).

While this post-2010 decline has often been ascribed to voter lassitude and to the intransigence of Tea Party members in Congress, we believe another hypothesis must be taken into consideration – that of an internal, organizational deficiency.

Since its emergence six years ago, the Tea Party movement has regularly prided itself on being a grassroots movement, denying claims that it is just another cog in the Republican political machinery. Our theory is that the Tea Party movement belongs to the category of 'hybrid organizations' described by Ori Brafman and Rod Beckstrom in *The Starfish and the Spider: The Unstoppable Power of Leaderless Organizations*, that is, organizations in which some parts can be termed 'organic', 'informal' or 'decentralized' while others reflect different leadership paradigms. In a business context, Brafman and Beckstrom have argued that these organizations are the most powerful because they are agile in implementation, more responsive to market forces and employee variety, and are consistently adaptive to innovative processes (Brafman and Beckstrom, 2006). Is this also true for political organizations and social movements? Doesn't the low degree of operational leadership, and more specifically the absence of grassroots-connecting leaders in their midst, hurt them in the long run? Should the post-2010 decline of the Tea Party movement be seen as testimony to its success or, on the contrary, as evidence of a structural failure? This chapter will seek to expand the existing body of both political movement and leadership literatures by providing a new interpretation of the Tea Party movement's rise and decline in terms of leadership patterns.

The Tea Party as a (seemingly) leaderless social movement organization

Ever since the early nineteenth century, populist social movements and third parties have frequently upset the tempo established by the two major parties by challenging 'politics as usual' and established elites. In this regard, the Tea Party is walking on a well-worn path. The main debate about the Tea Party movement, however, has to do with authenticity and leadership.

Conflicting interpretations of the Tea Party phenomenon

Tea Partiers generally insist that they are a mass movement of ordinary Americans who had not previously been involved in politics but are concerned about losing the right to live their lives as they choose.

There isn't one main phone number in Washington for the Tea Parties, they contend (Armey and Kibbe, 2010; Baker, 2009; Brody, 2012; Farah, 2010; Graham, 2010; Maltsev, 2013; Meckler and Martin, 2012).

Opponents argue that this 'mass movement' portrayal ignores the fact that the Tea Party includes elites that wield many millions of dollars in political contributions and appear all over the media claiming to speak for grassroots activists to whom they are not accountable (DiMaggio, 2011; Street, 2011; Parker and Barreto, 2013). What kind of mass rebellion is funded by corporate billionaires like the Koch brothers, is led by former GOP kingpins like Dick Armey, and is ceaselessly promoted by millionaire media celebrities like Glenn Beck?, they wonder. To these people, the movement is actually 'Astroturf populism'.[1] Former Speaker of the House of Representatives Nancy Pelosi notably questioned the legitimacy of the Tea Partiers' activism in 2009: 'It's not really a grassroots movement. It's Astroturf by some of the wealthiest people in America to keep the focus on tax cuts for the rich instead of for the great middle class' (Powers, 2009).

As in most cases, the truth lies somewhere in between. In fact, the Tea Party movement may well belong to the aforementioned category of 'hybrid organizations', described by Ori Brafman and Rod Beckstrom (Brafman and Beckstrom, 2006). To confirm this hypothesis, a qualitative assessment of the degree of operational leadership within the Tea Party is necessary.

Assessing the degree of operational leadership in social movement organizations

Inspirational vs. operational leadership

The term 'leaderless' is a misnomer; all social movement organizations have leaders to one degree or another. These leaders typically provide inspiration and/or operational direction (Hsu and Low, 2010). Inspiration is provided through a combination of charisma and ideology (Weber, 1968), or a doctrine that guides the organization (Ladkin, 2007). Inspirational leaders frame the movement's ideology by linking – through an effective use of communication – the organization's identity, grievances, and proposed solutions to moral values and cultural norms (cf. Introduction to this volume). Operational direction includes the planning and coordination of means to achieve tactical and strategic objectives (Ladkin, 2008). Sometimes inspirational leaders are also operational leaders; sometimes they are different people.

Varying degrees of operational leadership

A high degree of inspirational leadership can be found in both centralized and decentralized organizations. Centralized or hierarchical organizations typically have a high degree of operational leadership as well. Decentralized or cellular-type organizations, on the other hand, tend to rely on organization members to plan, coordinate, and even strategize for the organization. These, therefore, have a low degree of operational direction (Hsu and Low, 2010).

The Tea Party's leadership pattern

The Tea Party, like all social movement organizations, mobilizes individuals through its structure, connectivity to local networks, and framing of its ideology. Unlike a majority of social movement organizations, however, the Tea Party mobilizes individuals without a clear operational leader.

Organizational structure

Political action committees and advocacy groups with a policymaking infrastructure in Washington play a key role in local, regional, and national Tea Party efforts. A few of these national organizations were newly founded with the Tea Party label (for example, Tea Party Express, which stages media events and gives money to GOP candidates); most simply added the denomination on top of their long-standing organized efforts, or linked their activities to Tea Party websites.

As a whole, however, the Tea Party movement is best characterized as having a decentralized, cellular structure. Tea Parties are far from being as widespread as local chapters of classic US voluntary federations such as the Boy Scouts or the American Legion, which still have millions of members organized in an elaborate network of active local chapters. But a stock of more than 800 regularly meeting local groups could be found in 2010 after multiple online searches (Skocpol and Williamson, 2012). The current number seems to be around 600 (Blow, 2013). Some of them belong to Tea Party Nation, others to Tea Party Patriots, yet others to the Tea Party Federation.

A few states, like Vermont, Delaware, and the Dakotas, have fewer than three Tea Party groups. Fifteen states have more than 30 Tea Party groups; three states (California, Florida, and Texas) have more than 50 local groups. States in the northern Rocky Mountains, in the Ozarks or lower Appalachian range as well as states along the southwestern border seem to have an unusually high Tea Party density (Skocpol and Williamson, 2012).

The Tea Party's organizational structure is dependent upon both direct and indirect ties. Movement meetings, print publications, conference calls and the Internet are mechanisms that are commonly used to link individuals to the Tea Party ideology and spur collective action. An American citizen who desires to protest may come across a Tea Party website while searching the Internet where he or she can find all the information needed to take direct action. It is conceivable that the Internet can provide the 'salient' or strong tie that Doug McAdam references as so important to individual involvement in a social movement (McAdam, 2003).

Connectivity to existing networks

The Tea Party's organizational structure needs to be considered in the context of the larger conservative movement in which it exists.

To be sure, the spread of local Tea Parties was hardly anticipated in advance, not even by the right-wing media stars or national advocacy organizations trying to spur and exploit Tea Party activism in early 2009 (Rosenthal and Trost, 2012). But the Tea Party movement is nonetheless a new incarnation of perennial strands in US conservatism. The frustration of grassroots activists with new government initiatives such as the Patient Protection and Affordable Care Act coexists with unflagging endorsement of long-standing social programmes such as Social Security and Medicare, to which they feel entitled (Skocpol and Williamson, 2012). Tea Partiers display considerable bitterness over perceived federal government 'handouts' to 'undeserving' segments of the population, the definition of which seems to heavily rely on racial and ethnic stereotypes. More broadly, Tea Party concerns exist within a context of fear that Barack Obama, by bringing 'change they can't believe in', may threaten normative patterns and destroy what they believe to be the 'real' America: a heterosexual, Christian, middle-class, (mostly) male, *white* country (Parker and Barreto, 2013). Previous scholars, including Martin Gilens, have noted connections between racial stereotyping and opposition to parts of US social provision, particularly welfare for poor mothers (Gilens, 2009). Tea Party reactions and attitudes fit into this picture.

Inspirational leadership

While there may be no official Tea Party leaders, there are nevertheless authors and public figures who provide inspiration and ideological support. Among them are Ron Paul, Glenn Beck, Dick Armey, Sarah Palin, Michele Bachmann, Newt Gingrich, Ted Cruz, and Paul Ryan, whom the media have successively identified as the 'architects', 'masterminds', 'founding fathers', or 'standard bearers' of the movement.

These inspirational leaders within the movement frame the ideology to appeal to movement sympathizers and reinforce activist commitment. They maintain the frames through websites, TV shows, and communiqués. Two examples of inspirational literature come to mind: Ryan Hecker's 'Contract from America' project and Paul Ryan's 'Path to Prosperity: A Blueprint for American Renewal'.

In 2009, a Houston-based attorney, Ryan Hecker, launched a website to create a collaborative platform for the Tea Party movement. While paying homage to the Republicans' 1994 Contract with America – described as 'the nation's last intellectual economic conservative movement' – Hecker insisted that the new list was 'created from the bottom up. It was not crafted in Washington with the help of pollsters' (Becker, 2010). Out of the original 1,000 ideas that were submitted, Hecker chose 50 based on popularity, then reduced that number to 21 items with the help of former House Majority Leader Dick Armey (R-TX), whose multimillion-dollar non-profit group FreedomWorks had established close ties with many Tea Party activists around the country. After releasing the 21 ideas at the annual Conservative Political Action Conference on 18 February 2010, a final online vote was held to narrow the 21 ideas down to ten. Over two months, 454,331 votes were cast. The resulting document, including the vote percentages for each statement, was posted online on 14 April 2010. Box 12.1 shows the agenda items that it encouraged congressional candidates to follow.

While it was not signed by many Democrats or Republicans in Congress, some of the Contract's ideas were included in the list of proposed legislative items that Republicans pledged to pursue if they gained a majority of the seats in the House of Representatives in the November 2010 election.

More recently, in March 2012, House Budget Committee Chairman and former vice-presidential candidate Paul Ryan (R-Wisconsin) issued a budget plan entitled *Path to Prosperity. Blueprint for America Renewal*. Under this plan, which became Mitt Romney's plan in the 2012 presidential campaign, several items were listed as key to contain budget growth and debt increase over the next years, including a cap on discretionary federal spending at $1.029 trillion and dismantling the Obama administration's 2010 healthcare reform law. Similarly to the 2012 budget plan, Ryan's 2013 plan focused on cuts in federal

Box 12.1   The 'Contract from America', as unveiled on 14 April 2010

1. **Identify constitutionality of every new law**: Require each bill to identify the specific provision of the Constitution that gives Congress the power to do what the bill does (82.03 per cent).

2. **Reject emissions trading**: Stop the 'cap and trade' administrative approach used to control pollution by providing economic incentives for achieving reductions in the emissions of pollutants. (72.20 per cent).

3. **Demand a balanced federal budget**: Begin the Constitutional amendment process to require a balanced budget with a two-thirds majority needed for any tax modification. (69.69 per cent)

4. **Simplify the tax system**: Adopt a simple and fair single-rate tax system by scrapping the internal revenue code and replacing it with one that is no longer than 4,543 words – the length of the original Constitution. (64.9 per cent)

5. **Audit federal government agencies for constitutionality**: Create a Blue Ribbon taskforce that engages in an audit of federal agencies and programs, assessing their Constitutionality, and identifying duplication, waste, ineffectiveness, and agencies and programs better left for the states or local authorities. (63.37 per cent)

6. **Limit annual growth in federal spending**: Impose a statutory cap limiting the annual growth in total federal spending to the sum of the inflation rate plus the percentage of population growth. (56.57 per cent).

7. **Repeal the health care legislation passed on 23 March 2010**: Defund, repeal and replace the Patient Protection and Affordable Care Act. (56.39 per cent).

8. **Pass an 'all-of-the-above' energy policy**: Authorize the exploration of additional energy reserves to reduce American dependence on foreign energy sources and reduce regulatory barriers to all other forms of energy creation. (55.5 per cent).

9. **Reduce earmarks**: Place a moratorium on all earmarks until the budget is balanced, and then require a 2/3 majority to pass any earmark. (55.47 per cent).

10. **Reduce taxes**: Permanently repeal all recent tax increases, and extend permanently the George W. Bush temporary reductions in income tax, capital gains tax and estate taxes, scheduled to end in 2011. (53.38 per cent).

spending – except on national defence – aiming to reduce spending by $5 trillion and balance the budget by 2040. As can be seen in Table 12.1, resonance between the text's various frames was high, so as to maximize ideological cohesion.

Operational leadership

Though its ranks include committed, inspirational conservatives, the Tea Party movement is not operating under the direction of official GOP organizations. Instead, it comprises a mix of local networks and wealthy national bodies.

At the national level, two advocacy groups embody the Tea Party brand best: Tea Party Express and Tea Party Patriots (TPP). The latter has been more closely associated with grassroots activism than the former. Until recently, its unsophisticated website gave the impression of an entirely volunteer-run organization (the design was improved in 2013). Nonetheless, TPP is very closely intertwined with FreedomWorks. Tea Party Patriots operates under the motto 'Fiscal Responsibility, Limited Government, Free Market', which closely resembles the FreedomWorks slogan of 'LowerTaxes, Less Government, More Freedom'. As Jenny Beth Martin acknowledges, FreedomWorks was crucial to the group's original launch and was a primary funder for their national rallies (Meckler and Martin, 2012).[2]

Tea Party Express, Tea Party Patriots, and FreedomWorks are not the only Tea Party-linked conservative groups, however. Other national advocacy groups hunting in these woods include the American Liberty Alliance, an organization run by conservative campaign veteran Eric Odom, and Americans for Prosperity, an advocacy group that, like FreedomWorks, is a spin-off of the 1980s free-market, industry-funded think tank Citizens for a Sound Economy. Along with right-wing think tanks like the Heritage Foundation and the Cato Institute, they have been bankrolled by a small number of far-right businessmen, most notably the libertarian Koch brothers – sons of Fred Koch, a founding member of the John Birch Society. Thus the national organizations promoting the Tea Party movement are more tightly tied to pro-business conservatism than to religious, social conservatism – which does not preclude overlap with the Christian right at the local level (Brody, 2012; Rosenthal and Trost, 2012).

At the grassroots level, Tea Parties are small, loosely interconnected networks, set up by local and regional organizers who often make use of social networking portals such as MeetUp.com. From interviews and various public sources, it appears that these groups have often been launched by men and women who did not know one another

Table 12.1   The Tea Party's strategic frames

Identity frame (what America is)	This nation has faced many tests in its history – moments in time when the very idea of America was threatened by crisis at home and abroad. Each time, Americans rejected radical proposals to remake this exceptional nation in the image of less-free nations abroad. Instead, principled leaders and brave citizens rose to meet the difficulties they faced by applying the nation's enduring founding principles to the challenges of their times.
Diagnostic frame (who the enemy is)	Today, America is struggling to recover from a great recession. Her people's liberties are endangered by unwarranted expansions of government. And she is threatened by a rising tide of debt at home and fierce enemies abroad.
Prognostic frame (goals/ solutions)	Bold reforms that bring Americans together to build upon the solid foundations of security and liberty that have made this nation exceptional: • A military that keeps America safe by letting national strategic priorities determine spending levels, not the other way around; • A free enterprise system that is reinvigorated, with bureaucracy restrained, and corporate welfare eliminated; • A safety net that directs assistance to those who need it most, provides incentives to work and save; • Health and retirement programs that protect key commitments to seniors, and provide greater choices, better health, and real security for future generations; • A tax code that fosters growth and job creation by lowering rates and getting rid of special-interest loopholes; • A budget process that restrains government spending.
Maintenance frame (how to keep the move-ment going / why it cannot fail)	As the challenge grows, so does the opportunity to restore America's promise and prosperity. The choice of two futures presented in this budget is premised on the wisdom of the American people to build a prosperous future for themselves and for generations of Americans to come.
Motivational frame	In the words of Winston Churchill, this generation has the opportunity 'to rejoice in the responsibili-ties with which destiny has honoured us... and be proud that we are guardians of our country in an age when her life is at stake.' We must not let this opportunity slip away.

personally before they met in rallies and other protest settings. The founders of Tea Party groups acted out of like-mindedness and the desire to challenge the political status quo (Zernicke, 2010).

Leaders who launched local Tea Parties and keep them going are usually people of modest means – usually retirees, semi-retired, or unemployed individuals – who happen to have some flexibility in the use of their time (CBS News/*New York Times*, 2010; Skocpol and Williamson, 2012). Ironically, many of them are supported by Social Security, veterans' pensions, or a spouse's salary.

Most of the activists who have been interviewed over the years knew little or nothing about the national free-market organizations that have been crucial to the funding of the Tea Party phenomenon at the national level. Those who did have often sought to distance themselves from them. Links between the pro-business elites and local Tea Parties do not seem terribly strong, therefore, and are certainly not formal or simply hierarchical. The Tea Party as a whole appears to be a fairly leaderless social movement, meaning a social movement organization in which inspirational leaders exercise a low degree of operational direction.

Can a leaderless social movement organization be effective?

Competing views on the subject

Opinions regarding the effectiveness of leaderless social movement organizations are dichotomous. Some argue that they are less effective, that social movement organizations that adopt leaderless strategies do so as a 'last-ditch effort' to stay alive (Hsu and Low, 2010). Others argue that leaderless social movement organizations are more successful than organizations that have a clear leader because they are agile in implementation, more responsive to external forces, and are consistently adaptive to innovative processes.

In their bestselling book *The Starfish and the Spider*, Brafman and Beckstrom clearly support the second view. Traditional thinking, they explain, holds that hierarchies are most efficient at getting things done. Hierarchies, such as corporations, have leaders who can make decisions and set priorities; chains of command to hold everyone accountable; mechanisms to shift money and authority within the organization; rules and disciplinary procedures to prevent fracture and drift. This type of system has a central command, like a spider's brain. Like the spider, it dies if you thump it on the head.

The rise of the Internet and other forms of instantaneous, inter-personal interaction, however, has broken the spider monopoly, the authors argue. Radically decentralized networks – everything from illicit music-sharing systems to Wikipedia – can direct resources and adapt ('mutate') far faster than corporations can. 'The absence of structure, leadership, and formal organization, once considered a weakness, has become a major asset', they write (Brafman and Beckstrom, 2006: 7). Moreover, hierarchies are at a loss to defeat networks. Open systems have no leader or headquarters; their units are self-funding, and their members often work for free. Even in principle, you cannot count or compartmentalize the participants, because they come and go as they please. Knowledge and power are distributed throughout the system. As a result, the network is impervious to decapitation; it is like a star-fish: cut off an arm, and it grows (in some species) into a new starfish. Fragmentation, the bane of traditional organizations, actually makes the network stronger.

Again, we would argue that things are not so clear-cut and that there are specific conditions under which leaderless social movement organi-zations will be more or less effective.

Indicators of effectiveness

Roughly speaking, the effectiveness of a leaderless social movement must be assessed between two actors: the leaderless social movement organi-zation and its target, which may be the state, private corporations, or society as a whole. In an attempt to quantify the varying degrees of effectiveness we may use political scientist Rachel Einwohner's seven indicators (Figure 12.1) (Einwohner, 1999).

These indicators should be considered on a spectrum of varying degrees of effectiveness. In doing so, we do not imply that a low score

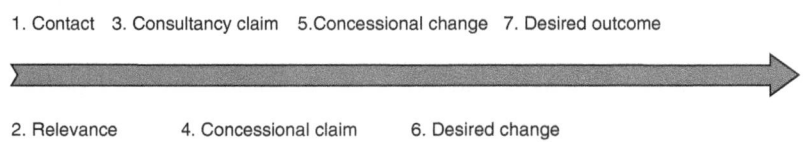

1. Contact   3. Consultancy claim   5.Concessional change   7. Desired outcome

2. Relevance   4. Concessional claim   6. Desired change

Figure 12.1   Indicators of social movement organizations' effectiveness

on this scale means that the organization does not consider *itself* effective. This tool is primarily meant for outsiders wishing to evaluate social movement organizations.

Assessing the efficiency of the Tea Party

Using Einwohner's scale, we would argue that the Tea Party has gone through stages 1 to 5.

Contact

Has the Tea Party taken action against the target (Washington, the federal government)? The answer is yes. The strategies that have been used so far to do so include demonstrating, petitioning or otherwise lobbying elected local and federal officials, entering a number of Republican (both House and Senate) primaries, and engaging in legal action against 'ObamaCare' on the basis of the 'commerce clause' and the 'compacts clause' of Article 1 of the Constitution (Godet, 2012).

Relevance

Has the target acknowledged the social movement organization as valid and relevant? Has it verbally indicated that the social movement organization is legitimate and worthy of a response? The answer is, again, yes. Barack Obama, while mocking the Tea Party at first and rejecting it on ideological grounds later, said he understood the Tea Partiers' anger at the economic situation in a March 2010 NBC interview with Matt Lauer (Capehart, 2010). The GOP, meanwhile, praised the movement as the new vanguard of the party. In 2009, John Boehner pressed fellow Republicans to get out in front of the movement or, at least, get out of its way. 'I urge you to get in touch with these efforts and connect with them', he told a closed-door meeting of the Republican Conference. 'The people participating in these protests will be the soldiers for our cause a year from now' (Boyer, 2010). Boehner seemed an unlikely clarion for an anti-establishment revolt. He had been in Congress since 1991 – long enough to have twice climbed from the backbench to a leadership position. He had been a friend of Ted Kennedy's, and a champion of George W. Bush's expansive No Child Left Behind legislation. After the economic collapse of 2008, he had reluctantly advocated for the Troubled Asset Relief Program ('a crap sandwich', he called it), the Tea Partiers' litmus test of political villainy. But Boehner was among the first Beltway Republicans to recognize that the rise of the Tea Party might represent – at least initially (see Alix Meyer and François Vergniolle de Chantal's chapters for a discussion of Boehner's complicated relationship with Tea

Party Congressmen from 2011 to 2014) – a near-miracle of good luck for Republicans.

Consultancy

Has the target consulted with the social movement organization? Has the target invited the social movement organization to negotiate a solution to remedy grievances? Yes. Boehner aggressively wooed the insurgents, spending much of the 2010 summer months travelling, often by motor coach, to campaign events – he attended more than 160 – and donating millions of dollars from his own campaign chest to the challengers. He even adopted the overheated Tea Party rhetoric in vowing to dismantle the Obama healthcare plan, which he dubbed 'this monstrosity' in front of Washington reporters in November (Boyer, 2010).

By the end of 2010 – particularly in the mid-term elections of that year – the Tea Party had made a powerful impact on both the Democratic and Republican parties. Tea Party voters helped create the new Republican majority in the House of Representatives and during 2011 quickly exerted influence on the Republican legislative agenda.

Concessional claim

Has the target made concessional claims or promises to act in accordance with the social movement organization's demands? Yes. When the 112th Congress convened in 2011, 86 Republican members were freshmen, bound to a mood of deep disaffection. To satisfy them after the election, Boehner announced a renewal of the Republican moratorium on budgetary earmarks and forswore domestic travel by military jet, a relished perk of his predecessors. As the transition to the new Congress began, in mid-November, Boehner avoided potential conflicts with his freshman colleagues by promising them a seat at the leadership table and two places on the steering committee that would choose committee chairs. When the freshmen told Boehner that they still felt underrepresented, he gave them a second leadership position and a third steering-committee seat.

From June to August 2011, Tea Party-backed politicians were at the vanguard of the attempt to force the federal government to default in the debt-ceiling crisis. Representative Michele Bachmann pledged unconditionally to vote against any increase in the debt ceiling. Ron Paul argued that defaulting on the national debt would actually be 'a good thing'. Respect for the Tea Party – or fear of it – led every leading Republican presidential candidate to oppose the debt-ceiling deal. When John Boehner, the House speaker, tried to cut a deal with President Obama that included some modest revenue increases, Tea Party freshmen humiliated him. After this latest agreement was finally struck – amounting to a near-complete capitulation by Obama — they went on Fox News to complain that it only called for $2.4 trillion in cuts, instead of $4 trillion.

Concessional change

Has the target changed its behaviour in the direction desired by the organization? Yes. To be sure, the Tea Party initially appeared to display little impact on the course of the 2012 Republican presidential campaign. Representative Michele Bachmann of Minnesota, who called herself a founding member of the Tea Party Caucus in Congress, bowed out of the presidential race after a disappointing finish in Iowa. Her Tea Party affiliation did little to help her campaign. Herman Cain, who also claimed the mantle of the Tea Party, and Rick Perry, whose conservative views were in line with many members of the movement, both dropped out of the primary race. But then, in August, Mitt Romney named Representative Paul D. Ryan of Wisconsin as his running mate. Mr Ryan's ascendancy to the No. 2 spot on the Republican ticket was a signal event for a movement that counts him as one of their own.

Following Romney's defeat in November, two conflicting theories were offered to explain the Republicans' failure to unseat Obama twice in a row. One of them was that the party alienated independent voters and was out of step with the demographic changes of the country as a whole. 'The GOP is becoming a *Mad Men* party in a *Modern Family* America', former George W. Bush campaign strategist Matthew Dowd famously told ABC reporters in November 2012 (Godet, 2013).[3] The other was that the party should never have nominated a 'big government establishment Republican' for president. 'Mitt Romney's loss was the death rattle of the establishment GOP. Far from indicating a rejection of the Tea Party or grassroots conservatives, the disaster of 2012 signals the beginning of the battle to take over the Republican Party and the opportunity to establish the GOP as *the* Party of small government constitutional conservatism', conservative figurehead Richard Viguerie declared in a statement released less than a week after the presidential election (Viguerie, 2012).

It seems therefore that the Tea Party, acting largely as a pressure group, has profoundly shaped the content of national political debate and has had a transforming impact on the Republican Party by pushing it further to the right. On this narrative most observers agree. Ideological polarization, defined as divergence on a broad range of issues based on a consistent set of beliefs (DiMaggio et al., 1996; Fiorina and Abrams, 2008) is now at an all-time high in the US Congress (see Figure 12.2).

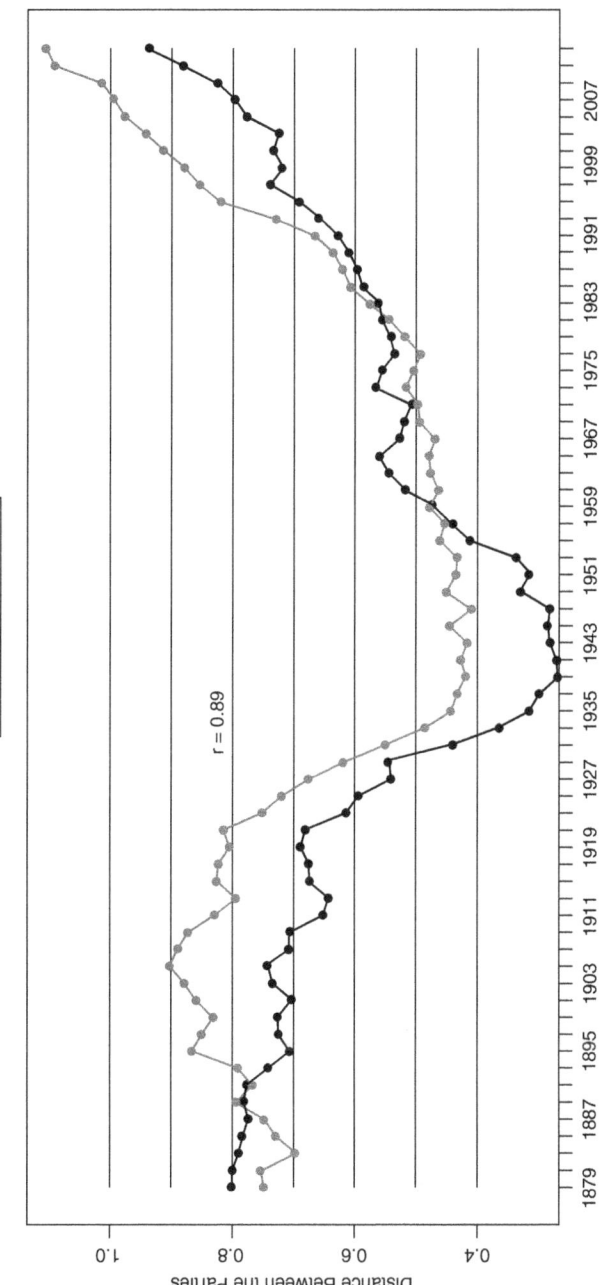

Figure 12.2 Ideological Polarization in Congress, 1879–2013[a]

Note: "r" indicates the correlation between polarization in the House and polarization in the Senate, with zero indicating no discernible trend and 1 showing they are moving in tandem. The 2013 figure of 0.89 casts serious doubt on the popular explanation that rising polarization is attributable to the redistricting (or 'gerrymandering') process, since only House districts are affected by this process and not state boundaries.

Source: Keith T. Poole and Howard Rosenthal, voteview.com, 2013.

Is this the change Tea Partiers really wanted, though? Has the target complied exactly with the demands of the organization? Has the social movement organization achieved its desired outcome or realized its overall goal? 'No' is the rational answer to all three questions.

The Republican Party certainly has adopted some of the ideas of the Tea Party movement, but the more ambitious parts of the Tea Party platform (strict constitutionalism, simplification of the tax code, suppression of earmarks, defunding of the Affordable Care Act, and so on) have been left out by Republican Congressmen, including some of the 2010 freshmen who got there on the movement's coattails. In October 2013, for instance, John Boehner overruled the 40 Tea Party supporters in Congress and allowed a deal to be passed with the help of Democrats to raise the debt ceiling and reopen the government after a fifteen-day budget showdown that led to a partial government shutdown.

It is now clear that the movement has not yet achieved its desired outcome or realized its initial goal, which was to break the bipartisan gridlock inside the Beltway and usher in a new era of 'fiscal responsibility' at the federal level.

Making sense of the Tea Party's failure to produce the desired change and outcome

This failure to achieve stages 6 and 7 may be ascribed to three main factors.

Overreach

Using a word that political scientist George Edwards recently chose to describe Barack Obama's presidency, the Tea Party has been guilty of overreach (Edwards, 2012). It set itself too ambitious a goal. Changing the US political system in the era of the 'permanent campaign' is close to impossible. The Tea Party's direct view of democracy is too idealistic or simplistic, as is often the case with populist movements (Kazin, 1998; Rosanvallon, 2011).[4]

Elite resistance

The movement has also overestimated its power to persuade the American people and the political elites. Though John Boehner has tried to accommodate Tea Party militants since 2010, the Republican Party elite as a whole has always taken a dim view of the movement. Most freshmen (the example of Marco Rubio comes to mind) shed the

Tea Party label after being elected or refused to join the House Tea Party caucus that Michele Bachmann founded in July 2010.

The ambiguous legacy of leaderlessness

Leaderlessness certainly allowed the Tea Party to achieve national prominence. More specifically, the movement benefited from the weak ties binding local groups to national advocates. Because there was no one centre or obvious source of authority and resources, the fate of Tea Party enthusiasm was not inextricably linked to the political fortunes of any one candidate or entity. Grassroots engagement was not undercut when particular candidates were defeated or particular organizations discredited. For instance, when Mark Williams, a leader of the Tea Party Express, was forced out of the organization for racist comments he posted on his blog, a Houston Texas Tea Party group responded with a blog post entitled 'Who Is Mark Williams?', which declared that Williams was perhaps a left-wing plant intended to make the Tea Party appear racist. Other groups ignored the controversy entirely.

But the Tea Party's organizational structure, in order to be fully effective, necessitates a consistent frame. In a 'broad' and 'deep' state such as the United States – that is, a state in which the government has established its authority in both urban and rural areas and exerts a great deal of control over society (Boudreau, 2005) – the key factor in the effectiveness of organizations with a high degree of operational leadership is the centralized structure itself. The key factor in the effectiveness of organizations with a low degree of operational leadership, on the other hand, is frame resonance (Hsu and Low, 2010). Strong resonance is the 'glue' that keeps the decentralized organization together. To succeed, in other words, leaderless social movement organizations must have a centralization of intent and purpose.

Whereas Tea Party rhetoric was relatively straightforward in 2010, it became more difficult to understand in 2012, with some Tea Party leaders – Missouri Representative Todd Akin and Indiana Senate candidate Richard Mourdock, most of all – engaging in a 'war against women' by campaigning against abortion and birth control. The statistical overlap between conservative Christians and Tea Party militants was a known fact (Jones and Cox, 2010), but what happened in 2012 was a sheer collapse of frame resonance. Abortion and immigration basically replaced economic and constitutional issues as the core of Tea Party rhetoric. This lack of a consistent frame may explain the Tea Party's travails since 2011.

Conclusion

Our assessment of the efficiency of leaderless political organizations and social movements will therefore end with a mixed verdict. On the one hand, the Tea Party movement's impact on the Republican Party has been very strong since 2009. At the start of the Obama era, writing the obituary of conservatism was a national pastime, and not just on the left. Declaring Reaganism dead, influential public intellectuals on the right such as David Frum urged a new conservatism that accommodated itself to the public's apparent acceptance of an activist government, suggesting such policy prescriptions as a national anti-obesity campaign (featuring a 'fat tax') and the payment of subsidies to working-class single men to make them more attractive marriage prospects. The emergence of the Tea Party forced upon Republicans, in one electoral cycle, a rebranding that otherwise might have taken the party a generation to achieve. The current Republican Party cannot exist without Tea Partiers, who make up a vital proportion of its core support network (in 2013 36 per cent of Republicans or Republican-leaning independents still said that they were members of the Tea Party movement). Fifty-four per cent of Republican and Republican-leaning voters actually want the party's leaders to move further to the right (Pew Research Center, 2013b).

On the other hand, the movement has failed to convince a majority of Americans that it is a force for good. Its popularity ratings are today quite low, with 49 per cent of the public now viewing the Tea Party unfavourably, compared with 25 per cent in February 2010 (Pew Research Center 2013a). The movement has also failed to modify the balance of power in Washington: Barack Obama is still president, the Democratic Party still intends to make the federal government a major player of the economic recovery scenario, and the House Tea Party caucus lost 18 of its members in the November 2012 Congressional elections (Michele Bachmann kept her seat, but Allen West in Florida, Scott Brown in Massachusetts, and Joe Walsh in Illinois did not, for instance). Finally, the Tea Party has failed to repair the US political system and counterbalance the power of the moneyed elites on US politics. The jury is out on whether or not it will vanish completely anytime soon, but research suggests that the Tea Party is declining as a social movement and is now a mere faction of the Republican Party, with little hope therefore of achieving its desired outcome: making the US political system more accountable to the people while preserving the legacy of the Founding Fathers.

Such an ambiguous outcome owes much to external factors – elite resistance, voter apathy, the difficulty of effecting change in an era of divided, 'do-nothing' federal government – but our belief is that it mostly springs from the movement's internal, structural weaknesses. While centralized operational leadership may not be necessary for a leaderless organization – be it a company or a social movement – to be effective, and indeed may spur its initial growth, strong inspirational leadership seems to be a better predictor of long-term success. The recent collapse of frame resonance among Tea Party ranks and ensuing decline of the movement can be viewed as corroborating this hypothesis.

Notes

1 The term 'Astroturf' came into political use in the 1980s to describe grassroots activism that is more artificial than authentic. Usually it takes the form of lobbying by corporations who organize campaigns that are made to appear to be spontaneous mass activism but are actually front organizations with names that disguise their true purposes.
2 Leaked emails have also suggested that, at least in early months, FreedomWorks retained control over significant aspects of TPP messaging (Roth, 2009).
3 Indeed, the GOP is undergoing a long-term ideological evolution – from the conservative backlash of the 1960s and the growth of the Christian Right in the Reagan years to the emergence of the Tea Party movement in 2009 – that goes against the political leanings of major growing US minorities. Even though the redistricting that followed the 2010 census tends to help Republicans in Congressional elections, current demographics in the US will make it increasingly difficult for a Republican candidate to be elected to the White House (Godet, 2013).
4 French political historian Pierre Rosanvallon actually argues that populism involves a triple simplification: a political-sociological simplification along the lines of homogeneous people versus corrupt elites; second, a procedural and institutional simplification directed against the messy world of intermediary powers; and third, a simplification of the social bond which is reduced to being a matter of homogeneous identity (Rosanvallon, 2011).

Bibliography

'Contract from America' (2010), date accessed 14 April 2010. http://www.thecontract.org/

Armey, D. and Kibbe, M. (2010), *Give Us Liberty: A Tea Party Manifest* (New York: HarperCollins).

Baker, B.L. (2009), *Tea Party Revival: The Conscience of a Conservative Reborn: The Tea Party Revolt Against Unconstrained Spending and Growth of the Federal Government* (Outskirts Press).

Becker, B. (2010), 'A Revised Contract for America, Minus "With" and Newt', *New York Times,* date accessed 14 April 2010. http://www.nytimes.com/2010/04/15/us/politics/15contract.html?_r=0

Blow, C. (2013), 'This Is Not 2009', *New York Times,* date accessed 24 May 2013. http://www.nytimes.com/2013/05/25/opinion/this-is-not-2009.html

Boudreau, V. (2005), 'Precarious Regimes and Matchup Problems in the Explanation of Repressive Policy', in Davenport, C., Johnston, H. and McClurg Mueller, C., (eds), *Repression and Mobilization* (Minneapolis, MN: University of Minnesota Press), 33–57.

Boyer, P.J. (2010), 'House Rule: Will John Boehner Control the Tea Party Congress', *New Yorker.com,* date accessed 13 December 2010). http://www.newyorker.com/reporting/2010/12/13/101213fa_fact_boyer?currentPage=all

Brafman, O. and Beckstrom, R. (2006), *The Starfish and the Spider: The Unstoppable Power of Leaderless Organizations* (New York: Penguin PortFolio).

Brody, D. (2012), *Teavangelicals: The Inside Story of How the Evangelicals and the Tea Party are Taking Back America* (Grand Rapids, MI: Zondervan).

Capehart, J. (2010), 'President Obama Hears the Tea Party', *WashingtonPost.com,* date accessed 30 March 2010). http://voices.washingtonpost.com/postpartisan/2010/03/president_obama_hears_the_tea.html

CBS News/ *New York Times* (2010), 'National Survey of Tea Party Supporters, April 5–12', date accessed 14 April 2010. http:/ / documents. nytimes. com/new-york-timescbs-news-poll-national-survey-of-tea-party-supporters?ref=politics

DiMaggio, P., Evans, J., Bryson and Bryson, B. (1996), 'Have Americans' Social Attitudes Become More Polarized?', *American Journal of Sociology* 102 (3), 690–755.

DiMaggio, A. (2011), *The Rise of the Tea Party: Political Discontent and Corporate Media in the Age of Obama* (New York: Monthly Review Press).

Edwards, G. (2012), *Overreach: Leadership in the Obama Presidency* (Princeton: Princeton University Press).

Einwohner, R.L. (1999), 'Gender, Class, and Social Movement Outcomes: Identity and Effectiveness in Two Animal Rights Campaigns', *Gender and Society* 13 (1), 56–76.

Farah, J. (2010), *The Tea Party Manifesto: A Vision of an American Rebirth* (Washington, DC: WND Books).

Fiorina, M. P., Abrams, S.J. (2008), 'Political Polarization in the American Public', *Annual Review of Political Science* 11(1), 563–88.

Formisano, R.P. (2012), *The Tea Party: A Brief History* (Baltimore, MA: Johns Hopkins University Press).

Gilens, M. (2009), *Why Americans Hate Welfare: Race, Media, and the Politics of Antipoverty Policy* (Chicago: Chicago University Press).

Godet, A. (2012), *Le Tea Party: Portrait d'une Amérique désorientée* (Paris: Vendémiaire).

Godet, A. (2013), 'La crise idéologique du Parti républicain' IFRI: Potomac Paper 17, 1–45.

Graham, M. (2010), *That's No Angry Mob, That's My Mom: Team Obama's Assault on Tea-Party, Talk-Radio Americans* (Washington, DC: Regnery Publishing).

Horwitz, R.B. (2013), *America's Right: Anti-Establishment Conservatism from Goldwater to the Tea Party* (Malden, MA: Polity).

Hsu, J.S. and Low, B.C. (2010), *The Leaderless Social Movement Organization: Unstoppable Power of Last-Ditch Effort?*, Master's thesis, (Monterey, California: Naval Postgraduate School).

Huret, R. (2014) *American Tax Resisters* (Boston, MA: Harvard University Press).

Jones, R.P. and Cox, D. (2010), 'Religion and the Tea Party in the 2010 Election: An Analysis of the Third Biennial American Values Survey', PublicReligion. org, date accessed 4 December 2014. http://publicreligion.org/site/wp-content/ uploads/2010/05/Religion-and-the-Tea-Party-in-the-2010-Election-American-Values-Survey.pdf.

Kabaservice, G. (2012), *Rule and Ruin: The Downfall of Moderation and the Destruction of the Republican Party, From Eisenhower to the Tea Party* (New York: Oxford University Press).

Kazin, M. (1998), *The Populist Persuasion: An American History* (Ithaca, NY: Cornell University Press).

Keyes, S. (2011), 'Report: Number of Tea Party Events Down More Than 50 Percent in 2011', *ThinkProgress*, date accessed 22 July 2011. http://thinkpro gress.org/politics/2011/07/22/273766/tea-party-events-declining/?mobile=nc

Ladkin, D. (2007), 'Leading from the Middle: Operational Leadership as Hermeneutic practice'. Paper presented at the 6th International Studying Leadership Conference, University of Warwick.

Ladkin, D. (2008), 'Leading Beautifully: How Mastery, Congruence and Form Contribute to Inspirational Leadership Performance', *Leadership Quarterly* 19(1), 31–41.

Ladkin, D. (2010) *Rethinking Leadership: A New Look at Old Leadership Questions* (Cheltenham: Edward Elgar Publishing).

Lepore, J. (2010), *The Whites of Their Eyes: The Tea Party's Revolution and the Battle over American History* (Princeton: Princeton University Press).

Libby, R.T. (2013), *Purging the Republican Party: Tea Party Campaigns and Elections* (Lanham, MA: Lexington Books).

Maltsev, Y. and Skaskiw, R. (2013), *The Tea Party Explained: From Crisis to Crusade* (Open Court Publishing Co.).

McAdam, D. (2003) 'Beyond Structural Analysis: Toward a More Dynamic Understanding of Social Movements', in Diani, M. and McAdam D. (eds), *Social Movements and Networks: Relational Approaches to Collective Action* (Oxford: Oxford University Press), 281–99.

McCarty, N., Poole, K.T. and Rosenthal, H. (2006), *Polarized America: The Dance of Ideology and Unequal Riches* (Cambridge: MIT Press).

Meckler M. and Martin, J.B. (2012), *Tea Party Patriots: The Second American Revolution* (New York: Henry Holt and Co.).

Parker, C.S. and Barreto, M.A. (2013), *Change They Can't Believe In. The Tea Party and Reactionary Politics in America* (Princeton: Princeton University Press).

Pew Research Center for the People and the Press (2013 a), 'Tea Party's Image Turns More Negative', *People-Press.org*, date accessed 16 October 2013. http:// www.people-press.org/2013/10/16/tea-partys-image-turns-more-negative/

Pew Research Center for the People and the Press (2013 b), 'Whither the GOP? Republicans Want Change, But Split Over Party's Direction', *People-Press. org*, date accessed 31 July 2013. http://www.people-press.org/2013/07/31/ whither-the-gop-republicans-want-change-but-split-over-partys-direction/

Powers R. (2009), 'Pelosi: Tea Parties Are Part of an 'Astroturf' Campaign By 'Some of the Wealthiest People in America', *ThinkProgress.org*, date accessed 15 April 2009. http://thinkprogress.org/politics/2009/04/15/37578/pelosi-astroturf/

Price Foley, E. (2012), *The Tea Party: Three Principles* (New York: Cambridge University Press).

Rasmussen, S.D. and Schoen, D. (2010), *Mad as Hell: How the Tea Party Movement Is Fundamentally Remaking our Two-Party System* (New York: HarperCollins, 2010).

Rosenthal, L. and Trost, C. (eds) (2012), *Steep: The Precipitous Rise of the Tea Party* (Berkeley: University of California Press).

Rosanvallon, P. (2011), 'Penser le populisme', *VieDesIdées.fr*, date accessed 27 December 2011. http://www.laviedesidees.fr/Penser-le-populisme.html

Roth Z. (2009), 'Freedom Works Says Jump, Tea Partiers Ask How High', *Talking Points Memo*, date accessed 11 August 2009. http://tpmmuckraker.talking-pointsmemo.com/2009/08/freedomworks_says_jump_tea_partiers_ask_how_high.php?reffpb

Ryan P. (2012), 'The Path to Prosperity: A Blueprint for American Renewal', date accessed March 2012. http://paulryan.house.gov/uploadedfiles/pathtoprosperity2013.pdf

Skocpol, T. and Williamson, V. (2012), *The Tea Party and the Remaking of Republican Conservatism* (New York: Oxford University Press).

Street P., and DiMaggio, A. (2011), *Crashing the Tea Party: Mass Media and the Campaign to Remake American Politics* (Boulder, CO: Paradigm Publishers).

Van Dyke, N. and Meyer, D.S. (eds) (2014), *Understanding the Tea Party Movement* (Burlington, VT: Ashgate).

Viguerie R., (2013), 'The Battle to Take Over the GOP Begins Today', *ConservativeHQ.com*, date accessed 11 January 2013. http://www.conservativehq.com/node/10743

Weber, M. (1968) *On Charisma and Institution Building* (Chicago: Chicago University Press).

Zernicke, K. (2010), *Boiling Mad: Inside Tea Party America* (New York: Macmillan).

13
Petra Kelly: Charismatic Leadership in the German Peace Movement and Early Green Party

Saskia Richter

Introduction: political leadership within social movements

Political leadership in Western democracies is often analyzed as leadership in governments, parliaments, parties and administrations (Helms, 2005; Helms, 2000; Glaab, 2007; Walter, 1997). Beyond these boundaries leadership research is an interdisciplinary field (Fiorina and Shepsle, 1989: 17). Social movements lack executive positions making leadership more difficult to characterize. The grassroots nature of social movements adds further challenges to the identification of influential persons. A way to overcome this can be to analyze leadership through the biographies of participants in social movements (Ferree, 2000: 111 ff.; Barker, 2001).

Social movements are defined as networks which are organized in a collective way and are based on a collective identity (Roth and Rucht, 2008; Daphie, 2012: 43ff.; Tarrow, 2005: 135). Social movements are successful when there is a kind of opportunity window for an issue in society, there is the possibility to mobilize support, and the activists are able to frame or communicate their claims (Smith, Wiest 2012: Chapter 1; Giugni, 2002:14 ff.). Activists and followers (Marg et al., 2013) organize or take part in citizens' initiatives, demonstrations or other protest activities. Owing to the grassroots nature of these movements, participants often have difficulties accepting authorities or leaders within the social movement. For this reason political scientists are developing the concept of key figures in social movements (*Forschungsjournal Soziale Bewegungen* 4/2013; Rucht, 2013: 32 ff.); but one could also use the term protagonist (Richter, 2012: 184 ff.).

The chapter looks at connections between leadership and social movement research in political science. This is why the term political leadership is used in the analysis of the early 1980s peace movement in continental Europe and West Germany. By way of example this chapter analyzes the leadership of the founder and first chair of the German Green Party, Petra Kelly. The chapter considers her position within the transnational peace movement in opposing the NATO Double-Track decision between 1979 and 1983 in West Germany and her period of greatest influence in the Green Party between 1979/80 and 1985.

Leadership is always a relationship between followers and leaders (Burns, 1978: 141 ff.; Jones, 1989: 41 ff.) in political parties, administrations and political movements. The history of political leadership is not just the history of great men, successful politicians and prime ministers (Schwarz, 1998) but also the story of failed politicians (Forkmann and Richter, 2007: 15 ff.; Schneider, 2006) and political activists. And while activists are often unknown and politically powerless, some, including Petra Kelly, rise to become popular with the public, some become more popular than pop stars (Richter, 2010; Robertsen-von Trotha, 2013). It is the task of political science not just to analyze political institutions and their functions of political leadership but also the biographies of the political leaders and the sociological and historical contexts in which they had to make leadership decisions (Hartmann, 2007).

Burns (1978) introduced the distinction between 'transactional' and 'transforming' leadership (141 ff.). Transactional leadership – as the editors point out – takes place when 'one person takes the initiative in making contact with others for the purpose of an exchange of valued things' (also Nowotny, 1997). In contrast – as the editors note – transforming leadership has a moral dimension. This idea is related to the leadership theory of Max Weber (2010) written in the early twentieth century. Weber made the distinction between legal, traditional and charismatic authority. He defined charisma as the specific quality of a person with exceptional strength that makes his followers view him as a political leader. Charisma is extraordinary, emotional and oppositional, i.e. not affected by economic interests (compare Lenze 2002).[1] It can but does not have to be revolutionary. The following analysis works with Weber's charismatic authority as well as the editors' definition that political leaders are understood as 'agents' to whom authority is delegated to oversee tasks that advance the goals of their followers or 'principals'. Weber assumes that charisma is not necessarily connected to power. Rather charisma can be a type of leadership that defines political directions, proposes new interpretations for contemporary challenges and provides an emotional connection.

Petra Kelly however was both: a political leader in a social movement to whom authority was delegated informally and a politician who took the initiative to change politics in an analytical and very emotional way (Edelman, 1990). This chapter is based on the research for the book *Die Aktivistin. Das Leben der Petra Kelly* (Richter, 2010). The analysis chose the term charismatic leadership – not charismatic authority – to explain Kelly's extraordinary position in the transnational peace movement against the NATO Double-Track decision between 1979 and 1983. During her time as a politician and political activist Petra Kelly was able to express emotions that were her own but shared by many of her followers: fear, hope and anxiety, the characteristics of the so-called *Zeitgeist* in the early 1980s. This emotional environment created her window of opportunity. Kelly never held a major executive national position, but she was an outstanding politician within the peace movement that stressed a key role within the German public during that time. The case study of Petra Kelly is a contribution to a more general theory of leadership because it addresses the question of whether leaders act as causal agents rather than agents of their followers, as proposed by the editors. The case study also analyses what leadership is in a social movement, and in particular what made Kelly's leadership possible.

Petra Kelly: founder and first chair of the Green Party in Germany

In the late 1970s Petra Kelly was one of the founders of the German Green Party. For 30 years the German party system was called a two-and-a-half party system, where the Christian Democrats (CDU), the Social Democrats (SPD) and the Liberal Party (FDP) were alternating between government and opposition (Jesse, 2001). The formation of the Green Party at the beginning of the 1980s as an *Anti-Parteien-Partei* was without doubt an innovation in the German party system (Markovits and Klaver, 2013; Markovits and Gorski, 1997). Kelly became the figurehead of the alternative party. In the 1979 election for the European Parliament she was the frontrunner of the predecessor to the Green Party 'Sonstige Politische Vereinigung – Die Grünen'. In 1980 she became the first spokesperson of the Green Party. In 1982 she coined the term *Anti-Parteien-Partei* in an interview with the German news-magazine *Der Spiegel*.[2]

As a political scientist Kelly was employed in the administration of the European Commission. In her role as a civil servant in the economic and social committee she focused her work on employment rights and job markets. She was also concerned with environmental issues and gender equality. After her half-sister Grace had died from cancer in 1970 Kelly started researching the effects of radiation. She got involved early in the emerging movement against nuclear power plants on the European level as well as the women's movement and the ecological movement. Later as a member of the German parliament Kelly politicized Grace's dying and made plain her sister was like the victims of Hiroshima in the end: remnants of a human being in a hospital room; Kelly considered this a sign of living in an atomic age during the 1970s.[3]

In Germany the emerging social movements provide a grassroots environment for the founding process of the Green Party. The report *The Limits to Growth* was published in 1972 by the Club of Rome (Meadows et al., 1972). The first oil crisis shocked Western industrial nations in 1973 (Doering-Manteuffel and Raphael, 2008: 31). Not just governments had to contemplate the changing world order: civil societies in the Western democracies were changing too. Citizens' initiatives became the form of organization of the decade. Germans tried to affect change in their communities through environmental initiatives and protests against nuclear power plants and other industry projects – a phenomenon that can be observed today too. In the late 1970s Kelly stood in the middle of this process not as a protest organizer but as an intellectual and politician. A former member of the SPD, she was also a member of the voluntary executive board of the umbrella organization Bundesverband Bürgerinitiativen Umweltschutz (BBU). This position allowed her to be on the first electoral lists of the 'Sonstige Politische Vereinigungen – Die Grünen'.

Within the new Green Party Kelly became a media star: she projected an image which was seen as relevant in society and had an effect on mass media (Lowry and Korte, 2000: 1–2). She was a small, well-educated and smart young woman, who eloquently spoke of her international involvement in the social movements, her work in the European administration and increasingly about her personal consternation about the fate of her sister. She was not without controversy – the early Greens focused on a grassroots organization without personalization, but the national and international media loved reporting on Kelly's stories and political statements. She was something of a counterpart to the establishment of male middle-aged politicians arguing rationally about policy decisions. Journalists described Kelly as fresh, striking and committed to finding solutions for humanity's problems: peace, ecology, human rights, gender equality and employment rights.[4]

While talking about alternative political visions Kelly displayed her feelings of sorrow about the suffering and death of her sister. It can be interpreted as political strategy that Kelly combined political statements and very private emotions to strengthen the relevance of her arguments. Through her media presence Kelly coined the term of the *Anti-Parteien-Partei* in a *Spiegel* interview. A report on German TV presented her as a young woman working till exhaustion for Green politics. There were a lot of other party members working hard too, but she was invited onto the influential American program *Meet the Press* on 10 July 1983 where she was introduced as the 'best-known leader of West Germany's Green Party'. More so than her colleagues in the early Green Party Kelly was able to present her political views alongside her biography. However, as one of the first chairs of the Green Party her power was limited (Richter, 2005: 169 ff.). The Green Party staffed leadership positions because the party rules required it to. As the story of Joschka Fischer 15 years later illustrates, power was always shared informally within the party organization (Raschke, 2001: 49 ff.).

The Green Party and the German Peace Movement during the early 1980s

During the founding process and pre-parliamentary phase of the Green Party the growing peace movement against the NATO Double-Track decision became a key force for the party's consolidation (Richter, 2011: 229 ff.). Between 1981 and 1983 thousands of people in several cities all over Europe but especially in West Germany protested against the NATO armament decision: in Belgium, 200,000 people on 25 October 1981 and 400,000 on 23 October 1983; in Amsterdam, 400,000 on 21 November 1981; in The Hague, 500,000 on 29 October 1983. In West Germany major demonstrations included 300,000 protesters in Bonn in October 1981 at the Bonner Hofgarten, and during the protesters' church conventions in Hamburg 1981 and Hannover 1983. Many Germans participated in the so-called *Ostermärsche* between 1981 and 1984 as well as in several protest activities such as the human chain between Stuttgart and Ulm with 200,000–300,000 people on 22 October 1983.

Why was the peace movement so important for the consolidation of the Green Party? During this pre-parliamentary phase the ambition of the new party had to be representation in parliament (Raschke, 1993: 592 ff.; Markovits, 1997 (1993): 283 ff; Müller-Rommel, 1993). Several federal elections were held during the early 1980s and national elections were held in 1980 and 1983. In 1980 the Green Party got 1.5 percent of the vote, which was far below the five percent hurdle for parties entering the German Bundestag. The founding of the party did not begin in the peace process. It is anchored more within the ecological, anti-nuclear and women's movement as well as with the issues of post-industrialization and new values of growth in society (Inglehart, 1977). But within the rising peace movement the Greens could articulate their political positions of ahimsa[5] and disarmament. The Green Party was represented in the coordination committee of the peace movement that was responsible for organizing the peace demonstrations.

Petra Kelly's political statements on peace and disarmament were connected to peace politics. During this early phase of the Green Party Kelly could use the strength of the peace movement to promote her own goals. Environmental issues became part of a wider concept of peace. Here Kelly distinguished herself from other Green politicians who emphasized environmental issues (Mende, 2011: 447 ff.). In her speeches Kelly articulated a deep desire for peace and asserted that the ecological movement could not be a comprehensive movement without integrating the aims of the peace movement. She brought forward her arguments against atomic weapons, military armament in East and West and the dangers of radiation. By using the aims of the peace movement for Green policy in general and for the Green Party in particular Petra Kelly very authentically enhanced her own sources of power.

The main demonstrations of the peace movement occurred in 1983, the year the NATO Double-Track decision was ratified and national elections were held in Germany. As the political scientist Helmut Wiesenthal pointed out, the evolution of the German Green Party to the fourth party of the Federal Republic took place in parallel to the formation of the larger peace movement in Western Europe (Wiesenthal, 1993: 95–142, 114). He presented the argument that the Greens were pushing forward the movement against the NATO Double-Track decision from the moment of their establishment. Together with the former general Gert Bastian who became her partner later (Schwarzer, 2001), Petra Kelly was one of the prominent voices supporting the controversial *Krefelder Appell* (Becker-Schaum, 2013, online) and the call for disarmament in Germany.

Petra Kelly: charismatic leadership in the German peace movement

Petra Kelly within the Peace Movement

During the pre-parliamentary phase the Green Party was organized as a movement party (Raschke, 1993: 499 ff.). The term emphasizes the personal and political linkage between party organization and social movements in several ways. As a party politician Petra Kelly was one of the activists who represented the aims of the movements first within the party and later in parliament. Together with the parliamentary group of the Green Party she meant to carry the interests of the social movements into the German Bundestag.

The section below, 'Charisma and emotional leadership in the German peace movement and the early Green Party' explains how the peace movement was meaningful beyond the wide stream of post-materialism in the late 1970s – in particular considering its support in society. Petra Kelly as a Green politician played a key role within the peace movement between 1979 and 1983. Returning to Germany from Brussels she became a star in the national in international media. Journalists portrayed her as the figurehead of the Greens; not everybody in the grassroots party that tried to avoid personalization accepted this description. Very early on Kelly polarized the Green Party: many colleagues did not accept her celebrity status. She developed alluring mannerisms very early as well. In parliament when Kelly did not share her mandate with a second representative who was delegated by the Greens for their parliamentary group she maneuvered herself into a margin position in the parliamentary group as well as in the party itself.

At the same time Petra Kelly was highly present in the media – in newspapers, magazines and TV shows. She was a Green politician who spoke English fluently and could represent the party in the foreign media and in movements abroad. Petra Kelly was one of the speakers – although less an organizer – at the important peace demonstrations, e.g. in the Hofgarten in Bonn. Kelly had an extraordinary sense of mission. Even without an office, she wrote press releases, open letters and articles for newspapers and movement magazines. Her grandmother supported her in her political work. When Kelly made a personal political decision she communicated it to the world: among others, her distance from the SPD in the late 1970s, her distance from the Catholic Church and an initiative against children's cancer in memory of her sister.

In order to gain profound knowledge of technical and political details, Kelly built an international network of experts that included scientists, activists, politicians and informed citizens. She spread information by writing letters and sending out copies – decades before the internet made international communication and the flow of information instantaneous and virtually free. In her communications she used symbols like paper-missiles, dead fir trees, peace-doves and flowers on military helmets to underline her political position for disarmament. Kelly manufactured T-shirts with political claims like one that said 'swords into ploughshares' which she wore on an official visit to the GDR head of state Erich Honecker on 31 October 1983.

Petra Kelly and categories of political leadership

The role of the media: Petra Kelly skillfully communicated her political positions via the German media. Press and radio/TV portrayed her as a politician working around the clock for a world without weapons where humanity lives in peace with nature without ever having time to enjoy nature in person. In 1983 *Time* magazine described her as the attractive star of the radical *Anti-Parteien-Partei*. The American program *Meet the Press* invited her to a media discussion about the military expansion in Europe and introduced her as the leader of the Green Party in Germany. This communication and media reception were attributes of Petra Kelly's political leadership. With her strong public presence in German and international media, which portrayed her as holding a leading position within the party, Kelly was able to develop a claim to political leadership. During her time not every party fellow supported her solo attempt; mostly she missed coordination with the parliamentary group or the party. Today her party colleagues remember her posthumously as a media star (Heinrich Böll Stiftung, 2007).

In office: Petra Kelly's official leadership positions included being the frontrunner during the elections for the European Parliament in 1979 as mentioned above, the chair of the Green Party between 1980 and 1982, and the chair of the parliamentary group of the Greens in 1983. The Green Party's founding principles included grassroots democracy, rotations of their parliamentary delegation and little personalization (Raschke, 1993; Markovits, 2013: 29 ff.). Nonetheless Petra Kelly managed to increase her popularity in Germany and beyond. Owing to her elevated status she had easy access to conferences, speeches and delegations. She could speak from a position of formal and informal leadership within the party and could place her issues on the official agenda. A 1982 newspaper article stated that the Green politician Kelly had a higher level of exposure in the US than the newly elected chancellor from the CDU, Helmut Kohl.[6] In 1983 she received letters from abroad addressed to 'Petra Kelly, Germany'.

Symbols and political actions: Petra Kelly was able to use her popularity in order to broadcast her political positions via symbols and political actions. With Lukas Beckmann, Gert Bastian and others Petra Kelly was one of the activists demonstrating illegally on the Alexanderplatz in East Berlin in May 1983. National and international media were reporting about the forbidden political activity of West German politicians in the GDR while peers were struggling for positions and holding a peace conference in West Berlin. Despite being detained briefly, Kelly and the others succeeded in making contact with some of the GDR's civil rights activists like Bärbel Bohley. They also arranged a meeting with Erich Honecker in October 1983 where they handed him a personal peace agreement that demanded abstention from violence and disarmament.

Symbols: The symbols Kelly used to underscore her political claims can be categorized as reference symbols (*Verweisungssymbole*) and aggregation symbols (*Verdichtungssymbole*) (Sarcinelli, 1987; Edelman, 1990; Richter, 2010: 245 ff.). Reference symbols point out objects or situations like the danger of missiles or the damage of fir trees. Aggregation symbols on the other hand address the observer's emotions; they could be flowers – as during the Alexanderplatz protest – or doves, as used for an act of protest in Washington DC. Both types symbolize peace and present political statements in a simple way with reduced and condensed complexity.

T-shirts: Petra Kelly's T-shirts with printed political statements were remarkable during this period. During official meetings Kelly could be sure of the media's attention. Through the statements on her T-shirts she was able to communicate her message without uttering a single word. In Moscow she wore a shirt with the slogan 'Respect human rights'. In Belgrade she supported dissidents with Rosa Luxemburg's slogan 'Freedom is always the freedom of dissenters'. In each instance the national and international media reported about the events and transmitted her message into the public sphere.

Petitions: The *Krefelder Appell* was one of the most important petitions of the peace movement against the NATO Double-Track decision in Germany. Together with Gert Bastian Petra Kelly was one of the initiators of the controversial initiative. The *Appell* also had initiators in the GDR and raised suspicion owing to its call for an end to military expansion in West Germany. Without discussing the meaning of the *Appell* we shall note that there were several other petitions Petra Kelly supported concerning civil-rights activity in the GDR and the peace movement in both East and West, etc.

Transactional and transforming leadership: Within the framework of transactional and transforming leadership Petra Kelly acted as a transforming leader. Her political vision was one of a world without weapons or at least without an arms race between East and West. A world where all people live in peace and freedom without discrimination based on birth, faith or gender. Listening to her, one realizes that she embodied a morally pure political vision of a world without repression, exploitation of natural resources, industrial pollution or ecological destruction. In that complexity she was a pioneer in the early 1980s and stood out among her fellow Green Party members. Her arguments were rich in facts and scientific evidence. But she also used emotions to accentuate her political statements. In her 1983 book *Fighting for Hope* she declared her vision of a nonviolent future. She stated that it was chiefly her life experience that empowered her political agenda in the Green Party. However, Kelly never held a major executive national position and indeed the peace movement failed in its aim to prevent the NATO Double-Track decision. But political leadership does not have to be successful to be identified as leadership and for civil society Kelly was a top-ranking politician who developed accurate responses to the challenges of her time.

Charisma and emotional leadership in the German peace movement and the early Green Party

In *Economy and Society* Max Weber described the categories of legal, traditional and charismatic authority. Interpreting the category of charismatic authority in connection with the study of Petra Kelly in the peace movement we start with the assumption that charisma does not need to have a connection to power. In contrast with charismatic authority, charisma can be political leadership that motivates people to follow their leader voluntarily. Petra Kelly did just that. She provided charismatic and emotional leadership using her ability to speak to people as a political activist and politician. Using the categories of this book, she was a communicator who spoke via media to the public and much more a grassroots connector who developed concise positions within the peace movement of the 1980s. Kelly was one of the few politicians who articulated the fear of her time. Maybe her biggest impact was in expressing the helplessness people felt against the backdrop of NATO's military operation. Not to everybody but to those who were receptive to her message Kelly became an emotional leader.

There were a lot of flaws in her informal charismatic leadership position too: she was very focused on her own person and her positions.

The more she had intuition for the time and society she was successful in, the less grasp she had on colleagues and forces and factions inside the Green parliamentary group and the Green Party. With Gert Bastian and her grandmother she had strong personal support. In addition she had close friends and a loyal office assistant who worked for her until 1990. But it was difficult for Kelly to organize insider relationships that could stabilize her political position. Also there was high employee turnover in her office. She had the reputation of being difficult in collaboration. After the peace movement had failed to prevent the NATO Double-Track decision, Kelly needed to develop new political issues and statements as she had done with human rights, Tibet, cancer, later right-wing extremism. But her activity had never been stronger than in the social movements during the early 1980s.

Within the context of the peace movement Petra Kelly had a talent for winning favors from the movement's supporters. In her political statements she asserted that there had to be a change in the military politics of NATO, the German government and the majority of the German Bundestag. Like thousands of citizens in the Federal Republic of Germany, Petra Kelly felt uneasy about the status of the military and the danger of nuclear weapons. But unlike others she had the capacity to articulate this unease in terms of political actions. The premise of wide popular support for Petra Kelly's emotional statements is validated by letters that can be read in the *Petra Kelly Archive* (*PKA*) and the *Archiv Grünes Gedächtnis* (*AGG*) in Berlin.[7]

However, the real power of her charismatic and emotional appeal was limited. As Weber wrote, charisma is dependent on a political constellation, a window of opportunity that makes the combination of leadership, followers and emotions possible. The situation in the peace movement against the NATO Double-Track decision, the personal experience of the effect of radiation, the articulation of the emotions of sorrow, fear and pain as well as the transfer of personal feelings into the political debate, explain the rise, strength and fall of Petra Kelly: with the protests against the NATO Double-Track decision she was able to develop her political personality and her positions of Green peace politics. But in late 1983, after the Bundestag voted in favor of military expansion, people lost hope that Kelly's words could translate into government policy. In losing her political battles Petra Kelly lost her audience. In 1985 she lost the support of her parliamentary colleagues and her own party when she refused to give up her seat during a rotation of the members of her parliamentary group. This was certainly one of the causes of her failure.

Conclusion

Was Petra Kelly's leadership effective? The appraisal of political leadership within social movements is challenging and the case of Petra Kelly has to be investigated from at least three perspectives: (1) the social movements, (2) the party founder, (3) the wider meaning for society.

(1) Jenkins and Form describe social movements as organized efforts to bring about social change (2005: 331). It has to be said that the peace movement was not successful in preventing the implementation of the NATO Double-Track decision. The missiles were positioned and the danger of a nuclear war on German territory was extremely high at least until the mid-1980s. Neither the protesters in the peace movement nor its key figures, protagonists or leaders like Petra Kelly and other politicians could stop NATO's strategy. But the social movements could point out the dangers of the military politics and paved the way for the civil rights movement in the GDR that would be successful later in 1989.

(2) As one of the founders of the Green Party, Kelly can be described as a successful politician. Especially during the early years of the young party in the so-called pre-parliamentary phase Kelly was able to communicate her viewpoints and the positions of the Green Party within the German and international media. In those early years Kelly was loved by the media and managed effective and successful election campaigns for the Green Party. She was smart and could eloquently discuss Green positions with established politicians on TV shows and in discussions within the alternative movements in the early 1980s. She did not have an executive position but here as well one should not underestimate the importance of public debates for social change in the long term.

(3) Potentially most notable – but maybe not within the category of effectiveness – was Petra Kelly's impact on society of the early 1980s. During her time as a politician she reached not just the activists in the social movements but also less politically informed citizens. Kelly had the ability to explain complex military issues in a personal way using not just technical details but also emotions. Kelly articulated the threat people felt in facing nuclear weapons in their backyards and the possible apocalypse.

In evaluating the importance of the peace movement and the rise of the Green Party for the contemporary history of the Federal Republic of Germany, Petra Kelly's importance stands out. In protesting the political strategy of nuclear armament the peace movement changed the political culture of the old Federal Republic (Kielmansegg, 2000: 233 ff.). West Germany had never seen so many protesters and demonstrations against military policies. The establishment parties were unable to integrate the opposition any longer. Social democrats were leaving their party. Christian democrats were also protesting. Members of the churches were organizing protest activities. Trade unions, women's groups and other citizens' initiatives were ruling the decade; with them civil society took on the challenge of political integration.

In brief, Petra Kelly was not a new, successful, smart politician who came out of nowhere to change the rules of representative democracy. She was a politician who called attention to the possibilities of participatory democracy. Because of her capacity of expressing emotions in a way people could relate to, she progressed to become an outstanding politician within the peace movement protesting against the NATO Double-Track decision and during the founding process of the German Green Party. Although the peace movement lost the battle on cruise missiles, the power of protest was a new force in the political culture of the Federal Republic of Germany. Since then the Green Party has been represented in the German Bundestag in every legislature except 1990–94. Four years changed politics in Germany. At the center of this change was Petra Kelly: a media darling and a controversial party colleague, but also the figurehead of a whole movement.

Notes

1 Lenze describes how brands could be charismatic in postmodern societies and how marketing and consumption could be keys for charisma. Postmodern charisma is organized charisma. In political sciences it could be relevant for election campaigning too.
2 Kelly, Petra, 'Wir sind die Antipartei-Partei', *Der Spiegel*, 14 June 1982.
3 Kelly, Petra Rede im Deutschen Bundestag, 10. Wahlperiode, 36. Sitzung, Bonn, 22 November 1983.
4 Freeman, Clive, 'Petra Kelly brings a fresh look to the German politics: American activism, '60s style', *People Weekly*, 22 November 1982.
5 In the 1980s the Greens listed four adjectives for their politics: ecological, grassroots democratic, social and nonviolent.
6 Schröder, Peter W. 'Deutscher Wahlkampf – Star in US-Zeitungen ist Petra Kelly', *Neue Presse*, 4 March 1983.
7 E.g. AGG PKA 1847, 1868, 1870, 1871.

Works cited

Barker, C., Johnson, A., Lavalette, M. (eds) (2001) *Leadership and Social Movements* (Manchester: Manchester University Press).
Becker-Schaum, C. (2013) *Die Grünen und die Friedensbewegung*, http://www.boell.de/de/demokratie/archiv-gruene-geschichte-friedensbewegung-1983–16647.html, date accessed 10 July 2014.

Burns, J. McG. (1978) *Leadership* (New York, Hagerstown, San Francisco, London: Harper & Row, Publishers).

Daphi, P. (2012) 'Zur Identität transnationaler Bewegungen', *Aus Politik und Zeitgeschichte*, 62, 43–8.

Doering-Manteuffel, A., Raphael, L. (2008) *Nach dem Boom: Perspektiven auf die Zeitgeschichte seit 1970* (Göttingen: Vandenhoek & Ruprecht).

Edelman, M. (1990) *Politik als Ritual: Die symbolische Funktion staatlicher Institutionen und politischen Handelns* (Frankfurt/Main and New York: Campus-Verlag).

Feree, M.M. (2000) 'Was bringt Biographieforschung der Bewegungsforschung', Miethe, I., Roth, S. (eds) *Politische Biographien und sozialer Wandel* (Gießen: Psychosozial-Verlag), pp. 111–28.

Fiorina, M.P., Shepsle, K.A. (1989) 'Formal Theories of Leadership: Agents, Agenda Setters, and Entrepreneurs', Jones, B.D. (ed.) *Leadership and Politics: New Perspectives in Political Science* (Kansas: University Press of Kansas), pp. 17–40.

Forkmann, D., Richter, S. (eds) (2007) *Gescheiterte Kanzlerkandidaten in Deutschland: Von Kurt Schumacher bis Edmund Stoiber* (Wiesbaden: VS Verlag für Sozialwissenschaften). *Forschungsjournal Soziale Bewegungen* (2013) 26.

Freeman, C. (1982) 'Petra Kelly brings a fresh look to the German politics: American activism, '60s style', *People Weekly*, 22 November.

Giugni, M.G. (2002) 'Explaining Cross-National Similarities Among Social Movements', Smith, J., Johnston, H. (eds) *Globalization and Resistance. Transnational Dimensions of Social Movements* (Lanham: Rowman & Littlefield Publishers), pp. 13–29.

Glaab, M. (2007) 'Politische Führung als strategischer Faktor' in *Zeitschrift für Politikwissenschaft* 17, pp. 303–32.

Hartmann, J. (2007) *Politik und Persönlichkeit* (Wiesbaden: VS Verlag für Sozialwissenschaften).

Heinrich Böll Stiftung (ed.) (2007) *Petra Kelly: Eine Erinnerung*, Berlin.

Helms, L. (2005) *Regierungsorganisation und politische Führung in Deutschland*, (Wiesbaden: VS Verlag für Sozialwissenschaften).

Helms, L. (2000) '"Politische Führung" als politikwissenschaftliches Problem' in *Politische Vierteljahresschrift*, 41, 411–34.

Inglehart, R. (1977) *The Silent Revolution: Changing Values and Political Styles among Western Publics* (Princeton, NJ: Princeton University Press).

Jenkins, J.C., Form, W. (2005) 'Social Movements and Social Change', Janoski, T., Alford, R., Hicks, A., Schwartz, M.A. (eds) *The Handbook of Political Sociology: States, Civil Societies, and Globalization* (Cambridge: Cambridge University Press), pp. 331–49.

Jesse, E. (2001) 'Die Parteien im westlichen Deutschland von 1945 bis zur deutschen Einheit 1990' Gabriel, O.W., Niedermayer, O., Stöss, R. (eds) *Parteiendemokratie in Deutschland* (Bonn: Bundeszentrale für politische Bildung) pp. 59–106.

Jones, B.D. (1989) 'Leader/Follower Interactions in Mass Democracies: Follower-Driven Models', Jones, B.D. (ed.) *Leadership and Politics: New Perspectives in Political Sciences,* (Kansas: University Press of Kansas), pp. 41–56.

Kelly, P. (1982) 'Wir sind die Antipartei-Partei', *Der Spiegel*, 14 June.

Kelly, P. (1983) *Um Hoffnung kämpfen* (Bornheim-Merten: Lamuv-Verlag).

Kelly, P. (1983) *Rede im Deutschen Bundestag*, 10. Wahlperiode, 36. Sitzung, Bonn, Dienstag 22 November.

Kielmansegg, P., Graf (2000) *Nach der Katastrophe: Eine Geschichte des geteilten Deutschlands* (Berlin: Severin & Siedler).

Lenze, M. (2002) *Postmodernes Charisma: Marken und Stars statt Religion und Vernunft* (Wiesbaden: Deutscher Universitäts-Verlag).

Lowry, S., Korte, H. (2000) *Der Filmstar* (Stuttgart: J.B. Metzler).

Marg, S., Geiges, L., Butzlaff, F., Walter, F. (eds) (2013) *Die neue Macht der Bürger: Was motiviert die Protestbewegungen?* (Bonn: Bundeszentrale für politische Bildung).

Markovits, A.S., Klaver, J. (2013) *Dreißig Jahre im Bundestag: Der Einfluss der Grünen auf die politische Kultur und das* öffentliche *Leben der Bundesrepublik Deutschland* (Berlin: Heinrich Böll Stiftung).

Markovits, A.S., Gorski, P.S. (1997) *Grün schlägt Rot: Die deutsche Linke nach 1945* (Hamburg: Rotbuch).

Markovits, A.S., (1993) *The German Left: Red, Green and Beyond* (Cambridge: Polity Press).

Meadows, D. H., Meadows, D. L., Randers, J., Behrens, W.W. III, (1972) *The Limits to Growth: A Report for the Club of Rome's Project on the Predicament of Mankind* (New York: A Potomac Associates Book).

Mende, S. (2011) *'Nicht rechts, nicht links, sondern vorn': Eine Geschichte der Gründungsgrünen* (München: Oldenbourg).

Müller-Rommel, F. (1993) *Grüne Parteien in Westeuropa: Entwicklungsphasen und Erfolgsbedingungen* (Opladen: Westdeutscher Verlag).

Nowotny, T. (1997) 'Aber was macht der Dumme schon mit dem Glück? Politische Führung durch Bruno Kreisky', Österreichische *Zeitschrift für Politikwissenschaft*, 26, 393–406.

Raschke, J. (2001) *'So kann man nicht regieren': Die Zukunft der Grünen* (Frankfurt/ Main: Campus-Verlag)

Raschke, J. (1993) *Die Grünen: Wie sie wurden, was sie sind* (Köln: Bund-Verlag).

Richter, S. (2005) 'Führung ohne Macht? Die Sprecher und Vorsitzenden der Grünen', Forkmann, D., Schlieben, M. (eds) *Die Parteivorsitzenden der Bundesrepublik Deutschland 1949–2005* (Wiesbaden: VS-Verlag für Sozialwissenschaften).

Richter, S. (2010) *Die Aktivistin: Das Leben der Petra Kelly* (München: Deutsche Verlags-Anstalt).

Richter, S. (2011) 'Der Protest gegen den NATO-Doppelbeschluss und die Konsolidierung der Partei Die Grünen zwischen 1979 und 1983', Gassert, P., Geiger, T., Wentker, H. (eds) *Zweiter Kalter Krieg und Friedensbewegung: Der NATO-Doppelbeschluss in deutsch-deutscher und internationaler Perspektive* (München: Oldenbourg), pp. 229–45.

Richter, S. (2012) 'Die Protagonisten der Friedensbewegung' in Becker-Schaum, C., Gassert, P., Klimke, M., Mausbach, W., Zepp, M. (eds) *'Entrüstet Euch!' Nuklearkrise, NATO-Doppelbeschluss und Friedensbewegung* (Paderborn u.a.: Schöningh) pp. 184–99.

Robertsen-von Trotha, C.Y. (Hg.) (2013) *Celebrity Culture: Stars in der Mediengesellschaft* (Baden-Baden: Nomos).

Roth, R., Rucht, D. (eds) (2008) *Die Sozialen Bewegungen in Deutschland seit 1945: Ein Handbuch* (Frankfurt/Main: Campus-Verlag).

Rucht, D. (2013) 'Schlüsselfiguren statt Führer. Zur (Selbst-)Steuerung sozialer Bewegungen', *Forschungsjournal Soziale Bewegungen*, 26, 32–43.

Sarcinelli, U. (1987) *Symbolische Politik. Zur Bedeutung symbolischen Handelns in der Wahlkampfkommunikation der Bundesrepublik Deutschland* (Opladen: Westdeutscher Verlag).

Schneider, W. (2006) *Große Verlierer: Von Goliath bis Gorbatschow* (Reinbek: Rowohlt)

Schröder, P.W. (1983) *'Deutscher Wahlkampf – Star in US-Zeitungen ist Petra Kelly', Neue Presse*, 4 March.

Schwarz, H.-P. (1998) *Das Gesicht des Jahrhunderts: Monster, Retter, Mediokritäten* (Berlin: Siedler).

Schwarzer, A. (2001) *Eine tödliche Liebe: Petra Kelly und Gert Bastian* (Köln: Kiepenheuer and Witsch).

Smith, J., Wiest, D. (2012) *Social Movements in the World-System: The Politics of Crisis and Transformation* (New York: Russell Sage Foundation).

Tarrow, S. (2005) *The New Transnational Activism* (Cambridge: Cambridge University Press).

Walter, F. (1997) 'Führung in der Politik. Am Beispiel sozialdemokratischer Parteivorsitzender', *Zeitschrift für Politikwissenschaft*, 7, 1287–336.

Weber, M. (2006 [1922]) *Wirtschaft und Gesellschaft* (Paderborn: Voltmedia).

Weber, M. (2010 [1922]) *Economy and Society* (London: Routledge).

Wiesenthal, H. (1993) 'Kapitel 5: Programme' in Raschke, J. (Hg.): *Die Grünen: Wie sie wurden, was sie sind* (Köln: Bund-Verlag), pp. 95–130.

14
Erika Steinbach: The Last Charismatic Representative of the Expellees?

Lionel Picard

Introduction

The expellees were the millions of Germans who were forced to flee their homelands or were sent to the Western part of Germany at the end of the Second World War. At the time of the Potsdam Conference (July–August 1945), the Allies established new German borders, and the German populations that lived on the east side of the Oder–Neisse line were deported to what remained of German territory (the Allied occupation zones, the future Federal Republic of Germany (FRG) and German Democratic Republic (GDR)). The legal uncertainty concerning the definitiveness of these borders elicited hope of return to their regions of origin among the expellees (for some of them up until the reunification of 1990). In 1949, the new German state of the FRG included millions of expellees who organized themselves in several associations on local and national levels. The associations pursued various objectives, including political demands, calls for relief programs and efforts to preserve their cultural heritage.

The expellees had such a significant demographic weight that they represented a non-negligible electoral lobby. Hopeful of returning to their homelands, they had high expectations for the foreign policies adopted by the federal government and, until the end of the 1960s, put considerable pressure on the parties in power to come to an agreement on the provisional status of the German–Polish border (Ahonen, 2003: 179). One political party in particular (Bund der Heimatvertriebenen und Entrechteten) claimed to represent them, but this was only briefly at the beginning of the 1950s. This party consisted of Bundestag members and ministers in Konrad Adenauer's government. The political integration of the expellees was successful because the group was represented by associations, rather than developing into a bloc of protest voters (Fischer, 2010: 272–85). The leaders of the expellee associations were important public figures, and in 1961 the group actually represented 21 percent of the population (Beer, 2011). Today, over 65 years after the expulsions, there remains only a small number of the original 12 million people of all ages who arrived as refugees or expellees at the end of the war. Nevertheless, interest in the expulsions and in the history of the expellees is strong, and the topic is kept alive through various media (literary works, television documentaries, scientific studies on the psychological consequences of the event and controversial memorials). From amid this contemporary debate, as media-centered as it is political, one leading figure stands out: Erika Steinbach, president of the Federation of Expellees (Bund der Vertriebenen (BdV)) since 1998.

Erika Steinbach has been a conservative party Bundestag member since 1990, which means that, except for five years spent as part of the opposition from 1998 to 2003, she has always been a member of the ruling majority. From 2000 to 2010 she even held a seat on the party's national board. She has thus played an important role inside the party in power, which has only strengthened her status among the expellees. Those who think that her actions are not effective or lack resolution, however, argue that Steinbach is too closely tied to her party to offer the BdV an independent political voice. She is, in fact, the link between the expellees (and the lobby they make up) and the conservative party. Many other representatives of the expellees are also members of conservative parties, but Steinbach's position as president of the BdV makes her the most important interlocutor for the government. Steinbach defends the close ties between the BdV and the conservative parties. According to her, the distancing that took place between the BdV and the government (SPD and FDP) in the 1970s was a mistake, leading to the isolation of the movement and the adoption of a hardline stance, which she judged 'understandable emotionally, but politically idiotic' (Steinbach, 2010: 89). If her loyalty to both her party and her association is clear, it does not prevent her from criticizing both groups: she distanced herself from the party's national board in September 2010 after being attacked by fellow party members, and when *Der Spiegel* magazine revealed that founding members of the BdV were more implicated in Nazism than had been previously imagined, she asked a renowned historical research center to investigate and shed light on this aspect of the group's past.[1]

Erika Steinbach's leadership role in the BdV is somewhat unusual in that it concerns both the political and private spheres. Steinbach holds a seat in the German parliament, but it is above all as president of the large national federation of expellees that she has become known to the general public and the media. The relationship she maintains with the members of her association is based on their genuine support for a charismatic leader such as defined by Max Weber (Weber, 1978). Her leadership has never been seriously questioned, and Steinbach knows that she can count on her base to defend her actions. The defiance and rejection she elicits from some segments of the population are proportional to the support she receives from the ranks of the BdV. Since the end of the 1960s the gap has been increasing between the expectations of the expellees and their treatment by large media outlets (Kittel, 2007: 147–69). Steinbach herself does not escape criticism; indeed, she often becomes the focus of it as the almost exclusive representative of the expellees. In that sense, the media, which participate in the demonization of the BdV and its president, play a non-negligible role in reinforcing the personal relationship between Steinbach and the members of the BdV. Steinbach's charisma is based, in fact, on the extent to which her individual qualities respond to the expectations of the group.

Before discussing how she became an indispensable leader, this chapter begins with an overview of Erika Steinbach's predecessors and the rivalries which marked the existence of the expellee associations. Then it focuses on her relationship with the media and her role in politics to show how her strategies tend to classify her as a grassroots-connector but also a communicator, following the typology presented in the introduction to this volume. This analysis concludes with a reflection on the strategic nature of Steinbach's position by showing, through a significant concrete example from the recent past, the effect that her name alone can have in the public sphere.

Figures from the past

The organization of the representation of the expellees

From the beginning, it had been extremely difficult for the expellees to get organized. In fact, following their arrival in the occupation zones after the war, the expellees did not have the right to organize themselves into associations as the Allies feared the formation of protest groups, which might risk becoming centers of revanchism. Furthermore, despite the end of the ban on organizations that came with the creation of the FRG, it took a decade for the expellees to succeed in establishing representative groups. It was not until the end of the 1950s that the organization of the expellees became a reality (Stickler, 2004: 33–99).

The main challenge was to choose between two opposite methods of organization. Would it be better to opt for national organizations for the expellees along the lines of their native regions (Silesia, East Prussia and so on) or a single organization for all of the expellees then living in a given region in the FRG (Bavaria, Lower-Saxony etc.)? Indeed, the sense of identity that comes from one's native region is very strong, and the expellees were not prepared to renounce it. The particularism was so intense that for at least one native region, two competing associations had to coexist (two provincial associations representing Silesia).[2] Instead of favoring a single organization that downplayed regional differences, thus making the group as a whole stronger, the expellees ended up organizing themselves into both national associations corresponding to their various homelands and provincial groups in which all expellees of a given part of the FRG were members. In the absence of a common structure for all expellees, it was impossible to find a leader who could speak for them all. Instead, rivalries began to form; the leaders of the different organizations were constantly competing with each other and a multitude of public figures tried to make themselves heard. Each association had its own political ideology and the lack of coordination reduced the effectiveness of the group as a whole. The leaders of each of the nationally organized regional associations tended to exaggerate the uniqueness of their movement at the expense of the collective project. The absence of a central leader and the rivalry between the different organizations explains, in part, why the expellees failed to mobilize effectively against the *Ostpolitik* at the end of the 1960s and the signing of the eastern treaties at the beginning of the 1970s.[3] In 1990, the price that had to be paid for the unification of the two German states was the definitive renouncement of any claims to the eastern territories; there was intense resentment among the expellees who regretted that the divisions within their own organizational structures was what, to a large extent, had made their actions ineffective (Gröger, 1991).

The rivalry among the representative organizations

Despite the large number of expellee associations, certain individual public figures had a stronger influence than others. The provincial organizations, in fact, played a marginal role and their voice carried little weight at the federal level. In terms of the larger national associations, it was still necessary to create a distinction based on the geographical origins of the expellees. Indeed, if the nationally organized regional associations of the Federation of Expellees had an equivalent status, their actual political weight was, however, very different depending on their numbers. The Germans from East and West Prussia represented a demographic weight (1,890,000 expellees) that was much more significant than that of those from Brandenburg (410,000) (Beer, 2011: 85). The Germans from Silesia or the Sudetenland were the most numerous, and their representatives were the most listened to in the media and the political sphere as they were considered the most representative of the expellees.

Two main leaders emerged and occupied prominent positions, both politically and in the media, during the 1970s and 1980s, and they alone came to symbolize the expellees as a collective group in the FRG as well as in Poland (Schumann, 2009). However, Herbert Hupka (Bundestag member affiliated with the SPD, 1969–72, and with the CDU, 1972–87), the founding leader of the association of Silesians (1968–2000), and Herbert Czaja (CDU Bundestag member, 1953–87), founding leader of the Federation of Expellees (1970–94), were not successful in collaborating as their rivalry was too fierce.[4] Rather than creating a bond, their common geographical origin only exacerbated their rivalry (Czaja was born in Teschen/Cieszyn in Upper Silesia, while Hupka grew up in Ratibor/Racibórz, also in Upper Silesia). While Czaja spoke in the name of all the expellees, as he was the head of the sole national structure which claimed to defend the interests of all expellees, Hupka was merely the representative of a nationally organized regional group, although it was also the largest (Silesians). Herbert Hupka's political influence was considerably reinforced by the fact that he was a Social Democratic Bundestag member (SDP) up until 1972 and changed parties in 1972 precisely because of his categorical opposition to the eastern treaties. Many other Social Democratic members of the Bundestag had similarly turned their backs on their party to join the CDU, endangering the fragile majority in the Bundestag of the center-left coalition (SDP and FDP).

The personal rivalry between the two main leaders interfered with their capacity for action and helps explains why the expellees did not carry much weight in German foreign policy — or rather why the expellees always had the official support of the right-wing conservatives, but without this actually giving them any real influence on governmental policy. Each of the two leaders was more focused on defending his own position than genuinely acting as the spokesman of all the expellees. Czaja led the BdV for a long time, and he appointed his successor, Hartmut Koschyk, with whom he quarreled in the end because he adopted a policy that was not uncompromising enough for Czaja. This example demonstrates the challenges faced by the associations when it became time for a renewal of leadership, which would sometimes involve taking a less hardline political stance. Above all, it became apparent that the political success of the associations was directly linked to the personality of their leaders and that the quarrels between them had detrimental consequences on their objectives.

The associations benefited from financial support from the state and from the Länder, and a lot of money was given to them each year. If a portion of the money was used to finance national meetings and other important gatherings, or even the organization of exhibitions or cultural events, another non-negligible portion was used to cover the living expenses of association personnel. As the associations were numerous, the official representatives of the expellees were legion. Many of them lived off public subsidies and were thus referred to as 'professional expellees' (*Berufsvertriebene*) or 'permanent association staff' (*Vertriebenenfunktionäre*) by their adversaries, as a way of discrediting those who defended the expellees without having an electoral mandate or any real democratic legitimacy. The representatives of the expellees were often attacked for making a career out of their political commitment and for being more interested in defending their own jobs than in doing anything substantial for their group. It was thus, to some extent, more the comfort of their official positions that interested them than the interests of the group they claimed to defend. Indeed, their daily preoccupations often appeared to be far from the concerns of the expellees.

The expellee associations, a primarily male-oriented world

It is not surprising to note that during the 1950s the leadership roles in the expellee associations were almost entirely in the hands of men and that women were very few in number. But in the 1990s the situation had not changed, and the main leaders of the associations continued to be almost exclusively men. Whether it was a question of the nationally organized regional associations or the provincial associations, all the groups were led by men, not only at the top, but also in the governing bodies. This can be explained, in part, by the fact that the close links between the associations and the conservatives tend to correspond with a general desire to see men lead as well as by a reluctance to renew the leadership (the generation that lived through the expulsion was not always willing to give up their positions to young people who had not experienced the event themselves and were thus considered less legitimate). This male dominance of the movement might seem unimportant, but it needs to be taken into consideration in order to better understand why the election of Erika Steinbach as the new president of the BdV constituted such a sharp break with past.

Erika Steinbach

Steinbach, president of the BdV

Erika Steinbach was elected president of the BdV in 1998 and has been re-elected since every two years. She is thus at the head of the largest organization representing the expellees. At the same time, the nationally organized regional expellee organizations no longer have a charismatic leader like Herbert Hupka. The leaders that still do have a presence in the media owe their notoriety to their extremism. Rudi Pawelka, president up until 2013 of the association representing expellees from Silesia, became known to the public through his support for the *Preußische Treuhand,* a trust that wanted to use any legal means possible to obtain compensation for the losses incurred during the expulsion. In addition, sensational declarations against Poland ended up isolating Pawelka within his own movement and leaving the door open for Steinbach to become the new representative of all the expellees.

It was primarily through an innovative initiative that Erika Steinbach was first noticed by the general public: in September 2000 she announced the formation of the Center against Expulsions.[5] According to the BdV, its function is to create a place that demonstrates how twentieth-century European history was marked by expulsions. This announcement immediately provoked uproar in Germany due to fears that the expellees would create an institution whose goal was the rewriting of the history of the Second World War, in which the expellees – and the Germans more generally – would be portrayed as victims. Indeed, with the extreme right often supporting such views, the question of Germans as victims of the war is highly controversial in Germany (Niven, 2006). While the arguments continued, Steinbach became an object of media attention, and she established herself as the sole spokesperson for all questions concerning the expellees. It was mainly the absence of serious rivals that allowed her to distinguish herself, but her resolute support for her controversial foundation helped her overshadow other leaders. The project, in fact, responded to an overwhelming desire on the part of the expellees to have their destiny symbolically recognized in a space dedicated to their memory. Many of their leaders had, indeed, regretted the fact that Germany did not commemorate the history of the expulsions, but none had demonstrated any intention of creating such a memorial. In fact, Erika Steinbach announced that the

BdV would come up with the necessary funding to create a site for exhibitions and information about the expulsions. This initiative provoked a very strong reaction in both German politics and the media and set off many arguments and debates that lasted for several years.

An eternal enemy in the eyes of Poland

For decades, the expellees have been demonized in Poland. As Germans, they represent the age-old enemy, but even after the war they remained a symbol of danger for the Polish who were concerned that they would return to retake possession of their former lands and homes. In fact, the expellees claimed the right to return and demanded the reintegration of the territories along the German borders lost at the end of the war (Demshuk, 2012). The revisionism embodied by the leaders of the expellee associations elicited much fear in Poland. Czaja and Hupka became symbols of revanchism, or even fascist imperialism, according, at least, to the communist propaganda. Today, it is Erika Steinbach alone who embodies this imposing legacy. Her legitimacy to speak in the name of the expellees is, however, frequently questioned. Steinbach was born in West Prussia in the city of Rahmel/Rumia in 1943.[6] Her family fled to the West in the spring of 1945. Her mother was a civil servant while her father was a soldier of Lower Silesian origin. The family lived in this region of Germany because of the war, and Erika Steinbach is often criticized for defending a region that was not really her own. Indeed, she was born in a region in which her parents had only lived for a very short time, and which, before the invasion of Poland, had not been a part of Germany for nearly 20 years. This criticism was made of various expellee representatives with the goal of denying their legitimacy to speak for a group of which they supposedly were not a part. Among the expellees themselves, however, such considerations were of no importance. If Erika Steinbach was regularly attacked by her political adversaries because of her native origins, her legitimacy was never questioned by the expellees themselves.

When the Polish media want to warn the public about the German expellees and their territorial or financial demands, it is systematically Erika Steinbach that they focus on. One controversial image in particular helped draw attention to her in both Germany and Poland. The Polish magazine *Wprost* outraged the public in both countries in September 2003 when it portrayed Erika Steinbach in a photomontage featuring her on the front cover wearing an SS uniform while straddling the back of Chancellor Gerhard Schröder. The Social Democratic chancellor was depicted as the Trojan Horse of the revisionist goals of the

expellees, even though Schröder and Steinbach were unwavering political adversaries (Schröder formally opposed the BdV's policies). Erika
Steinbach has herself also contributed to disrupting diplomatic relations
between Germany and Poland. It is indeed because she acquired a solid
reputation among the expellees and because she alone embodies the
media's representation of this group of the population that the CDU
continues to give her a choice role within the party. But Erika Steinbach
is an embarrassing presence as far as relationships with neighboring
countries go. For the Polish media she embodies the eternal enemy, and
her declarations are always interpreted through an anti-German lens,
whether her comments are overtly hostile or seemingly conciliatory
(Urban, 2010).

A double-edged status

Erika Steinbach has thus acquired a stature that has made her a major
personality in the world of German politics. What are the consequences
of the leadership she exercises over the expellees as a group? Does she
represent an asset or a liability for this group? In fact, her indispensable
position is both at the same time.

An asset

First of all, Steinbach's leadership allows the expellees to have a single legitimate spokesperson in its relations with German institutions,
contrary to the prevailing situation in the 1970s when the expellees
struggled in vain against the *Ostpolitik* of Willy Brandt. At that time, a
cacophony reigned among the expellees because the different organizations did not want to lose ground in the face of their rivals and the
leaders spoke without any unified organization. The multitude of
declarations caused by the rivalry among associations paradoxically
diminished the overall influence of the group, whereas Erika Steinbach
has guaranteed them a significant voice in the media as their sole representative. The project of the Center against Expulsions owed much
of its success, in fact, to Steinbach's personality. She made the project
a fundamental goal for the BdV and the expellees, and she would stop
at nothing to accomplish this task. As long as this goal had not been
reached, there was little chance she would step down from her position
as president of the BdV. As a conservative member of the Bundestag and
a member of national board of the CDU, she has served as an important
political link between the expellees and the conservative party, and
thus as an indisputable grassroots-connector. The CDU has not been

able to refuse to guarantee her a position as member of the Bundestag without running the risk of cutting themselves off from the expellees, whereas in the past, the most embarrassing leaders were left on the sidelines when other members of the party came forth as candidates in the legislative elections. Since Steinbach is now the only charismatic representative, her place is assured. She has made herself an indispensable member of the conservative party. And the risk of a break between her and her party could only come from Steinbach herself since she has already publicly criticized the CDU for not being far enough to the right. Similarly, refusing to support the construction of the commemoration site desired by Steinbach would also mean alienating a large part of the CDU's traditional electorate. Steinbach's provocations tarnish the image of her party in the eyes of general public opinion, but the CDU, as just stated, cannot afford to cut itself off from her and the millions of expellees she represents.

A liability?

The progress of the memorial site project was partly slowed down by Steinbach herself. She, in fact, associated herself with so many objects of fear on the Polish side that any controversial declarations made by her were immediately taken up by the media. Indeed, in the past, Steinbach has not exactly been very compatible with diplomacy. In the Bundestag, for example, she voted against the border treaty of November 14, 1990, which recognized the German–Polish border (the argument of the non-resolved question of lost possessions served as a pretext). And she indulged in scornful claims about Władysław Bartoszewski (Auschwitz survivor and former Polish minister of foreign affairs), who is widely respected,[7] but whom she claimed had a 'poor character' as he did not respond to her letters.[8] Her declarations regarding the Polish responsibility for the beginning of the Second World War put her at the margins of the political field and led to her being pushed out of the CDU national board. As a matter of fact, Steinbach thus exposed her project and the institution that she represented in the heat of the criticisms. It is also, however, in this way that she succeeded in imposing herself in the media and becoming indispensable. An unassuming weak and complaisant character would not have had the same impact. When the large governmental coalition (SPD/CDU) was succeeded by a center-right coalition (FDP/CDU) in October 2009, the new minister of foreign affairs (Guido Westerwelle, who thus became part of federal government for the first time) asserted his authority by declaring his opposition to Erika Steinbach's appointment to the collegiate governing body of the

Commemoration Foundation planned by the previous government. He refused to accept the idea of such a controversial figure – who was seen in Poland as the symbol of German revanchism – being in control of the new Center. This unacceptable affront for the BdV precipitated a serious crisis that threatened the survival of the entire project. Continuing the project would have been impossible for the government without the participation of the BdV, and impossible for the BdV without the financial support of the government. The BdV applied the 'empty chair' policy, refusing to participate in any discussions for several months, until a compromise was finally agreed upon: Erika Steinbach gave up her seat, which was normally hers by right as president of the BdV, in exchange for greater representation of the BdV in the Center's board of directors and an increase in the size of the Center's exhibition area. While she did indeed capitulate in giving up her seat, she also helped her organization gain more influence. In the end, it was a question of personality that determined the influence of the BdV on the project. From the moment Steinbach agreed to remove herself from direct involvement in the Center, the project lost its political dimension and the creation of a true exhibition and research center became possible (Douglas, 2012: 361).

Conclusion

Is Erika Steinbach the last charismatic representative of the expellees? Their numbers are dwindling, and what legacy they leave behind depends to a large extent on the actions of the BdV. The last victims of the expulsions are disappearing as the twenty-first century advances, and the BdV has taken on the mission of fixing the memory of the expellees in the German collective consciousness. The public and media are now paying closer attention to this population as they are rapidly decreasing in number, helping public leaders of the group make their voices heard. Will Steinbach really be the last? It is impossible to say with certainty, but that may very well be the case. Given the dwindling numbers, there is very little chance that this group will once again find itself at the center of public attention. Indeed, the heated debate over the memorial site no doubt represents the end of intense media focus attention on the expellees.

However, Erika Steinbach's important role as charismatic leader of the expellees is undeniable. No one has disputed her supremacy and she alone has become the embodiment of the millions of expellees, regardless of their opinion of the BdV, which expellees are far from supporting unanimously. Her replacement is clearly not a current priority, and there are no candidates stepping up to take her place.[9] There is thus little risk of a battle for control among leaders of the BdV. If there had been such a risk, a war of succession would no doubt have already occurred. Erika Steinbach was at the center of various media storms. No one challenged her role or actions as president of the BdV then. Her eminent presence within the CDU and her extremely conservative position have made her an easily identifiable figure who, along with others, embodies the most radical wing of the conservative party. She recently declared, on several occasions, that she did not see herself in agreement with the criticisms of certain members of the CDU. When Thio Sarrazin caused a controversy with an anti-immigrant book in 2009 (Sarrazin, 2010), the media speculated on the emergence of a new political movement to the right of the CDU (Hildebrandt, 2010). Erika Steinbach was inevitably cited as an indispensable figure for this new movement. She thus not only took hold of the group of expellees, but her influence goes well above and beyond this specific group to include the most conservative branches of the right-wing parliamentary group.

Notes

1   The Institut für Zeitgeschichte recently published the results of this work on the leaders of the BdV in 1958: Schwartz, M. (2012).
2   While the Landsmannschaft der Oberschlesier represented the Germans of Upper Silesia, the Landsmannschaft Schlesien – Nieder- und Oberschlesien e. V. claimed to represent the Germans of both Upper and Lower Silesia.
3   The political stakes were not the same for all expellees as they did not all pursue the same goal. The return to the borders of 1937 supported by the natives of Silesia did not, for example, satisfy the Sudeten Germans.
4   Hupka asserted that a Pole had once told him that in his childhood his mother would threaten him when he refused to eat by claiming that Czaja and Hupka would come and take him away.
5   Stiftung Zentrum gegen Vertreibungen.
6   In 1920, at the time of the Treaty of Versailles, this land belonged to Poland. It was occupied by Germany from 1939 on.
7   During a speech by Władysław Bartoszewski on April 28, 1995, in front of the Bundestag, the minister of foreign affairs even paid homage to the expellees. http://www.dpg-bundesverband.de/links_und_dokumente/bv_zeitgeschichte/1494279.html. Accessed on 8 June 2014.
8   A declaration made on the public television channel ZDF on September 16, 2010.
9   Of her two commitments (CDU and BdV), Steinbach clearly chose that in favor of the expellees in 2010, preferring a crisis with her own party rather than giving up her position as the president of the BdV.

Works cited

Ahonen, P. (2003) *After the Expulsion: West Germany and Eastern Europe 1945–1990* (Oxford: Oxford University Press).

Beer, M. (2011) *Flucht und Vertreibung der Deutschen. Voraussetzungen, Verlauf, Folgen* (Munich: Beck).

Demshuk, A. (2012) *The lost German East: forced migration and the politics of memory, 1945–1970* (Cambridge and New York: Cambridge University Press).

Douglas, R.M. (2012) *Orderly and Humane: The Expulsion of the Germans after the Second World War* (New Haven and Conn London: Yale University Press).

Fischer, W. (2010) *Heimat-Politiker? Selbstverständnis und politisches Handeln von Vertriebenen als Abgeordnete im Deutschen Bundestag 1949 bis 1974* (Düsseldorf: Droste Verlag).

Gröger, H. (1991) 'Das Ding mit der "Glaubwürdigkeit"', *Grafschafter Bote*, XII, 1.

Hildebrandt, T. (2010) 'Noch nicht. Eine rechte Partei gründen? Was die CDU-Enttäuschten davon halten', *Die Zeit*, XXXVIII.

Kittel, M. (2007) *Vertreibung der Vertriebenen? Der historische deutsche Osten in der Erinnerungskultur der Bundesrepublik (1961–1982)* (Munich: Oldenbourg Verlag).

Niven, B. (ed.) (2006) *Germans as Victims: Remembering the Past in Contemporary Germany* (Basingtoke, Hampshire: Palgrave Macmillan).

Sarrazin, T. (2010) *Deutschland schafft sich ab* (Munich: DVA).

Schumann, R. (2009) '"Scham als gemeinsame Chance". Aber auch die ist im deutsch-polnischen Verhältnis vertan, sobald oberflächliche Friedfertigkeit historischer Aufrichtigkeit das Wort verbietet', *Grafschafter Bote*, I, 1.

Schwartz, M. (2012) *Funktionäre mit Vergangenheit: Das Gründungspräsidium des Bundesverbandes der Vertriebenen und das 'Dritte Reich'* (Munich: Oldenbourg Verlag).

Steinbach, E. (2010) *Die Macht der Erinnerung* (Vienna: Universitas Verlag).

Stickler, M. (2004) *'Ostdeutsch heißt gesamtdeutsch': Organisation, Selbstverständnis und heimatpolitische Zielsetzungen der deutschen Vertriebenenverbände 1949–1972* (Düsseldorf: Droste Verlag).

Urban, T. (2010) 'Aufregung um die "blonde Bestie"', *Süddeutsche Zeitung*.

Weber, M. (1978) [1922] *Economy and Society* (Berkeley: University of California Press).

15
Edward Heath: The Failed Leadership of an Uninspiring Leader

Laetitia Langlois

Introduction

The question of leadership in contemporary Western democracies is a fascinating subject for the historian as it explores the emergence of a man or woman inside a party and the unique relationship he or she builds with the people. Leadership is commonly associated to Max Weber's theory of 'charismatic leadership' (Weber, 1995) and according to the French philosopher Jean-Claude Monod there is a persistence of the politics of charisma in contemporary democracies. (Monod, 2012: 58) Thus, leadership seems to be essentially construed around positive notions of power, success, domination and authority. Yet there exist other forms of leadership worthy of analytical exploration and the rationale of this article will be the failed leadership of the British Prime Minister Edward Heath. Edward Heath was leader of the Conservative party for ten years, Prime Minister for four years and member of parliament for nearly 50 years. Yet, today few people remember Edward Heath. The Conservative pantheon is inhabited by the great and imposing figures of Churchill, Macmillan or Thatcher but Heath has completely disappeared from the Conservative memory. At the heart of this exclusion lies the utter and complete disaster of his years in power. Yet, Heath was certainly a pioneer in many domains. He was the man who first talked of a devolved assembly in Scotland, the man who had Britain join the European Union in 1973, the man who launched a comprehensive reform of trade unions well before Margaret Thatcher. But history only retains his failures and broken promises. Minor leaders tend to be cast aside by historians but those tragic figures of failure shed an original light on the question of leadership and help to better understand the complex mechanisms at work between a leader and his

followers. As party leader or national leader, Heath confused his followers and dismayed people inside his party. He always stood between two
opposite trends and always hesitated between two political personalities. Torn between a moderate progressive form of Conservatism and a
more aggressive free market approach or torn between the status of the
tough moderniser and the cautious man of consensus, in power Heath
never really found his true self (Blake, 1985: 299; Campbell, 1993: xix).
This chapter focuses on this instability at the heart of Heath's leadership
and posits that all the difficulties and failures of his leadership stem
from this division at the heart of his political identity and his incapacity
thereof to project a coherent and clear image to his followers. Stephen
Skowronek's theory of leadership[1] provides a useful framework to guide
our analysis and will better highlight the structural contradiction of
Heath's political nature (Skowronek, 1993).

Repudiation and emancipation:
Edward Heath, the man of change

In 1965, for the first time in its history, the Conservative party organised elections to choose its leader and Edward Heath became the first
leader ever to be democratically elected at the head of the Conservative
party. Compared with Reginald Maudling, his main contestant, Edward
Heath stood out as a peculiar figure for he did not have the traditional
Conservative profile: at 49, he was still a bachelor; he came from a modest background and had been educated in a grammar school. Politically
speaking, Conservative MPs did not know much about him and his
political stance. Two points nonetheless had singled him out from his
colleagues. First, his European convictions were genuine and he conducted the negotiations for British entry to the European Union (EU) in
1963 with much vigour and passion. Second, in 1964, in spite of massive resistance from inside his own party, he succeeded in having the
system of Resale Price Maintenance[2] abolished (Ramsden, 1980: 236). It
was a highly controversial measure considering that it went against the
interests of small shopkeepers – a traditional Conservative electorate –
but he stood firm judging that '[it] would show us to be a dynamic,
modernising force' (Heath, 1998: 260). Why then did the party elect
Heath instead of a more traditional figure like Maudling? Who were his
followers and what exactly did they follow?

First, the press played a key role in Heath's election as head of the
party. John Campbell insists on the fact that Heath received 'flattering
profiles bearing very little relation to reality' (Campbell, 1993: 190).

He was presented as the young and tough moderniser, the champion of a new form of Conservatism and the representative of a new generation of politicians who would transform British politics. *The Economist* called him 'the abrasive man of change' (*The Economist*, 31 July 1965); in other newspapers he was commonly defined as the 'rough rider' or the 'tiger in the party's tank' (CPA, PPB 12, 26 July 1965). The press emphasised his modernising dimension and reforming spirit in order to instil a sense of novelty and renewal. Heath was usually compared to or seen as the new John Kennedy (Campbell, 1993: 190). Every epoch needs a hero and in the summer 1965, Ted Heath was the new hero (Sandbrook, 2006: 163). Nothing could be more ridiculous than comparing Ted Heath with John Kennedy but this is not simply an amusing anecdote. It reveals the sense of collective expectation that was pervading Britain in the mid-1960s. In terms of economic power or international influence, Britain was lagging behind and everyone was waiting for the politician who would restore Britain's prestige. And to the press in general there was no doubt that this man was Edward Heath.

Strangely enough, two years before he had not even been a serious contestant and was not particularly known to have a group of followers behind him. But in 1965 the situation was exceptional and circumstances worked in his favour. The Conservative party had lost an election and it needed not only a party leader but a leader of the opposition capable of rivalling Harold Wilson. Periods in opposition have always been difficult for the Conservative party because it has always considered itself 'to be the natural party of government in British politics' (Bale, 2010: 4) and that position was now being taken over by the Labour party. The pressure then to recover power was immense and one must point out the fundamentally pragmatic dimension of Heath's election. Samuel Brittan was amazed by the 'extraordinarily small part policy issues played in the choice between Heath and Maudling' (Brittan, 1968: 57), an argument shared by John Campbell who reveals that 'there was no ideological content to the contest at all' (Campbell, 1993: 180). His followers were not people bound by a set of common convictions, principles, values and ideas. They were a very vague indistinct group of people more concerned with finding the right candidate to beat Wilson than electing a leader with a coherent set of policies. Heath's choice was guided by the Conservatives' desperate attempt to come back to power (Ball and Seldon, 2005). A few days after the election, *The Economist* underlined the party's opportunism and wrote a prescient paragraph on the party's attitude towards its new leader:

Mr Heath certainly carries radical hopes in his baggage. But in electing him the Tories have primarily shown their instinct for power. They picked, by a narrow majority, the man they reckoned most likely to bullock their way back into power. They will remain united behind just as long as his pursuit of power looks promising. (*The Economist*, 31 July 1965)

Pragmatism and ambition made Heath's election, not enthusiasm, admiration or fascination. From the start, the union of his followers rested on a very fragile basis and the tensions that arose soon after derived from this original weakness. They did not particularly like Heath but they needed him because he was, as Tim Heppell explains, 'a symbol of a modern and socially representative Conservative party' (Heppell, 2008: 39). With him the party hoped to get rid of its elitist image and widen its electorate. Heppell also argues that Heath was 'an instrument of modernisation and meritocracy' thanks to his lower-middle class origins. (Heppell, 2008: 39) The use of the word 'instrument' reveals that Heath had a purely utilitarian function in the party. He had been elected to project a modern image but modernisation was still a concept that many Conservatives considered with caution and suspicion (Campbell, 1993: 199). Heath wanted to be the man of radical change in a party that defines itself as the 'guardian of national continuity' (Layton-Henry, 1980: xiii).This does not mean that the party is adverse to change but the real nature of the Conservative party is in a 'continuing dialogue between the themes of continuity and change' (Norton and Aughey, 1981: 13). Thus, the capacity for adaptation and change does not supersede an atavistic attachment to traditions. This combination of continuity and change is the soul, the essence, of the Conservative party but it is also its most complex feature, as Roger Scruton emphasises: 'the desire to conserve is compatible with all manner of change, provided only that change is also continuity' (Scruton, 1980: 22). Being leader of the Conservative party requires considerable skilfulness and an acute awareness that the past is not to be dispensed with but revered as a constant guide to the making of policy.

Though an admirer of Harold Macmillan, Heath did not at the beginning of his leadership envisage following in his predecessor's footsteps. Macmillan was a political father but Heath was not at the head of the party to perpetuate a tradition but to open a new chapter and start a new era of Conservatism.[3] Heath was never interested in the political philosophy of the party. He was a pragmatist at heart, a man who believed that common sense, political will and some dose of risk-taking were sufficient elements to make Britain prosperous again (Hurd, 1979: 12). He lacked one fundamental quality as far as the Conservative party was concerned: the sense of history, the sense of being the inheritor of a long and respected tradition of values, themes and ideals. Interestingly, Gamble explains that Heath was a man 'who rejected Conservatism as a political philosophy and argued that a Conservative party, to be an effective political force, had to turn its back on the past and become a party of progress' (Gamble, 1974: 91).

Stephen Skowronek raises the concept of 'repudiation' to describe the process of emancipation that animates a new leader wishing to impose his signature on the party. Repudiation is what best characterises Heath's intentions and state of mind when he became leader of the Conservative party. This repudiation took three forms: linguistic, human and political.

Soon after he was elected, Heath sent a letter to the Conservative Central Office indicating that he no longer wanted the term 'Tory' to be used but instead insisted on the use of the term 'Conservative' (CPA, CCO 4/10/152, 15 December 1967). The term 'Tory' conveyed an outdated image he wanted to get rid of. Also, during his years as leader of the opposition, from 1965 to 1970, reading all his speeches nowhere did I find a single reference to the One Nation tradition (CPA, PPB 14–17). He never mentioned this Disraelian legacy which was also so closely associated to the great figures of postwar Conservatism such as Churchill, Butler or Macmillan. One Nation Conservatism is a branch of the Conservative party which endorsed the postwar consensus and was primarily concerned with guaranteeing a fair and decent way of life to all citizens. One Nation Conservatives believed in Keynesian economics in the sense that, to them, the state had a major role to play as protector of its citizens. One Nation was a direct reference to Benjamin Disraeli, their icon, and they profoundly believed in a set of values such as social justice, prosperity for all and national cohesion (Green, 2002: 247–8). Philip Norton and Arthur Aughey sum up the One Nation philosophy as the reconciliation of the twin concepts of 'compassion and competence' (Norton and Aughey, 1981: 78). Edward Heath was always proud of identifying himself with the One Nation philosophy and was proud of having been one of the founding members of the One Nation group in 1951. Only during that short period in opposition did he play it down in order to project a more radical image. The concept resurfaced later, during his premiership when troubles increased significantly and tradition appeared a useful tool to unify the party and the nation. But at the beginning of his leadership, it seems that Heath did not consider that there could be a clever balance between a respect for tradition and an impetus for modernisation.

Repudiation was not just symbolised by the change in names but also by the change in people. Hardly a year after his election, Heath changed many men in the Shadow Cabinet with an avowed objective of marking 'a particularly significant stage in the transition towards a modern party' (Heath, 1998: 283). Some old warhorses such as Selwyn Lloyd, Duncan Sandys, John Boyd-Carpenter had to leave and were replaced by younger people who were to become – except one – Heath's closest colleagues: Robert Carr, William Whitelaw, Peter Walker and Margaret Thatcher. Edward du Cann left the chairmanship of the party and was replaced by Anthony Barber who was to become Heath's loyal Chancellor of the Exchequer (Ramsden, 1996: 250). Heath introduced a group of men he knew well and trusted for they had the same background and did not pose any threat. This group of men would later be known as the 'Heathmen' and became even more important when hostilities grew between Heath and the rest of the party[4] (Roth, 1972).

Finally, in terms of policies, Heath had a grand plan of reform and was determined to present a whole new programme that would, as he wrote in a letter, 'break our links with the past and build a new framework of policies' in order to achieve 'a fairly fundamental shift' (CPA, LCC Papers, 4 February 1970). To do so, Heath decided to retain all the posts he had held prior to his election. He continued to supervise the Economic Policy Group; he also stayed at the head of the Advisory Committee on Policy until 1968 and continued to control the Conservative Research Department together with Michael Fraser. He kept absolute control of the most strategic spheres of policy-making inside the party so much so that John Ramsden observes, 'Heath had more personal monopoly of authority in the Party than any leader before him since Neville Chamberlain' (Ramsden, 1996: 235). The modernisation of the Conservative party in his own image was at the roots of his commitment to politics. He exploited this monopoly to work out a new programme of radical policies. The document entitled *Putting Britain Right Ahead* was issued in 1965 and contained the main aspects of Heath's Conservative society (CPA, CCO 600/12/7, 1965). It presented a discourse based on dynamism, competitiveness and excellence. Heath's project was very clear: a European Britain whose prestige would lie in a dynamic recovery and a competitive modern industry. Thus, the maintenance of the postwar consensus no longer seemed a priority compared with Britain's economic excellence. Slashing public spending, reducing budget deficit and curbing inflation became the new priorities in Heath's Conservative discourse. As such, we can side with John Campbell when he affirms that his economic programme at the time was 'proto-Thatcherite' (Campbell, 1993: 267), hence the disappearance of the One Nation concept from his vocabulary to better enhance the impression of a radical departure. Another major twist was the overriding importance of Europe in Heath's vision: his ambition and greatest cause were to secure entry in the European Union to enjoy the benefits of the Common Market and emancipate the country from its historic ties with the Commonwealth and the USA (Heath, 1998: 361).

With the publication of *Putting Britain Right Ahead*, Heath not only wanted to impose his vision of Conservatism, he also wanted to cultivate the image of the innovator, the moderniser. Heath saw himself as a man of action whose role was to jostle the party out of its traditionalism. But not everyone in the party was satisfied with his sweeping behaviour and his irreverence towards the past. *The Times* reported an episode that illustrates this malaise inside the party. Lady Douglas-Home, visiting a local constituency, was applauded frantically by the audience when she warned Conservatives that 'they might become such a shiny bright new party that no one will recognize the true Conservatives in it' (*The Times*, 11 September 1965).

A very concrete illustration of his propensity to ignore tradition was his decision to convert the party to devolution in Scotland. In May 1968, attending a conference of the Conservative party in Perth, Heath announced that he would support the creation of a devolved assembly in Scotland. This would later be known as the Declaration of Perth, a major turning point in the Conservative party's approach to the Scottish question. The Conservative party had been heretofore a staunch defender of Unionism (the full name of the Conservative party being the Conservative and Unionist Party), therefore committing the party to the principle of Home Rule in Scotland was a revolutionary move (Bogdanor, 1979: 3). Inside the party there had been no consultation, only a few Shadow Cabinet members had heard of his intention, and everyone was presented with a *fait accompli*. Was this risk-taking, authoritative decision-making or simply opportunism in the face of poor electoral results in Scotland? The answer lies in all those three elements. There was a dose of opportunism in this pledge as Heath had never before really paid attention to the Scottish question, but the victory of the Scottish National Party (SNP) a year earlier at by-elections clearly precipitated this decision. It was also authoritative decision-making considering that he had not consulted his backbenchers before but Heath also enjoyed the image of the man who took tough decisions to carry the party forward. In his autobiography, Heath describes himself as a 'doer' and it was a waste of time for him to spend endless hours discussing the topic (Heath, 1998: 18). When he was convinced he could be in the lead on some questions he ignored the party and imposed his views. He could act independently in order to associate the party to a radical departure which would show its capacity for innovation and progress, this is exactly what he had done four years earlier with the abolition of the Resale Price Maintenance (Ball and Seldon, 1996: 21).

But it was not long before Heath met the massive resistance of the party. His modernising ambitions increasingly concerned Conservative MPs and some of them voiced their discontent in a forceful manner.

Disjunction: the collapse into indecision and elusiveness

Heath had been elected, and as such it gave him an undeniable legitimacy. After the much controverted emergence of Douglas-Home as leader in 1963, the election had been precisely aimed at giving 'an aura of authority over the Parliamentary Conservative Party and a perception of legitimacy as leader of the Conservative Party' (Heppell, 2008: 49). But legitimacy and authority are not equal and do not derive from the same sources. An election cannot give the natural authority that radiates from a charismatic and inspiring leader. Legitimacy, in Heath's case, was the result of the election. In Max Weber's terminology, his domination of the party was a rational legal process (Weber, 1995: 285). Authority, or 'charismatic leadership', has a more irrational dimension given that it has to do with the extraordinary qualities and skills of a man or woman (Weber, 1995: 320). 'Charismatic leadership' results from the confidence, the admiration and the devotion a leader naturally commands.

During his years as leader, Heath met considerable resistance from the traditional imperialist right and considerable hostility from those who refused the monopoly of modernisation. In *The Winds of Change*, John Ramsden explains that many Conservatives were hostile to this rhetoric of modernisation and change 'simply because they were natural conservatives who did not therefore see it as their Party's business to preach the opposite' (Ramsden, 1996: 11). Dominic Sandbrook adds that 'Heath's appeals to modernisation, rather than to tradition, did not fire up the Tory faithful' (Sandbrook, 2006: 159). The difficulty for Heath is that he was elected at a time of major transition. The party had lost two general elections successively, it had to adapt to the status of a party of Opposition, it also had to adapt to a society in flux. Defeat, introspection, anxiety: those three ingredients combined together provoked a Tory malaise that Heath, as leader, was supposed to allay and cure. For a great leader, this challenging and stimulating situation would have been an opportunity for excellence; for an awkward leader like Ted Heath those exceptional circumstances overwhelmed him.

During his years as leader of the opposition – from 1965 to 1970 – Heath faced a struggle between tradition and modernisation and was caught between several antagonist movements inside his party: new economic models were emerging and appealed to those who had grown exhausted of the postwar consensus. Andrew Gamble in *The Conservative Nation* dedicates a whole chapter to describe the 'growing ideological offensive of the New Right in the party' (Gamble, 1974: 104). The New Right blamed the postwar consensus for the economic decline of the United Kingdom and perceived it as nothing but a toned-down version of Socialism begetting a whole lot of evils: immigration, crime, violence, permissiveness and decadence. To the proponents of the New Right, the 'secret of national regeneration [...] lay in a radical new course that broke with the post-war settlement' (Gamble, 1974: 111). Others considered that progress was possible only through the maintenance of the Welfare State and the guarantee of cohesion and protection (Gamble, 1974: 99). In foreign policy too, conflicting stances vied with each other: the imperialist right wing best represented by people like Lord Salisbury or the Monday Club[5] clutched at the idea of a great imperial Britain while for others Britain's future could only lie in a strong union with Europe (Ball and Seldon, 1996: 215–29). Dealing with the party's heritage and at the same time handling the party's modernising spirit proved too difficult for Ted Heath. Thus, if repudiation characterises Heath's leadership at some points, disjunction, which is the inability to adjust to a party's past legacy according to Stephen Skowronek's classification of leadership, also casts light on Heath's leadership as he failed to master the combination of continuity and change that makes the essence of the Conservative party.

On many questions there was no doubt where Heath stood but faced with opposition and resistance Heath backed away in order to avoid conflicts. Also, when debates proved too divisive and inflammatory, he refused to resolve the question and eluded the subject. The difficulties of exercising power revealed the true nature of Heath's leadership: weakness, indecision and elusiveness. It was not so much a search for consensus as incapacity to decide and confront his party. It also revealed a lack of courage: elusiveness was preferable to direct confrontation but is it not the primary responsibility of a leader to confront his party when necessary?

One major episode – Rhodesia – clearly exemplifies Heath's difficulties in dealing with the party's past and enduring opposition from his colleagues. The Rhodesian crisis started only a few months after Heath's election. It represented the first act of provocation from the imperialist right and the first attempt to undermine his authority as leader. Many Conservatives had close emotional or family links with the former countries of the Empire, and the subject was highly sensitive as it involved a variety of feelings. Heath, as far as he was concerned, was totally impervious to the nostalgia or attachment that others in his party could feel. No one in his family had lived overseas and it was not before the 1960s that Heath first visited a Commonwealth country (Hurd, 1979: 41). As Andrew Roth explains he felt 'neither the "kith and kin" feeling of the traditional imperialist right' (Roth, 1972: 193). His beliefs in foreign policy also explain his detachment from the Commonwealth. Douglas Hurd affirms in his memoirs that 'Heath cared a great deal for Europe and nothing for the rest of the world' (Hurd, 1979: 41). The statement may seem extreme but it is nonetheless accurate as regards Heath's commitments and he made this clear in a series of lectures at Harvard in 1968 entitled *Old World, New Horizons*. In his autobiography, he reaffirmed his belief that nostalgia could not 'blind us to the real needs of our nation' (Heath, 1998: 225) and that 'our future lay in our own continent and not in distant lands which our forefathers had coloured pink on the map' (Heath, 1998: 177).

Problems occurred when Ian Smith declared the unilateral independence of South Rhodesia on 11 November 1965, an illegal decision that Harold Wilson immediately condemned. He first announced a series of economic sanctions before hardening his position and imposing in December an embargo on oil which would deprive Rhodesia of this precious source of energy. Heath also condemned the declaration of independence but refused to go further and used a very moderate vocabulary to refer to the new Rhodesian government. His natural sympathies lay with the more progressive branch who condemned the racist and authoritative government of Ian Smith. Heath abhorred all acts of racial discrimination but he never clearly articulated it as he knew that an important branch of his party supported Smith and the white settlers in Rhodesia. The letters sent to the CCO at the time of the crisis testified of the massive support of Conservative party members for Ian Smith. So when it came to take a decision on the Labour government's sanctions, Heath chose the most unsatisfying decision: limited but not punitive actions. The ambiguity of his position was accentuated by his decision to choose abstention on the vote on the oil embargo (Ball and Seldon, 1996: 229). His wish to maintain unity was crushed down as 80 Conservative MPs refused to follow their party's line and voted against the sanctions (*Hansard*, 21 December 1965, 722/1889). It was clearly from one branch of the party an act of betrayal and disloyalty. The divisions in his party were now exposed publicly in spite of his efforts to try and maintain unity. He was blamed for this disastrous spectacle and it was now obvious that he did not show enough authority to impose his views on the party. Here is how Tony Benn described Heath after the debate in Parliament: 'Heath is a pathetic figure, kicked this way and that, and is incapable of giving firm leadership. Home and Selwyn Lloyd are really running the Tory party now' (Benn, 1988: 354).

Heath was at a loss with this subject which was so far from his convictions, commitments and causes. To him, Rhodesia was an irrelevant waste of time and a serious brake on Britain's move towards modernity. He confessed in his autobiography that Britain's 'powerful, almost overwhelming historical background is still the main obstacle to modernisation in this country' (Heath, 1998: 258). Turning to Europe and breaking the links with the Commonwealth was a genuine belief and here was the best opportunity to affirm his position to his opponents inside the party but the search for unity prevailed over the expression of his deepest convictions. As Denis MacShane suggests 'the leader for whom unity predominates is the leader who ends up unsure how to lead' (MacShane, 2006: 52). This comment sheds an interesting light on the relation between leaders and led. A leader is expected to lead and that inevitably implies a degree of autocracy and domination. This is also the argument raised in Jean-Claude Monod's book, *Qu'est-ce qu'un chef en démocratie?* Monod describes modern politics as 'a never-ending struggle between two antagonist trends'[6] (Monod, 2012: 43). He suggests in his study that a democratic leader is an impossible concept, almost an oxymoron, and he highlights the tension of contemporary politics which extols democracy as the greatest form of government and yet is constantly in search of charismatic, almost domineering, leaders (Monod, 2012: 17, 31).

Heath's main fear was that the Rhodesian crisis could destroy the unity of the party as the Suez crisis had done a few years earlier. Heath was a whip at the time of the Suez crisis; he had been a witness to the havoc wreaked by this episode. The remembrance of those dark hours mitigated Heath's reaction: instead of asserting his position and clearly expressing his views, he chose a tepid in-between solution that did not satisfy anyone and did not resolve the tensions. At the time, he was not lauded for his sense of compromise; he was condemned for his weakness and indecision. This first episode announced and foreshadowed the other crises that blasted his years as leader of the Conservative party. Rhodesia is perhaps the most spectacular in the sense that the party was openly divided and a great number of MPs refused to vote according to instructions. It is also one of the most interesting to study as it involves the passions and fears of the Conservative party: the attachment to the Empire, the respect for the past, the reluctance and resistance to change. Heath's incapacity to take sides in a debate was again revealed on the delicate issue of incomes policy. The party was divided between the supporters of incomes policy and the antis, but Heath preferred to simply ignore the subject and wait until he was in power to decide on the relevance of incomes policy. This was Edward Heath at his worst: choosing escape rather than debate. No serious leadership has ever been achieved on such inconsistent behaviour and the severity of the criticisms against him originates from this major weakness.

Andrew Gamble argues that 'The crisis of leadership in those years was thus at the same time a crisis of ideology' (Gamble, 1974: 91). The major problem was that to the public at large Heath had no clear political identity: too many hesitations, a discrepancy between words and actions, a difficulty to define his political stance had blurred the political message.

The deconstruction of Heath's leadership

John Ramsden explains in *The Winds of Change* that many of the problems 'had to do with Heath himself, as a personality, as a manager of the Party, and as a controller of the debate about the future policy options' (Ramsden, 1996: 243). What this statement simply reveals is that Heath was no man to become one day leader of the Conservative party, let alone Prime Minister. The daily exercise of power brought to light the huge chasm between his alleged talents and the mediocre reality of his leadership. Heath had many qualities: he was determined, he was energetic, and exceptionally hard-working. All of these are professional qualities but his central, crippling handicap was that he lacked the charisma that radiates from the great men and women. It is a simple truth but an election cannot transform a shy and lacklustre man into a natural born leader. As we saw before, Weber's definition of 'charismatic leadership' rests on a series of exceptional qualities that set the leader apart and above ordinary men (Weber, 1995: 285). Eloquence, self-confidence, a sort of 'magic touch' with the people can be among those qualities, but Heath had none of these. He was a shy and introvert man who felt highly uncomfortable talking in public and was unable to inspire enthusiasm in the audience (Hurd, 1979: 11). It is crucial, I think, to emphasise the power of good communication skills in the construction of great leaders. Most of the major historical figures marked their times with famous speeches that had a worldwide echo. The power of words in politics should never be underestimated and Heath's uneasiness with words partly explains his failed leadership.

The first eminent member of the Conservative party to publicly express his bitterness and disappointment was Angus Maude, a representative of the New Right, in an article entitled 'Winter of Tory Discontent'. In this article, Maude unleashed a scathing criticism of the way Heath ran the party blaming him for his incapacity to show strong opposition to Wilson and to lack 'the Tory instinct for survival [which] depends on an ability to discern in doubtful situations what the people of this country really want'. The opening paragraph of his article encapsulates the gist of his grievances:

> It is obvious that the Conservative party has completely lost effective political initiative. Its own supporters in the country are divided and deeply worried by the failure, while to the electorate at large the Opposition has become a meaningless irrelevance. (*The Spectator*, 14 January 1966)

A week after, a Conservative party member from Sunderland sent a letter to the CCO in which he wrote that 'The truth of Mr Angus Maude's opening paragraph cannot unfortunately be questioned' (CPA, CCO 20/8/9, 20 January 1966). Maude's article was a very severe portrait of Heath's leadership but it also contained an element of truth when the article blamed Heath for speaking 'like a technocrat'. Ted Heath was indeed said to be a perfect technocrat: a lover of figures and tedious details who felt more comfortable with the civil servants in Whitehall than with his colleagues in the House of Commons.[7] Heath's place was in the background, in the shadow of great men, working on policy-making and administration. Not everyone can be a great leader but it could be simply argued that Heath was no leader at all. He was not a leader of men, of ideas, of change. He was overwhelmed and crushed by the prominence of the role and the weight of this exceptional position. And his former followers were dismayed by his incapacity to provide a satisfying leadership. A group of young Conservatives from Lewes included a motion on the agenda of their meeting which stated:

> This house believes that the present leadership of the Tory Party is not inspiring to Party members nor to the Nation and urges that steps should be taken immediately to provide this inspiration. (CPA CCO 4/10/150, 3 February 1967)

The key word of this statement is 'inspiration'. Heath was not an inspiring leader and his programme was too technocratic to secure the enthusiasm of the people. With Heath, no lyricism, no flame, no panache (Hurd, 1979: 11). His aim was to awaken people and show them the dire reality of their country. He alarmed people but he did not propose, as compensation for the grim picture he drew, an exciting project for Britain. The leader must be first and foremost an inspirer before being a doer and a thinker. He must inspire positive feelings such as enchantment, confidence and enthusiasm. He must be a myth-maker who takes people to another dimension, a dimension in which hopes and dreams are allowed in order to envisage a better life and a better tomorrow. And finally, the leader must create a positive narrative that appeals both to the people and his own party (Heppell, 2008: xiii). But this was not Heath's conception of leadership and politics. He had a too puritan and lofty vision of his mission to envisage a change of attitude. His favourite posture – and this is the one he always kept until the end of his career in 2001 – was that of the truth teller. Heath was the politician who told people the plain and unvarnished truth. This attitude is revealing of Heath's seriousness and integrity but inevitably it resulted in a disastrous effect in terms of public image. As *The Times* underlined, 'in the regard of the British public he has remained a strangely colourless figure with an elusive political personality' (*The Times*, 16 May 1970).

Heath's leadership was a non-entity and left a dangerous vacuum that worried Conservative party members, as the following letter highlights: 'One looks in vain for a leader at the head of the Conservative party' (CPA, CCO 4/10/150, 30 November 1967). But like nature, a political party abhors a vacuum. Enoch Powell, one of Heath's main rivals inside the party who had run against him for the leadership of the Conservative party, exploited this vacancy and sought to fill in the ideological and personal chasm created by Ted Heath. In 1968, the sudden popularity of Enoch Powell represented a real challenge to Heath's leadership. He imposed a real new tone and a new discourse in the national political debate.

Overnight, Powell became the central figure of British politics with the 'Rivers of Blood' speech but his provocations started well before April 1968 and one of them is revealing of his attempt to discredit Heath's leadership. In 1966, Heath entitled the Conservative manifesto for the general election *Action Not Words*. A few days later, Powell published his own manifesto entitled *Words Not Action*. This episode which, at first glance, could look insignificant was actually a biting attack against Heath and an explicit reference to the lack of dialogue and debates inside the party. The 'Rivers of Blood' speech is the most emblematic episode of the confrontation between the two men. The speech described in apocalyptical terms the dangers of massive immigration in the United Kingdom and the potential disintegration of Britishness. Powell was immediately sacked from the Shadow Cabinet but became overnight the hero of the working class, the defender of the most destitute and fragile people, the spokesman of the silent majority. Powell's feat was to be able to speak to a whole range of people who were usually totally impervious to the Conservative party's message. He did not speak like them but he spoke for them and everyone could feel familiar with the anecdotes he related in his speeches. Whereas Heath used the dry language of the technocrat, Powell brilliantly handled the language of the populist.

The effects of Powell's speech and popularity were momentous. Powell became the arbiter of the ideological debate and magnified the insignificance of Heath's leadership: he set the tone and forced Heath to change his language and adopt a different position. For instance, just a few months after the 'Rivers of Blood' speech, Heath explained in a speech in York that 'the number of immigrants entering Britain [...] must be severely curtailed' (CPA, PPB 16–17, 20 September 1968). His attempt to appropriate Powell's favourite theme was so obvious that he lost all credibility. In *For Conservatives Only*, Lord Coleraine writes that 'Those who set the trend, not those who reflect it, have the real power' (Lord Coleraine, 1970: 12). Heath was the leader of the party but he was not the intellectual, moral and spiritual driving force of the party. He never set the trend, he did try to impose a new discourse but he failed because it was too technocratic and dry. He was unable to communicate his project in simple and appealing language, hence the divorce between him and the rest of the nation. Only before the general election did he succeed but here again his success (as in 1965) rested on a major misunderstanding. While for five years he had been completely deconstructed by the pressures of opposition, he was suddenly reconstructed, in the words of Harold Wilson who nicknamed him

'Selsdon Man', after a speech he gave at the Selsdon Park Conference in which he emphasised right-wing themes: public spending cuts, tax cuts, selectivity in social services, reform of trade unions and above all, two words which caught attention: law and order (Blake, 1985: 307). Wilson immediately condemned this speech as a direct attack on the postwar consensus but unexpectedly it worked in Heath's favour. Thus, the dull and unidentifiable leader became the tough man bent on imposing law and order. 'Selsdon Man' was a grotesque political mask, a device to attract more voters on the right but deep down Heath fundamentally remained a One Nation Conservative. For the second time he donned a mantle that was not his and endorsed a political identity so far estranged from what he really was. But this character was more appealing than the real man and the 'law-and-order' discourse more exciting than his highly complex programme. In Ted Heath's career, success was possible only if he misrepresented his political identity and failure came inevitably when the exercise of power unveiled his real nature.

The real tragedy of Edward Heath's leadership is that he was an inspired leader with great ambitions but was totally uninspiring to the public. He was a moderniser, he was a determined and hard-working leader but he never managed to secure the enthusiasm of his party and never managed to communicate his vision to the nation. He was not liked nor understood and his two elections are the result of profound misunderstandings on his political personality; finally, as far as his legacy is concerned, apart from Britain's entry into Europe – his great historical success – he achieved none of his promises and ambitions. The failures and prevarications of a leader are extremely instructive for an historian as they provide an illuminating insight to unravelling the complexities of political leadership. Whatever the epoch, whatever the mode of designation, whatever the party and the country, there are unchanging fundamental elements about the nature of leadership: an ability to manage different coalitions inside a party, a clever balancing between tradition and change, and above all a natural authority that commands the devotion, respect and loyalty of the party (Weber, 1995: 320). But, in our view, there is one final element that transforms any leader into a great leader: the sense of history. Leadership is this ability to create a new narrative, to impose new economic or intellectual models and to change the course of history (Heppell, 2008: xiii). In spite of his central leading position, Edward Heath never dominated the national debate or controlled the set of events. He was a plaything in the hands of history, never its master. While the Conservative party reveres its great figures, Edward Heath suffered the cruel destiny reserved to the losers and minor transitional figures: the fall into oblivion and historical obscurity.

Notes

1 In this book, Skowronek divides leadership into three main categories: articulation, repudiation and disjunction. The last two categories are particularly helpful for our study of Edward Heath.
2 The Resale Price Maintenance was a practice which consisted in having a fixed price imposed by the manufacturer and the retailer was not allowed to sell the product at a lower price.
3 'I now had the chance to stamp my brand of Conservatism on the party and, in time, to make a bid for the job that would enable me to change the course of British history' (Heath, 1998: 269).
4 This group of men was composed of Anthony Barber, Peter Walker, John MacGregor, William Whitelaw. Some of them held important responsibilities in his future government.
5 The Monday Club was a right-wing group formed in the early 1960s to oppose decolonisation in Africa.
6 My translation.
7 When Heath became Prime Minister and political pressure started to grow around him, he drew very close to Robert Armstrong, a senior civil servant, who came to be known as the 'Deputy Prime Minister'.

Works cited

Primary sources

Conservative Party Archives

PPB 12: Speeches by Edward Heath, 1964–65
PPB 16–7: Speeches by Edward Heath, 1968–69
CCO 4/10/150: Criticism of leader, 30 November 1967
CCO 4/10/152: Heath's message, 15 December 1967
CCO 20/8/9: Correspondence with Edward Heath, 20 January 1966
CCO 20/8/10: Correspondence with Edward Heath, 12 June 1967
CCO 20/8/12: Correspondence with Edward Heath, 8 July 1968
CCO 600/12/7: *Putting Britain Right Ahead, A Statement of Conservative Aims*, London, Conservative Political Centre, 1965
LCC papers: 1970

British Press

The Economist, 31 July 1965
——, 9 October 1965
——, 28 January 1968

The Spectator, 15 October 1965
——, 14 January 1966
The Times, 11 September 1965
——, 23 April 1968
——, 16 May 1970

Official publication

Hansard, 21 December 1965, 722/1889

Autobiographies, memoirs and diaries

Benn, T. (1988) *Out of Wilderness: Diaries 1963–1967* (London: Arrow).
Heath, E. (1988) *The Course of My Life* (London: Hodder & Stoughton).
Hurd, D. (1979) *An End to Promises, Sketch of a Government 1970–74* (London: Collins).

Secondary sources

Bale, T. (2010) *The Conservative Party from Thatcher to Cameron* (Cambridge: Polity).
Ball, S., Seldon, A. (eds) (1996) *The Heath Government 1970–1974: A Reappraisal* (London and New York: Longman).
Ball, S., Seldon, A. (eds) (2005) *Recovering Power: The Conservatives in Opposition Since 1867* (Basingstoke and New York: Palgrave Macmillan).
Blake, R. (1985) *The Conservative Party from Peel to Thatcher* (London: Fontana Press).
Bogdanor, V. (1979) *Devolution* (Oxford: Oxford University Press).
Campbell, J. (1993) *Edward Heath: A Biography* (London: Pimlico).
Lord Coleraine (1970) *For Conservatives Only* (London: Tom Stacey Ltd.).
Freeden, M. (1996) *Ideologies and Political Theory* (Oxford: Clarendon Press).
Gamble, A. (1974) *The Conservative Nation* (London and Boston: Routledge & Kegan Paul).
Green, E.H.H (2002) *Ideologies of Conservatism: Conservative Political Ideas in the Twentieth Century* (Oxford: Oxford University Press).
Greenleaf, W.H. (1983) *The British Political Tradition, vol. 1: The Rise of Collectivism* (London: Routledge).
——, *The British Political Tradition, vol. 2: The Ideological Heritage* (London: Routledge).
Heath, E. (1968) *Old World, New Horizons: Britain, Europe, and the Atlantic Alliance* (Cambridge: Harvard University Press).
Heppell, T. (2008) *Choosing the Tory Leader: Conservative Party Leadership Elections from Heath to Cameron* (London and New York: Tauris Academic Studies).
Jessop, B. (1974) *Traditionalism: Conservatism and British Political Culture* (London: Allen & Unwin).
Layton-Henry, Z. (ed.) (1980) *Conservative Party Politics* (London and Basingstoke: Macmillan Press Ltd).
MacShane, D. (2006) *Heath* (London: Haus Publishing).
Monod, J.-C. (2012) *Qu'est-ce qu'un chef en démocratie? Politiques du charisme* (Paris: Editions du Seuil).
Norton, P., Aughey, A. (1981) *Conservatives and Conservatism* (London: Temple Smith).

Ramsden, J. (1980) *The Making of Conservative Party Policy: The Conservative Research Department Since 1929* (London and New York: Longman).

——, (1996), *The Winds of Change, Macmillan to Heath 1957–75,* (London and New York: Longman).

Roth, A. (1972) *Heath and the Heathmen* (London: Routledge & Kegan Paul).

Sandbrook, D. (2006) *White Heat: A History of Britain in the 1960s* (London: Abacus).

Scruton, R. (1980) *The Meaning of Conservatism* (London: Macmillan).

Skowronek, S. (1993) *The Politics Presidents Make: Leadership from John Adams to George Bush* (Cambridge: Harvard University Press).

Weber, M. (1995) *Economie et Société* (Paris: Plon).

16
When the President is not really the Boss: The Mysterious Case of Ronald Reagan's Presidential Leadership

Françoise Coste

In the classical theoretical debate regarding the balance between the leadership of political leaders and the strength of democratic institutions, the office of president of the United States offers a complex example. As one of the best contemporary specialists of the American presidency, Fred I. Greenstein, recently wrote in his study of presidential leadership, *The Presidential Difference: Leadership Style from FDR to Barack Obama*: 'The United States is said to have a government of laws and institutions rather than individuals, but ... it is one in which the matter of who occupies the nation's highest office can have profound repercussions' (Greenstein, 2009: 2). Few American presidents illustrate this conundrum better than Ronald Reagan. In many respects, he embodies the very definition of a successful leader. He came to power, in 1980, after years of political chaos in the United States, marked by the violent upheaval of the 1960s, the shocking corruption of Watergate and the humiliating defeat of Vietnam. Reagan astutely made the most of this difficult context in which American institutions seemed irretrievably broken, and the series of audacious economic reforms he launched in the spring of 1981 showed it was still possible to wield enormous power from the White House – in other words, his presidency tended to prove that when entrusted to an efficient leader willing to take risks to advance his ideological goals, American institutions, as in a mutually-reinforcing movement, could still work very well. This renewal of presidential power was made all the more dramatic by the formidable efforts of his communication team to convey the authority of the chief executive to the American public. For Mike Deaver, Ronald Reagan's main media consultant, 'the perception of what was done often mattered as much as what was actually done' (Deaver, 1987: 73). Deaver saw himself as 'the choreographer' and 'the director' of the Reagan presidency.

His main innovation was the 'photo-opportunity', or photo-op: the careful staging of every public event involving the president (Deaver, 1987: 141).[1] Deaver's favorite photo-ops were the ones which included what one of his aides once called 'a heroic situation', as if the president were the hero of a Hollywood movie: Ronald Reagan as a cowboy riding his horse, Reagan as a brave and patriotic GI touring the battlefields of Normandy, or preventing an invasion of South Korea by checking the movements of North Korean troops from the DMZ (demilitarized zone) (Hertsgaard, 1988: 25). The message was unmistakable: the American people could be proud of their president, he was the man in charge, the revolutionary and charismatic leader making history.

To this day, this is the vision millions of Americans have kept of him. Thanks to his undeniable impact on federal policies (economic but also military and diplomatic) and to his remarkable communication skills which allowed him to inspire pride and optimism in the American people, Reagan seems to have set the modern template for a successful presidency. Yet, when one goes beyond the shiny façade and studies the day-to-day inner workings of Ronald Reagan's White House, it becomes equally obvious that this man who knew, like few others before or after him, how to lead the country actually did not know how to lead men. In public, he may have radiated an image of uncompromising authority but, in private, his White House team was in a near-constant state of disarray for eight years. So where traditional leadership studies (as James McGregor Burns's very influential *Leadership* (1978)) often focus on the relationship between a leader and his followers, it seems necessary to include a third actor in the drama of leadership: the men and women working in the shadows around the leader. How do staffers participate in the construction and projection of leadership? Are they mere admirers of the powerful man/woman they work for or can they also become agents of change themselves? And, more importantly in the present case study, what happens when they work for a president who, behind closed doors, seems to abdicate his responsibilities?

When leading men is more difficult than leading a country

The most famous definition of presidential leadership in the United States was probably given by political scientist Richard Neustadt in his seminal book, *Presidential Power and the Modern Presidents: The Politics of Leadership from Roosevelt to Reagan* (first published in 1960, then updated in 1990). For Neustadt, the role of the people working with the president was crucial, as his 'strength or weakness turns on his personal capacity to influence the conduct of the men who make up government. His influence becomes the mark of leadership. ... Presidential power is the power to persuade'. Central to the relationship between the president and his staff was the notion of presidential choice. For Neustadt, a good leader was a man who knew how to make complex choices:

> He makes his personal impact by the things he says and does. Accordingly, his choices of what he should say and do, and how and when, are his means to conserve and tap the sources of his power. ... The outcome, case by case, will often turn on whether he perceives his risk in power terms and takes account of what he sees before he makes his choice. A President is uniquely situated and his power so bound up with the uniqueness of his place, that he can count on no one else to be perceptive for him. ... Useful information, timely choices may not reach him; he must do the reaching. (Neustadt, 1990: 4, 11, 150)

If this is the template of a successful presidency, then Ronald Reagan must be considered a failed president. In the 1990 edition of his book, Neustadt developed this notion at length. He admittedly recognized that Reagan could be praised to a certain extent as

> his Presidency restored the public image of the office to a fair ... approximation of its Rooseveltian mold: a place of popularity, influence, and initiative, a source of programmatic and symbolic leadership, both pacesetter and tonesetter, the nation's voice to both the world and us, and – like or hate the policies – a presence many of us loved to see as Chief of State. (Neustadt, 1990: 269)

But Neustadt's tone in his long chapter devoted to Reagan is generally severe, as the political scientist wrote extensively on the infamous and complex IranContra scandal which erupted in 1986 and nearly destroyed Reagan's presidency. For Neusdtadt, this political catastrophe was inevitably inscribed in Reagan's inability, from the very beginning of his first term, to fit the definition of an efficient presidency he had first exposed in 1960. Indeed, in the White House, Reagan displayed no capacity 'to influence the conduct of the men who make up government', he never realized he could 'count on no one else to be perceptive for him', and he never 'did the reaching' to find the useful information which could inform his choices.

At the most basic level, Neustadt's theory of successful leadership obviously requires a high degree of involvement on the part of the president as an individual who heads not only a country, but a large team of people working for the executive branch – the size of the White House staff, which had remained almost insignificant throughout the eighteenth and nineteenth centuries and in the early twentieth century (only 31 people worked for the White House in the 1920s), started to grow significantly during the Roosevelt administration, to reach around 400 people in the Reagan years (Kernell, 1989: 188; Hart, 1987: 21, 105). The managerial dimension of the presidency was precisely Reagan's first weakness: Reagan loved being the president, he loved performing during Deaver's photo-ops, but he hated the homework that goes with the presidency. Just before his election, when he was informed that presidents were briefed every morning at 7:30 by a National Security Council staffer, he replied: 'Well, he's going to have a helluva long wait' (Cannon, 1991: 144). This was not a joke. As he once said: 'Show me an executive who works long, overtime hours, and I'll show you a bad executive' (quoted in Cannon, 1991: 125) Accordingly, he adopted a rather light schedule in the White House: he would arrive in the Oval Office at 9 a.m., where he would be briefed by his closest advisors; then at 9:30, he would receive a short national security briefing; after another conversation with his advisors, he would take anywhere from 30 minutes to one hour to work alone (often to read official documents or answer his personal mail); around 11 or 11:30 a.m. came his first break of the day (as the White House could not admit publicly that the president, who was in his 70s, could not work for more than two hours without needing to rest, these breaks were euphemistically called in the official schedule distributed to the press 'personal staff time');[2] it was then time to lunch, most of the time alone; Reagan would often start his afternoons with another hour of solitary work, before attending some meetings and taking another hour or two of 'personal staff time' (devoted on most days to a nap); once rested, it was time to finish the day: one last short meeting, one last briefing by the staff, and by 6 p.m. at the latest he was back in the White House residence to have dinner with his wife and watch TV.[3] And Reagan could not wait for each day to be over: throughout the day, he would cross off every item on his schedule as if to make time go faster.[4] Despite this relatively easy schedule, Reagan tried his best to escape from the White House as often as possible. Almost every week, he would take his Wednesday afternoons off in order to go horse-riding in Virginia; as for the week-ends, they would most of the time start as early as Friday afternoon, when the Reagans would leave the White House to go to Camp David, where they loved watching old movies while eating popcorn; but nothing compared with the Reagans' passion for their Santa Barbara ranch – they flew there so many times between 1981 and 1989 that Reagan spent more than one full year of his presidency in California (Reagan, 2007: 11, 431; Reeves, 2005: 414).

Such idiosyncrasies had a great impact on Ronald Reagan's managerial style and choices as a team leader. His distance – which sometimes bordered on indifference – towards the minutiae of his function explains that he was not involved in the life and the work of his staff. He could not bring himself to care about who worked for him, even in the most sensitive of positions. For example, in 1983, James Baker, who had become Chief of Staff in January 1981 and who was getting tired of the inhumane pace of the job, approached him to say he wanted to leave. He suggested a new arrangement: he would become the National Security Advisor and media guru Mike Deaver would replace him as Chief of Staff. These probably are the two most eminent positions in the White House; and yet, Reagan did not think for one second about the stakes of Baker's proposal, and he accepted it in the blink of an eye. A few hours later, other staffers rebelled against this unexpected change. They complained loudly during a meeting with the president, and Reagan immediately reversed his position (Reagan, 1990: 448). So Baker remained the Chief of Staff until Reagan's re-election in 1984. After that election, Baker went back to the president with another exchange suggestion: why not pick Donald Regan, the Secretary of the Treasury, as Chief of Staff and Baker would replace him at Treasury? The president was about to lose his closest advisor and to replace him with a man he barely knew. This did not seem to worry him though, and without betraying any feeling of surprise or sadness, without asking any question, without 'doing any reaching' for 'information' to use Neustadt's terms, Reagan simply said 'Yes, yes – I'll go for it' (Regan, 1988: 229). Thus, Reagan gave the impression that the team who was supposed to help him lead the country did not matter. Both from a professional or human point of view, its members were interchangeable. The identity and the role of the men in charge of managing the White House and the administration did not deserve the slightest reflection on his part.

Reagan also forfeited another of Neustadt's famous conclusions, 'the power to persuade'. A leader must of course persuade his voters and his followers to support him, but as Neusdtadt stressed, 'the power to persuade' is maybe even more important when applied to the duty to persuade the people working for the three branches of the US government. This entails making decisions and convincing others to accept and implement them. But this too, President Reagan proved unable – or unwilling – to do. The many memoirs written by his advisors share a striking common point: the fact that Reagan always remained silent during meetings. His main economic advisor, David Stockman, was taken aback by their first meetings: 'We had a few informal sessions with the President-elect, during which he simply listened, nodded, and smiled. "We have a great task ahead of us," he would presently say, but never finished the sentence. He gave no orders, no commands; asked for no information; expressed no urgency' (Stockman, 1986: 81).

Equally surprised was Donald Regan. Before joining the administration, Regan had been the head of Wall Street powerhouse Merrill Lynch. When he became Secretary of the Treasury in 1981, he expected the Republicans in the White House to adopt rational corporate-like management techniques. He was flabbergasted when he discovered a system where 'I never saw President Reagan alone and never discussed economic philosophy or fiscal and monetary policy with him one-on-one'. For him, it was a 'baffling system, in which the President seldom spoke, while his advisors proposed measures that contradicted his ideas and promises. ... The President himself sent out no strong signals. He listened, encouraged, and deferred. But it was a rare meeting in which he made a decision or issued orders... He hesitates to ask questions' (Regan, 1988: 142,188). This reluctance to 'do the reaching' in order to assemble data enabling him to make choices was also what shocked the staffers working for the national security team, like Richard Pipes (this specialist of Russian affairs wrote in his diary after one of his first meetings with Reagan: 'RR totally lost, out of his depth, uncomfortable. ... Did not speak for forty-five minutes or so; when he finally spoke up it was to sigh "Oh boy!" ... He did not listen attentively, looking away or staring at the papers in front of him... All this – both the substance and human conflict – is above and beyond him.'), or like Geoffrey Kemp, a Near East expert: 'the reality of Reagan as a decision-maker is that he made very few decisions... The President never came in and said "Gentlemen, we have three tough decisions, a, b, and c". ... He was an extraordinarily passive participant' (Pipes, 2003: 166; Strober and Strober, 2003: 109).[5]

The lack of decision-making on the part of President Reagan may be one of the most troubling aspects of his leadership style. This does not mean that his presidency was devoid of significant reforms. As Neustadt correctly admits: 'We will not look back on Reagan as "passive" in policy terms. ... [He left] an active record... He championed the income tax cuts of 1981... He pushed a military buildup... He said no to tax increases... He said yes to summitry with Gorbachev. Reagan initiated the Strategic

Defense Initiative almost on his own.' But such political landmarks were not the result of carefully thought-out decisions and audacious risk-taking on the part of the president: instead of being the mark of active, ambitious, and innovative leadership, they were the inevitable and almost mechanical culmination of a lifetime of ideological commitments ('Reagan's no's and yes's ... welled up from the convictions he brought with him into office. ... These enabled him to act, despite his equally unusual disdain for detail. Commitments were his compensation: commitments drawn not from events but from prior convictions') (Neustadt, 1990: 276–7, 277, 278), Reagan cannot consequently be considered a revolutionary leader, he did not alter the political status quo in a profound manner – hence Stephen Skowronek's refusal to classify him, in his now classic *The Politics Presidents Make: Leadership from John Adams to Bill Clinton*, in the highest category of presidential action, 'the most promising of all situations for the exercise of political leadership', that of 'reconstructive' leadership (Skowronek defines 'the politics of reconstruction' as 'a great opportunity for presidential action ... harnessed... to an expansive authority to repudiate the established governing formulas... In this way, ... the order-creating capacities of the presidency [are] realized full vent in a wholesale reconstruction of the standards of legitimate national government') (Skowronek, 1997: 37). For Skowronek, since Reagan's conservative economic reforms were all concentrated in the spring of 1981 and since his other seven and a half years in office marked no real dismantling of the liberal welfare state born of the Roosevelt era, 'even before the end of the first year, the administration was a spent force so far as reconstruction was concerned. There was to be no second thrust as there had been for FDR in 1935; the Reagan Revolution turned out to be a single-jolt affair' (Skowronek, 1997: 421, 425).

Hypotheses

The deficiencies in Ronald Reagan's leadership style are inescapable. Over the years, observers have tried to reconcile them with the incredible level of popularity and the reputation for strong leadership that he enjoyed during and after his years in office. Psychological explanations have been largely put aside, as most analyses of the Reagan years agree with Neustadt's:

> I reject the cartoonist's answer: Reagan cannot have been stupid. No one is who governs for two terms this country's largest state, campaigns for the White House three times, wins twice, and bows out

after eight years the most popular President since Gallup Polls began. He may have been lazy, as many allege, and ill informed on many fronts. But he also must have been shrewd. (Neustadt, 1990: 309)

A more interesting and fruitful way of looking at the Reagan years is to go back to the traditional dichotomy stressed earlier by Fred I. Greenstein between individual leaders and institutions. Ronald Reagan is largely credited for having single-handedly restored the prestige of the presidency; yet this thesis may very well be inverted: in the 1980s, the American institutions which had been so derided in the previous decade actually proved strong enough to help the president, to protect him from himself by acting as a screen between his many failings as a leader and the population. More precisely, the modern organization of the executive branch, marked as it is by a constant increase in the number of people working for the president (see above), allowed Reagan to find a very helpful shield in his staff. This proposition may seem surprising as it goes against a widespread hypothesis often applied to Reagan's presidency – that according to which he was a puppet, a lazy and passive president who was so disinterested that he let his advisors do the governing in his stead, which would be a clear perversion of democratic leadership. This interestingly happens to be the prevailing interpretation of Iran–Contra in the US, as illustrated for example by the chapter Neustadt devotes to the scandal, in which he, like many others, mostly blames CIA director William Casey, and not Ronald Reagan, for this unconstitutional abuse of power (Neustadt, 1990: 280–9).

Such a vision is understandable. It is indeed hard to deny the fact that some staffers did amass considerable power at the expense of the president between 1980 and 1988. These men were painfully aware of Reagan's obvious limitations – especially in foreign policy matters (Reagan's closest ally, Margaret Thatcher, had let the White House know that his performance at the G-7 summit in Versailles in 1982 had been very poor – which could only hurt America's international legitimacy) (Shultz, 1993: 353). The only solution was therefore to organize catch-up study sessions, to prepare Reagan before each international event. Hence the multiplication of long and detailed briefings, which aides conceived as crash courses. This proved particularly important before the first summit between Reagan and Gorbachev, in Geneva in November 1985. For a month, Reagan was briefed several times a week about every dimension of the US–Soviet relationship. Some passages in those documents sound more like a 'Soviet Union 101' class than like a presidential briefing. Thus, Reagan was explained elements which should have been rather obvious to any relatively well-informed American politician of the Cold War period, like the fact that 'The Politburo is the top forum in which all national security questions are discussed and decided and serves as the highest policy-making organ in the USSR'.[6] Such lessons also included long developments about 'The Soviet View of the United States', thanks to which Reagan learned that 'the Soviets see the US as their main rival for influence in the world and the greatest single threat to their security ... American military pre-eminence since 1945 is also a major factor in Moscow's attitude toward the United States'.[7]

The accumulation of clichés and obvious remarks in those brief-ings leaves a rather unpleasant taste. They convey the impression that Reagan's staffers deemed him utterly incompetent. And indeed, when one studies the organization and preparation of international events by the White House in the 1980s, one is struck by the complete lack of trust and respect towards the president on the part of his aides. In his memoirs, Richard Pipes remembers his shock 'during the briefings which took place in the Oval Office, ... to see how little deference Deaver and Baker showed Reagan – they seemed to treat him rather like a grandfather whom one humors but does not take very seriously'. (Pipes, 2003: 176) It is true that the men surrounding Ronald Reagan in the White House did all they could to systematically minimize his autonomy in foreign policy matters. By far their main obsession was to prevent any improvised declaration by the president regarding foreign policy. To avoid the gaffes his aides deemed inevitable if Reagan were allowed to speak freely, every single one of his diplomatic meetings was tightly scripted. For example, every American–Soviet summit included a one-on-one discussion between Reagan and Gorbachev. Reagan's aides dreaded those sessions, convinced as they were that he would not be able to understand the remarks and proposals coming from the Russian leader, who had an impressive grasp of international questions. As a result, before each summit, the staff would prepare long briefings anticipating any possible idea on the part of Gorbachev, and providing Reagan with a verbatim ready-made answer – as in a Hollywood script learned by heart by an actor. For instance if, in Geneva, Gorbachev was to criticize Reagan's closeness to 'the military-industrial complex', then Reagan was to answer: 'to say that these sectors are the arbiters of public views toward the Soviet Union is far off the mark. The American people have no animosity towards the Soviet People. They want noth-ing more than peaceful relations with your country, and relief from the defense burden. They have no desire for endless confrontation and competition'; if Gorbachev was to criticize the social problems affecting the US (like 'poverty, unemployment, crime, racial discrimination'), then Reagan had to say: 'The United States isn't perfect. We have never made any secret that many of our citizens haven't been able to share in the prosperity enjoyed by the majority of Americans. But we're working hard to change that – and I'm proud of the record of my Administration. We've created some eight million jobs since I came into office.'[8] Such scripts ('talking points') were actually provided by the staff for every single meeting on the presidential agenda, from inconsequential photo-ops with children or celebrities to, more tellingly, every appointment with members of his administration or members of Congress[9] – in other words, the president's political margin of manoeuvre was virtually non-existent.

However, the puppet hypothesis is not wholly satisfactory. Several elements tend to prove that his staff did not rob Ronald Reagan of his presidential leadership. First, if the White House staff had really been intent on taking advantage of the president's passivity and manipulating it to advance their own political agenda, then they would logically have been highly satisfied with Reagan's disdain for the gritty dimensions of the presidential function and they could have very well organized a secret conspiracy, as Bill Casey and Oliver North were accused of doing during Iran–Contra. But the reality seems to be much more prosaic. When one looks at the relationship between Reagan and his staff, one reaches the inescapable conclusion that the president was actually surrounded by men who strongly respected the office of the presidency and what it stood for. They were highly aware that they were only political appointees, that they had not been chosen by the people. In their eyes, mere staffers could not replace a democratically-elected leader. As a result, many were dissatisfied with the inner workings of the Reagan White House. Interestingly this unease was present throughout the whole ideological spectrum of the Right. One of the most powerful centrists of the Reagan team, Deputy Chief of Staff Richard Darman, tried from the get-go to trigger Reagan's interest. In late 1981 for example, when the staff decided to organize what they called 'weekly updates' every Monday morning to discuss the events of the coming week, Darman asked, even begged, Reagan to give his input:

As you know, another 'Weekly Update' briefing meeting is scheduled for Monday. If there are any matters on which you wish to have additional briefing information or discussion, would you please note the issues or topics below? If you do not have any suggestions, you may be forced to endure an agenda made up solely of items chosen by your staff!

The stakes could not be more clearly stated, but despite the gentle warning, Reagan simply replied with a short hand-written sentence on Darman's memo: 'Haven't had time to think of any.'[10] Darman's unwished-for power as an agenda-setter for the president was consequently confirmed, which in turn bothered the conservative faction in the staff. One of those conservatives, speechwriter Terry Dolan, strongly criticized during the drafting of the 1983 State of the Union Address what he called 'a spoon-fed presidency', sounding in the process like the second-coming of Richard Neusdadt:

> I felt an absolute responsibility to present – as forcefully as possible – my reasons for believing the President should be given the opportunity to read this draft. ... I think it should be the President's decision to choose how much or how little – what combinations, what mix – of these rhetorical and thematic points he wishes to have in his speech. He is the best judge, only he can take the broad view, only his is the comprehensive look. ... I was somewhat shocked by Dick Darman's suggestion that if we do not pare down the President's options and restrict them to what appears to be a narrow field we 'have failed as a staff.' Far to the contrary, presenting only a few options based on the feelings of six or seven people – none of whom were elected and most of whom have no responsibility or expertise in these areas – is a disservice to the President and the country.[11]

In these tensions and petty rivalries within the staff may lie one unexpected answer regarding the enduring myth of Reagan as a puppet of his aides. Instead of seeing Reagan's hands-off management style as paving the way for a behind-the-scene conspiracy, it could also paradoxically be seen as an anti-body preventing the emergence of such a cabal – a probably totally involuntary confuse-and-conquer move. Indeed, the fact that Reagan was such a bad leader of men within the White House created uncertainties, doubts, and unease among the staff. As a result, the atmosphere in the White House was not very healthy or conducive to alliance-making and cooperation. It was difficult for most presidential advisors to reconcile their pride in working for the president, especially this historical president, with his diminutive leadership. Reagan was unquestionably a hero for these Republicans; he was after all the man who had conquered the White House after decades of Democratic domination in Washington. They sincerely admired him and like the millions of Americans impressed by Deaver's photo-ops, they too were in awe of his Hollywood charisma. Years later, Geoffrey Kemp from the National Security Council would still recall the incredible effect Reagan would have on his subordinates: 'After the assassination attempt [in March 1981], he used to work out with weights every day; he had terrific biceps. He would come in with these jodhpurs and a tennis shirt on, looking incredibly macho, presiding over the NSC meeting' (Strober and Strober, 2003: 109). When confronted with Reagan's passivity, these men did not see the situation as an incredible opportunity to advance their own personal agenda and to substitute their own leadership for that of the president's; the much more common reaction was rather one of distress: distress that the boss could never remember the names of those working with him, even those he had seen every day for years on end (Reagan, 1990: 391–2); or distress because of the nagging fear that the president may not be up to the job, both mentally and physically. For example Reagan was deaf and he could not understand a word pronounced by the Director of the CIA, William Casey, who mumbled a lot – which terrified Robert 'Bud' McFarlane, one of his National Security Advisors, who described almost tragic-comic scenes in his memoirs:

> Sometimes, we would sit through sessions in the Oval Office where Casey would sit at the President's side, mumble his way through a long monologue with the President listening intently and nodding while the rest of us in the room stared at each other in utter incomprehension. Afterwards, when the President had sent Casey off with authorization to do whatever on earth it was that he had been describing, [Chief of Staff] Jim Baker would say to me, shaking his head, 'God knows what he just approved.' (McFarlane, 1994: 283)

This sense of distress also derived from the constant fear in which the staff was working. Since Reagan would never give any order at the end of meetings, the staff was never sure of what they were supposed to do. They had to resort to guessing, which was mentally exhausting: what if they guessed wrong? What if they did the opposite of what the president was thinking? What if they got the Administration in trouble? What if they lost their job as a result? (Strober and Strober, 2003: 547.)

This proved too much for many people, to such a point that they decided to leave the administration. Any president will see a lot of advisors leave, especially after his re-election. But this phenomenon reached historical proportions in the case of Ronald Reagan.[12] For many historians, it is precisely this mass exile of competent staffers which paved the way for abuses like Iran–Contra. This consequently shows that the people who study the scandal and wonder (like the Congressional committee which investigated Iran–Contra) 'did Reagan know that the CIA was channelling Iranian money towards the Contras?' do not ask the right question. We will probably never know for sure, one way or another, whether Reagan knew, whereas there is absolutely no doubt about the terrible effects of his incompetent management and insufficient leadership of the White House. The very popular 'puppet theory' seems to have no validity at all: the staff was too divided, too paranoid, and too exhausted to set in place an elaborate, efficient, and coherent conspiracy. But in a way, the alternative may be worse: Reagan's inability to clearly manage the men around him sowed chaos and it is in this leadership vacuum that things like Iran–Contra happened.

This shows that the modern imperial presidency made famous by Arthur Schlesinger Jr should not be understood as an exercise in solitary and individual power. Presidential leadership in the case of Ronald Reagan may have looked to the outside world like the triumphant actions of one man, but this image actually depended on the ceaseless work of his policy aides and of his media team. So Reagan's leadership was the result of a group effort, a collective construction made possible by the institutional tools he found at his disposal in an enlarged White House staff. In other words, the institutional framework which was created in the eighteenth century to constrain the president's power and ambition has evolved throughout history to become a shield that can protect him and reinforce his prestige and power, even when he is not up to the task.

This extreme reliance on staffers is of course nothing new in modern management techniques and it is probably inevitable in the complex organizational structure that is the executive branch of the United States government. However, Reagan seems not to have been able to master this situation, which ended up weakening his presidential leadership. First, this state of things came into being regardless of his intentions: his lack of involvement in the life of the staff shows that it is the staffers themselves who set up this collective style of leadership and not the president who explicitly asked them to adopt such a system – they made him an executive leader, almost despite himself. Reagan was therefore lucky to find such willing participants, humble enough to work in the shadows and protect their boss from any bad light. But the introduction of pure chance in presidential leadership leads to a second, even graver, problem.

As long as Reagan was lucky enough to have devoted and competent staffers, men and women who greatly respected his office and were horrified at the very idea of encroaching on the president's power, he was able to ride on their behind-the-scenes work and appear as totally in charge in the eyes of the public. But this situation is a double-edged sword: when the staff took a mediocre turn, which was the case with the new team which surrounded Reagan when his historic aides left the White House after his re-election, then hiding the leader's flaws became harder and harder and the emperor was finally left with no clothes – as in the case of Iran–Contra. If this fiasco was ultimately his fault, it is because he never seemed to understand that if being so dependent on the staff does indeed lighten and facilitate the president's workload, it does not diminish his institutional responsibility. Far from it really, as it requires an ever greater vigilance on his part – something Reagan never displayed.

We therefore end up where we started, with Richard Neustadt. Reagan's many mistakes may offer the best illustration of his remark: 'he [the president] can count on no one else to be perceptive for him'. Reagan was a bad leader, and he surrounded himself as time went on with worse and worse aides, but he never noticed and realized it, and no one told him. And why should they? No one who works in the White House and who wants to protect their career is going to tell the president of the United States that he does not work hard enough, that he does not understand complex international issues, that other heads of state think he is ignorant, or that he does not always know how to pick good advisors. Reagan as a leader with a long political experience when he entered the White House should have known and anticipated that most people behave in the most sycophantic manner around the president – the letters from ordinary Americans that the staff would forward to him were systematically positive ones and the members of his administration regularly sent him the most obsequious notes (from Secretary of Defense Cap Weinberger: 'I am more conscious all the time what a great privilege it is to work with you here as we did in Sacramento. It is my honor to be on board with you';[13] or from Secretary of State George Shultz: 'Three magnificent summits that signify the profound ways in which you and your ideas have changed the world immensely for the better!! Thanks!! ... Your leadership continues strong and I am proud to be on your team').[14] But Reagan proved unable to see through these compliments. Instead of developing a critical and skeptical eye, and reflect upon his own incredible position at the head of the most powerful country in the world, he chose to bask in the prestige and the pleasures of the presidency. In other words, he ended up tempting fate, and fate came back to punish him with one of the worst crises in the history of the American presidency.

Notes

1 The staging required putting a cross on the floor to show the president where he should stand, calculating in advance the angles of the TV cameras, choosing the most flattering lights and so on (Regan, 1988: 247–8).

2 See for example: The President's Schedule, August 3, 1981, folder 'Presidential Briefing Papers, 07/31/1981–08/03/1981', Box 13, Darman, Richard, Series III-Presidential Briefing Papers, Ronald Reagan Library; The President's Schedule, September 16, 1981, folder 'Presidential Briefing Papers, 09/15/1981–09/16/1981', Box 14, Darman, Richard, Series III-Presidential Briefing Papers, Ronald Reagan Library.

3 See for example: The President's Schedule, March 9, 1982, folder 'Presidential Briefing Papers, 03/09/1982–03/10/1982', Box 17, Darman, Richard, Series III-Presidential Briefing Papers, Ronald Reagan Library; The President's Schedule, January 11, 1982, folder 'Presidential Briefing Papers, 01/11/1982–01/12/1982', Box 16, Darman, Richard, Series III-Presidential Briefing Papers, Ronald Reagan Library; The President's Schedule, December 10, 1984, folder 'Presidential Briefing Papers, 12/10/1984–12/12/1984', Box 36, Darman, Richard, Series III-Presidential Briefing Papers, Ronald Reagan Library.

4 The Schedule of President Ronald Reagan, February 9, 1987, folder '02/09/1987 (Casefile 527109)', Box 78, President, Office of the–Presidential Briefing Papers, Ronald Reagan Library; The President's Schedule, April 14, 1982, folder 'Presidential Briefing Papers, 04/13/1982–04/14/1982', Box 18, Darman, Richard, Series III-Presidential Briefing Papers, Ronald Reagan Library; The President's Schedule, June 19, 1981, folder 'Presidential Briefing Papers, 06/18/1981–06/22/1981', Box 12, Darman, Richard, Series III-Presidential Briefing Papers, Ronald Reagan Library.

5 Alexander Haig, Reagan's first Secretary of State, shared this negative assessment, explaining that 'Because of his habitual cheery courtesy, it is at times difficult to know when he is agreeing or disagreeing, approving or disapproving' (Haig, 1984: 57).

6 Soviet National Security Decision-Making, folder '(USSR) – Memoranda to the President from Robert C. McFarlane (2)', Box 7, Regan, Donald T – File Series I, Ronald Reagan Library.

7 Memorandum for the President: The Soviet View of the United States, November 5, 1985, folder '(USSR) – Memoranda to the President from Robert C. McFarlane (3)', Box 7, Regan, Donald T – File Series I, Ronald Reagan Library.

8 What to Expect from Gorbachev in Geneva memorandum, November 12, 1985, folder '(USSR) – Memoranda to the President from Robert C. McFarlane (3)', Box 7, Regan, Donald T – File Series I, Ronald Reagan Library.

9 See for some good examples: Meeting with Conservative Organization Leaders, February 17, 1981, folder 'Presidential Briefing Papers, 02/13/1981–02/18/1981', Box 10, Darman, Richard, Series III-Presidential Briefing

Papers, Ronald Reagan Library; Meeting on the Deficit with Business Representatives, January 15, 1985, folder '01/15/1985 (Casefile 318615)', Box 53, President, Office of the–Presidential Briefing Papers, Ronald Reagan Library; Talking Points – Senators Jackson and Warner, March 30, 1982, folder 'CFOA 415, Nuclear Freeze', Box 4, Meese, Edwin–Files CFOA 219, 375, 376, 414, 415, Ronald Reagan Library; Meeting with Republican Congressional Leadership, February 6, 1985, folder '02/06/1985 (Casefile 318706)', Box 54, President, Office of the–Presidential Briefing Papers, Ronald Reagan Library; Private Lunch with House Speaker Thomas (Tip) P. O'Neill, March 7, 1985, folder '03/07/1985 (Casefile 318807)', Box 55, President, Office of the–Presidential Briefing Papers, Ronald Reagan Library; Meeting with GOP Congressional Leadership, September 11, 1985, folder '09/11/1985 (Casefile 362310)', Box 61, President, Office of the–Presidential Briefing Papers, Ronald Reagan Library; Meeting with Republican Women Members of the Senate and House of Representatives, March 24, 1983, folder 'OA 11841 Women's Issues (10)', Box 52, Meese, Edwin–Files OA 11841, 11842, 11843, Ronald Reagan Library.

10 Note for the President, December 9, 1981, folder 'FG 001 (President of the United States) (052200–052599)', Box 38, FG 001, President of the US, Ronald Reagan Library.

11 State of the Union Address Memorandum for Michael Deaver, January 15, 1983, folder 'OA 10869 State of the Union (1982 and 1983) (3)', Box 22, Deaver, Michael K.–Files OA 8546, Ronald Reagan Library.

12 Most spectacularly, Reagan lost his three closest White House advisors who composed what was nicknamed the 'troika' during his first term: Chief of Staff James Baker, political advisor Ed Meese, and media guru Mike Deaver.

13 Cap Weinberger note, August 19, 1983, folder 'Folder 94 (8/19/83)', Box 7, Presidential Handwriting File–Series II–Presidential Records, Ronald Reagan Library.

14 George Shultz note, June 28, 1988, folder 'Folder 330 (6/16/88–6/28/88)', Box 20, Presidential Handwriting File–Series II–Presidential Records, Ronald Reagan Library.

Works cited

Archival documents

Cap Weinberger note, August 19, 1983, folder 'Folder 94 (8/19/83)', Box 7, Presidential Handwriting File–Series II–Presidential Records, Ronald Reagan Library.

George Shultz note, June 28, 1988, folder 'Folder 330 (6/16/88–6/28/88)', Box 20, Presidential Handwriting File–Series II–Presidential Records, Ronald Reagan Library.

Meeting on the Deficit with Business Representatives, January 15, 1985, folder '01/15/1985 (Casefile 318615)', Box 53, President, Office of the–Presidential Briefing Papers, Ronald Reagan Library.

Meeting with Conservative Organization Leaders, February 17, 1981, folder 'Presidential Briefing Papers, 02/13/1981–02/18/1981', Box 10, Darman, Richard, Series III-Presidential Briefing Papers, Ronald Reagan Library.

Meeting with GOP Congressional Leadership, September 11, 1985, folder '09/11/1985 (Casefile 362310)', Box 61, President, Office of the–Presidential Briefing Papers, Ronald Reagan Library.

Meeting with Republican Congressional Leadership, February 6, 1985, folder '02/06/1985 (Casefile 318706)', Box 54, President, Office of the–Presidential Briefing Papers, Ronald Reagan Library.

Meeting with Republican Women Members of the Senate and House of Representatives, March 24, 1983, folder 'OA 11841 Women's Issues (10)', Box 52, Meese, Edwin–Files OA 11841, 11842, 11843, Ronald Reagan Library.

Memorandum for the President: The Soviet View of the United States, November 5, 1985, folder '(USSR) – Memoranda to the President from Robert C. McFarlane (3)', Box 7, Regan, Donald T – File Series I, Ronald Reagan Library.

Note for the President, December 9, 1981, folder 'FG 001 (President of the United States) (052200–052599)', Box 38, FG 001, President of the US, Ronald Reagan Library.

Private Lunch with House Speaker Thomas (Tip) P. O'Neill, March 7, 1985, folder '03/07/1985 (Casefile 318807)', Box 55, President, Office of the–Presidential Briefing Papers, Ronald Reagan Library.

Soviet National Security Decision-Making, folder '(USSR) – Memoranda to the President from Robert C. McFarlane (2)', Box 7, Regan, Donald T – File Series I, Ronald Reagan Library.

State of the Union Address memorandum for Michael Deaver, January 15, 1983, folder 'OA 10869 State of the Union (1982 and 1983) (3)', Box 22, Deaver, Michael K.–Files OA 8546, Ronald Reagan Library.

Talking Points – Senators Jackson and Warner, March 30, 1982, folder 'CFOA 415, Nuclear Freeze', Box 4, Meese, Edwin–Files CFOA 219, 375, 376, 414, 415, Ronald Reagan Library.

The President's Schedule, June 19, 1981, folder 'Presidential Briefing Papers, 06/18/1981–06/22/1981', Box 12, Darman, Richard, Series III-Presidential Briefing Papers, Ronald Reagan Library.

The President's Schedule, March 9, 1982, folder 'Presidential Briefing Papers, 03/09/1982–03/10/1982', Box 17, Darman, Richard, Series III-Presidential Briefing Papers, Ronald Reagan Library.

The President's Schedule, April 14, 1982, folder 'Presidential Briefing Papers, 04/13/1982–04/14/1982', Box 18, Darman, Richard, Series III-Presidential Briefing Papers, Ronald Reagan Library.

The Schedule of President Ronald Reagan, February 9, 1987, folder '02/09/1987 (Casefile 527109)', Box 78, President, Office of the–Presidential Briefing Papers, Ronald Reagan Library.

What to Expect from Gorbachev in Geneva memorandum, November 12, 1985, folder '(USSR) – Memoranda to the President from Robert C. McFarlane (3)', Box 7, Regan, Donald T – File Series I, Ronald Reagan Library.

Secondary sources

Cannon, L. (1991) *President Reagan: The Role of a Lifetime* (New York: Simon & Schuster).

Deaver, M. (1984) *Behind the Scenes: In Which the Author talks about Ronald and Nancy Reagan... and Himself* (New York: William Morrow and Company).

Greenstein, F. (2009, Third Edition) *The Presidential Difference: Leadership Style from FDR to Barack Obama* (Princeton: Princeton University Press).

Haig, A.M. Jr (1984) *Caveat: Realism, Reagan, and Foreign Policy* (New York: Macmillan Publishing Company).

Hart, J. (1987) *The Presidential Branch* (New York: Pergamon Press).

Hertsgaard, M. (1988) *On Bended Knee: The Press and the Reagan Presidency* (New York: Schocken Books).

Kernell, S. (1989) 'The Evolution of the White House Staff', in Chubb, J.E., Peterson, P.E. (eds) *Can the Government Govern?* (Washington, DC: Brookings Institution).

McFarlane, R. (1994) *Special Trust* (New York: Cadell & Davies).

Neustadt, R.E. (1960, 1990) *Presidential Power and the Modern Presidents: The Politics of Leadership from Roosevelt to Reagan* (New York: Free Press).

Pipes, R. (2003) *Vixi: Memoirs of a Non-Believer* (New Haven: Yale University Press).

Reagan, R. (1990) *An American Life* (New York: Simon & Schuster).

Reagan, R. (2007) *The Reagan Diaries* (New York: Harper Perennial).

Reeves, R. (2005) *President Reagan: The Triumph of Imagination* (New York: Simon & Schuster).

Regan, D.T. (1988) *For the Record: From Wall Street to Washington* (London: Hutchinson).

Shultz, G.P. (1993) *Turmoil and Triumph: My Years as Secretary of State* (New York: Charles Scribner's Sons).

Skowronek, S. (1993, 1997) *The Politics Presidents Make: Leadership from John Adams to Bill Clinton* (Cambridge: Belknap Press of Harvard University Press).

Stockman, D.A. (1986) *The Triumph of Politics: The Crisis in American Government and How it Affects the World* (London: Coronet Books).

Strober, D.H. and G.S. Strober (2003) *The Reagan Presidency: An Oral History of the Era* (Washington, DC: Brassey's Inc.).

17
Conclusion

Agnès Alexandre-Collier and François Vergniolle de Chantal

All the chapters in this volume set out to address specific aspects of political leadership, with a common interest in the management of uncertainty. In our Introduction, we contended that this notion of uncertainty in politics could be understood in two ways: when the political, economic and geopolitical context is impossible to decipher (*contextual uncertainty*) and when division and confusion among followers and the public at large blur the messages sent to leaders (*social uncertainty*). Drawing upon neo-institutionalism, the common thread in all these contributions seems to be found in the use or misuse of their surrounding structures by leaders in building what they expect to be appropriate strategies of leadership. In order to shape relations with their followers and provide them with a reassuring framework, all leaders rely on specific structures which in turn exercise constraints upon them, as illustrated with political institutions (see chapters by Meyer, Vergniolle de Chantal on the US; Schnapper, Tournier-Sol and Leydier on the UK), the media (Heinemann on France; Frame and Brachotte; Bonnet on Italy), political parties (Avril and Alexandre-Collier on the UK) and civil society movements and associations (Godet on the US, Richter and Picard on Germany). Whereas the contextual and social environments are difficult to control, these structures display regularities and norms which are supposedly easier to identify. Yet they actually include constraints which leaders are forced to take into account when setting up a connection with their followers, which is the very process whereby, from being simply agents of their followers, leaders can become causal agents or actors proper. It is in this sense that structures and agency are intrinsically interrelated. Relying on structures which are assumed to be solid and stable enables leaders to bypass the contextual and social uncertainties in which they evolve and gives them at least an illusion of control. But at the same time, what can happen is that uncertainty eventually permeates structures to the point of what Schedler termed *institutional uncertainty* (2013[1]). Both types of uncertainty thus represent major threats. Particularly in times of crises, leaders have to deal with a timetable on which they have no grasp in a pragmatic effort to build up what would retrospectively seem to be coherent leadership. And when followers are divided, leaders can be tempted to sever the bond altogether, leading inevitably to failure (see chapters by Coste and Langlois respectively about Ronald Reagan and Edward Heath). This connection thus remains an essential precondition, justifying Burns's (1978) typology of leaders as being transactional transformers and power-wielders. The three categories are explicitly based on the nature of the relationship between leaders and followers, from negotiation and consensus (transactional leadership), to changing (transforming leadership) and even fracturing the relationship (power-wielders). Inevitably, leaders resort to various approaches to changing or controlling these structures along the following lines:

1. Limited/No use of conventional resources

There are only very few examples of leaders deliberately refusing to use conventional resources to establish their strategies, with the argument that evolving in exceptional circumstances allows them to act in an exceptional way. In one isolated case among our case studies, Meyer argues that John Boehner only rarely tried to use the traditional toolbox of the Speaker to impose his will on his followers. The same holds true, but to a larger extent, in the other chamber of Congress. Vergniolle de Chantal shows the extent to which leadership in the US Senate takes on surprising dimensions. Contemporary Majority Leaders in the upper chamber have come to accept a routine use of minority procedures (or threat thereof) by individual members so as to avoid a frontal assault on senators' privileges. Even though this may seem to be a way of avoiding a damaging showdown, Majority Leaders have often found their own tactical and timely advantages in a modest use of their resources. The landmark legislations – from the stimulus plan to Wall Street regulation and healthcare reforms – adopted under the 111th Congress illustrate this paradoxical legislative leadership.

2. Use of conventional resources

In most circumstances, however, the use of conventional resources is motivated by a need for leaders to normalize their leadership when

faced with uncertainty. However, the discrepancy between the stabilization of their leadership and the unstable frame in which they have to
act produces different results. In some cases, leaders rely on conventional devices, thus producing a paradox between the context and their
own strategies from which some of them fail to recover. Tournier-Sol
explains how John Major was forced to become a risk-taker by the
uncertain context of the Maastricht crisis. At the same time, he ended
up resorting to traditional institutional strategies, such as the leadership election in June 1995, which turned out to be an unwise decision
and eventually led to his discredit. For Avril and Alexandre-Collier, the
extensive use of party resources allows leaders to benefit from regular
means and act within normal boundaries, which provides them with
a conventional frame for exceptional actions. Alexandre-Collier shows
how Cameron resorts to institutional devices, such as referendums and
open primaries, even though they are rarely used in a parliamentary
democracy, in order to reach out to the party's grassroots. The May 2015
general election will show if this strategy has paid off.

In similar cases, the structural frame is considered to be somewhat
inadequate and leaders are even ready to act directly upon it. Schnapper
thus argues that Blair never hesitated to twist institutions so as to
make them adapt to his decision-making in the field of foreign policy.
Instead of adjusting his own leadership to the structures available, Blair
preferred to act directly on the surrounding structures so that they
could be moulded by his decisions. Similarly, Scottish First Minister
Alex Salmond can also be classified among the game-changers, to the
extent of being accused, like Blair, of excessive presidentialization.
Leydier suggests how the newness of Scottish devolved institutions has
allowed most First Ministers, and more particularly Salmond, to make
them pliable and flexible enough to adapt to their leadership. In other
words, the only way to manage uncertainty is to bend the structures
themselves. This is what Skowronek (1993) termed 'repudiation' which
finally amounts to trying to change structures without paying attention
to what followers want. In an extreme, even caricatural way, such was
also the case with Berlusconi, who set out to refashion the whole political system so that it could be adjusted to his own style of leadership. As
was pointed out in the Introduction to this volume, this category is the
most relevant when it comes to understanding the issue of uncertainty
management by political leaders but the result is also troubling since it
shows leaders as actors who are ready to refashion the context in which
they find themselves, making it impossible for followers to identify

familiar features. Leaders fitting into this category are clearly *transforming* leaders but, from a more cynical point of view, they also betray their original 'home' by reshaping the whole system which fostered them and made their leadership possible.

3. Misuse of conventional resources

Examples provided by the chapters also reveal the extent to which some leaders misinterpret and hence misuse conventional resources. Coste suggests that Ronald Reagan's disruptive leadership originated from his misperception of his aides and staff as being helpful and competent enough to act instead of him when his weaknesses were first exposed. His excessive reliance on his staff even deluded him into believing that they could take over, as soon as he became unable to perform as the US president. In a context of economic crisis and poor industrial relations, Edward Heath never succeeded in controlling the national debate and the set of events which overwhelmed him. As a result of his refusal to communicate with the public, Langlois shows how he eventually found himself cut off from his followers and public opinion at the end of his premiership, although he had initially intended to preserve this bond.

4. Use of unconventional resources

Political communication is therefore particularly useful in a context of uncertainty because, unlike institutions and party structures, it does not provide a normative framework with which leaders have to comply. It involves tools which are more flexible and easier to manipulate. Although, as Heinemann argues, General de Gaulle famously instrumentalized radio and television to devise his own legitimacy as a leader, these media were still new to the political landscape in the late 1950s, and political communication was primarily used by de Gaulle as an unprecedented instrument of (almost military) mobilization. Other leaders have relied on marginal devices, almost invisible details to challenge uncertainty. Frame and Brachotte show how most leaders, when relying on their wives/husbands' communication strategies, instrumentalize their partners in order to fill the gap between themselves and their followers, even though it would be more accurate to say that some of these women/men deliberately put themselves forward as communication tools while claiming to act as ordinary supporters. In a different case-study, Richter draws up a list of eccentric communication props (e.g. flowers, doves, t-shirts), used by Peace leader Petra Kelly to face uncertainty and not necessarily to convince people, since, as a 'grassroots-connector', she was already a popular figure and her leadership was deeply embedded in civil society.

As shown in the Introduction to this volume, strategies used by leaders range from performing as game-changers and stability-providers, communicators and 'grassroots-connectors'. Cases of executive leaders, i.e. prime ministers or presidents, are particularly relevant. To some extent, Tony Blair belongs to the first category of game-changers, while Berlusconi is perhaps the archetypal example of the communicator. Both leaders ended up being perceived as ignoring the needs of their followers, in other words as 'power-wielders' obsessed with achieving their personal objectives and ambitions. Yet, whether this perception is partly founded or not, it would tend to suggest that these leaders have become caricatural figures, trapped in the public's stereotypes. As a consequence, this typology should not be understood as a list of fixed categories. Categories indeed fluctuate, as a discrepancy often exists between the leaders' official intentions and their actual leadership or, to put it more bluntly, between a hidden and an official agenda. In the case of Berlusconi, even though he could be classified as a communicator, his hidden ambition was to appear as a game-changer. His reliance on existing institutions probably blinded him as to the extent of his room for manoeuvre. But the point is that Berlusconi's *fall* does not mean that he *failed* as a leader, as illustrated by his continuing popularity regardless of the scandals and affairs surrounding him. With the devolved institutions in Scotland, it was initially easy for Alex Salmond to appear as a provider not so much of stability as of *stabilization* in a context in which institutions were brand new and still considered as work in progress. However, the difference between Salmond and previous First Ministers is probably based on his communication skills. To some extent, he is also seen as the embodiment of the Scottish nation, which makes him at once a game-changer, communicator and grassroots-connector. On the other hand, David Cameron's official aspirations as a grassroots-connector have turned out to be an artefact. Openly claiming that he intended to reach out to the grassroots (members and supporters) actually enabled him to act upon the party structures. Today reforms concerning the selection of parliamentary candidates through the A-list and open primaries show that, beneath the surface, David Cameron wants to be remembered as a game-changer within existing party structures.

On the whole, even though the results of these strategies are different, leaders eventually appear as actors rather than agents of their followers and environments, and this is the very paradox which the book has tried to discuss. While endeavouring to take their followers into account, some leaders end up shaping forms of leadership which ignore what their followers want as well as the constraints imposed upon them by surrounding structures. Even in the cases when immersed in civil society, leaders like Petra Kelly and Erika Steinbach managed to reshape the aspirations of their followers so as to adjust to their own leadership agendas. In the case of the Tea Party movement, which was hijacked by its grassroots base, the need for leaderlessness only serves to blur the centralization of intent.

When uncertainty about their followers' actual needs becomes overwhelming, leaders eventually tend to act upon these needs, sometimes failing to the point of disjunction, to use Skowronek's term (1993). In other words, while uncertainty is being handled through a set of different strategies, and while leaders clearly endeavour to act upon this uncertainty, sometimes taking major risks, the common result is that it eventually disappears from the priority concerns of leaders. In spite of all efforts to render uncertainty in models and theories, it should only be taken for what it is: something that is, by essence, unknowable and elusive. Yet, if leaders refuse to take this variable into account, the major risk is that they fail altogether. On the other hand, when their whole strategy is based on uncertainty management, the chief result to be expected is for them to become causal agents who have managed to reach a position enabling them to ignore uncertainty. Thus one could argue that while uncertainty is integrated primarily as a key variable for leaders in devising their agendas, it eventually becomes something which has no influence whatsoever on successful leadership: a 'non-variable'. In other words, successful leadership is not determined by leaders' capacity to manage or control uncertainty but lies rather in the art of bypassing and even ignoring it.

Note

1 See the list of works cited at the end of our Introduction.

Index

Page numbers in *italics* denote a figure/table

Printed and bound by CPI Group (UK) Ltd, Croydon, CR0 4YY